Special Silver Anniversary
Collector's Edition

The Young and the Restless

BARBARA IRWIN & MARY CASSATA

Publisher: W. Quay Hays
Editorial Director: Peter Hoffman
Editor: Steve Baeck
Art Director: Chitra Sekhar
Production Director: Trudihope Schlomowitz
Color and Pre-Press Manager: Bill Castillo
Production Artist: Regina Troyer
Production Assistants: Tom Archibeque, Dave Chadderon, Gus Dawson, Russel Lockwood
Copyeditor: Carolyn Wendt

For information:
General Publishing Group
2701 Ocean Park Boulevard
Santa Monica, CA 90405

Library of Congress Cataloging-in-Publication Data

Irwin, Barbara J.
    The young and the restless / by Barbara Irwin & Mary Cassata. --
Special silver anniversary collector's ed.
    p.   cm.
ISBN 1-57544-045-8 (hardcover)
1. Young and the restless (Television program)   I. Cassata, Mary
B.   II. Title.
PN1992.77.Y635I78   1998
791.45'72--dc21   97-52077
                                                   CIP

Printed in the USA by RR Donnelley & Sons Company
10 9 8 7 6 5 4 3 2 1

General Publishing Group
Los Angeles

Table of Contents

Preface
by Jeanne Cooper

I venture to say, anything that survives 25 years in today's society has truly tapped into the "jet stream of miracles"!

I personally believe that all writers who script imaginary lives for real people for a quarter of a century should be canonized!!

It is my solemn wish that any performer who has survived the portrayal of the same character for 25 years be given a guaranteed berth in heaven, regardless of how many sinful deeds that character may have committed!

When *Y&R* burst upon the scene 25 years ago, the drama of daytime was forever changed. No longer was the "soap story" for just the shut-ins, housewives, or wishful dreamers for better lives, but it became the topic of conversation for college students, bankers, teenagers, athletes, teachers, showbiz elite—anyone, from every walk of life. You name it and daytime captivated it! The many loyal fans of years past grew in enormous numbers, and to this day these faithful viewers are the bulk support of daytime. I do not believe the creators of *Y&R*, Bill Bell and Lee Phillip Bell, ever dreamed their show would be the sensational cause for revolutionizing all of daytime, or that it would have the overwhelming appeal it has around the world.

This show called *The Young and the Restless* has given immeasurable reward not only to viewers, but to those who work to create it. And in a very tangible way, it has provided employment and financial support to so many, many others beyond the always recognized producer, writer, director, star. The artistic craftspeople—in every facet of the production—created and have maintained the quality of *Y&R*.

One could go on and on. I'm sure it would take 30 years to explain 25 years of *The Young and the Restless*! The better way to extol the virtues of this show is to express what's in the hearts of millions of our viewers: "Thank you for so many hours—through so many years—of joyful entertainment!"

Introduction

The Evolution of *The Young and the Restless*

March 26, 1998, marks the Silver Anniversary of the daytime serial drama *The Young and the Restless*. The show has always been known for its sensitive and enlightening treatment of social issues, slick production values, complex characters, and innovative use of music. Let's go back 25 years to where it all began.

It was the early 1970s and William J. Bell was head writer for *Days of Our Lives*. He'd accepted that position in 1966 after *Days* had been on the air for only 26 weeks and was near cancellation. Bell worked his magic, revamping the show and bringing it to the top of the daytime ratings within a few short years. Such an incredible success did not go without notice. The networks were all clamoring for Bill Bell to develop a new show. Bill and his wife, Lee, both felt an allegiance to CBS—Bill had worked in radio for CBS and had written for *Guiding Light* and *As the World Turns* for 10 years. Lee was an Emmy Award–winning broadcaster in her own right, having hosted *The Lee Phillip Show* on the CBS affiliate in Chicago for many years. CBS brought the Bell family to Los Angeles (they continued to make their home in Chicago until *The Bold and the Beautiful* went on the air) to talk business. With a commitment from CBS, Bill and Lee holed up in the famed Polo Lounge at the Beverly Hills Hotel, and with paper and pencil in hand, hammered out their story. The result of their efforts was a 65-page "bible" for the show, delineating the backstory, characters, and approximately two years' worth of storylines. The Bells had declared it was time for a change in the daytime serial, and their show, then tentatively titled *The Innocent Years*, would bring about that change. The bible reads:

My very firm conviction is that today, chemistry has replaced the "hospital life and death crisis" as the prime emotional force of daytime. Man–woman chemistry. Live, flesh-and-blood people who can get the adrenaline flowing. Damn nifty people who can turn you on and keep you turned on. That's what it's all about today as never before. Chemistry surging through our veins. Sure, there are those who deny themselves—or say they do. Those who turn away—or say they do. But don't you believe it. . . . Because either physically or emotionally, one way or the other, we all feel the need to be needed, of being wanted, of knowing the touch, conqu surrender of another human being.

That was the essence of *The Innocent Years*. Add to it music—to sustain and heighten the most dramatic of moments—and the show was on its way. But not before rethinking the title. It was now 1972, and the Bells knew that the innocence in our country had been lost. They thought the new title should be *The Young and the* "Something." The "Something" became "Restless." *The Young and the Restless*. The show went on the air on March 26, 1973, and was an immediate success. The story revolved around the lives of two families: the well-to-do Brookses and the struggling but proud Fosters. The setting was the midwestern metropolis of Genoa City, which was actually a small town in Wisconsin through which the Bells would drive on their way from Chicago to their weekend home in Lake Geneva.

Almost immediately after *Y&R* went on the air, CBS approached Bill Bell with the idea of expanding the show to a full hour. He resisted. The show was obviously working in its present form. Why tamper with success? But with an eye toward even greater success, the decision was made, and in 1980, *Y&R* went to an hour. There were some growing pains, to be sure, but the show quickly regained its momentum, and gained even more in the ratings.

The next challenge came when the show had experienced numerous recastings in the Brooks and Foster families. When actress Jaime Lyn Bauer (Lorie Brooks) informed Bill that she would not be renewing her contract, he surveyed the landscape of characters in Genoa City—and focused in on Paul Williams (Doug Davidson) and Jack Abbott (Terry Lester). He set out to create families for these characters, and within several months, the virtually seamless transition had been accomplished, and the Williams and Abbott families intersected with the marriage of Jack and Patty.

The Young and the Restless celebrated its 5,000th episode on October 29, 1992, which was officially declared William J. Bell Day in the city of Los Angeles. On that same day, CBS dedicated Studio 43 at CBS Television City to William J. Bell and *The Young and the Restless*. This dedication marked the first time in the history of CBS that a studio was dedicated to an individual and a series. The genius of Bill Bell cannot be overstated. He has created three of the 11 soap operas currently on the air: *The Young and the Restless*, *The Bold and the Beautiful*, and *Another World* (with the legendary Irna Phillips). His writing and producing has spanned nearly 15,000 episodes of daytime drama, on the air continuously for over 40 years.

Bill Bell is also the patriarch

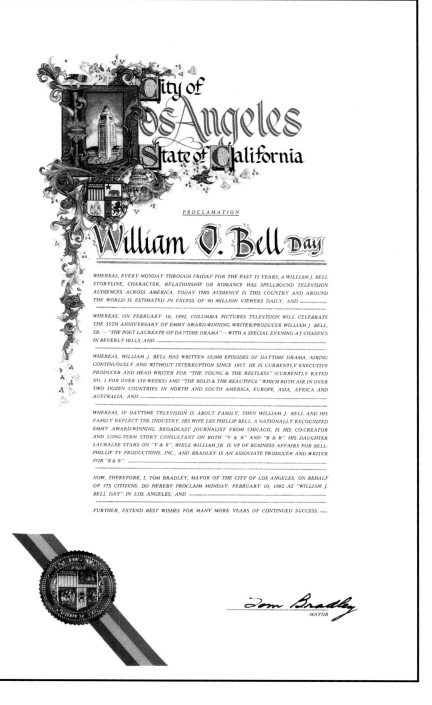

City of Los Angeles State of California

PROCLAMATION

William J. Bell Day

WHEREAS, EVERY MONDAY THROUGH FRIDAY FOR THE PAST 35 YEARS, A WILLIAM J. BELL STORYLINE, CHARACTER, RELATIONSHIP OR ROMANCE HAS SPELLBOUND TELEVISION AUDIENCES ACROSS AMERICA. TODAY THIS AUDIENCE IS THIS COUNTRY AND AROUND THE WORLD IS ESTIMATED IN EXCESS OF 40 MILLION VIEWERS DAILY; AND ——————

WHEREAS, ON FEBRUARY 10, 1992, COLUMBIA PICTURES TELEVISION WILL CELEBRATE THE 35TH ANNIVERSARY OF EMMY AWARD-WINNING WRITER/PRODUCER WILLIAM J. BELL, SR. – "THE POET LAUREATE OF DAYTIME DRAMA" – WITH A SPECIAL EVENING AT CHASEN'S IN BEVERLY HILLS; AND ——————

WHEREAS, WILLIAM J. BELL HAS WRITTEN 10,000 EPISODES OF DAYTIME DRAMA, AIRING CONTINUOUSLY AND WITHOUT INTERRUPTION SINCE 1957. HE IS CURRENTLY EXECUTIVE PRODUCER AND HEAD WRITER FOR "THE YOUNG & THE RESTLESS" (CURRENTLY RATED NO. 1 FOR OVER 150 WEEKS) AND "THE BOLD & THE BEAUTIFUL" WHICH BOTH AIR IN OVER TWO DOZEN COUNTRIES IN NORTH AND SOUTH AMERICA, EUROPE, ASIA, AFRICA AND AUSTRALIA; AND ——————

WHEREAS, IF DAYTIME TELEVISION IS ABOUT FAMILY, THEN WILLIAM J. BELL AND HIS FAMILY REFLECT THE INDUSTRY. HIS WIFE LEE PHILLIP BELL, A NATIONALLY RECOGNIZED EMMY AWARD-WINNING BROADCAST JOURNALIST FROM CHICAGO, IS HIS CO-CREATOR AND LONG-TERM STORY CONSULTANT ON BOTH "Y & R" AND "B & B". HIS DAUGHTER LAURALEE STARS ON "Y & R", WHILE WILLIAM JR. IS VP OF BUSINESS AFFAIRS FOR BELL-PHILLIP TV PRODUCTIONS, INC., AND BRADLEY IS AN ASSOCIATE PRODUCER AND WRITER FOR "B & B". ——————

NOW, THEREFORE, I, TOM BRADLEY, MAYOR OF THE CITY OF LOS ANGELES, ON BEHALF OF ITS CITIZENS, DO HEREBY PROCLAIM MONDAY, FEBRUARY 10, 1992 AS "WILLIAM J. BELL DAY" IN LOS ANGELES; AND ——————

FURTHER, EXTEND BEST WISHES FOR MANY MORE YEARS OF CONTINUED SUCCESS. ——

Tom Bradley
MAYOR

of an incredibly talented family that is something of a dynasty in the world of daytime television. His wife, Lee, is not only co-creator of both *Y&R* and *B&B*, but also serves as long-term story consultant on both shows. Their daughter, Lauralee, stars as Christine Williams on *Y&R*. Bill Bell Jr. is President of Business Affairs for Bell-Phillip TV Productions, while Bradley Bell is head writer and executive producer of *The Bold and the Beautiful*.

Today, the daily worldwide audience for *The Young and the Restless* is estimated at 100 million. These viewers are in more than 30 countries on six continents. The show's international markets include Australia, Bermuda, France, Greece, India, Indonesia, Israel, South Africa, Trinidad, and the United Kingdom. *The Young and the Restless* has been the top-rated soap opera in the United States for nearly 10 years and counting. With Bill Bell at the helm, and with the unprecedented commitment on the part of everyone connected with the show, The *Young and the Restless* continues to be the one truly revolutionary daytime drama. Here's to the next 25 years!

Acknowledgments

Over the past three years, we've lived a soap opera in the writing of our two books on *The Young and the Restless* (this 25th anniversary volume and its antecedent, *The Young and the Restless: Most Memorable Moments*), which seems to us to be something of a serial in itself: a beginning, mostly middle, no end. Just as producing the daily episodes of *Y&R* is an ensemble effort, a book of this magnitude must also be recognized as a group effort. There are many to whom we owe a great debt of gratitude for their contributions.

To Bill and Lee Phillip Bell for entrusting us to capture the spirit and essence of the show that has been such a significant part of their lives.

To Nancy Bradley Wiard for cutting through the red tape, running interference and opening doors for us, and for allowing us to make ourselves at home at *Y&R*.

To Kay Alden, whose infectious enthusiasm truly inspired us.

To Lucy Johnson, Senior Vice President of Daytime/Children's Programs and Special Projects at CBS, for her support.

To Ed Scott and David Shaughnessy for sharing their knowledge and expertise and for always being willing to answer our questions.

To Andrea Joel for her untiring efforts in digging up the documents and archival materials that have enriched our book, and to Barry Wittman for going out of his way to provide us with photos that filled in gaps. Special thanks also to Bill Hultstrom, Jennifer Johns, and Gail Camacho for going "above and beyond."

To the CBS Photo Department, especially to Francis Cavanaugh for his munificent cooperation throughout this project, and to Rouhi Taylor, who always came through for us no matter how impossible our request. To Margaret Wright and Kathleen Tanji, along with the rest of the staff, who were so tolerant of our disruptions when we made their space our home away from home for days and weeks on end.

To the on-screen talent who were never too busy to share their stories with us through the spoken and written word: Marla Adams, Lauralee Bell, Peter Bergman, Eric Braeden, Sharon Case, Tricia Cast, Signy Coleman, Jeanne Cooper, Michael Damian, Doug Davidson, Alex Donnelley, Jerry Douglas, Sharon Farrell, Jennifer Gareis, Sabryn Genet, Heath Kizzier, Kate Linder, Aaron Lustig, John McCook, Shemar Moore, Joshua Morrow, Sandra Nelson, J. Eddie Peck, Scott Reeves, Victoria Rowell, Melody Thomas Scott, Nick Scotti, Shari Shattuck, Kristoff St. John, Heather Tom, Jess Walton, Tonya Lee Williams, and William Wintersole.

To the *Y&R* talent behind the scenes, who were always willing to help: Eva Marie P. Arquero, Joe Bevacqua, David Bruce, Fred Cooper, Victoria Curea, Patti Denney, Brenda Garcia, Trina Gavieres, Hitomi Golba, Jez Davidson Guito, Robin Gurney, Randall Hill, Don Jacob, Annette Jones, Kathy Jones, Josh McCaffrey, Sally McDonald, Kathy Nishimoto, Michael Okamura, Jennifer Qualls, Nora Wade, and Ralph Wilcox. A special note of thanks goes to Josh O'Connell, whose conscientious and good-natured attention to so many details was invaluable.

To *Y&R* publicists Frank Tobin and Charles Sherman; Jack Westerkamp and Cindy Lin of SONY Signatures; and Shannon Donnelly of Columbia Tristar Interactive for their various contributions; and to *Soap Opera Digest* and *Soap Opera Weekly* for being incredible storehouses of soap opera information.

To Jeff York, for his artwork that graces the endpapers and page 8 of this book, and to Tracy Mulcahy Bloom for her tireless efforts in illustrating the map of Genoa City, thereby making this fictitious locale "real." To Barbara York for sharing with us her son Greg's renderings, which so beautifully add to the "Day in the Life" section.

To our editor, Steve Baeck, for attending meticulously to every detail and for his advice and encouragement throughout; to art director Chitra Sekhar, for her beautiful design work that captured the spirit and tone of *Y&R*; and to our support at General Publishing Group: Peter Hoffman, Quay Hays, Sharon Hays, Lori Rick, Marc Nobleman, and Harlan Boll, who were always there for us.

To Randolph J. Granat for his painstaking efforts in compiling the comprehensive cast list, and to our friends, colleagues, and students in the Communication Departments at Canisius College and SUNY Buffalo, especially Terry Fisher and David Lesinski of the Canisius College Media Center, and Pam Bruns. We especially want to remember Dr. Charles Petrie, our respected colleague whom we lost during the year.

Finally, there are no words that can adequately express our appreciation to our families, who gave us unconditional love and support, and who endured more than anyone should ever be expected to: James Klein, Frances Irwin, Doris Lueth, William Irwin, The Kleins, Mama and Sam, all of the Ballachinos and Cassatas, and the ever-faithful Magic and Hanchy.

With little more in mind than putting as much time and distance as quickly as possible between himself and Chicago, Brad Eliot didn't expect the first day of the rest of his life to come to this! After being mugged, left for dead, his car hijacked, his money and personal effects gone, Brad stumbled along the roadside, his clothing torn and dirt-crusted. There he was in the middle of nowhere. Lucky for him, the sympathetic driver of a semi was willing to take on a hitchhiker and drop him off at the next stop—Genoa City. There, Brad entered Pierre's Restaurant and sat down to a scrumptious meal.

Newspaper publisher Stuart Brooks and mysterious stranger Brad Eliot instantly connected.

Snapper and Chris had long discussions over their relationship, but no matter what Snapper said about the two of them becoming sexually intimate, Chris argued that they had to wait until they were married.

When Sally McGuire, the waitress, presented Brad with the bill, he said he didn't have the money to pay for it. His demeanor and self-assuredness caught the attention of Stuart Brooks, who was sitting at a nearby table. Stuart Brooks, civic leader and publisher of the *Genoa City Chronicle*, happened to be there, dissuading young medical student Snapper Foster from seeing his daughter, Chris.

Without a fuss, Stuart paid the stranger's tab. He engaged him in a few minutes of conversation, and offered him a job on his newspaper. He even gave him a salary advance, and then suggested he rent one of the rooms above the restaurant. Later, at the newspaper office, Brad intercepted his own photo and a stunning story coming over the wires: "Dr. Brad Eliot burned beyond recognition in car accident, identified through a few personal belongings." Brad pocketed the copy and decided he would remain "dead."

At 19, college student Chris Brooks was consumed with love. Being in love. Medical student Snapper Foster was her whole heart and soul. The only problem was that while Chris fantasized about having Snapper's babies, her own strict moral code prevented her from engaging in sex with him before marriage. But Snapper, his hormones raging, didn't want to wait for sexual gratification, though he did insist they couldn't marry until he graduated from medical school, when he'd be able to support a wife.

Enter one young lady, Sally McGuire, the waitress at Pierre's, who not only adored Snapper but was always his ready and willing bed partner.

Ultimately, a suspicious Stuart Brooks made it his business to find out all he could about Snapper Foster. It didn't take long for him to learn that Snapper spent many a night in Sally's room.

Stuart, who was an attentive and loving husband to Jennifer, was a very protective father with all of his daughters. He didn't want to see any of them hurt. In addition to his disarming Chris, there was the shy and introverted eldest daughter, Leslie, whose friendship and trust were being carefully cultivated by Brad Eliot. Leslie's life was focused on becoming a concert pianist. Sixteen-year-old Peggy, with les and red hair, was still in high school. As for Lorie, 21, she was studying hard in Paris, or so she said. Lorie was the aggressive daughter. She knew one day she'd be famous. What man could have a better family? And what family could have a better husband and father?

Liz Foster, whose husband, Bill, had deserted her and their three children (Snapper, 23; Greg, 21; and Jill, 18), worked hard at her factory job to put food on the table. Liz's honesty and unwavering goodness earned her the respect and friendship of many, especially those who touched the lives of her children: Chris Brooks, Sally McGuire, Stuart Brooks, and Katherine Chancellor. A woman who didn't complain very much, she tended to disregard her own needs. Noting his mother began to tire more easily, Snapper took her to see her internist, who discovered she had uterine cancer and was in immediate need of surgery. Snapper notified Liz's brother, Bruce Henderson, from whom she had long been estranged, but who immediately left Chicago to be at her side. Liz's surgery was successful, and Bruce's stay in Genoa City was short, but he did manage to reconnect with Jennifer Brooks, with whom he had had a brief but passionate affair many years before she married Stuart.

During Liz's hospital stay, Jennifer met Snapper, her daughter Chris's boyfriend, and took an instant liking to him. This, of course, would introduce one more point of conflict between her and her hus-

band, Stuart. As for Liz, who recovered nicely, life went on, but with a pleasant twist. After being alone for so long, she met Sam Powers. Liz had almost forgotten how much she enjoyed male companionship.

Leslie Brooks and Brad Eliot grew closer, and their warm regard for one another became obvious. Brad didn't like to talk about his own background. Indeed, none of his new friends knew precisely what this "mystery man" did before he came into their lives. But he seemed to have that special knack for drawing Leslie out of her shell and for making her laughter a more familiar sound in the Brooks household. He was sincere in his advice to her not to make the piano her entire world.

Brad was elated and became her biggest cheerleader when Leslie was notified by Maestro Fautsch that she had been selected as soloist for the Mid-America Symphony Fall Tour. Leslie's parents and siblings were also proud of her accomplishment. But Leslie's future travels to Chicago and elsewhere

Leslie Brooks loved to practice, but when Brad came into her life, she became aware that her career as a concert pianist was not the only important thing in life.

would provide several opportunities for her mother to cross paths with Bruce Henderson.

Sally McGuire was used to sitting on the sidelines, watching the rest of the world go by. Oftentimes, she shared her most intimate secrets with Brad Eliot, who had become a close friend and neighbor. Brad was well aware, for example, that her insular world revolved around Snapper Foster. He also knew about her past affair with Frank Martin, who was the father of the child she had given up for adoption seven years before. The sudden reappearance of Frank in her life threw her world into turmoil as he demanded help in finding their daughter to heal the emptiness of his present childless marriage.

With Snapper's turning to Sally for gratification, and her need to put him on hold because of this new problem, Sally inadvertently learned from the frustrated Snapper that nurse Jane Wilcox had been raising Sally's little girl right here in Genoa City. It was inevitable in the weeks that were to follow that

Sally and Frank would be thrown together in their common quest to find their child. It would also culminate (for the time being) in Frank's seeking a divorce from his wife and desiring a reconciliation with Sally.

Jane Wilcox, engaged to a man named Steve, refused to give up little Susan. When Steve informed her that he didn't want to make her adopted child a part of their life, Jane Wilcox chose to give up Steve and keep little Susan. But the roundelay was not to end here. Months later, when Sally was to find herself pregnant with Snapper's baby, and Snapper, not knowing she was pregnant, had proposed to Chris, Sally asked Frank if he was still interested in marrying her. By this time he was committed to marrying Jane Wilcox!

And then there was law student Greg Foster, the middle child in the Foster household, the reasonable one. Although he walked in big brother Snapper's shadow, still he was his own person, with love, compassion, honor, and fairness the guidelines by which he lived. For example, when Snapper missed that all-important Brooks family dinner because he was so tired and innocently fell asleep in Sally McGuire's bed, it was Greg who had advised the humiliated and angry Chris to be understanding and not crowd Snapper. But at the same time he assured her that Snapper wasn't interested in any other woman.

Snapper and Greg talked about many things—their respective careers as a doctor and a lawyer, and the family finances and problems—but most of all their talk centered on Chris Brooks, to whom both brothers were attracted.

Liz Foster tried her best to be an understanding mother to her daughter, Jill.

When Greg offered to help Chris with her college debate topic (because as a law student he knew how to do the kind of research she needed to do) and Chris went on to win the debate, they bonded in the most natural of ways: over a hamburger at Pierre's. And when Snapper showed up at Greg's graduation at Yale and confided that it was all over between him and Chris, and when Chris phoned to congratulate him, Greg's heart leapt with joy.

Then there was the exhilaration of moving into his very first law office, and showing it off to Chris (only to have Snapper also drop by and take her home). There was the snagging of his first client, and celebrating that milestone with Chris. And when Chris began to work for him (Stuart had asked him to hire her and promised he'd foot her salary, although Chris was not to know), Greg realized he had fallen head over heels for her!

Greg and Snapper had words over his new "employee," and for the first time, Greg admitted to his brother that he had fallen in love with Chris. But how could Greg say anything to her? After all, he did not know for sure how Snapper really felt about Chris and he wasn't going to do anything to ruin things for big brother. Then Chris found out her father was paying her salary and she told Greg she couldn't work for him any longer.

Later, Snapper began to see more of Sally, who went off the pill but didn't tell him. Then Greg was hired by a local corporation on a weekly retainer, and he asked Chris to celebrate by either returning to

work for him or marrying him. But Chris, of course, was still in love with her first love, Snapper, as he was with her (though Snapper was too headstrong to admit it). Chris told Greg she had to "find" herself before she could consider marriage.

The youngest of the Foster children, 18-year-old Jill, put her own ambitions and aspirations aside, working as a manicurist to contribute toward paying the family's bills and to help put her brothers through school.

And as it so often happens, a series of unfortunate events were to put things in perspective. First, there was the huge misunderstanding between the hapless, restless Jill and her big brother, Snapper. How was Jill to know that when her flashy customer, Gwen

Sally was always there to fulfill Snapper's physical needs when Chris held him at arm's length.

Sherman, invited her to visit the "escort service" at which she worked, it would turn out to be a brothel? Or that as she was hurriedly preparing to leave almost as soon as she had arrived, Jill would come face to face with Snapper! He was so enraged that he gave her a resounding slap across the face in front of Gwen and all those people.

And then there was Sally's on-again, off-again trip with Pierre to Paris (resulting from her on-again, off-again romance with Snapper). When she fainted in Pierre's presence, he called a doctor, who privately informed Sally she was pregnant. Later, in the States, Sally admitted her pregnancy to Pierre. With no spousal candidate in sight, the courtly Frenchman proposed and then married her. But his protective sister, Marianne, wasn't going to sit still for this; she asserted she'd be journeying to Genoa City!

And then the most traumatic event of all: Chris, after telling Greg that she had to get herself together before considering marriage, actually became more untogether than she had ever been in her 19 years. For, on her way home from a job interview, she had stopped at a singles bar for a hamburger. Having observed her from afar several times before, George Curtis engaged her in conversation. He asked if he could walk her home. His good manners clouded her good judgment, and she said yes. As she was closing the door to her apartment, he stuck out his foot to stop it and forced his way in. The brutality, shame, and humiliation of Chris's rape nearly destroyed her, emotionally, spiritually, physically. Stuart was constantly haunted by the sickening thought of what happened to her. Her sisters and her mother were thrown into a state of shock. Snapper, who had been on the verge of proposing to her, wanted to tear Curtis limb from limb. And Greg had to learn from two women at the Rape Crisis Center the shattering truth as to why Chris really went home.

Courageously, Chris, bolstered by her sister Leslie, took George Curtis to trial. But her testimony, under cross-examination, was twisted so as to make the jury believe she made absolutely no attempt to fight Curtis off or scream for help. The jury brought in a verdict of "not guilty," and Curtis was set free.

But one very good thing was to happen before the year would end: Snapper and Chris announced they would soon marry. This prompted Lorie Brooks to return home from Europe, marking another event that was sure to set into motion a chaotic and surprising new year for all her family and her friends.

As the year began, the most immediate concern of the Brooks and Foster families was the preparation for Chris and Snapper's nuptials. Smarting from losing Chris to his brother, Greg at first refused Snapper's request to be his best man, but he later relented when Chris used her powers of persuasion on him. Greg could never say no to her.

Chris and Snapper happily looked forward to their wedding day.

Lorie persuaded Stuart to offer her a position at the Chronicle, hoping to get close to the handsome Brad Eliot.

Meanwhile, Brad Eliot was trying to put out a fire in a different quarter by counseling Sally to keep mum about the fact it was Snapper's baby that she was carrying. What would be the point of hurting Chris, Brad asked, or, for that matter, Pierre, her new husband with whom she had yet to consummate her marriage? Sally remained silent for the time being, and under Pierre's threat to put a quick end to their brief marriage if she didn't immediately share his marriage bed, she moved into the bridal suite that very night.

Another worrisome development was the place that Lorie Brooks would occupy in the scheme of things. Would she accept her father's invitation to work for the *Genoa City Chronicle*, or would that only precipitate the inevitable? Stuart had already noted that within a few days of being back in the Brooks household, Lorie seemed to be harboring the same old jealousies she had always felt toward her sister Leslie, and with Brad Eliot rapidly becoming the focus of Leslie's romantic fantasies, trouble was inevitable. For, as everyone who knew Lorie had come to know at one time or another, there were no such words in her vocabulary as "Hands Off," "Unattainable," or "Off Limits." Lorie would take whatever she wanted, when she wanted it, whether it

was hers to take or not. And if someone got in the way, so what? There simply was no way of stopping her. And now Lorie was making noises to Stuart about wanting to accompany him to the *Chronicle* right after Chris's wedding. Her unspoken agenda, which she was making no effort to hide, was to get to know Brad better.

Somehow, before the wedding, Snapper had unintentionally listened to his mother's telephone conversation with Sally. Liz was expressing her appreciation for Sally's decision not to inform Snapper that he was the father of her unborn child. The news sent Snapper straight to Sally's side to find out what all of this meant. And although Sally admitted that the child was in fact Snapper's, she reminded him that she had decided to marry Pierre. She had also insinuated that Pierre believed himself to be the father, even though Pierre knew the child's true paternity.

The day of the Foster/Brooks wedding came at last. Chris had scripted the services. The vows that each said to the other were:

"I join you in marriage Chris (Snapper) to be my wife (husband), now and forever. To hold you and keep you, in joy and sorrow, prosperity and hardship, health and sickness, to honor and defend you, to love and cherish, and together keep holy the word of God."

These words seemed to validate the meanings and feelings behind the events the couple had already shared and experienced. What marred their wedding night, however, was Chris's spontaneous recollection of her heinous attack. As her groom began to make love to her, she was seeing in his face the face of her rapist. So Snapper sensitively and immediately held off, saying that they *did* have a whole lifetime ahead of them to make love.

Lorie's flirtatious behavior toward Brad became manifest on the first day of her appearance at the *Chronicle*. She told Stuart she would take on the job of Enquiring Reporter, and then proceeded to do just that as she questioned Brad about almost anything and everything. On the positive side, Brad showed complete disinterest and thought she was terribly immature and self-centered. But as the days passed, Lorie undermined his relationship with Leslie by sowing seeds of doubt in his mind that Leslie had any interest in him whatsoever. And, of course, not to be unfair to Leslie, Lorie did the sisterly thing of forewarning her that men were not to be trusted. Soon she tried to seduce Brad. Then she failed to pass along Leslie's phone messages. And in no time at all, Lorie unearthed the information that Brad was, in fact, a psychiatrist/neurosurgeon who had been "killed in an auto accident." She even traveled to Chicago to question Barbara Anderson, whose name appeared in the news story of Brad's death. Barbara Anderson freely admitted she had been in love with him.

Meanwhile, in Sally's life, the sudden intrusion of Pierre's sister was enough to turn her world

Pierre's relationship to his sister, Marianne, was more that of a dutiful son kowtowing to his overly protective mother.

topsy-turvy, especially after Marianne learned that Sally was expecting. She correctly guessed that Snapper was the father, but promised she'd not say anything. When Pierre could no longer stand his sister's interference, he sent her back to Paris.

As for Jill Foster, young as she was, she could not help but feel that life was passing her by. Her world was dull and drab—from her make-do job at Hazel's to her surroundings at home, which consisted of worn-out furniture, hand-me-down dishes, giveaway glassware, cheap clothing, and generally uninspired conversation. Until Kay Chancellor, a regular customer at the beauty shop where Jill worked, touched her life. The besotted Kay saw a longing in Jill's eyes, and eventually offered her a position at the

Chancellor estate as her maid, hairdresser, and paid companion. Suddenly Jill was transported into a world splashed with dazzling colors and filled with priceless antiques, fine silver, sparkling crystal, luxuriant furniture, and designer clothes. Great wealth, opulence, and impeccable good taste abounded.

Jill tolerated Kay's habits of regularly drinking herself into oblivion and smoking to such an extent that her husband, Phillip Chancellor, couldn't stand to be near her. Jill pitied Kay, and desperately wanted to do everything in her power to help her. If she could help her employer curb her drinking and smoking, maybe Kay could then do more to help herself. Maybe Kay could start relating to Phillip. Maybe she could get him to love her again as much as she

loved him. All of Jill's many acts of kindness and great patience toward Katherine did not escape Phillip's notice, and he became inexorably drawn to the refreshingly innocent and beautiful young lady.

On the surface, Stuart and Jennifer Brooks's lives seemed to be proceeding rather normally. But Bruce Henderson was trying mightily to insinuate himself into Jennifer's life again. Jennifer was managing to keep him at a respectful distance, but that distance would get shorter and shorter as time would go by.

While Jill practically lived at the Chancellor home, Gwen Sherman did make another attempt to persuade her to earn some extra money, but Jill turned her down. She remembered all too well her previous association with Gwen at the "escort service" and the breach it caused between her and Snapper. However, Gwen caught the interest of Greg Foster when she went to see him at his law office about an inheritance. Greg was immediately smitten: he had never seen anyone quite so gorgeous as Gwen. Of course, Jill had no idea that Gwen was the girl her brother began to date, just as Greg had no idea that Gwen was a prostitute. And when all the secrets unraveled, it was far too late to change things.

By this time Greg had fallen irrevocably in love with Gwen, but to her credit, Gwen tried many times to walk away from her life of sin. Unfortunately, her employers wouldn't let her. She longed to be the unspoiled, innocent girl Greg thought her to be. Greg's mother, Liz, liked her, which made Greg happy. But when Jill discovered who her brother had fallen

Jill knew her place and chose her words very carefully when it came to Katherine's excessive drinking.

for, she demanded that Gwen break off with Greg immediately. When this didn't happen, Jill told Snapper that their brother's fiancée was a hooker!

The ensuing confrontation between the two brothers was explosive. Greg refused to believe Snapper and the two came to blows. Greg still loved Gwen and asked her to marry him, defying both his brother and sister, while Liz remained in the dark as to what the fuss was all about. As time passed, Gwen made promise after promise to mend her ways and turn her life around. She had even taken up waitressing at Pierre's, but her employers were unwilling to lose such a rich source of revenue. They, at first, threatened bodily harm, not so much to her but to Greg, and when she didn't heed their advice, they severely beat him. Later, Gwen found herself in the hospital, the victim of a brutal attack.

Snapper, meanwhile, was having his own share of problems. He felt he had to be firm with Chris, who now wanted to start a family. He also had to endure the openly expressed criticisms of his father-in-law, who felt their apartment was too small, among other things. If Snapper resented Stuart's constant interference in their lives, then Chris resented it even more. To Stuart's credit, his grievances with Snapper were understandable; after all, Marianne had told him that Snapper was the father of Sally's unborn child.

And then there was the tragic turn of events that occurred in the lives of Pierre and Sally. One night, after the restaurant closed, a mysterious intruder clubbed Pierre over the head in an attempted robbery. For several days Pierre went in and out of consciousness. Sally cabled his sister, Marianne, about Pierre's accident, but advised her there was no need for her to come to Genoa City. Sally honestly believed

Pierre would soon recover, but the headstrong Marianne was angered by Sally's cable and made immediate arrangements to leave for the States.

There were some days when Pierre briefly regained consciousness and would tell Sally he loved her. Then, thinking that Pierre was sleeping, Sally was stunned to discover that her husband had expired. While Snapper was leading the grieving widow to the elevator to take her home, Marianne was exiting from another. She headed straight for Pierre's room where she learned from a nurse he had died. All of the pent-up hatred she felt for Sally spilled out as Marianne vowed Sally would pay. Marianne would turn her out of Pierre's restaurant; then she'd sell the restaurant, and return with Pierre's body to Paris.

Meanwhile, Lorie was getting closer to her goal of closing the gap between herself and Brad. She had been plotting over the past several months to break up Leslie and Brad, sowing seeds of doubt as to how each felt about the other. As an example, a love letter Leslie had written to Brad begging him to join her in Detroit for her big concert appearance went unacknowledged, unanswered. It broke Leslie's heart. Meanwhile, Brad wondered why Leslie hadn't sent him a concert ticket. Didn't she need him anymore?

The culprit was the heartless Lorie. She had intercepted Leslie's letter and then lied about ever having seen it. Then she told Brad that he was getting in the way of Leslie's realizing her dreams of being a concert pianist.

Leslie called Brad just before the concert, only to have Lorie tell her, "Brad is interested in me." Later that evening, on the concert stage, Leslie's hands poised in midair above the keyboard, it was Lorie's taunt that Leslie heard. Leslie was unable to continue.

Snapper spent many hours visiting Sally in the hospital, hoping to lift her out of her depression.

She lapsed into a catatonic state, and had to be led off the stage by Maestro Fautsch.

What happened next was one big blur. Leslie insisted she had to get away before her next concert performance in Boston. Completely disoriented, she had been found wandering around in a city park in New York in the pouring rain. A stranger snatched her purse, and a policeman, noting her glassy stare, took her to a New York psychiatric hospital where she was admitted as "Jane Doe." It was some weeks later before Stuart, frantic with worry, was contacted that their "Jane Doe" might be his missing daughter. Leslie was transferred to a private sanitarium closer to home.

At first, only Jennifer and Stuart would know where Leslie was confined. Her recovery took months of therapy, during which Brad had become engaged to Lorie, an act which clearly disturbed Stuart and Jennifer. They wondered how they could have had such a self-centered, selfish daughter who would snatch the great love of her sister's life. Then, when the full story had come out as to how Lorie had destroyed the letter Leslie had written to Brad, Brad broke off the engagement. He devoted his full attention to building up Leslie's self-confidence so that she'd play again. Lorie, on the other hand, quit her job at the *Chronicle* at the same time her first book was published, which Stuart labeled a piece of disgusting trash. He wrote an editorial damning it. Undaunted, Lorie laughed it off, knowing it would be

great for book sales. Brad then proposed to Leslie, who suggested they defer their marriage until she'd come to be more in touch with her own feelings. She thought she might give up her concert career and turn her energies to singing. She would buy Pierre's restaurant and call it The Allegro.

In the meantime, Kay was totally destroying Phillip's love with her excessive smoking and drinking. She absolutely reeked of the sickening smell of her debauchery. She challenged Phillip to take her—make love to her right on the living room floor. And when Phillip didn't respond, Kay carried on shamefully with Jeff, the stable boy. Meanwhile, Phillip and Jill were bonding together in their losing battle to return Kay to civility. Phillip showed his appreciation through his kindness to Jill. They went on memorable late-night swims, and Phillip found himself relating to the kind young woman. And before he knew what had happened—long before Jill, who was fighting it, knew—Phillip had fallen deeply in love with this angel.

Chris, in the meantime, became pregnant and was afraid how Snapper would react. Snapper had recently graduated from med school, and Sally gave birth to Charles Pierre Roulland. Chris learned that Sally's baby was not born prematurely, as she'd been led to believe, and came to the stunning conclusion that Snapper was the baby's father. This revelation so disoriented Chris that she fell, aborting the unborn

Leslie and Brad were good for each other. She loved his strong, protective nature and he loved to take care of her.

child inside of her. Snapper tried to comfort her at the hospital—they'd have other children—but Chris was inconsolable. She told Snapper she would not return home with him. She had to find her own way in life to know who she really was.

Chris turned to Greg, asking him if she could join him at the Legal Aid office. The cases she worked on involved people who needed people, people who helped people. Ultimately this brought her and Snapper closer together, and Chris would eventually go home again.

Much to everyone's surprise, after being away for years, Katherine's son, Brock Reynolds, came home again. Brock, a practicing lawyer, was her son from a first marriage. Kay had a hard time welcoming him back. He had said such hurtful things to her in the past. But now, with his newfound religion, Brock was dedicating himself to helping his mother regain her sobriety. He and Jill sat out Kay's withdrawal with

her. But it wasn't easy for someone as willful as Kay to accept help. Alcoholics Anonymous was out of the question. It was too embarrassing for her to admit publicly that she had been a drunk for years. So, she continued getting on and falling off the wagon.

As good as he was in solving other people's problems, Brad had to face up to the reality that he had to stop running away, and to begin living. He faced up to Barbara Anderson and endured her railing that he had allowed their son to die on the operating table. He accepted Leslie's help in reconciling with his parents, and having them see for themselves that he was alive. Leslie, of course, drew strength from Brad and she told her sister Lorie not to see Brad anymore; she was going to marry him!

By the time the year would end, there was one interesting new arrival in Genoa City—Liz Foster's nephew, Dr. Mark Henderson, who would be interning at Genoa City Memorial Hospital. Bruce had written Liz that he was hoping Mark would be welcomed into the family fold despite the estrangement that had existed between them.

If Brad could not understand that everything Lorie did was out of love for him, then he was welcome to have her mousy sister Leslie, as far as she was concerned.

For many of the major players in Genoa City, 1975 started out on a positive note, although as the year progressed, the winds of change would challenge their faith, courage, and resiliency. For example, Phillip Chancellor made a New Year's resolution to marry Jill Foster during the coming year. His wife, Kay, joined Alcoholics Anonymous in an attempt to turn her life around. After having it out with her sister Lorie, Leslie Brooks promised Brad Eliot she would marry him, and the couple set their wedding date. Greg Foster went to bat for the woman he loved, Gwen Sherman, extracting a promise from Leslie to give her back her old job waiting tables at The Allegro. He even got Stuart Brooks to promise not to use Gwen's name in a vice ring story set to run in his newspaper. Liz Foster was slowly but surely becoming closer to Sam Powers. And even the restless Lorie Brooks was becoming excited about a new romantic partner in her life who did not belong to someone else, Dr. Mark Henderson.

As it turned out, Kay's impetus for attending AA was her undetected glimpse of Phillip and Jill locked in a tight embrace! At first she couldn't wait to get back to her room to hit the bottle again. And over the next several days, she languished between bouts of seething rage (even though she knew it was her drinking that caused her to lose Phillip in the first place) and self-pity. Then she knew what she had to do. She called Vivian Anders, her sponsor at Alcoholics Anonymous, stunning both Phillip and Jill.

Phillip told Kay how proud he was that she was taking this all-important first step, and the very moment that Brock learned about it, he hurried over to her AA meeting to lend his support. Kay was impressed with the sincerity of the AA members, who, under Vivian's chairmanship, each in their turn, recited the program's 12 suggested steps before declaring themselves. When it was Kay's turn, Vivian noted with disappointment, her chair was empty. But Kay did return later to declare herself, just in time for Brock to witness it, with love and pride.

The process of withdrawal was both painful

Brock Reynolds, better than anyone else, understood his mother, Katherine Chancellor.

and scary, but Kay persisted. She was going to lick this problem if it was the last thing she'd ever do. She found comfort from reading the Bible, and as the days and weeks went by, she devised a strategy to land Phillip back in her arms. Inundate everyone with kindness—Phillip, Jill, Brock, Liz—that's what Kay would do. And in the process she'd make Jill feel even more guilty than she already was feeling for daring to fall in love with Katherine Chancellor's husband!

This new tact seemed to be a far cry from the sodden Kay who'd threatened to commit suicide if Phillip left her. Or the liquor-crazed Kay who'd held a gun on Phillip and Jill (without their knowledge, of course), which didn't fire because the chamber was empty. But the greatest irony of all was that for all of Kay's efforts, she could not rekindle the love Phillip once felt for her or match the new and joyful love he

was experiencing with Jill: a love that was reciprocated in measure and kind.

While this was going on at the Chancellors', grave psychological and physical problems were ready to manifest themselves at the Brookses. Jennifer had dearly wanted to visit the Hendersons in Chicago to be near Bruce, but Leslie's sudden rush to marry Brad overwhelmed Jennifer with a sense of emptiness over losing her daughter. And so she put the Chicago trip on hold. Add to this the anxiety she was feeling after hearing from Mark Henderson that his father and mother were on the verge of a divorce, and Bruce's sudden appearance in Genoa City begging her to leave Stuart and marry him! Jennifer summoned the courage to listen to her heart, and then announced this decision to her daughters, as she wanted them to hear it from her directly before telling their father. Just then, they found out that Stuart had collapsed, was rushed to Genoa City Hospital, and went into cardiac arrest. His life was saved only because Brad, who happened to be at his bedside with Snapper, quickly reached for a syringe and injected it directly into his heart. Snapper followed this up by massaging Stuart's heart, until a heartbeat was sustained.

Jennifer's only consolation was that though she had betrayed Stuart in her heart, and she'd have to live with it, she hadn't told him what she had

Although Jennifer Brooks seemed happy enough with Stuart and their four beautiful and engaging daughters, she wistfully thought of her lost love, Bruce Henderson, perhaps more than she should have.

intended to do. Her daughters—including Lorie, who of all of them, she thought, might understand—couldn't forgive her, and they made no secret of their resentment.

For weeks, Stuart remained in guarded condition. But sick as he was, he knew one thing: he trusted the opinion of Bruce Henderson, a top cardiologist, and asked that he be brought in as a consultant. This not only stunned Stuart's entire family, but served to heighten the tension between Jennifer and her daughters. Fortunately, Bruce had the sensitivity to realize that Stuart's heart couldn't withstand an emotional shock. Bruce returned to Chicago, knowing that Jennifer would want to see Stuart through this terrible ordeal. But there was always the hope that he and Jennifer could have a future together.

Snapper bitterly resented his father's leaving them nine long years ago, and hated to see Liz work so hard to keep the family together. He nearly went through the roof when he learned his mother was still paying the premiums on his father's life insurance policy when she should be collecting money from it instead. As it was, Liz was genuinely worried that she wouldn't be able to meet expenses, especially since rumors of layoffs at the factory where she worked were rampant. So when Greg brought up the same subject of paying the premiums on his father's life insurance policy, Liz's anger exploded. All these years, she had refused to declare William Foster Sr. legally dead, so what was the hurry now? In addition to the problem of cash flow, that "hurry" manifested itself in the person of Sam Powers, a "date" Snapper had arranged for his mother without her knowledge.

Despite her attempts to banish thoughts of male companionship from her mind, Liz had to admit she did enjoy Sam's company. And for the first time since Bill left, Snapper noted she was reaching out to a man. Perhaps the time had truly come for the Foster family to declare William Foster Sr. legally dead. But an unexpected letter bearing a Chicago postmark, which Snapper received, changed everything. The letter was from Snapper's father. Bill Foster was terminally ill with lung cancer and emphysema and wanted to come home. Liz felt compelled to take him in so he could spend his final days with his family. And Sam Powers, gentleman that he was, said he understood and would wait for her.

Thanks to Leslie, at least one of the more compelling problems that threatened to destroy her future with Brad was cleared up before they walked down the aisle. Leslie knew that Brad blamed himself for being unable to save his son in surgery, so Leslie persuaded nurse Barbara Anderson, the boy's mother, to solicit opinions and statements from the other doctors who assisted Brad on that ill-fated day. Their unanimous conclusion—that Brad had done all he could and should not hold himself responsible for the boy's death—helped to assuage much of the guilt Brad felt. But when Leslie asked Brad if he wanted to move to Chicago to resume practicing medicine there, Brad firmly replied that he wanted to begin his new life with Leslie right here in Genoa City.

Leslie's wedding was everything she wanted it to be and more: she insisted her marriage to Brad was all she'd need to make her life complete. Yet Brad couldn't help but be concerned that she'd find marriage not as fulfilling as she had hoped, that there'd be something missing. Brad mulled this over very carefully. He had to do something to get her to return to the concert stage. With this in mind, he deliberately arranged for them to honeymoon in Palm Springs, knowing that the Mid-America Symphony would be performing there. It would afford him the opportunity to arrange a reunion between Leslie and Maestro Fautsch. To Brad's great satisfaction, everything worked out just as he had hoped, and the inevitable happened. Maestro Fautsch extracted a promise from Leslie that she'd make another concert appearance. Leslie was thrilled and grateful.

Subsequently, Leslie flew to Buffalo, New York, to give a concert, but without Brad. In the meantime, Brad made arrangements with the Maestro not to let on that he'd be there, in the audience. His motive was to prove to Leslie that she could perform without having to lean on him. He wanted to build up her self-confidence so she'd truly believe that her natural abilities would carry her through. The concert was a great success, and after Leslie's superb perfor-

mance, Brad revealed himself and let her know how proud he was. More successes were to follow.

But there was more happening, over which Brad had limited or no control. He fretted over how Lorie's forthcoming novel—a story of two sisters, one of whom had suffered a mental breakdown—would affect Leslie. To exacerbate his worry, Leslie returned to the New York mental hospital in an attempt to deal with her past. She found that the same women who had terrorized her were still there; Brad had to go to her rescue before she became completely traumatized.

With Brad now out of her life, Lorie dedicated herself to writing her novel: she'd make the whole world stand up and take notice of her superior talents!

The worldly Phillip Chancellor had come to love Jill Foster, long before the young girl could bring herself to admit that she cared for him, too.

Then, there was the matter of Brad's own severe recurring headaches, which were affecting his vision and his perception. He was determined his wife would not know about them. Mark Henderson diagnosed his condition as a swelling of the optic nerve and later arranged for Brad to check himself into a Chicago hospital. After exhaustive tests, it was determined that the condition he suffered from was chronic neuritis, and he'd eventually go blind. If anything was a certainty, it was that Brad would do everything in his power to prevent Leslie from giving up her career.

Back at the Chancellors', Jill, unaware that Kay was onto her, was so guilt-ridden about her feelings for Phillip that she decided to leave there for good. Taking no chances, Kay went to see Liz, who knew about her daughter's affair with Kay's husband. Kay played on Liz's sympathy, professing her undying love for Phillip. Later, Liz advised her daughter that she couldn't build her happiness on someone else's misery. Then, in a supposedly gracious moment, Kay offered to pay for a college education for Jill as a farewell gift, but the heartsick girl burst into tears and declined to take her up on her offer.

Jill's brothers urged her to reconsider; she'd be making an investment in herself and in her future. Feelings of guilt and insecurity were flooding over her when Phillip took her in his arms at the bunkhouse and made passionate love to her. Jill didn't resist. Kay witnessed the indiscretion and it nearly destroyed her;

it took all of the strength she could muster to keep from hitting the bottle again.

However, Kay continued her façade of being kind to Jill. For insurance, she persuaded her son, Brock, who had been attracted to Jill, to propose marriage. Feeling unwanted, the confused young woman accepted, and Brock, a self-styled preacher, performed the ceremony. But the marriage wasn't consummated, and lasted only until Jill discovered she was pregnant with Phillip's baby.

When Jill told Phillip she was carrying his child and that her marriage to Brock wasn't legal, Phillip was overjoyed. He immediately investigated the matter of getting a divorce in the Dominican Republic, which sent Kay straight to the bottle.

In a drunken stupor, Kay signed the divorce papers, striking out any claim to a property settlement, which she didn't want if she couldn't have

If Phillip wanted a divorce, Katherine didn't want any leftover mortgages on their marriage. Property settlement be damned!

Phillip. Jill was on cloud nine; she immediately negated her invalid marriage to Brock, and told her family she was marrying Phillip Chancellor.

Upon Phillip's return from the Dominican Republic, a stone sober Katherine met him at the airport and offered to drive him home. On the way, she begged him for a second chance. When Phillip rebuffed her, she pressed her foot down hard on the accelerator as they were rounding a dangerous mountainous curve. The car plunged over a cliff.

As Phillip lay dying in his hospital bed, he asked the hospital chaplain to marry him and his beloved. Soon afterward, he was dead. Over time, Kay recovered, and waged an endless round of legal maneuvers. Ultimately, Jill's marriage to Phillip was declared invalid, and Jill and her family were evicted from the Chancellor estate, where they'd been living since Phillip's death. To put the icing on the cake, Kay offered the pregnant girl $1 million to raise Jill's unborn child as her own. At first Jill was repulsed by

such an absurd offer, but then thought better of it and relented for the good of the baby and her family.

Elsewhere, it was Regina, Bruce's estranged wife, who blew the whistle on Jennifer. After a bitter confrontation with Stuart, Jennifer admitted she loved Bruce and would have left Stuart had he not had a heart attack. Stuart asked her to get out, now, immediately. Jennifer took the next flight to Chicago to be with Bruce.

It wasn't long after that that Jennifer discovered a lump in her breast, which turned out to be malignant. Having a mastectomy was the worst experience of her entire life. Jennifer withdrew from having any contact with either Bruce or Stuart. Depressed

Regina and Bruce Henderson's marriage had been rocky for a long time. They argued over everything.

and alone, she was badly in need of companionship and counseling. It took time.

Jennifer moved into her own apartment and slowly began the process of rehabilitation. She confided in Lorie, telling her of her torrid affair years ago with Bruce Henderson. Lorie advised her to go after what she really wanted.

At the Foster residence, Liz vacillated between her feelings for Sam Powers and for Bill, each of whom was reluctant to place any pressures on her. In the end, Liz declined Sam's proposal of marriage, and Sam left Genoa City to pursue a substantially better job in Kansas.

Bill, meanwhile, took Brock's advice to work at the Senior Citizen's Home helping the seniors out in small ways. Brock also persuaded Kay to do what she could for the seniors. Appalled at the deplorable conditions she found there, she pledged to completely refurbish the recreation room.

The Foster family was now growing closer together. For the first time in years, they felt the warmth of a close family unit.

Lorie Brooks had been without a man for perhaps the longest stretch in her life. She lost Brad to Leslie; had a brief, nonsexual alliance with Phillip after Jill "married" Brock; and was unable to stir any interest on Brock's part because he, too, was trying to find himself. Her most serious prospect was the young doctor, Mark Henderson, who immediately piqued her interest by resisting her attempts at seduction. She later learned that Mark was impotent, and she promised to help him with his problem by using a

Liz was close to her two boys, Snapper and Greg, and they had a deep and abiding love for their mother.

sensory therapy technique she learned in Paris.

After a particularly painful visit with her mother after the mastectomy, Lorie asked Mark to spend the night with her. She assured him that although he couldn't be intimate, his being there with her was enough. Mark confessed he was falling in love with her.

After Lorie told her mother she was going to marry Mark Henderson, Jennifer, in a state of shock, told Mark he must immediately end his relationship with Lorie because his father, Bruce Henderson, was also Lorie's biological father. It was a secret Mark must never reveal—to Lorie or to anyone else. Mark told Lorie he didn't love her, and she left Genoa City, devastated.

During the year, Gwen Sherman, Greg's true love, entered a convent, and Chris Foster continued with her Legal Aid work. She and Snapper observed that Sally's baby was one year old.

Nineteen seventy-five had been a long and difficult year and no one was sorry to see it end.

There was never a year more in tune with the biblical verse: "To every thing there is a season and a time to every purpose under heaven." Phillip Chancellor III was born; Bill Foster died; Jennifer, Peggy, and Joann wept; Liz mourned; Lorie, Lance, Leslie, and Brad loved; Katherine and Jill continued to wage war; Snapper healed and Stuart was restored to health; and Brock sowed seeds of hope, love, and peace through acts of human kindness.

The Chancellor baby had to remain in the hospital several days after his birth because of a high fever. During this time, Kay constantly bugged Jill over the deal they had made that she would raise the child as her own in exchange for the sum of $1 million. It was a deal that Kay's son, Brock, and the Fosters violently opposed. Kay was also firming up her plans to leave the Chancellor estate to the Senior Citizens. She intended to leave Genoa City and the life she knew there to establish a new life for herself and the baby.

But when Jill held her son in her arms for the first time, she realized she couldn't go through with it. She bolted from the hospital with the baby, leaving a thunderstruck Kay behind. Not one to take things lying down, Kay created a mighty ruckus with the Fosters, who had returned her check.

Kay headed straight for her attorney's office to initiate proceedings to repossess the baby. Her attorney advised her to drop the suit. Fuming, her next step was to kick out the seniors from her estate; Kay then returned to her drinking. Brock, the eternal optimist, attempted to persuade her to make something of her life by helping the Fosters in their time of dire financial need.

Meanwhile, Jill was instituting a lawsuit of her own on behalf of her son for one half of Phillip Chancellor's estate. She also hocked her jewelry in an effort to get her parents to go to Arizona where the climate would be better for her father's emphysema. Liz, meanwhile, begged Kay to hire her as her housekeeper, but failed to tell Jill about it. Then Kay, feeling good about doing good, decided to accept Brock's challenge to come to the Fosters' aid. She was just about to set up a trust fund for Phillip when she was served with Jill's petition to recover her son's rightful

Katherine failed in her desperate attempt to gain custody of Jill's son, and was left feeling empty and alone.

share of the estate. Deeply hurt and feeling very much the fool, Kay, nevertheless, swallowed her pride and agreed to a meeting with Jill to iron things out. She'd drop her lawsuit, Jill said, if Kay would be willing to help out her family.

But, unfortunately, their amiable sparring completely fell apart when declarations of mistrust were hurtled back and forth. Katherine declared she didn't believe Phillip Chancellor was the father of Jill's baby, which sent Jill out into the night, half screaming and half sobbing. The courts would have to settle their dispute after all.

Jill's petition in probate court against the estate was a total bust, as there was nothing in writing to substantiate her claims. Even though Brock testified against his mother—admitting that she had offered him money to marry the then-pregnant Jill— and his testimony did Kay a great deal of harm, the judge nevertheless decided in Kay's favor, leading Brock to proclaim she was now truly alone with only the memory of her dead husband to sustain her.

Jill, of course, vowed to get even. Her first move was to call upon Katherine, badger her into admitting Phillip did indeed love her and that the son she bore was Phillip's. She then left, leaving behind a bag that contained a bottle of vodka. Her plan was to destroy Kay by pretending that things were as before: Phillip was still alive, there was no baby, and Kay was a hopeless drunk. Jill had cases of vodka delivered to gaslight her, and poor Liz, who was employed as a domestic at the estate, could hardly believe her daughter could be so devious. Even Brock was flabbergasted as to the extent Jill was taking this to drive Kay insane. He led his mother to Phillip's tombstone (he was buried on the estate) to show her that Jill's machinations to make her believe Phillip was still alive were utterly false!

When Bill Foster returned home to spend the final months of his life with his family, he vowed he would be as unobtrusive as possible. But he didn't want to be so unobtrusive that he would let another man propose to his wife and take her away from him! Bill proposed, too, and Liz accepted; they renewed their vows. It was a strong, quiet kind of love that Liz had for Bill, a love that he returned in kind.

When hospital treatment for Bill's lung cancer

and emphysema became too costly, Bill turned to smoking with the intention of hastening his death, until Snapper and Liz put a stop to it. He insisted upon being an organ donor, and signed a DNR (do not resuscitate) order as well. Bill quietly wrote one letter a year up to his 21st birthday to little Phillip, as well as a letter he wanted to be delivered to Kay after his death, thanking her for agreeing to pay for his hospitalization. He asked Jill to prepare Liz for the end, knowing how hard her mother would take it. And he asked Brock to deliver his eulogy.

Just when Bill thought he might go home one last time, he suffered a serious relapse and was put on a life-support ventilator. When he regained consciousness, he was in such acute pain that he begged Liz to pull the plug. This went against anything she would ever do—against her God, against herself, against her sense of justice and humanity. But she did as Bill asked—as an act of love—and watched as his contorted face relaxed in peaceful sleep.

Lorie Brooks dreaded the arrival of New Year's Eve; it was the day she had hoped to marry Mark Henderson. She confessed to Brock that her new philosophy was, "From now on I think of myself first; to hell with the rest of the world; and all men are now fair game!"

It was her brother-in-law, Brad, who put the pieces of the puzzle together. He knew that Lorie had taken a blood test at Mark's request. Then there had been that disturbing conversation between Mark and Jennifer, and then Mark's distraught words to Lorie. . . .

Lorie overheard the tail end of a disturbing conversation between Brad and her mother, and she demanded that Brad tell her what it was all about. Lorie knew it was more than the mastectomy that was sinking her mother into an emotional morass. It had to have something to do with Mark's refusal to marry her. And in a flash, Lorie, too, had come up with the answer! Why hadn't she seen it before? Mark was her brother!

Lorie tore into Jennifer not only for the loss of Mark but also for the loss of Stuart, the only real father she had ever known. When Lorie later faced Stuart for the first time after her revelation, he sensed there was something troubling his second child and reached out to comfort her. She bolted from his arms.

Later, unwilling and unable to walk away from Mark unless she gave it one more try, Lorie located him in a clinic on the outskirts of Cleveland, and

Bill Foster's illness took its toll on Liz, who struggled with the decision to put an end to her husband's suffering.

Lorie Brooks enjoyed the thrill of the chase as millionaire Lance Prentiss romanced her to the extreme.

proposed they resume their relationship. Mark sadly told her that it wouldn't work; it was contrary to the laws of man and God. It had to be good-bye. Lorie left, promising Mark she'd never trouble him again.

In Paris, where she was performing, Leslie ran into her old friend, Lance Prentiss, and invited him to visit her in the States. She wanted him to meet her husband, Brad, and her sister Lorie; Leslie intrigued him by saying she knew that Lorie and he would be incredible together. So what began in an unremarkable enough way, with Lorie and Lance sizing each other up and sparring with one another at a bar in Chicago, turned out to be a remarkable love affair punctuated by their pursuit of exotic adventures all over the world, with each of them an equal partner in a thrilling game of creating desire and longing, chasing and being caught, teasing and being teased, romancing and then refraining from the ultimate act. It was a dangerous game of the heart and mind they were playing until they finally realized

they had reached the point of no return in their relationship and had fallen madly and irrevocably in love. For Lorie, it was the perfect cure for getting over Mark Henderson. For Lance, it brought into sharp focus a new complication he had created, by having two women in the center of his life—the headstrong, independent Lorie and his possessive mother, the veiled Vanessa.

Vanessa Prentiss was a woman of mystery. As half owner of Prentiss Industries, she also made half of the decisions. The veil she wore across the lower part of her face covered the awful disfigurement she suffered when she saved her son Lance in a fire accidentally started years ago by her other

Leslie and Lance reestablished their friendship, which would grow ever deeper as the years progressed.

Vanessa Prentiss wore a veil to conceal the scars she suffered in a terrible fire many years ago.

son, Lucas. From that point on, Lance would belong to no one but her. Her dislike for Lorie was as undisguised as it was unreasonable, and Vanessa would fight tooth and nail to break up the couple. When Lance and Lorie married on the spur of the moment at Lake Tahoe, one might say it was done in part to best Vanessa.

Brad Eliot loved his wife, Leslie, so much, he couldn't bear the thought of burdening her with the reality that he was going blind. The news would only interfere with her career. So he simply didn't tell her he would soon lose his eyesight. He spun a web of lies to explain why he couldn't be with her at her concert sites or at family celebrations. And the more he lied, the more entangled he became in his deceitful web, until it was impossible to extricate himself. He would rather she thought he didn't love her than deny her the triumphs and acclaim she was winning. But as far as she was concerned, her success meant nothing without Brad. Soon he asked for a divorce, but when he found out that she was pregnant with his child, he was stunned, overwhelmed. He learned to read

braille, and when Lorie told her sister the truth, Leslie wrote him a letter in braille, telling him how much she loved him. It was the beginning of breaking through his defenses.

Although Jennifer's four daughters resented her betrayal of Stuart, the youngest, Peggy, was the most reluctant to forgive her. It was understandable, then, that Peggy should seek someone to whom she could unburden her soul. Peggy certainly couldn't discuss this with her father, who was still in the dark, although he was becoming more aware of certain enigmatic tensions.

Peggy turned to her tutor because Jack Curtis was easy to talk to, and he seemed to give her the kind of advice that led her to believe he had her best interests at heart. So Peggy found herself consulting with him frequently, unaware that he was altering his own personal schedule to accommodate her. It seems that his wife, Joann, a waitress at The Allegro, was desperately trying to lose weight, get it under control to please him, and put the romance back in their marriage. She had lost eight pounds, but had many more to go.

Brock was encouraging Joann and gave her some money to buy a new dress so she would look nice for Jack when they went out that night. But later Jack called to say he had to go to a meeting (he was meeting Peggy at the library) and he would be late. Too late.

When Jack returned home, he said he was too tired to do anything but go straight to bed. Forget dinner. Forget the movies. Then Joann tried to initiate

Joann slimmed down hoping to regain her husband's affections, but Jack was already involved with Peggy Brooks.

lovemaking, but he wasn't interested. Bitterly disappointed, Joann assuaged her frustrations by devouring the entire dinner she had prepared. Diet be damned!

On campus, rumors were flying that Professor Jack Curtis traded good grades for sexual favors, and Peggy confronted Jack about them. Jack said he was glad she brought up the subject, but that she shouldn't add to their credence by falling in love with him. Peggy said it might already be too late.

Meanwhile, back at The Allegro, Brock was trying to cheer up Joann. It was her birthday and she thought Jack had forgotten it. Actually, Jack remembered while he was out with Peggy. He cut their date short and rushed off to buy Joann a gift before going home.

Months passed. Neither Joann nor Peggy was aware of what Jack was doing. Each thought she was the only woman in Jack's life. When they found out he was leading both of them on, they were outraged. Joann had been working so hard to make herself attractive to Jack that she was gradually becoming a much more self-assured young lady. That Jack was cheating on her was more than she was willing to accept. She demanded that he remove all of his things from their apartment and get out—go after Peggy if he wanted her.

Chris Foster first encountered the Becker family through Legal Aid when Nancy, a diabetic, sought advice for her husband, Ron, who was being held in jail on a possible rape and burglary charge. Nancy insisted that Ron was completely innocent, and that the charge was the result of a setup by a woman whom Ron had shunned. Disbelieving Ron's story and recalling her own shattering experience of being a rape victim, Chris was repulsed by even the

The support Peggy received from her sister gave her the courage to report her assault to the police.

sight of Ron. But her heart went out to Nancy and her little girl, Karen. Ron was freed of this charge because of insufficient evidence. Foolishly, Chris asked her father to help find a job for Ron to help get the family back on its feet. Ron secured a job as a woodworker, and the compassionate Chris asked him to make a table for her.

Peggy wanted to confide in someone about Jack Curtis, so she went to Chris's apartment. When she found her sister wasn't home, Peggy let herself in with her key, intending to wait for Chris. An intruder got there first, and raped her!

Jack, meanwhile, was racing over to the Brookses to tell Peggy he was going to be free to marry her, but her family turned him away.

Chris insisted that her sister report the assault to the police. Ron Becker had been arrested as a suspect, and Peggy identified him in a police lineup. A hearing was scheduled and Ron asked his wife to have his work clothes cleaned for the hearing. Emptying his pockets, Nancy found a note with Chris's address on it and realized her husband did, in fact, know where Chris lived. Shattered, she began to doubt him. It turned out that the case did go to trial, but the jury returned a verdict of "not guilty," concluding that Peggy's case was not proved beyond a reasonable doubt.

The Beckers' home life became a shambles, and was often punctuated by violent arguments. Nancy argued in favor of leaving Genoa City, but Ron, wanting to get even with the Brookses, wouldn't hear of it. One of Ron's verbal attacks was so vicious that Nancy fell into a catatonic state and had to be institutionalized. Ron then left town, and Chris and Snapper took little Karen in, becoming more and more attached to the enchanting little girl the longer they kept her.

Jennifer went home at last and her doctor pronounced that there was no evidence that her cancer had recurred. However, a previously undetected heart condition would take her life within the coming year, after she and Stuart celebrated their 30th anniversary and made peace with one another. And as for Gwen Sherman, she was now Sister Magdelene. She was ready to take her final vows—until Greg Foster walked into her life again. The Mother Superior, noting there were feelings that the young nun was trying to suppress, cautioned her not to go to God with half a heart, but to pray for guidance.

It was certainly a year that tested the mettle of many; perhaps next year would be more tranquil.

Chris Foster believed she and Snapper could provide a more stable home life for little Karen Becker. Ron had had more than one brush with the law.

After their elopement, Lorie and Lance flew to the Prentiss estate at Lake Geneva to inform Vanessa and to pack for their honeymoon trip. Vanessa tried valiantly not to show her dismay and alienate her beloved Lance. Privately, she did remind Lorie that she had broken the truce they had forged, and Lorie'd have to work doubly hard to regain the ground that was now lost. However, the newlyweds continued on their way, taking the time to drop in on Brad and Leslie to tell them their happy news. The two couples congratulated each other: a wedding and a reconciliation were indeed occasions to be toasted!

Even as Lance and Lorie were honeymooning, Vanessa began to lay the groundwork for destroying their marriage. The first thing she did was to invite Leslie to her home, letting her know she was not exactly pleased with her sister. (Vanessa would have preferred to have Leslie for her daughter-in-law.) But Leslie staunchly defended her sister, pointing out that Lorie, in putting the brakes on her second novel, had given up fame and fortune because of what the book might do to Leslie's life. Vanessa made a mental note to check into this, and as soon as Leslie was gone, called her private investigator to track down Lorie's second book.

The rivalry between Vanessa and Lorie escalated to alarming proportions. Lorie's taunts that Vanessa's veil was covering up a perfectly lovely, reconstructed face were canceled when Vanessa lifted her veil to reveal her ugly scars. Lorie scoffed that she had learned from Vanessa's doctor that she didn't have a heart condition as she claimed and that she could have had her plastic surgery 10 years ago but decided against it in order to hang on to Lance. Vanessa countered that if Lorie breathed one word of this to anyone, she'd reveal to Lance how Lorie had written a book, *In My Sister's Shadow*, using her sister's misfortune to earn a fortune for herself.

Eventually, an obsessed Vanessa devised a ploy to send Lance to Chicago on business, during which time she would shoot Lorie but say she thought it was a burglar.

After Vanessa fired two shots, she was horrified to find that she had shot her own son, who was not out of town as she'd expected. Again the women worked out a quid pro quo: Lorie would take the

Leslie and Brad made sacrifices for each other, but the fates were not kind to them. Brock helped Leslie pick up the pieces after her divorce.

blame, but Vanessa would have to move out. For Lorie, the agreement backfired: Lance indeed forgave his wife (for a crime she didn't commit), but he refused to allow his mother to move out.

Meanwhile, married life for Leslie and Brad seemed to be getting back on track, with both of them adjusting to his blindness. They were equally enthused about her pregnancy. And she intended to do her part in honoring the pact they made: she'd go on with her career if that's what he wanted. Then one day, Brad was helping Leslie pack for a concert tour when he accidentally and unknowingly hit her in the stomach with a valise. Leslie didn't let him know for fear that he'd only fall back into his old ways: blaming himself for holding her back and depriving her of the fulfillment he was sure she craved. So when the pains started shortly afterwards, she checked herself into the hospital instead of going to the airport as planned. Leslie swore she'd never tell her husband of his role in her miscarriage. She'd simply tell him at some point that she lost the baby.

When Leslie finally got around to telling Brad, he accepted it as one of life's bad things that happen to good people. He comforted her. But later, when he learned the truth behind the "truth," he realized he was the one that caused her to miscarry. Suddenly, everything else fell into place: he couldn't remember the last time he heard her practice, which made it clear she was sacrificing her career as a gifted concert pianist to care for him. And he wouldn't—couldn't—let that happen. He'd file for divorce, and then leave and never come back, if one last solution didn't pan out.

Brad boarded a plane for Chicago and persuaded the same doctor who initially worked on his case to rerun some tests. He underwent a high-risk, no-guarantee surgery, in the hopes that his eyesight might be restored and that he and Leslie could begin life anew. Brad had a letter written to be given to Leslie if he didn't make it about how much she meant to him and how she must carry on through her music if his operation wasn't a success. But he survived the operation, and the doctors said his prognosis seemed promising. At the same time, Leslie was home in Genoa City, being served divorce papers. Fortunately, Brock was there for her, to pick up the pieces.

Liz Foster wasn't adjusting well to Bill's death despite her strong religious conviction that it was God's will. She did receive much comfort, however, from meeting David Mallory, the young man who received Bill's eyes: it was as if Bill lived on. The burden of Bill Foster's death also weighed heavily on Snapper, who often dropped in on his mother to check on her mental state. He was the only one who knew she had pulled the plug on her husband's respirator. After all, there was no one else he could talk to about this—not Liz herself, not Chris, not Greg, not Jill. No, he had to keep it to himself.

An investigation was launched, with Snapper emerging as the prime suspect. He was then charged with murder. Poor Liz! How could her act of love for her dying husband, whose wishes she was obeying, be considered murder? She confessed everything to Jill (who couldn't bring herself to forgive her mother), and then suffered a minor stroke that wiped away any memory at all of what she had done! Snapper was devastated: not only did his brother blame him, but his mother lashed out at him, with hatred in her eyes, for making Bill die! But Snapper was freed on a technicality: the State couldn't prove the time of death and all charges against him were dropped.

At first, the hospital refused to go along with the court's decision, and Snapper was suspended. Then Liz remembered everything and wanted to tell the police she had pulled the plug, but Snapper wouldn't hear of it. It was over and done with. Snapper's suspension was finally lifted, but he left the hospital to open a free clinic in the poor section of town. He relied on Brock to plead his case with the hospital board to obtain much-needed equipment.

As if he didn't have enough on his mind, Snapper was also extremely

Snapper knew that he could count on Chris when the investigators turned their attention toward him regarding his father's death.

concerned about the growing attachment between Chris and little Karen. What if the Beckers suddenly showed up and demanded Karen's return? Even Stuart was helping Chris out, by tracking down information on little Karen's background. And when Stuart received a call from a nurse at the state psychiatric hospital that a patient who called herself "Mrs. Fran Jackson" might really be Nancy Becker, he hurried over to the hospital to check on it. He couldn't believe what had happened to Nancy; she was almost unrecognizable and was suffering from severe mental distress. The doctors suggested that bringing little Karen in to see her mother might jolt Nancy back to reality, but Chris initially rejected the idea of subjecting the little girl to such trauma. Later, Chris did relent, but Nancy remained unresponsive; Karen just cowered and clung to Chris's skirt.

Upon receiving the doctors' advice that Nancy'd probably never recover from her psychoses, Chris made up her mind right then and there to take further steps to legally adopt Karen. But Ron Becker returned to Genoa City and informed the Fosters, and his lawyer, that he wanted his daughter back. Ron failed to mention to his attorney that Nancy had reacted violently toward him when he visited her. The lawyer, deprived of this knowledge, told Ron that he'd have a stronger case if he were to reconcile with his wife. Ron exercised his legal right to remove her from the sanitarium, and threatened her that if she didn't go along with him, she'd never see Karen again.

Once he got her home, Ron overmedicated Nancy to make her appear more coherent, to make a good impression on the court. The dosages Ron was administering could possibly kill her, but she wasn't part of his long-range plans anyway. His only interest was Karen. Nancy's appearance began to improve so

radically that Ron's lawyer recommended taking the next step—living by themselves in a more suitable apartment. After that, they would go to court.

The effects of her medication would last only a few hours, Snapper informed Brock, who was representing the Fosters. On their day in court, Brock requested a two-hour delay so the court could see what Ron was really doing to Nancy. The tactic worked, and everyone went back to square one.

Ron snatched Karen from the school yard, telling her he was going to take her on a trip, and that her new mommy, Chris, would be joining them. But Karen got sick at the bus terminal and Ron took her to a neighborhood clinic that, he was surprised to discover, was run by Snapper. He deposited Karen there and quickly left. Later, he faced possible charges of kidnapping. Feeling like there was no point in living, Ron swallowed poison and had to be rushed to the hospital. At first Snapper refused to treat him, but he then gave in for Karen's sake.

When Ron's mother told him how sorry she was for making him feel unloved as a child, he felt he had a new lease on life. Ron told Snapper and Chris he believed the best thing for Karen was for her to stay with them; he would help with the adoption and then leave Genoa City with his mother to start over. Chris and Snapper were relieved that their nightmare would finally be over.

Ron next apologized to Nancy for the pain he caused her. Ron's words—that Nancy was a good wife and mother but he just couldn't see it—brought Nancy out of her catatonic state. She said she wanted to start a new life with Ron and Karen. But when Ron told her that Karen would be staying with Snapper and Chris, Nancy demanded to see her daughter one

last time. She had to say good-bye. Nancy became hysterical when the little girl didn't recognize her, and vowed she'd get her daughter back. Chris tried desperately to convince the judge that the Beckers were unfit parents, but the court psychiatrist declared that both Ron and Nancy had recovered. Chris's worst fears came true when Karen decided, after spending some time with Nancy, that she'd rather live with her real parents. Devastated by the court's decision that Karen would have her wish, Chris left town to find herself despite Snapper's protestations.

The Brookses had every reason to be concerned over Peggy's emotional state, and advised their daughter to seek professional counseling. But Peggy reacted in anger. She was absolutely adamant: she did not need it. She insisted that if everyone would just stop pressuring her, she'd be all right. Then she went

to Jack with her plan. They should get married right away, elope . . . and they couldn't tell anyone about it. It would have to be their secret. She'd still live at home but would visit Jack as often as possible. It would be a part-time marriage that would eventually evolve into a full-fledged domestic union. This way, if her family didn't know they were married, they wouldn't be knowingly asking her, "How are things going?" And she was sure that without their pressure, she'd achieve a normal relationship with her husband. Peggy and Jack were married immediately.

Things went along reasonably well until the night that Stuart stormed over to Jack's apartment, thinking Jack had conned his daughter into spending the night with him, without the benefit of a marriage license. Peggy listened from her sanctuary in the bathroom, as her father berated Jack, accusing him of being sex-crazed and selfish. Unable to stand it any longer, Peggy came out into the open, clad in only Jack's pajama tops, and lashed out at her father for treating Jack so unfairly. She told Stuart they were married, and that she was trying to get over her sexual hang-ups by sleeping with her husband. It was not going to happen now because he had ruined the moment! She then went home with her father, but only to pack her bags. She moved in with Jack, determined to be a wife to him in every way. Afterwards, she lied to Stuart, telling him she and Jack had consummated their marriage.

But then one night, Jack got tired of waiting

Despite the concerns her family expressed, Peggy couldn't wait to marry Jack Curtis.

for her to come around, and took her by force. Feeling degraded and used, she screamed that he was no different than Ron Becker! Angry and aroused, Jack turned his attention to Joann, who by now had become a beautiful, trim young woman. Still in love with her former husband, Joann gave in to his ardor, later berating herself for being such an easy mark.

Going to the Eliots' for tea and talk, Peggy didn't get much sympathy from Brad. He suggested that her sexual hang-ups might not have had as much to do with her rape as with taking Jack away from Joann in the first place. It was time to stop playing house! Meanwhile, Kay had become excessively possessive of Joann, transferring her own antipathy toward men to the younger woman. So when Jack went over to Kay's to tell Joann that his marriage to Peggy was over, Kay lied to him, telling him Joann was interested in another man.

The appearance of hairdresser Derek Thurston in Genoa City had a profound effect on Jill and Kay, who would fight tooth and nail for his love. Although Jill saw Derek first, Katherine's influence and money were enough to tie him up in a complicated marital knot. And the reappearance of Lucas Prentiss, on the other hand, would have particular meaning for Leslie. The coming year would certainly be a year to watch.

Lorie Brooks located Lucas Prentiss in Hong Kong and brought him back to Genoa City. His presence would have a profound influence on the lives of many.

While Jill Foster was falling in love with handsome hairdresser Derek Thurston with a full heart, Katherine

Chancellor was attracting him with a full pocketbook. Jill saw herself working side by side with Derek to

achieve his dream of owning his own beauty salon, which he would call The Golden Comb. She also saw

herself as his soul mate—marrying him, bearing his children, sharing in his triumphs and failures, growing old

with him. But Katherine had a different vision and proceeded to put every obstacle she could find in Jill's

way. First, she offered Derek the money to open up his own beauty shop. Then she got him drunk and tricked

Derek Thurston's arrival in Genoa City brought the rivalry between Katherine and Jill to the boiling point. Each saw herself as the woman for him.

him into marrying her. Later, she denied that they had married at all, telling Derek he was in her bed because they had made love—no strings attached. That is, until Jill said she wanted him, and he said he wanted Jill.

Characteristically, Katherine went into her drinking mode; then she revealed to Derek that they were indeed husband and wife. When he reacted in unadulterated outrage, Katherine turned to an even more extreme measure. She attempted suicide. Derek wasn't so callous as not to be moved by Katherine's desperate attempt to hold on to him. He rushed to her side, which indicated to Jill that he still had feelings for Katherine.

When Katherine recovered, she came up with this proposal for Derek: they would live together, platonically, if he wished, for one year. She would set up a $100,000 trust fund for Jill's son, little Phillip, on the condition that Derek not reveal this to Jill. Then, at the end of the year, she would let him have full ownership of The Golden Comb, and his freedom. Derek agreed to this arrangement, knowing full well that Katherine would contest the divorce that he so desperately wanted.

Jill was no fool. She suspected that Katherine might actually be able to gain Derek's affection, and Jill would only end up wasting a year she could otherwise put to better use. She turned her attention to Stuart Brooks. With his standing in the community, he had power and the respect of many. He'd provide Jill and her son the security and money they needed to live comfortably.

Katherine truly loved Derek, and desperately wanted him to love her in return. She'd learned he had a young son, Jamie, whom he hadn't seen in years, and thought helping Derek to reestablish a relationship with his boy would make him love her. She managed to locate Derek's ex-wife, Suzanne Lynch. Suzanne warned Katherine to forget her plan and leave Derek. She explained that the syndicate was after him for killing the kingpin's brother and sending another one of them to jail. When the syndicate moved in to get their revenge, Katherine wound up taking a bullet for Derek that left her paralyzed. Despite the tragedy, it became clear to her that Derek really did care. He wasn't about to leave her now.

Not until she could walk again.

After a short time, Katherine had, in fact, regained feeling in her legs. But she kept silent because, according to their agreement, Derek would be free to go and her marriage would be over. She had also decided to pay off Suzanne to keep her distance. At this point, Katherine didn't want to share Derek with anyone—not even his own son. More and more, however, Derek began to wonder how his boy was doing. Feeling pressured by all of his questions, Suzanne agreed to come to Genoa City to talk with him in person.

In the interim, with Lucas now by her side, Vanessa underwent the surgery that would free her from her veils. She assured Lucas he had no reason to feel guilty about the fire that caused her scars so many years ago.

After Lorie persuaded Lucas to come back to Genoa City, Vanessa saw there was more to her daughter-in-law than the evil woman she'd made her out to be. Unfortunately, Lorie's book, exposing Leslie's trauma and institutionalization, was well on its way to becoming a best-seller, and would probably bring about the end of Lorie's marriage to Lance.

Lorie's book, exposing Leslie's nervous breakdown, was too much for Leslie to handle and she cut short her concert tour.

Vanessa tried desperately to buy up all the copies, but it was impossible. Lorie panicked when she saw the book in the stores, and, to complicate matters, Lucas had suddenly discovered that she was the only woman in the world for him.

Meanwhile, Brad regained his eyesight just as his divorce from Leslie was to be finalized. By this time, Brock had come to love Leslie. He presented her with a ruby ring—an engagement ring to wear when she was ready. Brad tried one last time to romance Leslie—he was still in love with her. But she confessed that her feelings for him had changed. She was a different person now. She no longer loved him.

As Leslie was turning a new page in her life, Lorie's world was falling apart. Brad and Stuart were both furious with her for exposing Leslie's past. Sure, she'd changed the names, but everyone would know that Leslie Brooks was the concert pianist whose life was detailed in the book. The one person who seemed to understand Lorie was Lucas. She could only hope Lance would understand, too. When Stuart broke the news to Leslie about Lorie's book, Leslie said she could never forgive her sister for doing this to her.

Lance rushed to Leslie's side to comfort her, and decided he'd postpone the second honeymoon he'd planned with Lorie to accompany Leslie on her concert tour to Denver. She'd need his support, he reasoned. Leslie was grateful to her brother-in-law for caring, but after her first concert was a resounding success, she assured him she would be all right. Lance then jetted off to Trinidad with Lorie.

But when a reporter in Denver confronted Leslie about Lorie's book, Leslie fell apart and canceled the rest of her concerts. Learning about this turn of events, Lance cut short his trip with Lorie and flew to Denver to be with Leslie. He convinced her to give her next concert. But she couldn't go through with it. The thought of everyone in the audience knowing about her collapse caused her to freeze, and she ran off the stage. Lance was there to comfort her. Perhaps he comforted her too much. They made love. Lance admitted he felt a deep and special love for her. But she convinced him they must go on with their own lives; they must forget their night of passion. They shared one final kiss good-bye—a kiss that Lorie witnessed. That was all Lorie needed to see. She quickly decided to go on tour to promote her book. After all, fame and fortune awaited her. Lorie didn't need to stick around for this—to see her husband taking more than a friendly interest in Leslie. Nonetheless, Lorie was surprised and hurt when she returned to Genoa City after her book tour to find that Lance and Leslie had fallen in love.

Leslie, meanwhile, was waiting for the right

time to tell Lance she was carrying his baby. Brock knew the situation, and nobly stepped aside to allow Leslie her happiness.

Meanwhile, no one was more content than Vanessa to see Lorie and Lance's marriage crumble. Vanessa had always believed Leslie was far better suited to her older son than was Lorie. But Lance was torn when he discovered the real reason Lorie left in the first place was because she'd witnessed him kissing Leslie—a good-bye kiss that was, for him, a confirmation of his commitment to his wife. Lance decided the time had come for him to get his marriage back on track. Leslie, reeling from Lance's decision, traveled to Seattle for a concert date. Lucas followed her. And Leslie confirmed his suspicions that the baby she was expecting was Lance's.

At this low point in her life, Leslie was grateful for Lucas's support and friendship. She accepted his gallant proposal and they wed. Leslie vowed she'd never tell Lance the baby was his. She owed it to Lucas to make their marriage work. Meanwhile, Stuart was shocked by his daughter's sudden decision to marry Lucas, and the ever suspicious Vanessa realized there had to be a compelling reason for the two to wed so hastily. Vanessa planned to find out what that reason was.

Few besides Lucas knew the truth about Leslie's pregnancy. Maestro Fautsch did, and offered Leslie his villa in Switzerland. It would be a safe haven for the couple, a place where they could keep the baby's birthdate a secret. But before the couple departed, Vanessa managed to find out the real reason behind Leslie and Lucas's marriage. She vowed to keep the couple's secret. After all, Vanessa owed her son

With the encouragement of youngest son Lucas, Vanessa underwent the surgery that freed her from her veils.

Lucas much for helping to "unveil" her, for persuading her to have the surgery, which proved to be successful.

Greg decided to move back to Genoa City. In no time at all, he reopened his office and was back in business as if he had never left.

Liz Foster found herself in a situation that was entirely new to her. Two men, Stuart Brooks and Maestro Fautsch, were both taking an interest in her. And as it would come to pass, she would end up in competition with Jill over Stuart, who offered Jill a job managing the classified section of the newspaper. Jill was grateful. Stuart's compassion reminded her so much of her late husband, Phillip Chancellor.

Sensing that her mother was starting to have deep feelings for Stuart but also that Stuart might not feel the same, Jill told her mother she might be setting herself up to be hurt. The ever cautious Liz took note of her daughter's comments. But Stuart was able to lift Liz's spirits when he invited her to dinner. The couple had a wonderful time together, and began to see more of each other. Despite the hardships they

Lucas followed Leslie to her concert date in Seattle and proposed marriage, knowing she was carrying Lance's baby. Leslie gratefully accepted.

both had endured, Liz and Stuart were now experiencing some of the best times of their lives. They felt alive. They were connecting.

Stuart was confused, however, when he found himself drawn not only to Liz, but also to Jill. Liz Foster was down-to-earth and unpretentious, while Jill ignited in him a passion he thought he could never recapture. Jill, banking on getting Stuart away from Liz and to the altar, made love to him. Stuart told Jill she must forget it ever happened, that it had been a huge mistake. He didn't want to hurt Liz.

But Jill was relentless. She wasn't going to have her mother beat her at a game in which she herself excelled. Coming on to Stuart, Jill urged him not to suppress his real feelings for her. She tracked him to a convention in Las Vegas, hoping to make him forget about Liz once and for all. Stuart certainly felt young again in Jill's arms and in her bed. Jill presumed that her mother and Stuart were history. Despite Jill's

proclamation that age meant nothing, Stuart felt uncomfortable about the fact that he was old enough to be her father. Jill nevertheless managed to get Stuart as far as the wedding chapel. However, he couldn't go through with it. If they ever *did* marry, Stuart said, it would have to be in the presence of his daughters.

Tired of keeping their relationship a secret, Jill insisted it was time to bring their feelings for each other out into the open. She was sure their families would put up a fuss, but she was prepared to deal with it.

Liz, meanwhile, was upset over Stuart's seeing another woman, even though she didn't know that woman's identity. She was prepared to go on the offensive. She accepted Katherine's birthday present of a makeover from The Golden Comb, hoping it might help her win Stuart's heart completely, once and for all. Katherine assured Liz this other woman was probably some young, sexy tart interested only in Stuart's money. And that surely Stuart would come to his senses soon.

Lorie managed to figure out that Jill was the new woman in her father's life. She confronted Stuart and prevailed upon him to see Jill as a gold digger. With his wounded ego, Stuart certainly wasn't interested in hearing his daughter's opinion, and resented her interference in his life. Lorie and Chris decided it was time for a family powwow to talk some sense into Stuart. Peggy, who'd been away at school, was summoned home, and Leslie, though reluctant to come because her pregnancy was farther along than it "should" be, nevertheless flew back to Genoa City. The meeting proved successful, and Stuart broke up with Jill. Or at least he tried. But Jill had one more ace up her sleeve. Desperate to trap Stuart into marrying her, Jill told him she was pregnant and wondered what he planned to do about it.

Meanwhile, Snapper was feeling lonely over Chris's departure, and decided to move into the resident quarters of the hospital. Casey Reed, a beautiful and gifted doctor, occupied the room adjoining his. Snapper was attracted to Casey, but she had no interest in becoming involved with Snapper or any other man. Snapper was simply seeking friendship. Casey's feelings were tempered by her father's mistreatment of her mother when she was growing up, as well as by some other vague disturbing "intuitions" that she couldn't quite put into words. Snapper learned Casey had a younger and much wilder sister, Nikki, and that Casey's primary goal was to turn Nikki's life around. She asked Brock to give Nikki a job at The Allegro, and in exchange, comforted him over his breakup with Leslie, assuring him she'd always be there when he needed a friend.

Nikki Reed had been seeing Paul Williams, who was as promiscuous as she was. When Nikki contracted gonorrhea, Snapper expressed his concern to Casey over her sister's lifestyle. Nikki, who was down on herself, just wasn't interested in hearing any words of wisdom from Casey. After all, Nikki said, Casey was just as messed up as she was. That it wasn't normal for someone Casey's age to be a virgin. That she was using her commitment to her work as an excuse to avoid establishing relationships with men.

No one was more surprised than Stuart that he should find himself involved with the beautiful, much younger Jill Foster.

Undaunted by Nikki's verbal lashing, Casey allowed Snapper to set up Nikki with a young intern named Scott Adams.

Nikki was surprised that a man like Scott would have any interest in her—especially when he pronounced that he wasn't interested in her body. The young girl had never met anyone like him. When Nikki protested she was no good for him, Scott assured her she *could* be the woman for him. That she *could* change, if she really wanted to. Scott dared Nikki to tame her wild ways, and, good sport that she was, she took him up on his dare. Nikki was determined to leave her past behind and move her life in a more positive direction. Paul Williams had no use for this tamer version of Nikki. He told her to call him when she was ready to have a good time again.

Nikki managed to keep on the straight and

Snapper Foster and Casey Reed, both on staff at Memorial Hospital, could share their innermost feelings with one another. They established a deep and meaningful friendship.

narrow with Scott's help, but slipped in a major way when she slept with her English professor in the hopes of salvaging a passing grade. Ashamed of her actions, she was ready to pack it in, but Brock encouraged her to stick with college and look to the future rather than dwell on the past. Brock also wished he could help Casey overcome her fear of men. By this time, Casey had come to the disturbing conclusion her father was at the root of her problems, but she couldn't explain why.

It was inevitable, that over time, Snapper and Casey would grow closer and feel more than friendship for each other. Just when Snapper finally confessed his feelings for Casey, they were interrupted by a telephone call from Chris, who had just returned home. Snapper rushed home to see her. Chris said she would make no demands on her husband, and would fully understand if his feelings for her had changed. When Snapper returned to Casey, she told him she was ready to follow through with her feelings for him. Now it was Snapper who asked for time to sort things out.

Chris visited the hospital to meet Casey, this other woman who obviously meant so much to her husband. The two women immediately found they shared a mutual liking and respect for one another. They decided it was up to Snapper to choose between them. When Snapper came down with appendicitis and Chris was wiping his brow after surgery, Snapper whispered Casey's name. Devastated, Chris believed that Snapper had made his choice. She quietly began divorce proceedings. Casey and Greg both pleaded with Chris not to rush into such a decision. Not long after, when Casey got word that her mother had been killed in an automobile accident, Snapper was there for her. But Casey assured Snapper she could manage without him, and Snapper reconciled with his wife.

Brock was always there for his friends—ready to lend a helping hand. After Casey's mother died, he was at Casey's side, helping her with the heartrending task of sorting through her mother's personal belongings. He came across a letter from Nick Reed, Casey's father, begging his wife's forgiveness for causing their family so much pain. Brock thought it would do the Reed sisters some good if he brought Nick back to Genoa City. Nikki, especially, would benefit; she desperately needed a father's influence.

Nick did return. But he asked his youngest daughter to wait a while before telling Casey he was back in town.

In the meantime, Casey had come to realize that the man standing over her bed in her nightmares was her father. How she loathed him for taking advantage of her so many years ago—if she never saw him again, it would be far too soon to suit her!

When Nick did approach Casey, he threw her world into turmoil. Casey demanded that he leave town immediately, or she'd tell Nikki what he had done to her! But Nick turned out to be rather persuasive. He acted hurt that Casey didn't believe he was a changed man. He no longer drank. He no longer chased after women. Furthermore, he totally regretted what he had done! He begged Casey to believe him. And she did.

But when Nick realized that his youngest daughter was interested in Greg Foster, all those old for-bidden feelings came rushing back, and he didn't know how to curb them. And there was one thing of which he was certain: he was not about to let Greg or anyone else get close to his daughters. Nick began drinking heavily again. Casey decided she couldn't remain silent any longer. She had to warn Nikki—reveal how Nick had violated her, his own daughter! But Nikki refused to believe her, and was convinced that Casey was trying to make her father the scapegoat for her own inability to relate to men. That is, until Nikki came face to face with the awful truth one night and realized that Nick hadn't changed at all. He came home drunk and tried to force himself on Nikki. She fought him off and he fell, unconscious. At the hospital, Nick said he was sorry, that he never meant to hurt his daughters. Before he died, he told Casey and Nikki he loved them.

Greg consoled Nikki. He convinced her to forget the past, and to get on with her life. They grew

Nikki Reed was happy to have her father back in her life, but Casey didn't share her sister's enthusiasm.

closer, though Nikki protested she wasn't good enough for him. But Greg persisted until Nikki said yes to his marriage proposal. Liz and Snapper worried that Greg was moving too quickly, and could only hope that the wild Nikki had changed her ways. And when Paul Williams surfaced in Nikki's life again, and told her he loved her and that he was sure she still had feelings for him, he put her life in turmoil. But Nikki married Greg.

Meanwhile, Vanessa was moving ahead in her scheme to wreck Lorie's marriage to Lance. First she announced to Lorie that she had information that would jeopardize Lorie's happiness. Then she called Lucas and invited him to join Prentiss Industries, knowing Lucas's jealousy of his more successful brother would play right into her plan to dethrone Lance. Although reluctant, Lucas did agree to work at Prentiss, rationalizing that it would strengthen his relationship with his mother. Encouraged that her plan was working, Vanessa began to transfer more and more stock to Lucas, severely undermining Lance's power.

Leslie cringed when Lorie told her of Vanessa's threat to reveal some truth that could destroy Lorie's marriage to Lance. Leslie pleaded with Vanessa to keep her promise not to reveal the secret—that Lance was the father of her unborn child. Meanwhile, Leslie's recent return to Genoa City prompted Lorie to do some calculations of her own. She came to the inescapable conclusion that

Leslie's pregnancy was too far along—the baby had to be Lance's! As Leslie returned to Europe to give birth to the child, Lorie calmly told Vanessa that she indeed knew the truth about the baby. But she also assured her mother-in-law that her marriage was strong enough to withstand it!

In Switzerland, Leslie gave birth to Brooks Lucas Prentiss. She lost no time in acknowledging to Lucas that he had met his "obligation," and that she would be forever grateful to him for giving her son his name. She also admitted that she felt guilty and could no longer detain him. He was free to go. But Lucas said he wanted to stay, and a relieved Leslie prayed that perhaps someday she would come to love him in the same way she loved Lance.

With Lance's ouster now complete, and with Lucas at the helm of Prentiss Industries, Leslie and Lucas decided to give their marriage a real chance. They began living as husband and wife. But Lucas was not without a conscience; he could not help agonizing over his brother's loss of power. Vanessa tried to reassure him that things were exactly as they ought

Greg Foster proposed to Nikki, though Liz and Snapper thought he was moving too quickly.

Maestro Fautsch was always there for Leslie, offering her guidance not only in her career, but also in her personal life.

to be. Besides, it would secure Brooks's future as the rightful heir to the family business. Still, Lucas was uncomfortable with the situation, and offered his brother a position heading Prentiss Industries' European Division from the Paris office. Lance immediately rejected the offer, and began looking for other businesses to buy. He and Lorie moved out of the family home into a penthouse apartment in an effort to distance themselves from Vanessa's manipulating ways. In addition, Lorie told Lucas she could no longer be friends with him for the way he treated Lance. Lucas was forced to admit to himself that he was still in love with Lorie. All the while, Vanessa maintained that there was one way Lorie could guarantee Lance's reinstatement: Divorce him.

Lucas soon realized he just wasn't cut out to head a major corporation. He decided to travel to Australia to meet up with Leslie and Brooks during her concert tour.

Stepping up her efforts to drive a wedge between Lance and Lorie, Vanessa convinced Lance that Leslie would appreciate a visit from him. Leslie was thrilled to see him. Over dinner, he told her he was committing himself to Lorie—and he suggested to Leslie that she do all she could to save her marriage to Lucas. Furthermore, Lance told her he'd reconsidered Lucas's job offer and planned to accept it.

As fate would have it, Lucas witnessed the intimate conversation from a distance, and presumed the worst. When the two brothers met up again in Genoa City, Lucas rescinded his original job offer, but, in a deliberate attempt to keep Lance and Leslie apart, told Lance that if he truly wanted to help Prentiss Industries, he'd go to war-torn Santa Domingo where the company was in desperate need of leadership.

Maestro Fautsch later told Leslie that Lucas had seen her with Lance in Australia. Leslie then understood the reason for Lucas's change of heart, and was touched when Lucas told her for the first time that he loved her.

Knowing how unhappy Lance was, Lorie tried to convince Vanessa to reinstate him at Prentiss Industries. But Vanessa insisted that there was only one way for that to happen. This forced Lorie to make a very painful decision. She had to convince Lance she didn't love him anymore. By divorcing him, he would regain his rightful place in the family business. Lance was stunned by Lorie's decision, but he granted her the divorce she said she wanted. He also promised himself that he would win her back by buying another business and proving he was still the same successful man with whom she had fallen in love.

In another part of town, Derek's ex-wife, Suzanne Lynch, tricked Katherine into revealing she was able to walk again, after months of Katherine's keeping it a secret. But this boomeranged on Suzanne, who was hoping to reconcile with Derek; it freed him to propose to Jill instead. Jill, on the other hand, was tricking Stuart Brooks into thinking she was pregnant with

Stuart Brooks and Liz Foster weathered the troubled times brought on by his involvement with her daughter, Jill.

his child. Before she'd give Stuart his freedom, she demanded a guarantee from Derek that he would marry her. Once again, Katherine intervened by "creating" a family emergency for Suzanne and Derek that would remove them temporarily from the scene. Furious that Derek left town without an explanation, Jill realized how foolish she was for having trusted him in the first place. So she married Stuart, vowing to get pregnant for real. This left Derek, upon his return, with little choice but to retreat to Katherine's eager arms. Derek never knew that Katherine had engineered the entire caper in the first place.

As for Liz, she just couldn't believe Jill could actually have planned to marry both Derek and Stuart on the same night! And she doubted Jill had any real feelings for Stuart. When Stuart admitted to Jill that their marriage was nothing more than an "arrangement" because of her condition, Jill decided it was time to move out. Stuart implored her to stay until the baby was born, thinking it best to keep up appearances. But Jill sought much more from her marriage. She had needs and desires, which Stuart wasn't fulfilling. Although Stuart's attitude could have provided her an out—she wasn't even pregnant, after all—she grew even more determined to conceive. But how? Jill then read an article in the *Genoa City Chronicle* about a clinic in New York that performed artificial insemination. She went to New York.

In the meanwhile, Greg had a hunch that Stuart married his allegedly pregnant sister out of a sense of obligation. When Greg confronted Stuart,

Stuart confirmed his suspicions, and Greg tried to figure out a way to get Stuart and Liz back together.

When Jill returned, she was infuriated at Stuart's allegations that she'd gone to New York to have an abortion. They fought, and Jill tumbled down a flight of stairs, suffering internal injuries and a concussion. Stuart asked the doctor about the baby's condition and was shocked when the doctor informed him that Jill wasn't pregnant. He made up his mind right then and there: this was not to go on! As soon as Jill came home from the hospital, he ordered her out of the house and informed her that he was seeking an annulment.

But Jill was not to be deterred. Stuart could say he wanted an annulment all he wanted to. She knew him well enough to know that a man of his highfalutin moral principles was not about to admit they'd slept together before they were married. He would do anything not to have his daughters or Liz find this out. In the meanwhile, Stuart sought out Liz and apologized for hurting her. He told her she was the only woman he'd truly cared for since Jennifer's death a few years earlier. And he admitted he had made a grave mistake in marrying Jill, but that he was about to set things straight by ending the marriage.

With Jill's marriage to Stuart in shambles, she was now encouraging Derek to divorce Katherine, and to seek a whopping settlement. But she also warned him that they wouldn't be able to see each other until her own divorce was finalized, because

Katherine was committed to Fairview Sanitarium when Suzanne drugged her and caused her to lose touch with reality.

Stuart's daughters would be watching her every move! When Stuart offered Jill a $25,000 settlement, Jill's lawyer advised her to demand a lot more. A frustrated Stuart confided in his daughter Lorie the real reason behind his marriage to Jill; together Stuart and Lorie began to make plans to prove that Jill had in fact tricked him into marriage.

As Jill was working to get a larger share of Stuart's fortune, Suzanne was setting her own plan in motion to get her hands on Katherine's money. She was drugging Katherine by feeding her tainted chocolates. Katherine began behaving so erratically she had to be committed to Fairview Sanitarium, where doctors opined she would need years of therapy. Suzanne not only continued to drug Katherine, but she used her absence to seduce Derek. Katherine finally realized Suzanne was poisoning her and vowed to make Derek's ex-wife pay.

When Fairview burned to the ground, Suzanne thought her problems were over. Another patient had set fire to Katherine's room and perished in the blaze. Unbeknownst to all, Katherine had slipped her wedding ring on the charred remains and escaped.

While Derek mourned, Katherine decided to remain "dead."

Katherine attended her own funeral in disguise, and then showed up at Liz's house and begged her startled friend to keep her secret. She had to find out how Derek really felt about her. Now that he had all the money he ever dreamed of having, Katherine would be able to judge his true colors.

Katherine went to the mansion, unseen, of course, and overheard Derek defending her to Suzanne.

Katherine would soon get her revenge. Before too long, voices from the grave (by way of telephone calls), phantom visits, and a bed full of tarantulas came close to pushing Suzanne over the edge.

Derek continued to vacillate between Suzanne and Jill. Meanwhile, Katherine was insisting she was through with Derek, and put into motion a plan to drive Jill and Derek together so that Liz could resume her relationship with Stuart.

But even though Derek was now available to Jill, Jill refused to let Stuart off the hook so easily. While arguing over their divorce as Stuart was eating, Stuart began to choke. A panicking Jill had enough presence of mind to call Snapper, who led her through a tracheotomy. Jill saved Stuart's life. Stuart made a full recovery, and now wondered how he could ever repay Jill. Jill suggested they give their marriage another try, but Stuart insisted he couldn't do this and urged her to proceed with her plan to divorce him. Feeling no animosity toward Jill, he then offered her $100,000. But Jill demanded more—she wanted half of his estate as well as the Brooks home. Stuart then rescinded his offer and decided to force Jill into a lengthy court battle—something she wanted to avoid now that Derek had declared his love for her and proposed marriage. Anxious to have the ultimate revenge on her

Brock squared off with Derek when it was clear to him Derek's primary interest was his mother's fortune rather than her happiness.

"deceased" rival, Katherine, Jill signed the divorce papers. She got nothing from Stuart, but became Mrs. Derek Thurston!

Jill and Derek were thunderstruck when Katherine revealed herself to them, and reveled in celebrating her revenge! Not only was Jill left without a single cent, but she didn't have Derek either! Katherine at first dismissed Derek's protestations of love, but soon found she was still vulnerable to his charms. She allowed him back into her bed.

Meanwhile, Brock was certain Derek was out to hurt his mother, and hired a private investigator who turned up not only photos of a cozy tête-à-tête between Derek and Jill, but also an audiotape of them plotting against Katherine. Katherine, however, refused to believe she was being used, and resented Brock's interference.

While Stuart was straightening out his tangled love life, his daughter Chris was doing an investigative report on prostitution for the *Chronicle*. Snapper was concerned over the potential danger of such an assignment. Chris dismissed his concerns and became involved with two young teenage girls caught up in a prostitution ring run by Rose DeVille. Rose denied knowing the two girls in question—Julie and Sharon—and had her henchman, Vince Holliday, trail Chris, who was asking too many questions. When Chris returned to the shop, Vince chloroformed her and took her to the basement where he was also hid-

ing Sharon. Rose's plan was to now sell Chris as well as Sharon to another ringleader in South America.

Snapper and Brock, fearing for Chris's safety when she was nowhere to be found, went to Rose's. Rose claimed she hadn't seen Chris, but slipped up, calling Snapper by name. Snapper and Brock rescued Sharon and Chris, and Rose and Vince were arrested. They wouldn't be able to hurt anyone else. At least not for now.

The otherwise happy news that Chris was expecting was tempered by her fear that she had been exposed to German measles. When Chris finally broke the news to Snapper, he assured her that they would face whatever would come their way, together. They were relieved to learn the tests were negative; their baby would be all right.

Always one to help those less fortunate, Chris soon turned her attention to their new neighbor, April Stevens, who was only 19 years old and was raising a child alone. Chris intended to help April in any way she could.

Meanwhile, Leslie was having a difficult time convincing Lucas she could love him the way she loved Lance. Vanessa, however, was encouraging Leslie to free Lucas from their marriage so he could find someone who would truly love him. When Leslie's attempt to be a real wife to Lucas failed, she was shattered, and Lance offered her and Brooks a place to stay at the penthouse. Furious over her sister's intrusion in her life, Lorie unleashed her anger on Leslie, who became suicidal and left town.

Despondent over his crumbling marriage, Lucas was drowning his sorrows at The Allegro when Casey approached him. He looked like he could use a friend. Lucas was immediately attracted to her. They bared their souls to each other, and made love that night. Casey was left unfulfilled, but Lucas was fascinated with the beautiful doctor.

No longer in touch with reality and no longer in Genoa City, Leslie wandered rain-soaked into an unfamiliar bar. The owner, Jonas, a man with a rough demeanor and a kind heart, said he would take care of her until he was certain she was all right. He made her over into a sexy blonde, and Leslie began her new life as a piano player and singer at Jonas's club. She had a new name, too: Priscilla.

Greg had always encouraged Nikki to make something of herself, and was more than happy to support his wife's decision to pursue a modeling career. Nikki answered an ad for Rose's Modeling Agency (yes, Rose DeVille was back in business!), not knowing it was a front for a drug and prostitution ring. Greg had warned Nikki not to enter into any kind of contract without giving him a chance to read it first. But Nikki

was so anxious to start her new career that she disregarded his warning and signed on the dotted line. She was then upset to discover she owed Rose $1,800! Rose assured her she'd earn much more than that, and she could simply pay the fee out of her earnings.

Greg didn't appreciate Nikki's first job: modeling lingerie. And when he heard Snapper and Chris were expecting, Greg thought he and Nikki should start a family, too. But Nikki argued that he was just trying to quash her budding career.

When Nikki found herself in the hotel room of prominent businessman Walter Addison, she quickly learned he wasn't there to help her with her modeling career as she'd thought. She refused his advances, and in the fight that ensued, Addison fell dead of a heart attack.

So as 1979 was coming to an end, Nikki hoped she could straighten out the mess she'd gotten herself into and still keep her marriage intact; Katherine was blissfully in love with Derek while Jill was getting tired of waiting for him; Lance toasted the end of a terrible year; and Stuart and Liz were anticipating the good things to come. They all wondered what the new year had in store for them.

Derek Thurston wasn't the only one plotting to dupe Katherine Chancellor out of her millions. It seemed Derek's ex-wife, Suzanne Lynch, and con artist Douglas Austin each had hatched schemes of their own to get their hands on Katherine's money and failed, before they decided to join forces to carry out a more successful venture. Derek thought he was well on his way toward reaching his goal as the unsuspecting Katherine appointed him chairman of the board of Chancellor Industries. Once there, he quickly aligned himself with Judy Wilson to oust George Packard, who, as president, had been running the company since Phillip Chancellor's death. A takeover by Derek seemed virtually within his grasp.

In the meantime, Casey Reed and Lucas Prentiss were growing closer to one another, with each trying to fill the gaps that existed in their own lives, each seeking a deeper understanding of the meaning of pure love as opposed to physical attraction. But even as Lucas found himself connecting with Casey on a metaphysical plane, he had come to the realization that he wasn't cut out to run Prentiss Industries alone. He badly needed Lance's help. But now that Lorie's divorce from Lance was final, Vanessa dispatched her eldest son to the Paris office.

Elsewhere, Leslie was overcoming her objections to Jonas's transforming her into the new person she had become. She found great satisfaction making the bar patrons happy with her music. Through her relationship with Jonas, she was able to loosen up. Jonas taught her not to take life so seriously. Leslie also decided she had no interest in knowing her past. She wanted only to look ahead. However, when a minor surgical procedure revealed Leslie had had a baby, Jonas realized there were people somewhere who needed her. He vowed to help her regain her memory. But, at the same time, Leslie found herself falling in love with Jonas.

Lorie, despondent over Lance's relocation to Paris, needed to feel some purpose to her life, so she convinced Lucas to allow her to take care of Brooks. When the young child fell during an argument between Vanessa and Lorie, and was rushed to a near-by hospital, Leslie, miles away, awakened from a nightmare, sensing something had just happened to her baby. Thankfully, Brooks quickly recovered.

Lucas and Jonas were thrown together when Dr. Sebastian Crown persuaded them to continue the fight they had begun some time ago against the dictator of Santa Leandro. Lucas provided money and the Prentiss jet, and flew to Santa Leandro with Jonas and Crown, unaware that "Priscilla" had stowed away on the plane. Lucas was shocked to see that Priscilla was really Leslie, but it was obvious she didn't recognize him. Lucas also could tell she was in love with Jonas.

When they returned to Genoa City, Leslie did not recognize her sisters, or her son. Lorie was torn, because she strongly believed the truth about Brooks's paternity might be the key to bringing Leslie back to reality. Despite Vanessa's pleas that Leslie regain custody of Brooks, as she still had a vendetta against Lorie, Leslie believed in her heart that Brooks, this child she didn't even know, was better off with Lorie. Leslie granted her sister legal custody.

Convinced that her life as Leslie Brooks was truly buried in the past, Priscilla prepared to return home with Jonas. And to her singing job at Jonas's bar. As she was saying her good-byes, she accidentally encountered Maestro Fautsch at Vanessa's. The maestro gently prevailed upon her to play the piano for him. Suddenly, the most mellifluous strains were being coaxed by her fingers as they flew over the keyboard. And it caused her to wonder if someday she might draw out all the memories of her life as Leslie that remained hidden in the deep recesses of her mind. She felt she had little choice but to remain in Genoa City. And she convinced Jonas to run The Allegro for her.

And so it was that Lucas and Leslie decided to give their marriage another chance, compelling Casey

to break off with Lucas and turn to Jonas for commiseration and comfort. Soon after the reconciliation of Leslie and Lucas, Lorie's fear of losing Brooks intensified. But as time passed, Lorie detected the telltale signs of a marriage in trouble. Even the principals knew, in their heart of hearts, that not everything was as they pretended it to be. For Lucas knew Leslie could never love him as she did Lance. And Leslie, though working hard to regain her status as a virtuoso pianist, still struggled with the thought that she may have had something to do with Lance and Lorie's divorce.

The introduction of the mysterious business tycoon Victor Newman to Genoa City society portended the enormous gains in wealth and worldly power he was to assume with each passing year. Brock got to know Victor and his wife of 10 years, Julia, when he represented the 16-year-old who stole Victor's car. When the case was settled, Julia was admitted to the hospital with injuries suffered in a fall caused by Victor, and she wondered how long she could endure his jealousy and insecurities. Wanting more from life, Julia approached Brock about obtaining a divorce, but when Victor apologized and promised he'd change, Julia couldn't bring herself to sign the papers. She'd married Victor when

The wealthy and powerful Victor Newman and his wife, Julia, had a passionate and volatile relationship.

she was only 16, and could never, ever imagine life without him.

But Julia was also coming to care deeply for Brock, who, unlike Victor, treated her like a friend and not a possession. And with Brock, Julia felt alive. She sparkled. They spent a great deal of time together, and Brock helped Julia realize she should work to rebuild her marriage. Victor, assuming his wife was having an affair with Brock, took up with Lorie. Lorie then asked Victor if he'd consider financing a photo studio for Michael Scott, her book publicist: he'd become unhappy in that role and decided it was time to renew his career as a photographer.

As accustomed as she was to the day-to-day struggles of making ends meet, and terribly uncertain she'd fit in circulating amongst Stuart's well-to-do friends and business associates, Liz accepted his proposal of marriage with more than a modicum of trepidation. Jill didn't waste much time undermining her mother's happiness. In the most matter-of-fact way, she told Liz she didn't have what it would take to satisfy Stuart in bed. Then, in a fit of anger, Jill blurted out that Stuart had married her because she was pregnant. Liz didn't want to believe Jill. She knew that if it were true, she could never feel the same way about Stuart.

It was Lorie's admission that she was not Stuart's daughter—that she had forgiven her mother's indiscretion—that gave Liz all the reason she needed to forgive Stuart. Jill saw the error of her ways and set about repairing her relationship with her mother. She admitted she'd tricked Stuart into marrying her, and wished Liz and Stuart happiness together. With subdued joy, Liz and Stuart wed on the same day they became grandparents, when Chris gave birth to a daughter. Chris and Snapper named their baby Jennifer Elizabeth Foster.

The youngest Brooks daughter, Peggy, was totally against her father's new marriage. She felt in her heart that no one could ever replace her mother. With tenderness and understanding, Liz sat Peggy down and assuaged her fears by assuring her she had no intention of taking Jennifer's place. Liz invited Peggy to return home from San Francisco and share the Brooks home with them, and Peggy accepted.

Meanwhile, on the other side of town, Rose DeVille and Vince Holliday cursed Nikki for the mess she'd gotten them into. They had a dead man on their hands! They quickly dumped Walter Addison's body in an alleyway. Nikki's husband, Greg Foster, was appointed to defend the murder suspect, a young thug named Tony Baker, who the police caught rifling through Addison's wallet. All Rose and Vince needed was for Nikki to talk, which would then not only expose their role in the Addison case, but their illegal activities overall! They threatened Nikki that Greg

Lorie had a heart-to-heart talk with Liz. She knew Liz and Stuart loved each other, and hoped they would build a future together.

would be a dead man if she didn't continue to keep her mouth shut. Things got even stickier for Nikki, whose husband was still unaware of her involvement with Addison, Rose, and Vince. She left Greg a note of explanation, then drove off, intending not to return. Unfortunately, Nikki was involved in a one-car accident, and for weeks hung on to life by a thread.

Rose and Vince were eventually linked to the Addison case and arrested, but only after Rose had engaged a hitman to take care of Greg Foster. Nikki's role in the death of Addison came out, and Greg was a broken man, unable to comprehend how his beautiful young wife could have gotten herself involved in such a sordid affair. With Greg unable to forgive her, Nikki had no choice but to walk away from her marriage. The hitman, meanwhile, was still on the prowl, and inadvertently shot Greg's mother, Liz, instead of Greg.

Liz recovered, and as for Nikki, Paul Williams found her on the street selling flowers for the New World Commune. With no direction in his own life, all it took was a little friendly encouragement from Nikki—Paul decided to join the commune, too. Steve Williams tried to talk some sense into his younger brother, but Paul didn't want to hear it. He could never live up to his brother's standards and, as far as he was concerned, there was no point in trying. As Paul was getting ready to leave home, he and Steve scuffled. Their mother, Mary, who was hiding the fact that she'd recently discovered she was pregnant, got caught in the middle of their fight and brushed off her injuries as nothing—until the boys were gone. She lost the baby, and her own condition became critical.

Paul donated blood to save Mary's life, but blamed himself for the miscarriage. Nikki assured the unhappy Paul he could start a new life, as she had, in the commune. And while Casey tried to bring her sister back, Greg assumed his wife had resumed her relationship with Paul. He decided he was better off without her.

Steve Williams and Peggy Brooks teamed up to write a series of stories about cults, and Peggy went undercover to conduct her research. The story exposed the New World Commune as a scam, but not before its leader, Sumiko, grew suspicious of Peggy and almost killed her. Paul rescued her just in time. When the commune members dispersed, Nikki felt more lost than ever. She resigned herself to the fact that her marriage to Greg was over, and Paul was there to help pick up the pieces.

In the meantime, Jill had grown tired of waiting for Derek to leave Katherine. She briefly dated Steve Williams, who liked her honesty and directness. He also encouraged her to make more of her life. Jill left the salon and landed a job at Jabot Cosmetics, where she was determined to succeed. She was quickly promoted to head of merchandising when she impressed Jabot's owner, John Abbott, who recognized her talents.

Nikki signed on with Rose's Modeling Agency and got a lot more than she bargained for when she and Rose and Vince became entangled in the death of a prominent businessman named Walter Addison.

Jack Abbott, on the other hand, John's womanizing son, had no interest whatsoever in the family business. Until, that is, Jill asked him out for a drink as a thank-you for his understanding when Liz was hospitalized. She confided that she liked ambitious, successful men, which prompted Jack to tell his father he wanted to join Jabot. John was grateful to Jill for prodding Jack; he had been looking forward to this day for a long time. He assigned the pair to work together on the new Jabot ad campaign.

Without really intending to, Peggy and Steve had grown close while working on the cult series, and it was only natural that they started dating. But when Steve announced that he was taking a job at a newspaper in Washington, D.C., Peggy got upset and turned to Jack for comfort. In a moment of weakness, she slept with Jack. But Steve came to realize how much Peggy really meant to him, and he decided to keep his job at the *Chronicle*. He also planned to propose to her. Peggy, however, continued to see Jack, and, in spite of herself, was taken in by his charming ways.

Meanwhile, Chris was doing her best to be a good friend to April Stevens, who finally told Paul he was the father of her baby. Stunned, Paul made it perfectly clear he had no interest in April or their daughter. April's parents didn't know the father's identity, but felt that he should take responsibility and marry their daughter. April begged them not to interfere. To further complicate April's life, her mother, Dorothy, impulsively admitted she'd given up April's twin sister for adoption when she was a baby.

With his marriage to Nikki at an end, Greg began to date April, who, in turn, was beginning to feel more in control of her life. April decided not to put Heather up for adoption as she had considered doing.

Greg was stunned to learn that his nemesis, Paul Williams, was Heather's father, but came to the conclusion that even his long-standing resentment for Paul could not undermine his commitment to April.

Julia, meantime, told Victor she wanted to have a baby. Without confiding in her, Victor proceeded to have a vasectomy. Victor's coldness caused Julia to turn to Michael Scott, for whom she was now modeling. Victor, of course, suspected something was going on between Julia and Michael, although neither one had crossed the line.

As if Victor didn't have enough problems with Julia, Eve Howard, his former secretary, returned to Genoa City with her six-year-old son. Eve confessed to Julia that she had initiated one night of passion with Victor while they were on a business trip in Acapulco, during which Charles Victor Howard (Cole) was conceived. Her only reason for returning to Genoa City now was that she needed money, and she knew Victor would want to provide for his son. Shocked that Victor could have been unfaithful to her, Julia turned to Michael for comfort. They made love, while Victor confronted Eve and vehemently denied Cole was his son.

John Abbott and Jill Foster saw some of Michael's photos of Julia and instantly recognized Michael's talent and Julia's beauty. They immediately asked them to work for Jabot. Michael not only turned the job down, assuming Victor would never allow Julia to model, but he warned Victor that his obsessive jealousy would ultimately cost him Julia's love. The ever unpredictable Victor surprised Michael by agreeing to let Julia accept the assignment.

Katherine, meantime, found herself attracted to Douglas Austin, an old associate of Victor's. Douglas encouraged their dalliance by saying that if

Michael Scott was a talented photographer. Victor set him up in business and kept close tabs on his work while Michael grew closer to Julia.

she could make Derek jealous, Derek would appreciate her more. Douglas challenged Derek to a duel over Katherine's honor (Derek got shot in the rump!), and then teamed up with Victor to get Derek out of Katherine's life. Victor was distressed that Derek was using her, and thought that a fine woman like Mrs. Chancellor deserved better. Katherine trusted Victor implicitly, and asked him to keep a close watch over Chancellor Industries while she was away on the second honeymoon Derek had planned in an effort to hold on to his job.

By this time, Douglas had fallen in love with Katherine and wanted to marry her. He followed Katherine and Derek on their cruise. When Derek saw Douglas, he became jealous and returned to Genoa City in a huff. Confused over her feelings for Derek and Douglas, Katherine jumped overboard, determined to end it all. When the ship's captain informed Derek that Katherine wasn't on the ship, Derek sought to have her declared dead so he could have his share of her fortune. Katherine's longtime attorney, Mitchell Sherman, informed him that without a body, the legal process would take five years. Out of respect for Katherine's wishes, Mitchell left Victor in charge of Chancellor Industries.

Felipe Ramirez and Katherine Chancellor were an unlikely match, but it was his friendship that helped her to build her inner strength and return to Genoa City a changed woman.

Genoa City mourned Katherine, not knowing she'd been rescued by Felipe Ramirez, a Cuban revolutionary hiding out in Jamaica. Felipe hated people of wealth, and put her to work on the island—cooking, cleaning, fishing, and helping him with his English. Eventually, the two grew close, and Katherine came to appreciate the simple life. When a severely infected cut on Katherine's leg threatened her life, Felipe risked his own to get her to a hospital. Katherine made a miraculous recovery. She hoped to take Felipe, whom she'd grown to love, back home with her. But he penned a good-bye note and left. Katherine learned Felipe's boat had been bombed, and, mourning him, decided to stay forever in Jamaica. Much to her surprise and joy, she found Felipe alive. But he insisted she return to the life she knew, while he would continue his political work. He told her that if it were to be, they would meet again someday. Katherine sadly returned to Genoa City, ready to begin a new life without him.

Peggy Brooks accepted Steve Williams's proposal of marriage, and the two set the date for their wedding. All the while, Jack Abbott tried to undermine their engagement, filling Peggy with enough doubt to make her question whether she was doing the right thing. Even though Steve tried to reassure her that their love was strong enough to overcome her doubts, Peggy couldn't help feeling the way she felt about Jack and secretly hoped she was making him jealous. But Jack didn't seem to notice. When the big day arrived, Peggy felt she was being pressured into a marriage she really didn't want and she left a hapless, heartbroken Steve stranded at the altar. Steve quietly walked away, leaving Genoa City for good, as he headed for Washington, D.C., to accept the newspaper job he'd been offered.

Another couple found themselves at odds when differences over business matters collided with their personal feelings. John Abbott was known for being levelheaded, yet he fired Jill in a disagreement over the new Jabot ad campaign. It was clear that something more was going on, when John gave her her job back over lunch, after which he kissed her passionately. No one could have been more surprised than John himself, but it made Jill realize that she was attracted to John much more than she thought. However, when John decided against taking her on a business trip, she felt rejected and spent the night with Jack, nursing both her wounded heart and her pride.

At her apartment the next morning, Jill found a letter John had left in which he had expressed his deep feelings for her. She was moved. But she'd gone and ruined things again. It seems John had seen her with Jack the night before, and now didn't want to have anything to do with her. Disillusioned, John left Genoa City to run Jabot out of the New York office. And as for Jill, she thought it would be best if she quit Jabot. Which she did.

When Jill complained that Jack was moving too fast for her, she sent him right into the arms of 17-year-old Patty Williams. Patty, the younger sister of Paul and Steve, hadn't adjusted well to having her life upset by all the attention her family was paying to Paul and April's daughter, Heather, so an affair with

an older man—like Jack Abbott—fit in well with her rebellious nature.

When Heather became desperately ill, Greg put his own feelings aside and urged Paul to do the right thing. Greg thought Paul should marry April and give the daughter he shared with her a name before she died. Paul struggled with the decision, but finally agreed to marry April. Heather's condition improved, and Paul was beginning to accept his responsibilities as husband and father. He put off going to school, got a second job, and tried his best to make ends meet. But once Heather was well again, April and Paul mutually agreed they would end their marriage. Paul, at least for the time being, did not stand in Greg's way when Greg said he wanted to pursue his relationship with April.

With John out of her life now, Jill decided she wanted to pick up where she'd left off with Jack, while

Greg and Paul nearly came to blows over April and her daughter, Heather. Greg wanted what was best for them; Paul wasn't certain he was ready for the responsibilities of marriage and fatherhood.

up-and-coming singer Danny Romalotti, who'd just begun his career with an engagement at Jonas's club, befriended Patty. But Patty couldn't resist Jack's gifts or his irresistible charm, and though Jack was shocked to learn the "woman" he'd tried to seduce on more than one occasion was only 17, he had to admit he found her a refreshing change from the other women he'd dated. One afternoon, Patty caught Jack with another woman. He tried to cover, professing his love for the young Ms. Williams, but he also reminded her he had needs that she couldn't fulfill. When Patty insisted she would make love to Jack, he refused, saying one of the reasons she was so special was because she was saving herself for marriage. The fact that Patty's father, Carl, would kill him if he crossed the line undoubtedly had an influence on Jack, too.

Jack had reason to be upset with Jill. First, she lied to him when he asked her if she had any children. Then she fanned the Williams family's flames concerning his relationship with Patty. But the straw that really broke the camel's back as far as Jack was concerned was that Jill had the audacity to apply for a position with a competing cosmetics firm! It's no wonder he gave her a poor recommendation. Jill reacted by going straight to her brother Greg to file a

Danny Romalotti began his singing career at Jonas's, with Paul helping out as his manager.

sexual harassment suit against Jack for causing her to lose her job at Jabot in the first place. Even though at the time she had refused to let Jack cover for her by offering to take responsibility for the Jabot ad campaign that had gotten John so angry. . . even though it was all an out-and-out lie. . . even though Jill had quit of her own free will! What a woman!

Meanwhile, handsome but shady Jerry "Cash" Cashman had come to Genoa City from the East Coast and offered Nikki a job in the "entertainment" business. She'd have to dance the striptease, he told her, but that would only be to get attention. Once his new nightclub, the Bayou, took off, he swore that Nikki would be dancing in legitimate productions. He'd even help her get to the big stage in Vegas! A starstruck Nikki accepted the job, much to the disappointment of those who loved her. And when Jonas learned of Cash's sizable gambling debt, he, too, warned Nikki that she might get hurt. In time, Cash also became Katherine's paid escort, and Nikki and Katherine later became friends when they realized they shared a vested interest in Cash.

Greg and Paul eventually squared off when Greg wanted to wed the still-married April. Paul wanted to be a father to Heather after all. Then, when April learned her twin sister was alive, she left Greg behind and set out with Paul to find her. They grew closer again. Peggy Brooks, in the meantime, became interested in Greg, who had by now left Legal Aid to set up his own private law practice. It was clear April and Greg were separately pursuing new chapters in their lives.

Before too long, Paul and April would learn her twin's name: Barbara Ann Harding. April and Paul located Barbara in New York, but before they could

Jerry "Cash" Cashman promised Nikki fame and fortune to entice her to dance at the Bayou. It was there she would meet Victor Newman.

connect with her, she was heading back to Chicago to interrogate her father, whom she hadn't seen in almost 10 years. Barbara's father confessed that she'd been adopted—something she didn't know—and gave her the names of her biological parents: Dorothy and Wayne Stevens of Genoa City. Barbara headed there, and Dorothy and Wayne were shocked to learn that their new boarder, "Bobbie Smith" as she'd introduced herself, was actually their daughter. When Barbara met Paul, she wanted to have a relationship with him, but he told her he was married. He would soon learn that Barbara was April's sister.

Leslie, who was still trying to regain her memory, found that little Brooks had no recollection of her as his mother. She tried to reestablish a relationship with him on several occasions, to no avail. But when "Aunt Leslie" played a lullaby on the piano, it was obvious that a bond did exist between them. Lance gently revealed to Leslie the real reason she'd left Genoa City:

she was in love with him. Remorseful, humiliated, ashamed, Leslie immediately apologized to Lorie for interfering in her marriage. But this still left a burning question unanswered: Did she and Lance have an affair?

While Leslie was watching Brooks one night, she fell and hit her head. The blow immediately triggered memories of her night of passion with Lance. Maestro Fautsch quickly reminded her that she had never told Lance of Brooks's true paternity. During this emotional time, Leslie made two painful decisions. First, she decided to initiate divorce proceedings so that Lucas could be with Lorie, with whom he was deeply in love. Then she decided to fight to get her son back. Unfortunately for Leslie, the court ruled that Brooks was better off with Lorie, the only mother he'd really ever known. But the judge determined that, in time, after psychiatric counseling, Brooks would be able to handle the news that Leslie was his real mother. Vanessa would later tell Lance that Leslie could have prevented the entire court battle, but she refused to explain how.

Convinced that Eve was blackmailing him, Victor Newman denied that Cole was his son. Meanwhile, Julia found out she was pregnant. At first, she was ecstatic that she was carrying Victor's child. But then she remembered the one night she'd spent with Michael Scott, and now she couldn't be certain who the baby's father was! The last thing Victor expected or wanted was to be a father. He'd had a vasectomy to ensure it wouldn't happen, though his doctor told him the operation could never be 100 percent foolproof.

The thought of Julia with another man enraged Victor. He insisted Julia choose between him and the baby. When Julia pressed him as to why he hated the idea of a baby so much, Victor poured out the story of his heartrending past. He'd grown up in poverty. When his mother became pregnant again, his father took off. And his mother left her son in an orphanage where he spent the next 10 years. Victor never trusted anyone again—until he met Julia. And now he feared he'd be alone again. Julia crumbled. Later, Victor apologized. He begged her to believe that he'd love and take care of her and the baby.

Katherine returned to Genoa City a changed woman. Perhaps for the first time in her life, she was in control of herself and her emotions. She owed a debt of gratitude to Felipe, who'd shown her she needn't rely on Derek, or Douglas, or any man for that matter, to be fulfilled. Derek thought he was hallucinating when he saw that Katherine was alive. And she would quickly prove she was for real when she put Judy Wilson in charge of Chancellor Industries, with all decisions to be made by Victor Newman. Katherine then gave Judy her first assignment: Fire Derek.

It was only natural that Derek would conspire with Eve to destroy Victor. They got their hands on Victor's vasectomy report, which confirmed that Julia must have conceived *after* the operation. They sent a copy to Julia, who realized that Michael Scott was now in grave danger of facing Victor's wrath. Julia decided to play along with the charade as if Victor were the baby's father, and she could only hope that Victor would be none the wiser.

Victor had a plan, too. He sent Julia to the hospital for some rest, but he also arranged to have her hospital room bugged. He was soon rewarded when he learned Julia intended to leave Genoa City with Michael. Victor then hired a contractor to build a fallout shelter in a basement at his ranch, complete with video cameras and monitors. He lured Michael to the shelter and locked him in. Then he sent Julia a good-bye telegram from Michael. When Victor said he'd still been fertile when they conceived their child, and also promised to have the operation reversed, Julia believed Victor had truly changed. Until, that is, she turned on the monitor by accident and discovered Michael was a prisoner right in their own home!

After some time, Michael managed, with Julia's help, to free himself from the dungeon. But before he could escape, Victor returned. The two men scuffled, and Julia, caught in the middle, fell. She miscarried. Michael then trapped Victor in his own lair. When Paul went to the ranch to ask Victor for a job, Victor's absence aroused his suspicion. Paul did some snooping, and rescued Victor from the shelter.

Julia's condition was critical. Victor made a pact with God: Let Julia live and he'd give her her freedom. Julia recovered and left Genoa City with Michael.

As far as Eve was concerned, Victor seemed to be coming around. He made up his mind to give Eve $50,000, but only if she'd agree to his terms: Cole would attend the best school in Switzerland; Eve was to tell people that she was widowed, and that Cole's rich uncle was paying the boy's expenses. And, finally, she had to accept that Victor was not the boy's father. Eve agreed to Victor's terms, and left Genoa City with her son in tow.

Elsewhere in Genoa City, Vanessa learned that she had only two months to live. She'd have to move quickly if she were to get her revenge on Lorie.

Julia Newman was distraught when she received a copy of Victor's vasectomy report, and feared for Michael's safety. Who was the father of her unborn child?

And above all, she had to be sure Lance would find out he was Brooks's father. Vanessa burned her medical records, and then encouraged Lance's new French fiancée, Simone, to pressure Lance into setting a wedding date, knowing full well that this would upset Lance. So far so good: Vanessa's plan was working. Simone returned to Paris, alone. Vanessa's next step was to suggest to Leslie that if she were to tell Lance the truth about Brooks, they would most likely regain custody of their son. Then they could live together as the family they rightfully should be.

Leslie's career was beginning to take a positive turn. She accepted an invitation to perform at the premier summer concert event in Europe, which stalled her divorce proceedings. Leslie asked Stuart (who insisted on going despite his heart condition), Liz, and Lance to accompany her to Europe. Katherine Chancellor would go along, too, taking advantage of the trip to seek out potential plastic surgeons on the continent. Leslie's performance created a sensation, but Lorie managed to steal the thunder from her sister. Dressed in a most revealing gown, Lorie made a grand entrance. All eyes were on her as she waltzed in on the arm of French filmmaker Jean

Paul Vauban, who was interested in making a film of Lorie's book, *In My Sister's Shadow.*

Leslie's divorce from Lucas became final when she returned to Genoa City. Lucas then proposed to Lorie. But she'd become involved with Victor and turned him down. Victor, however, had more on his mind than romance when it came to Lorie. He'd been buying up Prentiss Industries stock with plans for a takeover. He asked Lorie to consider selling him her stock, promising her wealth and power. But despite her growing personal relationship with Victor, Lorie refused because she couldn't bear the thought of Lance losing control of his business again. Fearing Lorie would succumb to Victor's pressure, Leslie, wanting Lance's happiness above all else, told Lorie she'd relinquish any claim to Lance and Brooks if Lorie would agree not to sell out to Victor. Victor resigned himself to Lorie's decision, and promised he would burn her proxy. He told Lorie he would always be there for her. Lucas, knowing how much Lorie loved Lance, put his own feelings aside and encouraged his brother to propose to Lorie. Lucas then announced he would be leaving Genoa City.

Lance planned to take Lucas's advice. Vanessa, meanwhile, tried to convince an indecisive Lorie that Lance had every right to know Brooks was his son. She urged Lorie to tell Lance the truth, reasoning that if he were to find out from someone else, he'd never be able to trust her again. But time was running out, and Vanessa could no longer wait for Lorie to make up her mind. *She* would have to make it happen!

Using Lorie's typewriter, Vanessa typed a note addressed to herself and left it where Lance would be sure to discover it. She then lured Lorie onto the bal-ny and made a ruckus, screaming that Brooks and

Leslie and Lance made a grand entrance at the ball after the European Music Critics Gala Concert . . .

Lance were living a lie. She jumped to her death, making it look as if Lorie had pushed her. Lorie was arrested on suspicion of murder. The police also suspected Lorie of extortion when they found money in

. . . but Lorie made an even grander entrance on the arm of the handsome Jean Paul Vauban.

Brooks's bank account—money the prosecution said Vanessa was forced to pay Lorie in order to see her own grandson.

Lance believed in Lorie's innocence. He gave her an engagement ring and promised they'd be spending the rest of their lives together once the trial was over.

Chris and Snapper talked about having another baby, unaware of the turmoil they were about to face. Sally wrote Liz that her son, Chuckie, was ill—she was bringing him to Genoa City to see a specialist. She also confessed she was still in love with Snapper, Chuckie's father. With Sally and Chuckie in town, Snapper told Chris it was a bad time to think about having another baby. As Chuckie's condition worsened, Chris worried that Snapper would become more involved in his son's life, particularly because he had grown up without his own father most of his life. Sally assured Liz she had no intentions of acting on her feelings; she was respectful of Snapper's marriage to Chris. But Chris accused Sally of using Chuckie's illness to get closer to Snapper, which Sally vehemently denied.

Looking for something to make her life more tolerable, Chris was pleased when Jack Abbott offered her the opportunity to model for Jabot. Her first assignment was a shoot in Hawaii, which infuriated Snapper. Chris insisted it was something she had to do for herself. But she was taken ill at the last minute and couldn't go. Snapper spent more and more time with Chuckie as his son's condition became critical, putting more strain on his marriage. Greg warned Snapper not to lose sight of his wife and daughter, because Greg, who cared deeply for Chris, might be there to take over in his absence.

Nikki, meanwhile, found herself on the receiving end of a crazed secret admirer. He turned out to be her neighbor Eddie, who had some rather bizarre habits (like talking to his mother's ashes!). Paul, his father Carl, and Jonas rescued Nikki from Eddie's apartment just as Eddie blew himself up. Much later, after she got over the traumatic episode, Nikki sensed Jonas's compassion. Desperately wanting to be in love, Nikki wondered whether Jonas might be the man for her. She had no idea her life was about to take a dramatic turn.

Out at the Newman ranch on the outskirts of Genoa City, Douglas sensed Victor needed some cheering up, so he took his friend to the Bayou, where Victor was immediately smitten with Nikki Reed. Victor made a deal to buy the club, on the condition that his ownership would not be made public. He also insisted Nikki be signed to a guaranteed contract, and he had a dressing room fit for a queen built for her. Nikki happily accepted the new terms of her employment, and Victor, who was masquerading as the interior designer, showed an awestruck Nikki her new dressing room. Victor, later posing as Douglas's servant, instructed Douglas to shower Nikki with gifts to determine whether Nikki had a price. When he was certain Nikki passed the test, Victor revealed his true identity. He invited her to stay at the ranch, where he planned to make her over into the perfect woman.

While Nikki was on the cusp of an incredible adventure with Victor Newman, Jill, with her lawsuit in place against Jack, found herself enjoying the company of Andy Richards, a nice guy who was hiding a painful past. But Jill would soon discover her future wasn't to be with Andy; her former boss, John Abbott, was the reason.

The events of 1982 led to the departure of several longtime Genoa City residents, while the Abbott family came into prominence. As of old, the Abbotts were back together again under one roof. To all outward appearances, Jack, the oldest and the only son, seemed to be settling down in both his personal and his professional life. Lovely Ashley, the middle child, with college degree in hand, joined the family cosmetics business, in product development. And Traci, the youngest, decided to enroll at Genoa City University to stay close to budding rock star Danny Romalotti. Even the senior Abbott, John, seemed to be doing his part to contribute to the picture of two-parent family solidarity and would marry by year's end.

Despite the tension caused by Sally and Chuckie's presence in their lives, Snapper and Chris vowed not to give up on their marriage. They suggested to Sally that they raise Chuckie as their own. Sally wouldn't hear of it: the boy was all she had. When Chuckie was desperately in need of a kidney operation to save his life, Sally urged Snapper to tell him the truth—Chuckie should know who his father was. Snapper decided to wait, and when the boy recovered from his operation, Snapper thought it best not to say anything. Chris, meantime, had called Stan Harris, Sally's boyfriend, and encouraged him to come to Genoa City to be with Sally. Stan proposed, and Sally accepted. Chuckie returned to Michigan with them, after bidding Snapper a tearful good-bye.

Snapper apologized to Chris for being so insensitive, and assured her that nothing meant more

Snapper bid a tearful good-bye to his son, Chuckie, as Sally and Stan planned to start a new life together in Michigan.

to him than his wife and daughter. But when Snapper accepted a three-month fellowship in London to teach and conduct research, Chris refused to go with him. She had to give her modeling career a chance. Snapper left without her, but soon afterwards, Chris realized her place was with Snapper. Jack released her from her contract, and Chris and Jennifer Elizabeth joined Snapper in London.

After Vanessa's death, Lorie told her fiancé Lance that she had been framed by Vanessa in a grand scheme to keep them apart. Lance wouldn't believe it, and asserted that, at the trial, the truth would be revealed. Lucas, meanwhile, found a piece of evidence that seemed to implicate Lorie—the letter stating she'd do anything to keep Vanessa from telling Lance the truth. Leslie hoped that Lucas wouldn't divulge the letter, for then the truth of Brooks's parentage would be known to all. To further complicate matters, Lance found a bottle of Vanessa's pills and discovered, much to everyone's surprise, that Vanessa had been suffering from a terminal illness.

At Lorie's trial, Leslie testified that Vanessa did indeed hate her former daughter-in-law. And when the prosecutor presented "Lorie's letter" to Lance on the witness stand, the courtroom erupted. Lance was in a state of shock when he learned that Brooks was his son, and began to doubt Lorie's innocence. Lorie *could* have committed the crime, he surmised, out of fear that Vanessa would break them up. Lance couldn't contain his anger toward Lorie for keeping him from his son for all these years. How could she say she loved him? He'd never believe her again, even in light of Lorie's insistence that she didn't write the letter.

After his testimony, Lance confronted Leslie, who admitted she'd kept the truth from him because she didn't want to interfere with the happiness he'd found with Lorie. She also confessed that she still loved him. In the final moments of the trial, young Brooks took the stand and told the court he saw his grandmother typing at Lorie's typewriter—with gloves on! Lance then realized that his mother *did* frame Lorie.

Although Lorie was cleared of all charges, Lance hated Lorie for causing him to lose Prentiss Industries. It seems Victor, upset with Lance for not giving Lorie the support he felt she needed during the trial, used Lorie's proxy to seize control of the company. Lorie tried to convince Lance that she would never have done such a thing to him, that Victor was a double-crosser who ruthlessly deceived her when he had assured her he'd burned the proxies.

At first, Lance vowed to regain the company. But when Brooks refused to accept anyone but Lucas as his father, Lance decided to leave Genoa City. Both his personal life and his professional life were a shambles.

Lorie promised herself she'd get Prentiss back

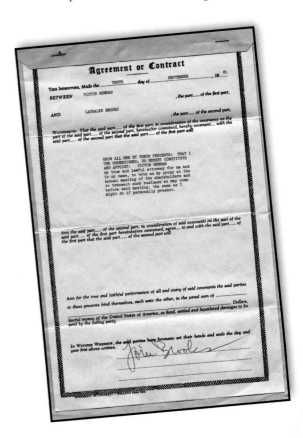

for Lance, somehow, some way. Victor tried to explain to Lorie he'd taken over Prentiss Industries for her sake—to teach Lance a lesson for mistrusting her the way he did. He agreed to give Lorie a job as a writer, reasoning that her work could enhance the image of the company. Before long, Victor and Lorie were reinvolved personally as well as professionally. What Victor didn't know was that Lorie would use her position to gain access to information in confidential files in order to write a scathing exposé about his life, thereby forcing him to return Prentiss Industries to Lance.

At the Newman ranch, Nikki was undergoing her transformation, and made several attempts to initiate a romantic relationship with Victor. But Victor rebuffed her advances, saying he planned to fix her up with a younger man. He arranged for Nikki to go out with handsome architect Kevin Bancroft, who was working for Victor on the Newman Towers building. Nikki went along with it, hoping to make Victor jealous. When Kevin found out Nikki was an exotic dancer, he told Nikki it would never work between them—she wouldn't fit into his upper-crust world. Nikki felt she let Victor down, and admitted to Victor that she was falling in love with him. Victor asked Nikki to stay with him, and they made love. Victor, though, stressed he wasn't looking for any kind of commitment.

Meanwhile, Katherine had been bailing Cash out of some of his gambling debts, but she didn't realize how much trouble Cash was in. She loved Cash; she wanted to marry him and take off for Paris. But their plans were brought to an abrupt end when Cash was killed by his angry creditors. Nikki and Katherine consoled each other—they'd both lost someone important to them.

Before long, Nikki found herself pregnant, but she knew Victor had no interest whatsoever in children. Victor insisted that Kevin admit he was the father of the baby. Kevin decided to do the right thing by Nikki and proposed to her, knowing how this would devastate Caroline Harper, his fiancée in San Francisco. Kevin's high-society parents then came to Genoa City, and promptly forbade him to marry someone with such a "colorful" past as Nikki. Kevin's mother, Alison, tried to buy Nikki off, but Nikki refused her offer. The couple wed. Caroline, hurt but impressed by Kevin's noble sacrifice, vowed to win him back.

It wasn't long before Nikki realized how terribly unhappy she was and sought to end the marriage. Katherine advised her young friend the only way out would be to admit the baby she was carrying was Victor's. But if she did that, Nikki would surely lose Victor for good. Desperately in love with Victor, Nikki was further distressed to learn that he was seeing Lorie Brooks. Upset with Nikki's meddling in his affair with Lorie, Victor told Nikki there would never be anything between them; she should get on with her own life and leave him alone.

Victor decided he wanted a commitment from Lorie, so he presented her with a brilliant engagement ring, and lavished her with expensive gifts. When they talked about wedding gifts, Lorie told Victor that her gift should be Prentiss Industries, and that if he trusted her, he'd give it to her *before* the wedding. He did. Lorie promptly burned her manuscript. But she stood Victor up on their wedding day, leaving behind a note explaining that her past meant too much to her to begin a future with Victor. Lorie then left Genoa City to be with her true love, Lance.

Snapper was glad Jill was suing Jack (she sought $1 million) for the way he treated her. Snapper felt that it was about time the world knew what a scoundrel young Mr. Abbott was. Jack protested that he never demanded sex from Jill to ensure her position at Jabot. Jill knew she'd never be able to substantiate her fabricated claim, but still managed to trick Jack into paying a $10,000 settlement to drop the lawsuit.

Much to her parents' dismay, Patty continued to see Jack, who professed his love for her. She cele-

brated her 18th birthday by making love with him. Patty was thrilled when Jack soon promised he'd make her a top model at Jabot. Mary Williams, meanwhile, was distressed when Patty announced that she was moving in with Jack. It violated all of Mary's most basic precepts that her own daughter would be living in sin. Besides, Mary knew that Jack was all wrong for her. But Patty didn't want to hear it.

When John told Jack he thought he ought to settle down, Jack promptly proposed to Patty. Overjoyed that her dream to marry her prince charming was coming true, she accepted. John was happy to see Jack had changed, and decided his wedding gift to his son would be the presidency of Jabot. Jack's sister Ashley, recently home after graduating from college, was surprised to hear of Jack's wedding plans. But she was pleased when Patty asked her to be her maid of honor. Patty also asked Jack's younger sister Traci to be a bridesmaid, hoping they would all grow close.

Jack's coworkers threw him a party the day before the wedding. He had too much to drink and spent the night with one of Jabot's models, Diane Jenkins. Hung over, Jack never would've made it to his own wedding if Ashley hadn't found him. Unfortunately, she found Diane, too—in his bed!

The Abbotts—John and his children Traci, Jack, and Ashley—were one of the most prominent families in Genoa City.

Ashley threw Jack in the shower to sober him up, and told Diane she hoped she'd never see her again. Ashley then warned her big brother that she would personally see to it that he'd be ousted from Jabot if he ever hurt Patty.

Never one to pass up an opportunity, Diane decided to use her night with Jack to her benefit. She warned Jack that unless he made her Jabot's number one model, she might just have to expose their tryst to his new bride. Jack agreed to hire Diane for the summer campaign, but he also scored a coup by signing on Julia Newman, capitalizing on her recent successes as a leading fashion designer to promote Jabot's fragrances.

While Nikki was stewing over Victor, Kevin's mother, Alison, was mired in problems of her own. Alison's husband, Earl, confessed he'd had an affair with Katherine when they were in college together, and was now smitten with Katherine all over again. Katherine returned his ardor. Hoping to break up Mr. and Mrs. Bancroft, Katherine had Douglas agree to court Alison. Alison slyly agreed to consider divorcing Earl if Katherine would help her to become more attractive to men. But what Katherine didn't know was that Alison hoped to use those tips to win back Earl's affections.

Alison also hoped Caroline Harper would win Kevin back. She told a devastated Nikki that Kevin was in fact in love with Caroline.

When part of the building at the construction site collapsed on Kevin and he was rushed to the hospital, Nikki prayed he would recover, promising herself she'd leave him so he could be with the woman he truly loved. Nikki's prayers were answered and Kevin recovered from his injuries. She then told him the baby she was carrying was Victor's. Kevin confronted Victor, who said it was not possible because he'd had a vasectomy. Alison demanded that Nikki relinquish the Bancroft name and fortune, or she would go public with word that the baby was Victor's. Nikki, furious at Victor for denying that he was the father, pawned a bracelet he'd given her and left Genoa City for parts unknown. Victor, meanwhile, reminded by his doctor that he could've fathered the child, was determined to uncover the truth about the baby's paternity.

April's twin, Barbara, was at first reluctant to get close to her newfound family. But she did grow close to them, and had the means to support them comfortably. Dorothy and Wayne left Genoa City and moved with her to New York. April followed. She thought it would be good for Heather, who could go to the finest schools and have all of the advantages Barbara's money could offer her. April asked Paul for a divorce, and Paul agreed, hoping Heather would never forget him.

Diane Jenkins rendezvoused with Jack Abbott, but promised to keep it a secret if he would give her Jabot's top modeling job.

Paul then decided to take his life in a different direction and joined the police force, which pleased his father. But Carl Williams's career was turned upside down when he got a little too close to breaking up Pete Walker's vice racket. He was framed and subsequently suspended from the force.

Captain Frank Lewis believed Carl's case was related to department corruption, so he asked Paul to infiltrate the mob to find out. Paul staged a falling-out with his family and went undercover. Paul and Andy Richards both got jobs working for Tony DiSalvo, who ran The Golden Touch bar, headquarters for Walker's prostitution ring. Paul met Cindy Lake, one of Tony's girls, and befriended her, hoping to expose that another prostitute, Pam Warren, had framed Carl. In the midst of his undercover work, Paul and Cindy fell in love. Cindy would do just about anything for Paul, and urged him to leave town when Pete Walker took out a contract on his life. Paul got the big boss to free Cindy from prostituting herself and promised her they'd spend quality time together once this nightmare was over.

This was a traumatic time for Mary Williams. Not only was she heartbroken over Paul, who had severed all ties with his family without explanation,

but then she discovered a lump in her breast. She went into the hospital, hoping Paul wouldn't find out about her circumstances. But Frank Lewis thought Paul should know, and told him. Paul went to the hospital to see Mary while she slept, and tearfully left a rosary with her. She awakened after dreaming that Paul had come to see her, and was surprised to find the rosary. Mary refused to sign a form consenting to a mastectomy should the lump be found cancerous. Thankfully, the biopsy proved it was benign.

Paul's undercover work was reaching deadly proportions. Pete Walker ordered Paul to kill Pam to keep her quiet, so Paul took her home to the Williams home to hide out. Pam saw firsthand how she'd helped destroy his family's happiness. Remorseful, she agreed to talk, hoping to rectify things. The police placed her under protective custody. When Paul was unable to produce proof Pam was dead, Pete ordered Paul killed, then and there.

Andy, who had been helping Paul break up the racket, found his personal life was becoming ever more complex. It seemed that whenever his estranged wife, Karen, called him crying she was all alone, Andy, fearing she would harm herself, would rush to her side. Their marriage had been a painful one for Andy, for Karen was forever seeing other men. Andy finally managed to convince Karen to grant him a divorce. He then proposed to Jill, and though Jill accepted his ring, she was not entirely happy about it. Andy was a good person, and he would make a good father for

Paul, Andy, and Jazz helped to break up the syndicate in Genoa City. Kingpin Tony DiSalvo and his cohort Wayne were unaware of their plan.

little Phillip, but he would never have the kind of money Jill was looking for in a man.

Then there was John Abbott, who had returned to Genoa City. Jill arranged a "chance" meeting with him, but found him to be preoccupied over Jack's ineptitude in running Jabot. She was happy when John said he'd be staying in Genoa City to oversee the company. Jill canceled a date with Andy to dine with John. John confessed he was falling in love with her. They agreed to start over, and Jill broke her engagement to Andy. John would be able to give her everything she'd ever want in life.

Jack tried everything to break up John and Jill. He paid Diane to find another woman for John. When that didn't work, Jack told his father about Jill's son, Phillip. John was angry Jill had deceived him. But when Jill told him the sad story of Phillip Chancellor's death and admitted she didn't like to burden others with her problems, John was moved and proposed marriage. He wanted to give Jill and her son a better life.

Jack then tried to find his mother, Dina, who had walked out on the family 11 years before. Maybe *she* would be able to divert John's attention from Jill. But when an impostor showed up in Dina's place, Jack sent her packing.

Next, Jack persuaded Katherine to tell Ashley about Jill's attempt to get her hands on the Chancellor fortune through a paternity suit. But Ashley refused to get involved in Jack's plots; she didn't want to see John hurt.

After Jill convinced her mother she was in love with John Abbott the man—not his money—Liz agreed to be matron of honor. John and Jill tied the knot, and when they returned from their honeymoon, Jack surprised everyone by welcoming them with open arms.

After all, he was confident that it would only be a matter of time before Jill would end up hanging herself.

Meanwhile, Patty was becoming increasingly unhappy in her marriage to Jack. She wanted a home of their own; he wanted to stick around the Abbott household to keep an eye on his father's new bride. She wanted to start a family; he had no interest and even threatened to get a vasectomy to prevent it.

Robert Laurence had successfully defended Lorie and cleared her name in the death of Vanessa. By the end of the trial, he'd grown close to Leslie. He decided it was time to get on with his life. The doctors at the mental institution where his wife, Claire, had been for 15 years concurred. But when Claire finally spoke her first word, "Robert," after so many years, the doctors were hopeful she might be brought out of her catatonic state. Robert kept this news from his daughter, Angela. He thought it best she believe her mother had died when she was a baby, just in case the miracle drug the doctors were administering to Claire didn't work. The doctors were surprised and pleased that the drug took effect and Claire was showing the first signs of recovery. Robert decided to tell Angela the truth; Claire, at first confused that her daughter was all grown up, apologized to Angela for not being there to raise her.

Angela was thrilled when Claire came home, but Robert and Leslie professed their love to one another, and Angela was devastated to learn her parents were no longer legally married. She ran away from home and would have gotten into serious trouble at The Golden Touch if it hadn't been for Andy and Paul. Robert and Claire were grateful that Angela was returned safely to them, and they decided to give their family one more chance. Robert ended his relationship with Leslie, who decided to plan a concert tour of Europe in the hopes of getting her mind off her failed romance.

Ashley put her college training to work as a chemist developing and testing new fragrances at Jabot. Not wanting any "special" treatment from her coworkers, she went by the name Susan Ashley. Brian Forbes, who worked with Ashley, was smitten with her, and warned her to keep her distance from the company's president, Jack Abbott. Brian was shocked when Jack told him that Susan Ashley was really his sister, Ashley Abbott. Suddenly, Brian feared that Ashley was there to spy on him for Jack. Ashley warned Jack that he wouldn't be sitting in the president's seat for long—she would be—if he interfered in her relationship with Brian.

Nikki was on her way back to Genoa City, and Katherine and Victor anxiously awaited news as to whether she'd had her baby. She had had a baby girl, whom Alison suggested she name Victoria, after Earl's mother. Nikki, certain that Victor was the father, wanted a blood test to prove it. The results confirmed her instincts, but before Nikki could learn the truth, Victor persuaded Katherine to tell Nikki that Kevin was the father. Nikki was stunned, but decided it best to move back in with her husband, even though she didn't love him.

Traci Abbott, president of Danny Romalotti's fan club, thanked Danny for the friendship he'd shown her over the summer, and decided she cared too much for him to go away to college. John was happy when his youngest daughter enrolled at Genoa City University. Now he had all of his children back under one roof.

After five years away, Gina Roma, Danny's older sister, returned to Genoa City, but when she showed up on her brother's doorstep, Danny wasn't

When Nikki returned to Genoa City with baby Victoria in her arms, she was told that a blood test proved Kevin Bancroft was the father. She moved in with him to build a life for their new family, but would soon learn the truth—that the baby's father was in fact Victor Newman.

overjoyed to see her. She explained she'd wound up in jail after pulling a scam with their crooked father. When Danny realized what a beautiful voice Gina had, he suggested she stay in Genoa City and start a singing career as he had. Gina agreed to stay. She quickly saw the benefit of Danny cultivating a relationship with Traci: the Abbott money would come in quite handy for an up-and-coming rock singer.

Danny, however, would never think of cashing in on his friendship with Traci. He gave Traci the opportunity of a lifetime when he invited her to join him on stage for the final number at his concert. Traci was an instant success, but their plans to celebrate were ruined when Danny never showed because he had to bring Patty Williams to the doctor's. Traci was hurt, and she wasn't interested in his apologies.

By year's end, Danny found himself caught between two young women, both of whom he cared for a great deal, while Liz and Stuart's marital problems escalated. Jill suggested that her mother consider a divorce.

"Victor was right as always," Nikki thought as she dashed over to Victor's to tell him how happy she was to at long last be Kevin's lover as well as his wife. She was now prepared to believe Victor's prediction that they would have a happy life ahead of them. What Nikki didn't know was that Victor was ready to acknowledge that he was the father of baby Victoria and that he was going to claim both her and the baby as his, because he loved them so.

Alison, on the other hand, was determined to break up Kevin and Nikki. When Leroy at the Bayou told Alison that business there was bad, she persuaded Leroy that Nikki might agree to strip again, if approached in the right manner. When Leroy then told Nikki that he felt suicidal because of his business woes, she felt sorry for him and agreed to appear, only a few times, to help business pick up.

After asking Kevin to watch the baby while she went out to meet a few friends, Nikki performed at the Bayou before a worked-up audience, not knowing that Alison had dropped in and made a hasty retreat. Of course, Alison ran straight over to tell Kevin, and Kevin, with his baby girl in his arms, checked it out for himself. He, too, quickly departed in shock. Nikki broke down and wept on stage.

To make matters worse, Pete Walker threatened to beat and possibly kill both Leroy and Nikki if Leroy didn't make a tape of Nikki stripping! Leroy had his back up against the wall. He'd have to make arrangements to have the tape done amid great secrecy because he knew Nikki would never go along with it.

Alison continued to stir up trouble every chance she got. At Victoria's christening, she figured out that Victor was the baby's father, and later confirmed that Victor's vasectomy didn't work! She promised herself if it was the last thing she'd ever do on this earth, she would put an end to her son's marriage to Nikki! With this in mind, Alison hired Rick Daros to pass himself off to Kevin as an investor. Her plan was for Daros to become romantically involved with Nikki.

Paul Williams was really in a heap of trouble as the syndicate was ready to rub him out for not killing Pam as ordered. To his surprise, he received a call from the police to identify Pam's body! Paul couldn't believe his eyes: the one person who could

For months, Paul would continue to work undercover, desperately trying to protect Cindy, as both of them bounced between being hunted down by the police and the mob. His mother was kidnapped by the syndicate and Carl negotiated a deal—Mary for Paul—if he could find his son! In a stunning denouement, Alex, the crooked cop, and Pete, the syndicate boss, shot and killed each other as Mary was rescued and reunited with Carl and Paul. Cindy hid out in a convent for a while, but came forward to testify against the mob, only to have her testimony set aside. Paul proposed to Cindy and they looked forward to spending the rest of their lives together.

Patty Abbott knew she had to tell Jack she was pregnant, but she was waiting for him to be in the right frame of mind. She did tell her mother, however, but asked her not to say anything to Carl until she had a chance to tell Jack first.

Meanwhile, Patty's playboy husband continued to have romantic liaisons with Diane in his office. Jill knew about this because she had had his office bugged, and deviously encouraged Patty to surprise Jack at work. Patty went to Jack's office and got the surprise of her life: Diane was undressing her husband! Blinded by her tears, Patty rushed down the hall and stumbled over a huge potted plant. Carl, still suspended from the force and temporarily working as a security guard at Jabot, was making his nightly rounds, saw her tumble, and hurried to her side. But Patty said she was all right and wanted to go home. A

help free Carl was lying on a slab in the morgue—dead! But this called for a celebration, with the syndicate welcoming Paul as a member of the "family." Paul couldn't be more uncomfortable: he was hugged and kissed in godfather fashion, getting all the attention as a brooding Tony DiSalvo got none.

What disturbed Paul more than anything else was the thought of Cindy meeting the same fate as Pam. Yet, when he begged Cindy to get out of town, she refused to leave. Then, when she didn't see Paul for a few days, she started putting out feelers, and Pete Walker definitely didn't like a nosy broad checking up on Paul. In the meantime, Frank Lewis had been critically wounded while on duty and came out of his coma only to have a heart attack and slip back into it; Stuart Brooks wrote an editorial on Paul's gangland connections; Cindy was put back to work as a prostitute; and Pete chose a classier lady for Paul to date.

few minutes later, Carl saw Jack and Diane leaving the office together and figured out what Patty must have seen.

Later, when an intoxicated Jack returned home, Patty tried to tell him she was carrying his child, but he muttered he was too tired and was going to bed, where he passed out. It was Ashley who found Patty doubled up with severe abdominal cramps and who got her to the hospital. When Jack overheard a nurse telling Patty they were doing everything possible to save the baby, he demanded to know from Patty why she didn't tell him about the baby. Her explanation—that she had seen him with Diane—made him feel like a worm. His marriage was a complete mess, and he didn't know how to make it right. Patty miscarried.

Danny, meanwhile, was going through his own private heartbreak. For as long as he could remember, he loved Patty, and he was bitterly disappointed to learn of her pregnancy. Although Danny never wished her anything but happiness, he feared her condition would bring her and Jack closer together, and that he'd never be more than a friend to her. Unfortunately, his pining over Patty meant he was unwittingly hurting the infatuated Traci Abbott. Danny spent endless hours at the hospital just to be close to Patty, and he told her he'd always be there for her. When he asked Patty if Jack was responsible for her being in the hospital, she didn't answer him. Carl and Mary Williams wished their daughter had been married to Danny instead of Jack; they were sure she'd have been much happier.

When Victor's ex-wife Julia happened to hear, through crossed telephone wires, a man's voice saying, "Victor Newman must die," she hurried over to Victor's to warn him. Victor dismissed it as being so much balderdash, and invited Julia to stay for dinner.

He was captivated by Julia's beauty and femininity, noting that she had acquired a new strength and maturity, which he liked.

Victor had recently rehired Eve Howard as his personal secretary, warning her that if she were to cross the line into his personal affairs again, she'd be out of there in a flash. Their relationship had to focus on work, period. Unbeknownst to Victor, Douglas had once confided to Eve that Victor had a particular fondness for her son, Cole, and had written him into his will to inherit one half of his estate. Victor also didn't know the intensity of Eve's loathing for him. She wanted to see him dead—to get her hands on her son's inheritance, sooner rather than later.

It so happened that Victor's personal cook, Charlie, was on an extended vacation, and it fell to Eve to prepare Victor's meals. She had her friend, Max, a chemist, prepare a lethal culture, which she could start giving him right away. As the days wore on, Victor was slowly, methodically being poisoned. When he fell from being weak and dizzy, Julia called his doctor, who said all Victor needed was rest and relaxation. Victor made plans to go to Tahiti with Julia. Then, Max drugged Victor's horse, hoping to cause a fatal accident.

The next time Julia called on Victor, Eve handed her a note saying that Victor had decided to go to Tahiti alone because he didn't want Julia "cramping his style." In reality, he didn't want her to take a vacation with an "invalid." But all the while he was right there at the ranch, languishing in his own bed. And when Julia tried to call Victor in Tahiti, a severe tropical storm prevented calls from going through.

Victor asked Eve to call a doctor. Dr. Schmitt was actually Max the chemist. Max charmed Victor into believing he'd be as good as new in no time at all. Max then concocted a new formula that actually made Victor feel better, but the shots were addictive, and they only masked the deterioration brought on by the bacteria that Eve had been feeding him. Victor was now too weak to eat at all.

As a deathlike pallor settled over him, Victor gave part of his dinner to his dog, Albert. Victor thought he dreamed Julia was hovering over him, only it wasn't a dream—she was really there. And when Julia saw Albert lying comatose on the floor, she immediately figured that Albert had been poisoned! Julia had the food analyzed, confirming her suspicions.

Victor devised an even more bizarre plot to entrap Eve. He proposed to her, making it clear that as his wife, she would inherit his entire estate. When she told Max she was going to marry Victor, Max went ballistic. Julia helped Eve to get dressed in her wedding finery, but by the time they had reached the house, paramedics were carrying out a covered body on a stretcher. They were told Victor had expired!

A wake was held; the casket was closed. Victor hid in an alcove and observed the mourners. After the burial, Eve and Max returned to the cemetery and dug up the grave. If there was an autopsy, and traces of the poison were found, Eve could go to prison, Max warned. He ordered her to have the body cremated.

When Eve returned to the ranch to survey

"her" property, she began to "imagine" things: Victor was everywhere, smiling at her. She built a shrine in Victor's bedroom and had the coffin placed on his bed. Then Max and Eve got married by a drunken judge who thought it strange to have a dead man in attendance. After the ceremony, Eve decided to say good-bye to Victor, and Max decked her on the chin and stuffed her body into the coffin, which he had assumed was empty because Eve had already arranged for the cremation.

The police arrived and in a scuffle in the barn, Max impaled himself on a pitchfork. Eve, completely deranged, was removed from the coffin, and Victor felt so sorry for her he had her committed to a private mental institution.

Just as Alison planned, Rick Daros was growing closer to Nikki. He took her on picnics, whispered sweet nothings in her ear, and arranged for private dinners in the Colonnade Room. He was always at the Bayou, enthusiastically applauding as Nikki stripped, and afterwards, he'd ply her with kisses as they carried

Eve Howard came back to Genoa City seeking child support from Victor for her son, Cole. She then set out to destroy Victor, but he outsmarted her, and it was Eve whose life fell apart.

on in her dressing room. It was during a rendezvous with him that Nikki heard a report on the radio that Victor had passed away. She was grief stricken.

Kay Chancellor, all the while disturbed with Nikki's dalliances with Rick, constantly said and did things to hasten the affair's end. She wondered, now that Victor was dead, whether she should tell Nikki who Victoria's real father was, but she had given Victor her word she'd keep silent. At first she did. But after Victor's funeral, Nikki left Genoa City to get away for a few days, and it was then that Kay, thinking Victor was really dead, sent Nikki a letter telling her the truth about Victoria's paternity. Victor, not dead, of course, demanded that Katherine intercept it before Nikki returned. But Rick found the letter and pocketed it.

Once Nikki returned, she visited Victor's grave for one final good-bye, and was overwhelmed when he appeared, in the flesh, and told her about his hoax!

Just when Nikki had decided to give up Rick to concentrate on making her marriage to Kevin work, Kevin and Rick got into a terrible fight over her, which prompted Nikki to ask Kevin for a divorce after all.

Kay brought Victor up to date on the entire situation with Nikki, Kevin, and Rick; and Victor spoke to each of them, resolving

John Abbott and his children were shocked when Mme. Mergeron turned out to be his wife and their mother, Dina, who'd left them many years earlier.

nothing. After much agonizing, Nikki flew to Haiti with Rick to finalize her divorce.

But other problems were erupting all over the place. Tony DiSalvo surfaced with a porno tape, *Hot Hips*, which both Alison and Nikki freaked out over. Part of it showed Nikki stripping and part of it used a double—Boobsie—engaging in sex acts, making it look as if Nikki was involved in the entire film! Alison then wrangled a temporary custody arrangement out of Nikki for Victoria, and took the little girl to San Francisco.

Victor was on an extended trip, leaving Nikki to deal with the porno tape situation without his help. She figured the best way to get DiSalvo to give up the tape was to seduce him into making a marriage proposal, and then hold out for the tape as her wedding gift. Paul, Andy, and Jazz, who were still attempting to bust the syndicate, tried to prevent Nikki from marrying DiSalvo, but Nikki was not to be deterred.

After the ceremony, DiSalvo went down to

Ashley couldn't forgive her mother for deserting the family. How would she now react to the news that she and her mother were both involved with Eric Garrison?

the storeroom to fetch the tape for his bride, where he ran into Paul and Andy. He got the drop on them and was about to shoot Paul, when Cindy barged in out of nowhere and took the shot intended for Paul. Jazz sneaked up behind DiSalvo and shot him dead. Nikki hid out at Victor's until Boobsie signed a legal document that cleared Nikki of all blame.

In the meanwhile, Alison had taken off with Victoria and they were nowhere to be found. Rick Daros remembered Alison talking about Appleshaw, her favorite small town in England. Rick flew there, found Alison with Victoria, and showed her Kay's letter stating that Victor was Victoria's father, which proved that Alison had no claim to her. He returned Victoria to her distraught mother. At this point, Rick was holding all of the cards: he had told neither Kevin nor Nikki about Victoria's paternity, and once again he had emerged as Nikki's hero.

Determined to find out more about Rick Daros, Kevin hired Paul and Andy to look into his past. They learned Rick had been married before, and that, according to newspaper reports in 1981, his wife died in a tragic swimming accident. Later, Andy, vacationing with Diane on the island of Maui, found out about a young couple who had had a terrible scuba diving accident—an equipment foul-up in which the wife's tanks had been filled with carbon monoxide. The young woman died and her husband was crazed with grief.

Back in Genoa City, when Ashley informed the advance representative of the European Mergeron

Corporation, Eric Garrison, that John Abbott had absolutely no interest in selling Jabot, Eric was stunned. Jack Abbott had led him to believe otherwise.

After John blasted his son for being so Byzantine, he clutched his chest and collapsed to the floor, unconscious. He suffered severe arterial blockage, which required immediate surgery. The near-tragedy drew the family closer; even Patty wanted to reach out to Jack to offer him physical comfort. But she couldn't. As John's health improved, he became aware of some notable changes that had taken place: his daughter Ashley had fallen deeply in love with Eric and he, himself, had come to the realization that selling Jabot might well be a good move after all. Eric returned to Genoa City, and when the negotiations were completed, they all awaited the arrival of Mme. Mergeron to personally close the deal. When she arrived, John almost had another heart attack: she was none other than Dina Abbott, his first wife who had deserted the family 12 years before!

Eric proposed to Ashley, who later discovered

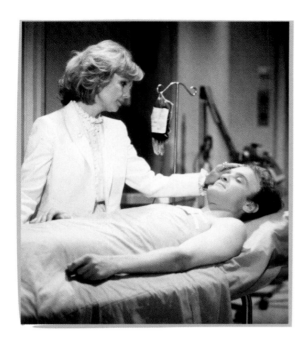

Dina was with Jack as he recovered from the gunshots inflicted upon him by his young wife, Patty.

Lauren and Danny gave a concert at the Regency Theatre in Genoa City. From the fans' reactions, there was no doubt that they had an exciting future ahead of them.

that he was once involved with her own mother! Then Dina asked her son Jack to head Mergeron America for her and he said he would think it over.

After Patty returned home from the hospital, she began seeing a psychiatrist to help her to mend her broken life and marriage. On the morning of her first wedding anniversary, she told Jack she wanted to have his baby. She thought everything was all right until she overheard her husband making an appointment for a vasectomy and boasting to Jill he married Patty only to get his father's wedding present: the presidency of Jabot. Later, Patty hysterically confronted Jack at his office, holding a small caliber handgun that she had purchased, and shot her husband three times. She then totally dismissed the shooting from her mind. Jack survived a long and delicate operation but faced the real probability of never

walking again. Patty became the perfect solicitous wife. She would love him in good times and bad, in sickness and in health. Fearful of what Patty might do once he went home, Jack consulted her psychiatrist and together they mapped out a strategy: a complete reenactment of the same scenario, gun and all. At the point where Patty was going to shoot him, however, she remembered everything, and recalled the original shooting as an exclamation mark for all of the rotten things he had done. In the end, Patty was the strong one. She divorced Jack and left Genoa City to begin her life anew. Turning his attention once again to Diane, Jack would soon find out that she was no longer available. Diane had married Andy Richards.

Traci Abbott was beginning to have romantic

fantasies about Danny Romalotti, and constantly battled with Lauren Fenmore for his attention. Both girls sang with Danny's band, and constantly clashed over who would be chosen to sing with him. Knowing Lauren to be far more attractive and sophisticated than she, Traci put herself on a strict diet and exercise regimen, hoping Danny would take notice. But the cunning Lauren used every trick she could think of to tempt Traci or publicly humiliate her by calling attention to her weight. Discouraged over not losing weight fast enough, Traci turned to popping pills, supplied to her by Sparky, the campus pusher.

But soon the pills took their toll. Traci could neither eat nor sleep, and she felt dizzy and irritable. She was terrified. Lauren, meanwhile trapped Danny into becoming engaged to her, leading Traci to pop more pills and to constantly be on the lookout for Sparky. While high on pills, Traci crashed her car and was arrested. She went into convulsions and sustained serious heart damage. Trooper that she was, Traci agreed to take part in a campus drug bust, and when Danny asked her to sing a song for his concert, which was dedicated to fighting drugs, she chose instead to address the audience, telling them of her near disastrous experience. Her message was that there were more sensible ways to solve one's problems.

During this time, Jill had another bruising argument with Mamie Johnson, the Abbotts' live-in maid, in which Jill laid the blame on Mamie for Traci's addiction to diet pills. In reality, Mamie had constantly fretted over Traci's lack of appetite. She

Jack was there to comfort Jill on a cold winter night, but neither of them had any idea that their most intimate moments were being photographed!

would always prepare healthy salads for Traci, only to see them shoved aside. Mamie couldn't stand Jill's harping anymore, so she packed her bags, and wrote a good-bye note to John in which she explained her inability to withstand Jill's accusations. When John drove home in a blinding snowstorm, tired and tense, there was hell to pay. He told Jill to get Mamie back, no matter what the cost! To compound Jill's problems, she listened in on a phone call between Dina and John in which Dina teased John about becoming a father yet again. Jill had recently told Dina that she was pregnant, but it was a deliberate lie, one that had been intended for Dina's ears only.

Panicked, Jill fled. She became stranded in the blizzard and phoned her stepson, Jack. He went to her rescue, and they found a bungalow, where they holed up for the night, locked in each other's arms, making passionate love, comforting each other. What they didn't know was that a stranger was at the window snapping pictures, and that soon there'd be hell to pay.

This was the year of memorable moments: big, powerful, dramatic moments that packed a wallop, and small everyday kinds of moments that tugged at the heartstrings. The year would be one that would not soon be forgotten.

While Lindsey Wells wanted payment in a big way for the lurid photos she took of Jack with his stepmother, Jack couldn't have asked for a more loyal employee than Carole Robbins.

Cricket Blair, Jabot's teen model, handed Jack the large gray envelope, which someone in the parking lot asked her to deliver. At the Abbotts', Mamie found an identical envelope on the wrought iron fence addressed to Mrs. John Abbott. There were no markings or return address. Each contained the same identical photo: two pairs of thighs almost touching. The next day, another photo was received; and the day after, another; until the final one revealed the participants to be Jack Abbott and Jill Foster Abbott in a very explicit pose. It was clear that John's son and wife were going to be blackmailed and that they had plenty to worry about. When the last envelope was received, Jack was still at home and he fought with the drunk who delivered it, as he tried to find out who sent it. Mamie told John about the ruckus, and when John asked what was in the envelope, Jill explained that it contained obscene letters, and that Jack simply wanted to put an end to it. John called the police to file a complaint.

The next day, Jack received a scrapbook of eight photos of him and Jill, with a note. It read,

"You'll hear from me tomorrow." And when tomorrow came, John Abbott introduced Lindsey Wells to Jack as the daughter of an old friend who had come back to work for them. Then Lindsey dropped her bombshell: she said that although it had been six years since Jack had seen her (he didn't remember her at all), she had recently caught a peek of him in the blizzard. Jack immediately realized that she was the blackmailer. Her payoff? A quick climb up the corporate ladder!

Jill was still in the dark, however, and suspected that Kay was behind the whole fiasco. When Jill confronted her, Kay didn't know what Jill was raving about, but she made a mental note to keep her eyes and ears open. Then things got complex and very messy very fast. Carl Williams began to poke his nose in to find out who the obscene-letter sender might be. He didn't like Jill and he hated his former son-in-law Jack even more! Jack launched an investigation of his own and hired Jazz to track down the negatives. But for naught.

As time went by, Carl suspected that something really ugly was going on between Jack and Jill, and speculated that John Abbott would be the one to get hurt. And by now, Lindsey was growing impatient, threatening to show John the incriminating photos unless Jack came through on his promises to her. On her threat of sending John an incriminating envelope every day, Jack gave her a plum advertising job. Suspiciously, there was a break-in at Lindsey's apartment. It was evident that the burglar was after some specific something.

Then Jack got Jazz to write Jill an anonymous obscene letter, and Jill's histrionics—throwing herself in John's arms and sobbing on his chest—were worthy of an Oscar. Carl was getting dangerously close to discovering the truth. He began questioning Jill about the night her car broke down and he continued to investigate the break-in, speculating a link between the two incidents. He was also wondering how Lindsey was climbing the corporate ladder so quickly.

But Lindsey was getting even hungrier. She offered to sell Jill the negatives for $150,000. Jack scoffed at the ridiculousness of it all, but he turned on the charm when it was clear that she was serious. He spent the night with her. Things began to get even stickier. Diane Jenkins was suddenly available (she had separated from Andy) and she demanded an exclusive relationship from Jack. Jill, meanwhile, was getting antsier by the minute: she told Jack his involvement with two ladies at the same time could get both of them blown out of the water.

Then Jack had a brainstorm. He proposed to Lindsey and quickly married her, and of course Lindsey turned over the envelope of incriminating negatives. The next morning, when Lindsey awoke, Jack was gone. He had left her a note explaining that the marriage ceremony was a fake—thanks for the "negative" memories! Lindsey vowed to get even. She sent Jack another complete package of negatives, and promised there were more where those came from. Lindsey's next move was predictable: she sold Kay the entire portfolio for $150,000!

Now it was Kay's turn to negotiate. She told Jack she saw nothing to be gained from hurting her dear friends John and Dina. But as for Jill, that was a different story. Jill had destroyed Kay's marriage to Phillip and Kay wanted retribution—and now Kay had the means! First, Jill pleaded with Kay that if this were to come out, it would destroy John! Then, just for insurance, Jill devised a plan to get Kay back on the bottle.

Andy made plans to meet Kimo, the head of the scuba diving task force, at his office to review the accounts of the accident that befell the American couple, and to learn their names. His suspicions were confirmed: the couple was none other than Rick and Melissa Daros! Andy quickly called Paul, told him there were too many extenuating circumstances, and asked Paul to join him in Maui right away. Then Paul and Andy checked out the story of the only two witnesses to the drowning, a couple who had pulled Daros out of the water after Melissa had drowned. The couple couldn't recall anything unusual about the drowning; it appeared to them to have simply been a tragic accident. Since there was nothing more for Paul and Andy to do in Maui, they headed home.

Rick Daros, meanwhile, persuaded Nikki to take a trip with him to Chicago, neglecting to tell her that their final destination would be St. Croix.

Andy, still running down leads, made another discovery. He found a story by a Rory Davis called "Death in Paradise," in which a jealous man kills his wife in a swimming accident. Andy soon learned that Rory Davis and Rick Daros were one and the same! There just were too many coincidences here, so both he and Paul raced over to tell Victor, who had his pilot fly the three of them to the Caribbean at once.

Once Rick and Nikki reached St. Croix, a storm prevented them from going scuba diving; instead they went souvenir shopping. At a sidewalk café, a local flirted with Nikki, causing Daros to make a big scene. Humiliated, Nikki wanted to return to the States, but Rick apologized, saying he'd never behave like that again. Rick then persuaded her to wait for

the weather to clear so they could make one more dive before returning to the States.

Nikki's rescuers touched down in St. Croix and the hunt to find her was on. The waiter at the café remembered the commotion Rick had caused, and was able to direct the three men to the village of Easterly, where Nikki and Rick Daros were staying. But the roads were washed out and the would-be rescuers had to find a schooner captain who'd be willing to risk the choppy waters to take them there.

When Victor finally got through to Nikki by phone, her jealous suitor yanked the phone from the wall, tied her up, and began to call her by his dead wife's name. Knowing that he had no place in Nikki's life, Daros told her that Victor was Victoria's natural father. She somehow managed to calm him down, and got him to untie her. Panicking, Nikki grabbed an iron skillet and hammered him over the head with it, and then ran out into the storm. Daros ran after her, dragged her back into the house, and promised her that tomorrow would be D-Day.

The next morning Rick got the scuba gear ready, and ordered Nikki at gunpoint to get ready. She heard a hissing sound; Rick was letting the air out of the tank! He was dragging her toward the surf when Victor, Paul, and Andy arrived. Nikki broke away from Daros, who shot Victor in the groin with a spear gun. Paul and Andy plucked Nikki from the water while Daros disappeared into the ocean. Victor was rushed to the hospital where Nikki kept a vigil, praying for the recovery of the man she truly loved, the father of her baby.

After he performed emergency surgery on Victor, Dr. Steele assured Nikki that Victor would survive, but that the nerve damage he'd sustained

Nikki's life was in danger when crazed Rick Daros took her scuba diving. Victor, Andy, and Paul would come to her rescue.

But Nikki's happiness was short-lived. While Douglas was helping him prepare for his wedding, Victor took the opportunity to study his medical chart. And what he read shocked him. "Get Nikki! Get Dr. Steele!" he commanded. He told Nikki that his chart indicated there was a real possibility he might be impotent. Dr. Steele told him he'd already informed Nikki. Nikki said it didn't matter. But Victor called the wedding off, anyway. He wasn't going to cheat Nikki: she deserved much more than half a man!

Victor wallowed in anger and self-pity; he wouldn't see or talk to anyone. Nikki took it for as

might make him impotent. Nothing mattered to Nikki but that his life was spared. When Victor opened his eyes, Nikki held his hand and quietly promised she'd never leave his side again. And when baby Victoria was brought into his hospital room and placed in her father's arms, Victor held her close, tears of love and gratitude filling his eyes. Then, Victor proposed to Nikki, and she accepted without a moment's hesitation, saying she wished to be married right then and there. Victor smiled weakly; there were a few technicalities that had to be attended to first. Besides, he knew she'd prefer to have a nicer setting. But Nikki was insistent, because she knew that if he discovered he was impotent and unable to perform the conjugal act, he'd choose not to marry her at all. She remained adamant, told him she had waited too long as it was, refused to accept any further delay! So Victor finally agreed—they'd get married that very day!

Nikki and Victor shared a love unlike any other, and their wedding day was the event of the year in Genoa City.

Victor and his mother, Cora, reconciled shortly before her death. She'd left him in an orphanage years ago when she was no longer able to provide for him.

long as she could, and then she let him have it with both barrels. What father would be doing what he was doing to his child? Suddenly they were in each other's arms, clinging tightly together, holding on to each other for dear life. But still he wasn't going to marry her. He ordered Douglas to drive him to the airport, and occupied himself on the way by looking at sensuous photographs of Nikki stripping. Within moments, he ordered Douglas to turn the car around and return him to Nikki: he no longer thought he had a problem!

Victor and Nikki's wedding was the most spectacular, grandest, and lavish wedding Genoa City had ever seen. No expense was spared. Top designers were engaged to create Nikki's wedding gown, using 70 yards of French silk-faced satin and organza, with a 10-foot train and royal crown—all hand beaded with over 20,000 small beads and pearls. A veritable who's who of wedding guests were invited: Arab sheiks, oil barons, and Japanese businessmen. But family and close friends, including those from earlier years, were considered the most important wedding guests of all.

If there was a fly in the ointment, it was Eve Howard, who escaped from the asylum to which Victor had committed her and who effectively disguised herself as one of the caterers. But her evil plan to harm Nikki and retaliate against Victor was ineffectual. There was absolutely nothing that could spoil their day!

Not long after her fairy-tale marriage to Victor, Nikki wanted to do something special to please him; his substantial wealth certainly took care of all his material needs. Perhaps, she thought, she could reunite him with his family! So Nikki hired Paul and Andy to investigate Victor's beginnings, knowing that he had been left in an orphanage in Buffalo, New York, some 30 years ago. After considerable digging into old records, legal documents, and newspaper morgues, the two investigators learned that Victor's father had died in 1962, but they discovered that his mother, Cora Miller, still lived in Buffalo in relative poverty.

Nikki brought Cora to Genoa City, where Victor first rejected her for abandoning him. But when Cora was hospitalized and found to be dying of cancer, Victor took her home to the ranch, where she spent her remaining days surrounded by love. From this bittersweet experience Victor learned a valuable lesson: love doesn't die and as long as one remembers, they would not be separated.

Dr. Jacobs told Kay Chancellor she was a good candidate for cosmetic surgery, but to ensure its

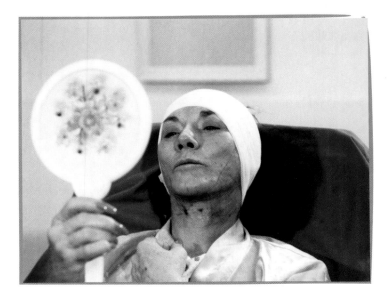

Katherine Chancellor sees herself for the first time as the bandages are removed after her cosmetic surgery.

success, he recommended a change in lifestyle. Kay decided to begin by softening the hate lines on her face, so she went straight to Jill to try to become friends. But Jill, showing no sympathy, lashed out at her, saying that Kay's ugly face was a reflection of all the carousing she'd done. Kay didn't let Jill's cruel words deter her; she put her affairs in order and rewrote her will to include young Phillip, Jill's son.

The surgery was a success, but when Kay saw her bruised and battered face in the mirror, her heart sank. Dr. Jacobs assured her that it would only be a matter of time before her face would heal and she would look lovelier than ever.

Elsewhere in town, Jazz felt he was always getting the short end of the stick. He saw and loved Amy Lewis first, but his educated, better-looking younger brother, Tyrone, came along, and Amy fell for him. Jazz was always broke because he used every dime he'd ever earned to pay for Tyrone's law school tuition. Tyrone didn't know that

Jazz worked for the mob—or that Jazz wanted to go straight and the mob wouldn't let him. The kingpin, Mr. Anthony, expected Jazz to get information from Tyrone, who worked in the county prosecutor's office, on the investigation that that office was conducting on mob activity. Mr. Anthony threatened to maim or kill Tyrone if Jazz didn't come through.

Jazz lied that the investigation was all a hoax perpetrated to throw the mob off to see if they'd make a slip. Mr. Anthony knew Jazz was lying, and he tore up the check for Tyrone's final tuition payment and had Jazz beaten up for good measure.

Tyrone was selected by the county prosecutor's office to work undercover and to infiltrate the mob, while Jazz was ordered by Mr. Anthony to break into the prosecutor's office to microfilm telltale documents. Jazz did his job and delivered the documents to Mr. Anthony, hoping he'd be off the

Brothers Tyrone and Jazz vied for the affections of Amy Lewis. Amy chose Tyrone.

hook. Meanwhile, Tyrone donned a disguise and became Leon Monroe, drug pusher.

A series of miscues and mishaps pitted brother against brother—operationally at least, for each loved the other dearly. When Jazz was ordered to kill "Leon Monroe," the two brothers concocted a scheme to make it appear that the deed was done. They substituted for Tyrone a murdered man whose face had been blown off. A grief-stricken Amy went to church on Christmas Eve to pray and find solace; Tyrone, dressed as a monk, comforted her!

In the romance department, 1984 was filled with movement and change. Some hearts leaped with joy, while others experienced pain and despair. And sometimes the same hearts felt the full range of emotions. Ashley, for one, couldn't decide between Eric Garrison and Marc Mergeron, and she ended up with no one. Patty, divorced from Jack, was heartbroken when Danny married his dear friend Traci (who was pregnant with Tim Sullivan's child)—but Danny really pined for Patty, while Tim broke Traci's heart. Lauren Fenmore married Paul; and Andy Richards divorced Diane; and Diane pined for Jack. Dina wanted John, and John wanted Jill to behave like a proper wife.

A man named Brent Davis came back into Dina's life. Douglas fell in love with Boobsie, but she was too enmeshed with the mob to extricate herself.

Romance abounded when Douglas Austin couldn't resist the charm of Boobsie.

And by year's end, there were hints that Jack was becoming interested in Nikki and Victor in Ashley.

On other fronts, Julia found the perfect surrogate husband and had a beautiful baby girl. Traci and Jill lost their babies through miscarriages or natural abortion. Katherine and Jill continued their rivalries as did Lauren and Traci.

And on the horizon there was big trouble, as a new man in town named Shawn Garrett prepared to possess Lauren—mind, body, and soul!

Jill started off the new year with a visit to Kay's, suggesting that they bury the hatchet once and for all. But Kay said she wasn't ready to be friends. Kay's one resolution for the New Year, which she intended to carry out, was to show John her damning collection of Jill and Jack photos! Jill screamed at Kay: she hoped 1985 would be the year Kay drank herself to death! Then Jill stomped off. The next day Jill tried to bribe Kay's housemaid, Esther, into retrieving the photo album for her. Kay got wind of it and that scheme fell apart, but only after Jill had hocked some jewelry to raise some of the money for the bribe.

Then Katherine called John and manipulated him into accepting a dinner invitation for both him and Jill at the Chancellor estate. On the day of the dinner, Kay instructed Esther to set up the slide projector in the living room while the rest of them would still be at the dinner table, promising they'd have a show Jill would never forget! When Kay ushered them into the living room after dinner, Jill immediately realized what Kay was up to and pretended to get wretchedly sick to her stomach, upstaging Kay. John took her right home.

The hocked jewelry caused a whole other set of problems. Jill had to tell John the jewelry was stolen, and John called Carl Williams again. Later, Jill said she had misplaced the jewelry and found it packed away in a travel bag. Miffed over the fiasco, John returned to the office to take his mind off of things, where he ran into Lindsey Wells, who was in

There was no greater rivalry than that between Jill Foster Abbott and Katherine Chancellor.

tears. It happened to be the anniversary of her father's death. John did the kindly thing and invited her to Gina Roma's restaurant, Gina's Place, for a little drink and gave her a shoulder to cry on. And she gave him a little innocent kiss in return, which Jill saw. Jill approached him about this later, and John couldn't help feeling like a schoolboy who was being asked to explain his every move. He felt defensive, obstinate, and refused to apologize.

Months went by and Katherine still hadn't acted upon her resolution. She instructed Esther to have the most provocative of the photos enlarged and cut into a puzzle. She'd send one piece a day to John until he received all 10 of the puzzle pieces. On the day she was to send the final piece—the piece that would reveal the faces of Jack and Jill—Kay was persuaded by Dina to restrict her rancor toward Jill and have Jack's face removed from the puzzle photo. Kay agreed. She'd also have Jack's face removed from all the negatives, slides, and photos. Then she called a special messenger, and she knew positively she'd have her revenge within the hour.

But when John received the final puzzle piece, he thought it was a pornographic photo and threw it out in disgust, without realizing it was Jill in the

photo! Later, when Kay realized what John had done, she relentlessly badgered him to get him over to her place, saying it was urgent that she see him. What was wrong with that woman? he wondered. What could be so important that he had to go there upon command? When Kay showed him slide after slide, photo after photo of Jill in various compromising positions, he just couldn't believe it. He hurtled the projector to the floor and stormed away to confront his wife.

When John got home, Jill was sunbathing by the pool, and he couldn't find her. Later, when she went to her room to change, she found John lying face down on the floor. John was rushed to the hospital.

At the hospital, the family huddled together, anxiously. All they knew was that John had suffered a stroke and that the doctors were still assessing the extent of its damages. Even Kay appeared on the scene, out of genuine concern for her dear friend. But she didn't miss out on the opportunity to let Jill know that John had seen the photos. Jill told Jack and both knew it was all over for them. But later, Dina told Jack she had persuaded Kay to have his face removed from all the photos, negatives, and slides, so John wouldn't know his son had been his wife's lover!

When Jill finally had the courage to visit John, she told him how much she loved him. But he became so agitated he had to be sedated. Later she told him the pictures were taken long before she met him, that she'd never been unfaithful to him.

The more Jill professed her love for him, the more John came back to that single question: Who was the man in the picture with her? Weeks passed. Then the doctor said John was well enough to go home. The first thing John said to Jill was that he wanted her out of the house in 30 days, and that he was filing for divorce. Jill was crushed, but Brock, back from out of town, encouraged her to put a positive spin on this: she had 30 days to save her marriage.

Jill came up with a new story. She claimed the man in the picture was her former fiancé, Andy Richards. She told John they'd made love when they were engaged—never before that and never after. John went to see Andy to check on Jill's story. He found out that Andy had never made love to Jill in the wintertime in a log cabin! At the end of his rope with her lying, John told Jill to see a lawyer. He wanted her out of there and he wanted her out of there, fast!

Jill's next strategy was to fake being sick—too sick to move out or see a lawyer. She studied a book on the different symptoms of depression. Jill was never seen leaving her room, and she said she didn't want to eat. This went on until her doctor pronounced her to be emotionally disturbed and he advised John to postpone the divorce for her sake. They called in a psychiatrist, whom Jill was willing—even eager—to see. He pronounced her "suicidal." It was Kay who came up with the idea to call Jill's bluff: Threaten her with shock treatments. Well, it worked—Jill hopped out of bed in a flash and was out of the house by the end of the day.

Jill retained Michael Crawford to represent her, and the lawyers dickered over what would constitute a reasonable settlement. Michael's figures were not acceptable to the other side, and when John saw what Jill had submitted as her expenses, he went through the roof. He immediately put curbs on what she could spend. The final figure Michael submitted was $132,000 a year, but John said that was patently ridiculous, and wondered whether the nude pictures could effect a more equitable solution.

As president of Lauren Fenmore's fan club and her biggest fan, Shawn Garrett dedicated himself to making Lauren a superstar and to ridding her of her husband, Paul. Shawn was so obsessed with Lauren that he couldn't stand not knowing what she was thinking about or doing every single minute of the day. He had her apartment bugged so he'd always know what Lauren and Paul's plans were, what they were doing, and what they were talking about. And it drove him absolutely wild to know that they were being intimate.

Lauren had a number of deep-seated hang-ups and insecurities. But she was fiercely competitive and would do almost anything to reach the top, including decimating her competition—Traci Abbott. Lauren was also a troubled young woman in that she deeply resented her mother, JoAnna, for not playing a normal role in her life. When her parents—Neil and JoAnna—were divorcing, Lauren had overheard JoAnna express regret about having had Lauren in the first place; JoAnna wished she'd had an abortion.

Neil Fenmore contacted his ex-wife in Milan, Italy, to invite her to return to Genoa City because he felt that the unevenness of Lauren's behavior and her unpredictable mood swings were indicative of her need for a mother's influence. He also let JoAnna know that Lauren's husband, Paul, was having a serious problem; although Paul wanted his wife to be happy, her compulsion to achieve success was destroying their marriage. JoAnna reluctantly agreed to return, but had little confidence she could be of much help. Lauren's first glimpse of her mother after all those years of separation came about when JoAnna attended Lauren's concert. Lauren reacted in shock when she saw her mother in the audience. Eventually, the two would grow close.

Shawn had to overcome several hurdles standing between himself and Lauren: Paul, Neil, JoAnna, Danny, other close friends, and Lauren, herself. His strategy was to methodically remove the obstacles that stood in his way, one by one. He used drugs to badly impair and nearly destroy Danny's singing voice. He made and carried through on threats to eliminate Paul as a competitor for Lauren's love. He confused Lauren as to how she felt about her marriage: she loved her husband; she resented her husband. She loved her career; her career was not as important to her as her marriage. She wanted to have the baby that Paul wanted them to have; she didn't want to have a baby. She wanted to sign the exclusive contract with Victory Records; she regretted signing the contract. She wanted to sing with Danny; she wanted to sing solo. And on and on.

Shawn bought Lauren expensive presents: a $7,500 gold star, a 5-carat diamond, a sable coat. Presents that Paul certainly couldn't afford. But these material things didn't mean much to Lauren. When it came right down to it, she truly loved Paul and was terrified of Shawn. Shawn forced Lauren to move out of the apartment she shared with Paul and to move in with him on the threat that if she didn't, Turk, Shawn's hit man, would kill Paul.

It was Christmas Eve. Under the pretense of getting some of her clothes from the apartment, Lauren left Paul a note saying she'd meet him in church. Shawn was hiding in the apartment and retrieved the note. Lauren went to church alone. She expected to meet Paul there, but Shawn showed up instead and sat next to her. Later, Paul walked in with his mother, and spotted Lauren and Shawn, and they sat several rows behind them. Paul watched Lauren throughout the entire service. The next day, Paul couldn't get it out of his mind that he never saw anyone look as unhappy as Lauren. Paul was now certain she had left him for some reason he knew nothing about. And with the New Year approaching, he promised himself he was going to find out why.

JoAnna and Lauren bonded over their disapproval of Gina Roma, to whom Neil had become engaged. Mother and daughter became strong allies in a plan they developed for JoAnna to win Neil back. Danny, meanwhile, urged Gina to contact their father

Gina Roma was thrilled that Neil Fenmore loved her as much as she loved him. But JoAnna and Lauren, his ex-wife and troubled daughter, would conspire to break them up.

in prison to let him know of the joyful turn her life was taking. But Gina wouldn't hear of it. The last thing she wanted was to have Neil know her family background, including her own brushes with the law. Lauren, who relied heavily on Tamra, her psychic, for direction, told her mother of Tamra's revelation of a deep, unsavory secret in Gina's past. Shawn arranged for JoAnna and Neil to be interviewed for a fan club function, which resulted in the awakening of new feelings they had never before experienced.

An investigator, hired by Lauren, discovered Gina's criminal record. Lauren's compulsion to break up Gina and Neil led her to New York City, where she interviewed Frances, a former cellmate of Gina's, and paid her off handsomely to appear in Genoa City on the day of the wedding. Frances created a terrible scene before an assemblage of wedding guests at a prenuptial brunch, and blurted out to Neil that she had shared a cell for three years with his bride-to-be in a New York State prison. Bitterly disappointed that Gina had not been honest with him, Neil announced to the guests that there would be no wedding.

Weeks later, when Gina confronted Neil for the first time since their breakup, she tried to tell him she was a different person now. She told him she wished she could change her past, but she couldn't. And if he could not accept her, she wanted a clean break. She slowly removed the engagement ring from her finger, placed it on his desk, and walked away. Neil said nothing.

The manipulative Shawn went into action. He wrote a fake letter addressed to Gina from Frances, in which Frances invited Gina to come to New York to see her. Gina went, hoping that Frances would reveal the name of the person who paid her off to break up her relationship with Neil. Although Frances had

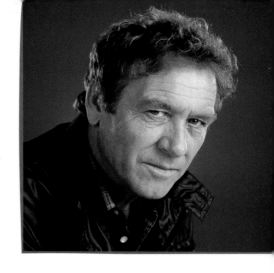

Ashley couldn't believe it when she learned that Brent Davis, and not John Abbott, was her father.

nothing to do with writing the letter, she did implicate Lauren and agreed to accompany Gina to Genoa City to back up Gina's accusation. Once again, Paul was dealt a blow when he learned what his wife had done. Paul walked out on Lauren. Shawn, tuning in with his listening device, felt he had taken another step toward making Lauren his.

The intrusion of Brent Davis in Dina Mergeron's life gave her cause to worry that Ashley might learn the secret that had long been kept hidden from her and the rest of the Abbotts, including John. Dina's favorite gemstone was garnets, and when Ashley received a garnet necklace from an "anonymous" source, Dina immediately suspected it was from her old suitor, Brent Davis.

Brent admitted that he sent the necklace. For Brent determined it was time that Ashley Abbott find out she was his daughter! He let a number of opportunities slip before he could summon the courage to tell her, and when he did, Ashley was shaken, thinking he was some kind of kook. He tried on several other occasions to tell her, and when she complained he was harassing her, he finally sneaked into her garage one night and waited for her to come home. He cornered her, and told her to check with Dina. Then he left.

Traumatized, Ashley staggered out into the rain-drenched street and through the park, where a

Victor and Ashley, and Jack and Nikki—two couples whose relationships would develop and grow to unparalleled levels over the years.

young punk snatched her purse. She wandered onto the highway, where a sympathetic truck driver, Hank (with a lecherous partner, Vince) picked her up, intending to drop her off at the next town. When their truck developed mechanical trouble, they stopped a nearby truck stop for repairs. They spent the night at a motel, with Hank making certain that two rooms were rented—one for Ashley and one for him and Vince. The next morning, Hank took off with Vince, leaving Ashley behind as he thought she would be safer there.

Meanwhile, Brent was so depressed over his encounter with Ashley that Kay decided that she and Brent should take a short vacation—a cruise. Dina, too, was depressed, but Victor got her to open up just enough for him to figure out that Brent Davis was Ashley's father. Victor began to search for Ashley, forgetting the birthday party Nikki was giving him. For that matter, he forgot Nikki!

Back at the truck stop, a hooker drove Ashley to the next town and dropped her off at a diner. Tom, the owner, felt sorry for Ashley, who told him her name was Annie. He offered her a job and a place to stay.

What happened next might briefly be described in a montage of scenes: first Vince, then later Victor, raced to the truck stop motel; Ashley listed "Annie's Apple Pies" on the chalkboard; and then Vince, and later Victor, learned about the diner and

rushed there. Vince arrived first, waited for all of the customers to leave, and then dragged Ashley to a back room, where he threw her on a bed, ready to rape her.

The screeching of tires in the parking lot prompted Vince to quickly bind and gag Ashley. Then he showed up at the counter in a chef's cap and apron to face Victor. Vince managed to send Victor away, saying Ashley had taken off with a couple of guys headed for Iowa. But it struck Victor, as he was driving, that the A's in Annie's Apple Pies matched the A's in Ashley Abbott. Victor headed back and rescued her. He brought her with him to the ranch, and notified the Abbotts that Ashley was safe. But Victor also told them that she had no memory of who she was, and needed to be with someone she trusted until she was better.

Katherine and Brent returned from their cruise to face Dina, who found it reprehensible that Brent had told Ashley that he was her father. Dina whipped out a gun, intending to shoot Brent, but Kay got in the way and took the bullet instead. Brent wrestled the gun away from Dina, leaving his fingerprints on it, intending to take the blame as atonement for the way he had treated Dina and Ashley. Kay absolved Brent, but didn't reveal who shot her. Ashley regained her memory when Victor reunited her with Dina. Ashley described her encounter with Brent in the garage, and said she hated both her mother and father (Brent). She clung to Victor. A lonely Nikki bonded with Jack Abbott, and Victor bonded with Ashley. Brent died of a recently diagnosed liver ailment, and Jack figured out that Ashley was his half sister.

With the demise of his Leon Monroe persona, young black law student Tyrone Jackson was forced to assume a new disguise if he was to persist in his mission to infiltrate the mob and break Mr. Anthony's syndicate. Only this time he became Robert Tyrone—a white man! Although still in love with Amy Lewis, who still believed him dead, Tyrone was fortuitously thrown together with Alana Anthony, Mr. Anthony's daughter. It was the perfect setup. All he had to do was to pretend to fall in love with Alana to get closer to Mr. Anthony.

Things were moving along smoothly for the two young people. They lived in the same apartment complex, where Tyrone worked as an assistant sales manager and had rented an apartment to Alana. Educated in Switzerland, Alana had been shielded from really knowing the kind of business her father was engaged in. She thought he ran a legitimate import company.

Alana and Robert shared many good times together—eating at Gina's and attending Danny Romalotti concerts. When Robert Tyrone lost his job, Alana put in a good word with her father, who noticed that a deep affection had developed between the two young people. Mr. Anthony offered Robert a position in his import company and, as easy as that, Robert was in! The only problem was that by this time, Robert Tyrone and Alana Anthony were really falling in love. And when Mr. Anthony saw the two young people kissing, they admitted their fondness for one another. He announced their engagement, and set the wedding date for two weeks away.

As Tyrone handed the keys to Mr. Anthony's office over to Jazz and Andy, he implored them to work fast. They had to if he was to accomplish his mission and take off before the wedding ceremony. Although he had indeed fallen for Alana, Tyrone couldn't in good faith go through with such a deception.

On the day of the ceremony, while the wedding party was in church, Andy and Jazz entered Mr. Anthony's secret room, which tripped a remote control alarm system that sealed them behind a concrete door. They soon lost consciousness due to lack of oxygen. Once Alana and Robert Tyrone were pronounced husband and wife, Mr. Anthony hastily left for the secret room, with Robert following closely behind. Andy and Jazz's execution would have been a certainty had the police not arrived in time to rescue them. Mr. Anthony was shot and killed in the shoot-out, instead. Afterwards, Tyrone had to tell his wife what happened and disclose his true identity. Crazed with grief and reeling from her husband's deception, Alana shot Tyrone, hitting him in the arm as he professed his love for her. Shortly afterwards, although she admitted a part of her would always love him, Alana walked out of his life forever.

Tyrone Jackson went undercover and became Robert Tyrone. His mission was to break up the mob, and Mr. Anthony was killed in the crossfire.

The mysterious shooting of Andy Richards, critically wounding him, and the claim afterwards that it was all a mistake, convinced Lauren she couldn't tell Paul (the bullet's actual target) about the threat Shawn was holding over her head. For, unless she divorced Paul and moved in with Shawn, Paul would be the target of Shawn's hit man, Turk! For his own protection, Lauren had to make Paul believe she no longer cared for him, and that her future was now with Shawn. There was no reason for Paul to disbelieve her, considering all of the bizarre things they had been doing lately—but Paul had more urgent things to attend to and hurried over to the hospital to be with his best friend, Andy.

When Paul learned that Andy might die, he raced over to the Rendezvous to pick up Andy's girlfriend, Faren. The two of them waited, cried, and prayed together while Andy was in surgery. Shawn had the unmitigated gall to go to the hospital to express his condolences, and he and Paul nearly came to blows. But Paul's actions told Shawn exactly what he wanted to know—Lauren had truly left him!

Lauren didn't know how to act around Shawn anymore. He had become so intense, angry, and manipulative; he had truly become psychotic! Lauren was afraid he'd want to make love to her, but he assured her he couldn't, even if he wanted to. He didn't want to say another word about it! Lauren badgered him with questions about his past, and all he'd offer was that until he'd met her, he'd never loved any woman except his mother.

When Shawn found out Lauren told her psychic, Tamra, who couldn't speak as a result of a mysterious hit-and-run accident, how much she really hated Shawn and was only humoring him until she could find a way to be reunited with Paul, he went berserk. He secretly canceled the worldwide concert tour he'd planned to promote her career. They flew to San Francisco where his mother had lived, and where she died in a fatal fire in 1972. Lauren managed to track down Mark Wilcox without Shawn's knowledge. Wilcox had married Shawn's mother while Shawn was away at summer camp during that fatal summer of '72. Wilcox told Lauren that he had suspected, but was unable to prove, that Shawn had started the fire. He warned her to run for her life, that Shawn was extremely dangerous. Moreover, inasmuch as Lauren was a singer just as Shawn's mother had

Shawn Garrett was obsessed with Lauren, and buried her alive. Paul, Jazz, and Andy rescued her.

been, Shawn might be thinking Lauren was betraying him just as he imagined his mother had betrayed him by marrying Wilcox.

By this time, Paul, Jazz, and Andy (now out of the hospital) were already in San Francisco, tracking down leads. But Shawn managed to elude them. He had Turk take Lauren to an abandoned garage, where Shawn tied her up. Then he gathered some of her clothes, doused them in gasoline, and set a match to them. But Turk rescued her because she was pregnant. Later, Paul, Jazz, and Andy caught up with Shawn and Turk, who were lying on the pier, where they'd been wounded in a shoot-out with the police. As he lay dying, Shawn mumbled that Lauren had three hours to live. The men raced over to the cemetery where Shawn's mother was buried, and found Lauren in the grave beside her, buried alive! Lauren survived, but lost the baby. Eventually, she and Paul reconciled.

Attorney Michael Crawford informed Jill that John was worth much more than they originally thought, and that they should up the ante on the divorce settlement to $5 million, plus $150,000 a year in support. Meanwhile, John's lawyer thought they should subpoena Kay Chancellor to testify regarding the photos she had of Jill, which Kay had ordered Esther to dispose of, but which Esther didn't. Lindsey worried that, as the photographer who took the pictures in the first place, she'd antagonize so many of the Abbotts that she was in danger of losing her job. Kay advised her to fess up, especially to John, but not to implicate Jack.

Esther began to compose an anonymous letter addressed to Kay, using words clipped out of the newspaper, indicating that she had the photos and would return them—for $100,000! But in the end, she bungled the job and returned the photos to Kay for free.

John was "thrilled" to have the photos in hand, certain they'd go a long way in reducing the amount of the divorce settlement to practically zero.

When Michael Crawford received his copy of the photos, he was fit to be tied. He had repeatedly asked Jill if there was something she wasn't telling him that he ought to know. It was now obvious his client had lied to him.

On the eve of the divorce hearing, Jill badgered John into listening to what she had to say: that if he insisted upon introducing the photos of her making love to another man, then she'd have to say who that other man was, wouldn't she? John scoffed. It could be the devil himself, for all he cared. So Jill told him that it was his son, Jack! But surprise of all surprises: John didn't believe her—not for a single moment! How could she stoop so low?

But Jill was not about to give up. She phoned several TV stations, newspapers, and the tabloids to set up a press conference. Then she called John to tell him what to expect. John was incredulous; he could not believe she'd make such an embarrassing public announcement. He decided to call her bluff. But Kay wasn't so sure Jill was bluffing, and felt John should be told the truth.

The next day, John rethought what Jill had told him. He passed his son's bedroom before leaving for work and saw Jack naked. He matched Jack's body to the body he saw in the photo. At the office, he asked Lindsey point blank if Jack was the man in the photo. Although Lindsey skirted his question, John knew it was, in fact, Jack.

Jill began the press conference by making a lengthy statement regarding her divorce from John Abbott. Just when it appeared she was going to release all the steamy details, complete with visuals, John marched to the front of the room and led her away. Now she'd have everything she wanted: sweet revenge, plus 20 percent of Jabot stock, a seat on the board of directors, and a cushy executive position with Jabot that would pay her $150,000 a year! John ate humble pie, but then he confronted Jack and threw him out with a vengeance, saying he couldn't stand the sight of him. He wanted him out of his house and out of his life. Jack stormed over to Jill's, filled with rage. He tore into her with such rancor, he literally left her shaking in her boots.

Jill's tensions were soon relieved when Sven, the master masseur at the Genoa City Hotel, gave her one of his soothing massages. However, she found he was getting too familiar, with a touch here and a touch there, and kisses that were becoming too demanding. When he wouldn't stop, she had him thrown out of her hotel suite, and had him fired. He went over to Gina's and belted down a few drinks.

Meanwhile, Michael Crawford dropped by early for their date and let himself in with the key Jill gave him. When he heard the shower running, he poured two glasses of wine. He went into the bathroom to give Jill her glass, and was mortified to find that Jill had been shot several times! For several days, Jill lay in intensive care, near death. Carl Williams had three main suspects: John Abbott, who was smarting from the recent divorce; Jack Abbott, whose life had been ruined by her disclosure; and Kay Chancellor, who just plain hated Jill.

Jill's mother arranged for little Phillip—whose rare blood type enabled him to donate blood—to be taken out of boarding school to be near his mother. But the angry and troubled boy could care less whether his mother lived or died.

Gina's had been beset by prowlers and Jack was rooming there for the time being. When Jack realized that the .38 revolver he had borrowed from Leo, the bartender, was the same kind of gun Carl Williams was looking for, he tossed it into the lake. When Carl fished it out and had it tested by ballistics, his suspicions were confirmed: It was the weapon that had been used to shoot Jill. Jack was arrested. Jill identified him as her attacker, even though she didn't actually see him. Jack confessed to the shooting although he was innocent; he just didn't want the case to go to court, and have his affair with Jill come out for public scrutiny. And he didn't want to subject his father, who had a heart problem, to more stress.

Jack was sentenced to five years' probation, with one year to be spent in a work-release program. He was assigned to a soup kitchen during the day, working under the supervision of its director, Ellen Winters, while at night, he was locked up. But what bothered him was that the real assailant was still on the loose.

Jill had also come to the realization that Jack was not her assailant, and she panicked at the thought that some nut might strike again. She came to realize, too, that the culprit was Sven when he let it slip that Jack had borrowed Leo's gun—a fact known only to Jack, Leo, and Gina. Soon enough, there was Sven banging at Jill's door again!

At almost the same time, Jack realized Jill's life was in grave danger, so instead of reporting to the lockup, he became a fugitive. Sven persuaded Jill to go over to his place for a private massage. When Jack finally traced Jill to Sven's, she was nowhere to be found. Jack scuffled with Sven in an effort to find out what he did with her, but he had to flee when Carl Williams showed up. Carl took off in pursuit.

Sven, meanwhile, had stuffed Jill in a meat locker in his kitchen, and turned it on full blast. He fled, and was last seen walking off a plane in Mexico. Jack saved Jill, and was later vindicated. John apologized to his son after Jill explained that the real reason Jack confessed was to spare him. But he still couldn't forgive him.

Mollie and Nina were pregnant teenagers who were roommates in Rose DeVille's boardinghouse, a front for the baby-selling ring Rose headed.

Nina Webster was on the streets and pregnant when she was taken in by Rose DeVille, who ran a baby-selling ring.

At the most vulnerable time in her life, Nina told Rose she'd be willing to give her baby away, as she'd be unable to care for it. Rose had a wealthy couple lined up who wanted the baby immediately after its birth. When Nina changed her mind, it was too late; Rose lied that her baby boy had died. But Cricket had seen a couple leave with a newborn baby. From that day forward, Nina became obsessed with finding her baby and would look for him everywhere she went.

Mollie, on the other hand, was a runaway; she didn't want her mother to know she was pregnant or be a burden to her. Danny Romalotti's summer concert, with its theme IT'S OK TO SAY NO TO SEX, featuring recording artist Michael McDonald, was the setting for a touching reconciliation between Mollie and her mother, who pledged to support her daughter. The two went home to prepare for the

Danny and Traci performed in concert, helping to spread the word to young people that IT'S OK TO SAY NO.

birth of Mollie's baby, while, for years to come, a restless and sorrowful Nina would continue her quest to find her son.

Victor Newman couldn't get Ashley Abbott out of his mind. In his past dealings with her, he knew her to be the strong-willed, capable, beautiful young corporate executive that she was, and he admired her for that. Her recent trauma, however, showed him her softer, more feminine, and more vulnerable side, and his admiration turned to love. She needed someone strong to take care of her, and Victor thought that he was that someone. It wasn't that he didn't love Nikki—he would always love her. But, for now, he was in love with Ashley.

So, while Victor was caught up in Ashley's spell, Nikki turned to Jack, who was having problems of his own with his father and his stepmother. Nikki and Jack found comfort and solace in each other's arms. When it became all too evident that Nikki had lost Victor to Ashley, she asked him for a divorce, which sent Victor straight to Ashley with a proposal of marriage. Perhaps, now, the diamond solitaire pendant he had given her could be made into an engagement ring, if she would have him. And Nikki told Jack that if only he'd pull himself together and shape up, they could have a nice life ahead of them. But Jack

didn't want a long-term commitment; he wanted to know what was wrong with just having sex.

Wishes aside, it was not to be for either couple. Nikki's sister, Dr. Casey Reed, discovered that Nikki had a fatal disease and that there might not be much time left. Victor was remorseful: he hadn't given Nikki the time or attention she deserved during the course of their marriage. He'd have to work quickly to repair the damage he caused, to make her feel that the love he was going to demonstrate now had been there all along. But he demanded one thing of Casey: Nikki was not to be told of her illness and risk marring the happiness she was to enjoy.

While she was on a routine business trip to Paris, Ashley found out she was pregnant. She couldn't get home fast enough to tell Victor the good news. But all her dreams crumbled when she learned Nikki was dying. How could she take Victor away from her when Nikki needed him so? She didn't tell Victor about her pregnancy or her decision to have an abortion.

Matt, Victor's brother, played a gallant role in all of this. He had a great affection for both Nikki and Ashley and couldn't stand to see either one of them hurt. He wanted to be there *for both of them*. In fact, Matt, not Jack, would have been precisely the man Victor would have chosen for Nikki had he married Ashley. At one point before Ashley decided to have the abortion, Matt had actually stepped forward and offered to be a father to his brother's baby.

Victor found out about Ashley's decision too late. The deed was done. He was furious that Ashley

Ashley was found wandering the streets of New York. John eventually located her and brought her back to Fairview Sanitarium where she could get the best care available.

would make such a weighty decision without talking it over with him first. He rushed to the cabin and found her there; they argued violently, and Ashley ran out in a savage, windswept rainstorm. Nikki, on the other hand, couldn't have been happier with the change in her life; it was as if her husband had fallen in love with her all over again! So, while Nikki was anticipating a second honeymoon, Ashley, with the sounds of a baby crying, ringing in her ears, was found wandering the streets of New York. She was committed to a mental hospital.

After Andy Richards's divorce from Diane Jenkins, he fell really hard for Faren Connor, who'd survived a serious automobile accident. The only problem was that Faren was not only not her real name . . . she didn't even know who she was or where she came from. Faren submitted to a number of neurological tests, hoping to find some answers, but the tests revealed nothing. She was advised to live for the future and forget the past. Andy and Faren married, and soon their dream of having a family and buying a home seemed to be coming true—until Evan Sanderson showed up on their doorstep. Evan claimed that Faren was his wife, Michelle, and that

she had a small daughter in Pittsburgh who missed her mother very much.

Former Abbott groundskeeper Brad Carlton proved that he was worthy of John Abbott's faith in his abilities, when, under the greatest of odds, he achieved fantastic results in selling the Jabot line of products in the most difficult territories. Jack Abbott thought Brad was a manipulative fortune hunter, and feared that his kid sister, Traci, would end up getting

Victor Newman's brother, Matt, was hand-picked by Victor to marry Nikki when Victor made plans to spend the rest of his life with Ashley. Jack was concerned about what was best for both Ashley and Nikki.

Traci Abbott and Brad Carlton fell in love. She met him when he was a groundskeeper at the Abbott home. Jack was always suspicious of Brad's motives.

hurt. Instead, Traci blossomed into a happy young woman who thrived on Brad's love. They were married in a simple ceremony before a small gathering of family and close friends. Brad told Jack it would mean a great deal to Traci if he could put in an appearance. Jack, still alienated from his father and banished from the family homestead, did manage to catch a glimpse of Traci getting married. But no one saw him but his father. John replaced Jack in the Jabot hierarchy by appointing Brad director of sales.

By the time the year had ended, many other noteworthy events took place. Jill worked hard on the men's line at Jabot; and Cricket befriended Nina and put up with her shenanigans. Katherine, meanwhile, took in Phillip, arranged for him to transfer to Genoa City University, and took steps to have him take on the Chancellor name. Cricket and Danny were becoming more than good friends; and the irrepressible Lauren managed once more to humiliate her husband, Paul. She entered him in a tabloid centerfold contest for Outstanding Professional Male, which he won, forcing him to have to resign from the mayor's Commission on Pornography.

Paul Williams got the shock of his life when his mother showed him his "centerfold." He felt betrayed by Lauren.

When Nikki went to refill her prescription for vitamins, she discovered she'd been taking an anti-inflammatory drug instead. She checked her file in Casey's office, and was further shocked to learn she had been seriously sick for a long time and was possibly dying! When Casey returned from her medical convention, she confirmed it, but protested that she was only trying to protect Nikki by not telling her. Casey soon told Victor that Nikki knew.

Nikki's most immediate concern became finding a suitable replacement for herself so that Victoria and Victor might be cared for in the manner she wished. Her first candidate was Casey, on whom she performed a "Nikki Makeover." But when Victor suggested that Casey go after his brother, Matt, Nikki knew Victor had no interest in Casey. She then turned her attention to her second candidate: Victor's first wife, Julia, whom she had to summon from Paris. Both Julia and Victor humored Nikki for a while, but once again Nikki struck out. Julia suggested she consider one final candidate, the most logical choice of all: Ashley Abbott! This, of course, blew Nikki's mind. But when yet another medical examination indicated that Nikki's condition was not improving, for there was more scar tissue on her lungs, Nikki attempted to locate Ashley.

Ashley had been in a mental hospital in New York City, where she was taken after being found roaming the streets. In that institution, she had deteriorated to an even sorrier mental state. She was constantly hearing in her head the sounds of a baby crying, and she was malnourished because her roommates were stealing the food off her tray.

Dr. Steven Lassiter, a psychiatrist assigned to the facility, attempted to obtain background information on his Jane Doe. The Abbotts, in their efforts to find Ashley, heard about Lassiter's patient, and contacted him to compare notes. John was shocked to find his daughter reduced to such a pathetic state, and worked expeditiously with Dr. Lassiter to have Ashley transferred to Fairview, the private institution closer to home. At the Abbotts' request, Dr. Lassiter came to Genoa City to continue treating Ashley. The family agreed to protect her by keeping her confinement a secret.

It was Paul Williams who tipped Nikki off as

to where she might find Ashley, and Nikki was shocked to discover that the strong young Jabot executive could have such overwhelming problems that would land her in a mental institution. But Nikki couldn't get to first base with Dr. Lassiter watching over her. He simply wouldn't let Nikki see her. And then Nikki got really depressed when, by checking the dates of the onset of her own illness and of Ashley's breakdown, she came to the inescapable conclusion that Victor didn't come back to her because he loved her, but because he knew she was dying! He didn't choose her over Ashley; he simply acted out of guilt. Why go on living? Nikki thought. The sooner she died, the sooner her husband and his lover could get back together. Throwing all caution to the winds, Nikki stopped taking her medication and really tied one on at Gina's, where she ran into an old friend

from her Bayou days. In no time at all, Nikki began to strip away her inhibitions as well as her clothes right in the middle of the dance floor. Gina tipped off Victor, and he hurried over to her place where he wrapped his coat around his wife and took her home.

Even as Casey was advising Nikki to seek a second opinion on her medical condition, Ashley decided the time had come for Victor to know the truth about why she aborted his child. She got permission to leave the hospital and went to the ranch where she was told Victor had gone horseback riding. Ashley saddled up and went looking for him, finding him in a remote corner of the ranch. She told Victor she had found out about Nikki's terminal illness and couldn't bear to add to his agony by telling him she was pregnant. Then she told him she thought abortion was the only logical solution, and she was telling him now to free both of them from further pain. Each asked the other for forgiveness, and they kissed passionately, just as Nikki, unseen, had come to tell Victor she'd learned she was in remission! Stunned, Nikki left the scene.

It's said that hell hath no fury like a woman scorned, and the sight of Victor and Ashley kissing made Nikki boiling mad. So mad that she decided she'd let Victor continue thinking she was going to die. She even applied ghastly makeup to make her look sicker, and Victor was truly troubled. When Victor suggested a second opinion, Nikki refused, for that would expose her fraudulent ways. Why bother? she asked, explaining that she was going to die anyway. She then

One of the most intense of all love triangles in Genoa City: Ashley, Victor, and Nikki.

had a ball playing the dying game to the hilt. She made an emotional good-bye videotape for Victor to find, which reduced him to bitter tears of remorse. Then, with Jack as coconspirator and lover, she arranged for a mortician to come to the ranch to make funeral arrangements, distressing Victor even more.

Nikki shared picnics with Jack, enjoying great food, great sex, and great plotting! But she slipped up, arousing Victor's suspicions when she asked for a sizable chunk of Mergeron stock to have something of her own to leave to Victoria. It was far too calculating for Nikki to think of all this by herself, and soon the ruse would be up and it would be Victor's turn to play games. But he decided she should twist slowly in the wind for a while. When Nikki wolfed down a tuna fish sandwich in her room, she got food poisoning. Other than an inconvenient trip to the hospital, she was pronounced perfectly healthy. Nikki confessed, saying she did it because she loved him.

Victor told Nikki he was suing for divorce, and then ran straight to Ashley to tell her there was hope for a future for them. But Ashley had gone on a short trip with Steven Lassiter. For Christmas, Victor gave Ashley a large pearl pendant and a unicorn—a symbol of dreams. Steven, on the other hand, gave her an engagement ring. Ashley decided to accept Steven's proposal.

If it weren't for Lauren's butting in again, Faren and Andy's marriage would have gone merrily on its way, but Evan kept pestering Lauren to put him in touch with Faren, whom he was sure was his missing wife. When Lauren set up an "accidental" encounter at the Rendezvous, Evan instantly knew he had found his wife, Michelle, again! But Faren (Michelle) didn't recognize him and she sent him away. As luck would have it, the Richards's happiness was marred by Faren's miscarriage, and though she dearly wanted to have another baby with Andy, Andy knew from her doctors that the risk was high. Another pregnancy might well lead to serious medical problems.

Hearing about her miscarriage, Evan again went to visit Faren, this time with their small daughter, Betsy, in tow. Seeing the little girl whom she could not remember really upset Faren, and once again Evan returned home to Pittsburgh. This time he promised Janet, Betsy's nanny, he would initiate divorce proceedings, unaware that Faren was now beginning to remember little things. When Faren received her copy of the divorce papers that Evan filed, she took exception to the wording that she had "willfully abandoned and deserted Evan and their daughter, Betsy." In no time at all, it was she who was on Evan's doorstep, and Janet could not prevent her from barging in to see Betsy. She wanted visitation rights. Faren was remem-

bering more things, albeit in bits and pieces. She confided in Paul, and Paul suggested she tell both Andy and Evan. Then Andy took exception that he had to hear this from Paul instead of directly from his wife, while Evan wondered whether he was rushing into things with Janet, who was already making plans for them to marry the day after the divorce was final. When Faren asked Evan to help her fill in the gaps in her memory—to tell her why she had been in an accident so far away from home—he sadly told her she was having an affair at the time. He said that they were at the point of breaking up, and that he and Betsy had gone to Europe to get away from all the ugliness. Both of them agreed that Betsy needed to know that Faren was her mother, and Betsy took to Faren right away.

On the chance that he and Faren might be able to work things out, Evan told Janet he didn't love her and that he wanted to call things off. The enraged, rejected woman packed her bags and left Evan's home, but she immediately sought out Faren, gun in hand. Afraid that Janet's paranoia would lead to something like this, Evan had followed her to Faren's

Phillip Chancellor found himself in the middle of a huge battle between Katherine and Jill over his custody.

Andy thought he'd finally found true happiness in his marriage to Faren, but it wasn't all smooth sailing for the couple.

hotel room, and he tried to reason with Janet. He couldn't reach her, so he jumped in front of Faren, taking the bullet intended for her.

Janet was taken away in a catatonic state, and as Evan lay dying, he told Betsy that Faren was her real mother and would always take care of her. Andy and Faren decided to relocate to Pittsburgh, rather than cause further disruption in little Betsy's life.

Young Phillip was caught in a maelstrom of charges and countercharges in Jill and Kay's legal battle over his custody. He was forced to listen to the entire hearing. How Kay used her power and money to win impressionable young men. How his father, Phillip Chancellor II, often threatened to divorce Kay if she didn't clean up her act. How his father and Jill fell in love, out of which he was conceived. How Kay's drinking and vindictiveness caused his father's fatal accident. How his father tried to legitimize him by marrying Jill on his deathbed. And perhaps the

Cricket and Danny were best of friends. They fell in love and Danny proposed, but life's complications would get in the way of his plans.

most telling blow of all, how Kay had Jill's marriage annulled, resulting in his losing the Chancellor name! Phillip III learned that Katherine was not the blameless person he thought her to be! Jill's fight for survival after she was stripped of her inheritance was also exposed. In the end, the judge awarded temporary custody of Phillip to Katherine, though she was denied the right to adopt him. This all left a thoroughly confused young man feeling as if both women were responsible for his father's death!

If there was one descriptor that fit young Phillip to a T, it was his shyness. His sheltered life left him with virtually no friends, so he chose the safe haven of staying with Katherine.

Phillip was attracted to Cricket but he was afraid she was too far above him. Besides, Cricket was dating Danny, and how could he compete with a rock star? But Cricket was a good listener, and Phillip hoped there'd be a chance for him. His heart soared when Danny suggested to Cricket that they use the summer to date others, after which they would reevaluate their relationship in the fall. To bolster his courage when he was around her, Phillip began to drink. Although Cricket didn't approve of his drinking, she switched places with him and claimed to be

Phillip Chancellor III also proposed to Cricket. Although painfully shy, he was able to open up to her, and she returned his love.

the driver when he was speeding and ran a stop sign. She saved him from a serious DWI charge—it would have been his second offense. Then, one night when Danny and Cricket were discussing how they might help him, Nina told him Cricket was seeing Danny again. Then Nina plied the vulnerable Phillip with booze and seduced him.

With support from Katherine, Jill, and Cricket, Phillip turned to AA and admitted he was an alcoholic. Cricket told him how proud she was of him, and the two young people realized they were in love. Phillip proposed to Cricket, and with the summer drawing to a close, so did Danny. Cricket was in

a dilemma, and didn't know which one to choose until Nina told her about her one-night stand with Phillip. Cricket was about to break off with Phillip, but reconciled with him when she realized that the reason Nina's announcement upset her was because she truly loved him. Kay and Jill were thrilled and began to plan the wedding, but Nina gloated she was pregnant with Phillip's baby.

There were other noteworthy happenings in 1987. Nina extracted a promise from Rose DeVille that she'd return her baby for $20,000, which Phillip borrowed from Kay, but later Nina found she was scammed. Michael Crawford proposed to Jill, but was turned down. Jill was far too busy causing trouble at Jabot. Lauren and Paul decided to remarry but

John enjoyed the company of Ellen Winters, whom Jack had dated after the completion of his community service at her soup kitchen.

Paul and Lauren had been married once, and considered giving it another try, but decided they made better friends than lovers.

didn't go through with the wedding. Mary Williams, in the meantime, tried to fix Paul up with a nice girl, Dana, from her church group. She turned out to be a siren. Brad began to move up the corporate ladder at Jabot, incurring Jack's enmity, while wife Traci moved to California to attend graduate school at Stanford, where Tim Sullivan was teaching. Lauren took advantage of Traci's absence by dating Brad. John Abbott began to date the director of the soup kitchen, Ellen Winters, whom he had met through Jack, and he also took some interest in JoAnna. Jill and her assistant, David Kimble, fixed Katherine up with Rex, a bum they found on a park bench—Kay tried to repay the favor by fixing Jill up with Skip. Neil Fenmore died of a heart attack and left Lauren to take over the reins of Fenmore Department Stores. Finally, Leanna Randolph, a former mental patient of Steven Lassiter's, showed up in Genoa City and tried to insinuate herself in Steven and Ashley's lives.

As the new year got under way, the lives of Ashley, Victor, and Nikki would continue to become entangled.

Ashley knew she would always hold Victor dear to her heart. For Victor Newman was a man no woman

could resist, let alone forget. How could she tell him now that she was going to wed Steven Lassiter? Steven

made her feel secure, and she felt it was high time that she move on, even if she still. . . . Steven, of course,

sensed the private torment Ashley was going through, but he was also confident that they could handle the

Victor Newman problem. For, from Steven's point of view, Victor posed no threat whatsoever.

Thus, it was that Ashley and Steven were quietly wed in the Abbott home. John couldn't be happier than to welcome his new son-in-law into the family. As for Victor, he could only feel betrayed, while Nikki saw renewed hope for a reconciliation now that Ashley was no longer in the picture.

Meanwhile, it was no accident that Leanna Randolph, a former patient of Steven's, should find herself in Genoa City. After all, she had tracked him there. And when Jack Abbott, who was attracted to the

beauteous newcomer, told her that the doctor had married his sister Ashley, Leanna followed the newlyweds to Hawaii! The way Leanna saw it, Steven belonged to her, and she was determined to do whatever it took not to let Ashley have him—even if it meant killing her (by sending Ashley poisoned leis, no

Dr. Steven Lassiter helped Ashley recover from her breakdown. She appreciated his kindness and compassion.

less). When the Lassiters returned to Genoa City after their honeymoon, Leanna resumed her relationship with Jack, arousing Steven's suspicions. The good doctor believed Leanna was desperately in need of further psychiatric care.

But there was more than romance on Jack's mind. Brad and Jill were seriously eclipsing him at Jabot with their success with one of the company's new lines. Jack had to come up with something big. So he plotted to buy Mergeron from Nikki and transform it into a premiere cosmetics company to compete with Jabot. Jack convinced Marc Mergeron to romance Nikki so she'd agree to sell him her stock. Then, armed with Nikki's stock certificates, Jack secured the necessary bank loans and resigned his post at Jabot, only to learn that the stock was never

even Nikki's to sell! In fact, the stock was in trust for Victoria, and Victor had supplied false documents to foil Jack's plan. Jack vowed to get his revenge on Victor, if he did nothing else!

Meanwhile, Ashley and Douglas reminded Victor of all of the good times he'd shared with Nikki. Victor quickly forgave Nikki for "selling out," but he didn't hide his pleasure over Jack's humiliation. Jack bounced back when he brought Leanna into a scheme to bring Victor down. He hired her to write an exposé of Victor's life, knowing she'd have to get close to the "Black Knight" (Jack's nickname for Victor) in order to pull it off. Leanna, who didn't like men to begin with, tried her best to catch Victor's eye.

Nikki planned to tell Victor of her pregnancy, but when Victor, who she suspected was seeing someone else, said he saw no future for them, Nikki decided to withhold the news. Leanna, meanwhile, managed to befriend Nikki, who suspected nothing and told everything. How Ashley was Victor's true love and how tragic their love affair had been! Leanna had the tape recorder rolling; she knew this was best-seller material, and she intended to use it! Leanna, whose pen name was Nora Randall, insisted her publisher protect her by not revealing the source of the juicy chapter entitled "Victor's Forbidden Love."

Victor, unaware of Jack's scheme but aware that eventually a book would be written about his life, wanted to ensure the truth be told, so he asked Leanna to write his authorized biography. Seeing this as an

Nikki had no idea that when she disclosed some of the most intimate secrets of Victor's life to Leanna that they would turn up in print in Leanna's new book.

opportunity to advance her writing career, Leanna agreed, deciding to worry about the sticky details later.

When Leanna's first book, *Ruthless: The Story of Victor Newman*, was released, John was ready to sue until Ashley confessed that much of it was true. Victor, too, was enraged and vowed revenge on "Nora Randall" for hurting Ashley.

Reporters hounded Ashley, and when Ashley told Victor she had confided their past to Nikki, Victor assumed Nikki had leaked the information. He was so enraged that he found a way to have their divorce finalized immediately. When news of the dissolution of their marriage was leaked, the press had a field day speculating that Victor and Ashley would reconcile. To deflect attention away from Ashley, Victor proposed to Leanna, who said, "Why not?" They wed in Las Vegas, but Leanna told Victor she was a virgin and had no intention of changing that.

Nikki, surprised that Leanna was Victor's new bride, learned that Victor could not legally marry until six months had passed from the time of his divorce, but she kept this information to herself, biding her time. Steven, meanwhile, didn't like Ashley's obsession with Victor Newman, but she assured her husband that her future was with him—and that Victor was in her past. Steven had planned to tell Ashley the truth—that Leanna wrote the book. But he was gunned down by the distraught son of a patient and died before he had the chance.

Traci wanted to check on the status of her mar-

Brad had married Lisa Mansfield when she was only 16. She came back into his life an obsessed woman, convinced that she could make him love her again.

riage to Brad, so she used the excuse of celebrating her victory in a writing contest to return to Genoa City. Brad was seeing Lauren, his wife's archenemy, but Traci's visit put his affair on hold. Traci told Brad she had grown close to her professor and mentor, Tim Sullivan, but felt she had to give their marriage another chance. Brad tried to understand how important Traci's writing was to her, but he didn't want her to return to Stanford. Traci then suggested that they have a baby. Brad initially objected, but gave in when he realized Tim might otherwise be a threat to his marriage.

Jack, always suspicious of Brad, hired Paul to investigate his background, and was pleased with what Paul turned up. Seems "Golden Boy" (Jack's nickname for Brad) had been gardener to the wealthy Mansfield family years ago, and married their daughter Lisa when she was only 16 years old. Lisa's father had the marriage annulled and told Brad to get lost. Jack now had proof that Brad was the gold digger

he'd always suspected him to be. Ashley urged Jack to keep this information to himself and allow Traci her happiness. But when Traci became pregnant, Lisa began to worm her way back into Brad's life by asking him to straighten out some paperwork regarding her father's estate. She promised she'd leave him alone once it was done. Instead, she drugged him and put him to bed. Then she took incriminating photos of them in bed together, and later told him they'd made love.

Things weren't going well for Brad at work, either. When sales of the men's line were down dramatically, John brought Jack back as CEO in an attempt to turn things around. Fearing for his job, Brad considered an offer in Chicago, which he rejected as soon as he found out that Lisa was the company's lead stockholder. Meanwhile, his job at Jabot was eliminated and he was only too happy to accept the job Lauren had offered him some time before.

Brad ordered Lisa to stay away from him and Traci, but Lisa vowed he'd be sorry he ever rejected her. She knew he could love her again if only he'd give it a chance. So she bought a remote lodge, had a cage built in the living room, and actually hired Rich Little to tape an impersonation of Brad explaining why he'd quit his post at Fenmore's and left town (to be with his true love, Lisa). She had one tape delivered to Traci and one to Lauren. Next, she marched over to Traci's, incriminating photos in hand, and told Traci she and Brad were in love and planned to marry. Lisa's thugs then knocked Brad out, took him to the lodge, and locked him in the cage. Devastated when she heard the tape, Traci doubled over in pain and was rushed to the hospital, where she miscarried. Meanwhile, Lisa cooked for Brad, talked to him, and told him how much she loved him. Brad decided if he

ever wanted to get out of this trap, he'd better change his tune and act nice. Traci, meanwhile, started divorce proceedings. Tim was there to comfort her. He planned to ask Traci to be his wife.

While Brad was locked in the cage, Nina was going stir crazy locked up in Katherine's attic awaiting the birth of her baby. When Phillip finally discovered her whereabouts, he was fit to be tied. How could Katherine do such a thing? Jill, desperate to prove that Phillip was not the baby's father, hired Paul to locate all of Nina's boyfriends from the past year.

Gina was stunned to discover that her father was in Genoa City. He assured her he'd turned over a new leaf: he was making a clean break from his crooked ways, and was now going by the name Rex Sterling. Danny didn't believe Rex's act at first, and warned Katherine that Rex was a con artist by whom she was being taken in. But soon Danny saw his father really had changed and they reconciled. Jill found herself attracted to Rex and vowed she would have him, despite the fact she was paying him to woo Katherine. Rex eventually told Jill their deal was off, and then charged an engagement ring to her credit card. Jill assumed it was for her, but the fur flew when Rex told Jill that he and Katherine planned to marry. Jill wasn't about to let Katherine have Rex when she wanted him for herself! She presented Katherine with her wedding gift—a box of receipts as evidence that Jill paid to have Rex romance Katherine. To convince Katherine of his sincerity, Rex had a prenuptial agreement drawn up that would leave him with a one-dollar settlement should he and Katherine ever divorce. Soon afterwards, Katherine and Rex were married. Nina went into labor during the ceremony and the couple spent their wedding night in an empty hospital room.

Nina's son was delivered by an emergency cesarean section, which left Nina in critical condition. Her thoughts of building a life with Phillip and their baby gave her the will to live, and she pulled through. And although the paternity test proved Phillip was indeed the baby's father, Jill and Katherine continued scheming to get Nina out of Phillip's life. They offered her $1 million to leave Genoa City for good, but to everyone's surprise, Nina turned it down. Now that she and Phillip shared a son, she'd find a way to get Phillip interested in her. Meanwhile, Phillip tried to have Cricket set a wedding date, but she broke their engagement, insisting his place was now with his son.

Jill's next plan was to divert Nina's attention from Phillip by setting her up with someone else. Chase Benson, a young man anxious to climb the corporate ladder at Jabot, was happy to go along with Jill's request. He courted Nina, and took her sightseeing in Los Angeles—just what Katherine and Jill thought they needed to build an abandonment case against Nina. Nina was starting to fall for Chase, until she saw through Katherine and Jill's scheme. She moved out from under Katherine's thumb and kept her

The bum Jill found on a park bench turned out to be Danny and Gina's father. He'd left behind his days as a con artist and now went by the name Rex Sterling.

whereabouts a secret from Jill. Phillip, meanwhile, still hung onto the hope of reconciling with Cricket. But Cricket, Rex, and Danny started to transform Nina into the kind of woman Phillip could be interested in.

Jessica Blair returned to Genoa City after many years of estrangement from her daughter. When Cricket was very young, Jessica had shipped her off to live with her grandmother, who died when Cricket was 13. A few months living with her mother then were enough, and Cricket ran away to live with her cousin, Joe Blair. Needless to say, Cricket wasn't happy to have her mother waltz back into her life now. Katherine offered Jessica a place to stay, hoping she and Cricket would be able to mend fences.

Jessica conferred with her doctor and knew that if she were ever to reconcile with Cricket, the time had to be now. Jessica told Cricket her father died in Vietnam before she was born, but Cricket was skeptical. She hired Paul to investigate. When Cricket confronted Jessica after Paul determined that her mother's story didn't hold up, Jessica admitted Cricket was conceived in one night of passion with a boy whose name she didn't even know.

John Abbott was attracted to Jessica, but Jessica kept her distance. She knew she was dying of AIDS and didn't want to lead John on. She also didn't want anyone to know of her illness. When Cricket came down with the flu, Jessica nursed her back to health. They spent considerable time together and grew much closer. John proposed to Jessica, and after struggling with her conscience, she accepted. When Jessica's condition worsened, she left John her engagement ring and a note saying she was returning to Kansas City. Before the flight, she collapsed and was hospitalized with pneumonia. Although she begged Dr. Scott Grainger not to tell John or Cricket the truth, Jessica herself reluctantly admitted to Cricket that she had AIDS. When Cricket tearfully told John, he was devastated. But John astonished Jessica with another proposal. She accepted. Immediately after the wedding ceremony, John and Jessica gently informed the rest of the family about her illness. They embraced her and Jessica was touched by their unconditional love.

Amy Lewis's New Year's eve prediction that a beautiful woman would walk into Paul's life and steal his heart was about to come true when he met Cassandra Hall at an art exhibit. Learning she was an interior decorator, Paul decided to engage her to redo his office. After a few months passed and the job was almost finished, Paul next asked her to redecorate his apartment. Their romance soared. Lauren did her best to attract Paul's attention, but he had eyes only for Cassandra, who admitted she was in love with Paul. Paul proposed, and Mary was afraid her son was moving much too fast.

Paul got the shock of his life when his friend George Rawlins, for whom he'd done some security work, asked him to dinner and introduced him to his wife. It was Cassandra! George then made it his business to try to find a nice woman for Paul. Maybe his niece, Brittany, who happened to be interested in Paul, would be the right girl for him. Cassandra discouraged the match, and soon Jack Abbott expressed an interest in Brittany. Brittany was directing an IRS audit of Jabot's books; perhaps Jack was hoping she'd go easy on them.

George later confided in Paul that he was impotent and feared Cassandra would leave him for a younger man. His comments resonated with Paul. George thought maybe motherhood would keep his wife from straying, and he came up with the idea that Paul could sire their child. Much to George's disappointment, Paul refused.

While Brittany suspected Cassandra didn't really love George but wanted him for his money, Mary came to the conclusion that Cassandra was

Cricket bonded with her mother, Jessica. The time they shared together would be even more precious when Cricket learned Jessica had been stricken with AIDS.

George Rawlins was unable to satisfy his wife, Cassandra, whose love affair with Paul Williams would be all-consuming.

good for Paul and wanted Lauren out of her son's life. Until, that is, Mary found out that Ms. Rawlins was a married woman. When Cassandra finally mustered the courage to ask George for a divorce, he collapsed with a heart attack, and she couldn't be sure he'd heard her. She'd now have to wait for the right moment to ask him again. George recovered, but his doctor discovered George was suffering from a terminal illness. His condition would deteriorate quickly. George was told he had very little time left to live.

Skip Evans and Carole Robbins both worked at Jabot, he as their talented photographer, and she as the ever loyal receptionist. Both were reserved, but they were a good match. She wondered, though, whether he could be comfortable with her disability: she wore a leg brace as a result of a childhood illness. They decided to take it slowly, and fell in love. With the support and love of the Abbott family, they had a fairy-tale wedding and began their life together.

In other happenings, Amy Lewis and Nathan Hastings professed their love for one another before Amy was forced to leave town to tend to her father, Frank Lewis, who had been stricken while on vacation. Jill wanted handsome attorney Michael Crawford back in her life, and though she learned he was engaged, she wasn't going to let a little thing like that stop her. Christmas was a bittersweet time for Ashley. Victor found a gift card Steven had written Ashley before he died. Victor ordered a pendant with

the infinity symbol on it to go with the card and gave it to Ashley, leading her to believe the pendant was from Steven. Ashley was touched that Steven had planned to give her such a beautiful and meaningful gift, while Leanna was touched by Victor's kindness. Chase filled Brad's job at Jabot, and since he was now answering to Jack, Jill lost her leverage with him regarding Nina. Chase took an interest in Cricket, who was also being wooed by Phillip and Scott Grainger at the year's end. Nina, meanwhile, was improving herself—her walk, her talk, her dress—in an effort to win over Phillip. Rex and Katherine were happy to have found each other, but were concerned that Phillip's separation from the baby might lead him to drink again. Finally, Rex's old cellmate, Clint Raddison, came to town, rented a room over Gina's, got friendly with the boss, and would soon turn Rex and Katherine's life upside down.

From his vantage point in the office he had rented, George Rawlins fixed his high-powered binoculars on

Paul Williams's office across the street. The image he saw threw him into a fit of blinding rage. His young wife,

the beautiful Cassandra, and Paul, whom he'd come to regard as a son, were locked in each other's arms,

in a torrid embrace! Just as he suspected, they had become lovers! They were betraying him!

George grimly plotted his revenge. Nothing could go wrong; it had to be absolutely foolproof. Painstakingly, he filed down the safety on his gun and then asked Paul to take it to the gunsmith to be repaired. Next, he wrote a letter stating that Paul had committed fraud. He created false invoices showing Paul had overcharged him for the security work he'd done, and replaced the real invoices in Paul's office with the fakes. He then cleverly staged an argument with Paul when he knew Victor would overhear it. Paul later returned George's gun to him, and not long after, Brittany found her uncle. He had been shot dead!

An incredulous Paul, the evidence mounting against him, found himself a primary suspect in George's shooting. He realized that if the authorities ever found out he and Cassandra were having an affair, he'd be convicted for sure. Unknown to Paul, he wasn't the only one Cassandra had been seeing. All the while she was having an affair with him, she was also having clandestine

The somber-faced trio—the widow Cassandra; Cassandra's lover Paul; and George Rawlins's niece, Brittany— mourned George's death.

WEATHER

Genoa City Chronicle

PUBLISHED DAILY

FINAL
EDITION

Price: 25 Cents

VOL. XXVII - NO. 18

WILLIAMS TRIAL BEGINS TODAY

PAUL WILLIAMS   GEORGE RAWLINS

City Leaders Confer on Vital Soil Conservation Program

Record 813,600 New Claims for Jobless Benefits Filed

DIPLOMATS FETED AS IMPORTANT ISSUES GO BY THE BOARD

meetings with a mysterious stranger, who'd soon be unmasked as her lover, Adrian!

It was Victor Newman who saw that George's story contradicted Paul's. He surmised that Paul was being set up, and offered to help Carl, who was forced to work "unofficially" on the case because of his personal involvement. But word got out that someone matching Paul's description was seen burying a gun. It turned out to be the murder weapon, and Paul was arrested.

Cassandra paid Paul's bond and warned that they mustn't see each other so as not to raise suspicions. When the gunsmith said George's gun had been tampered with, Paul knew he'd been framed. The treacherous Cassandra claimed to be relieved that Paul would soon be proven innocent, but Carl, Victor, and Brittany were suspicious of her grieving widow act. Cassandra continued to have numerous secret meetings with Adrian, who was growing ever more anxious to run away with her. But she insisted they

Believing they were now in the clear, Cassandra and her mystery lover, Adrian, stole away to Bermuda— away from everything that would remind them of the ordeal they had faced back home.

must wait until Paul was convicted. In the meantime, phone records led Paul to Adrian, and Paul found files in Adrian's house linking him to George. But there was nothing that would suggest murder.

Cassandra took the stand in Paul's trial. Under oath she admitted that she and Paul had had an affair. Desperate to clear himself, Paul faked his own death with Carl and Victor's help. He then went undercover to find the real killer. The court believed Paul's "suicide" was an admission of guilt and closed the case. Cassandra figured she was in the clear and jetted to Bermuda with Adrian. Paul revealed to his grieving mother that he was in fact alive, swore her to secrecy, and then he and Carl followed the couple to Bermuda.

Meanwhile, Victor was on a mission to uncover the scoundrel who wrote *Ruthless*. Leanna was worried, not only because of the book, but also because Nikki came home with her baby and Leanna feared she'd lose Victor to his ex-wife. Her attempt to win over the children to ensure keeping Victor probably wouldn't work, either. Victor was introduced to his son, Nicholas Christian Newman. He was touched

by Nikki's thoughtfulness when she brought in the same minister who'd married them to christen their son. Nikki then dropped the bomb: Victor's marriage to Leanna was not legal because they had not waited the requisite six months after his divorce!

Leanna felt the walls closing in around her and tried her best to hang onto Victor. Ashley, who'd recently learned that it was Victor who had ordered the necklace from Steven, was touched by his kindness. So Ashley and Nikki teamed up to undermine Leanna's relationship with Victor.

Jack started to sweat, too, when Victor's investigators turned up a connection between him and the publishing company. He decided he'd get away for a while. A ski trip might just be the ticket!

Lisa was finally living out her fantasy. She re-created her wedding night with Brad decked out in his tuxedo and she in her wedding dress. They shared a romantic dinner, and then moved to the bedroom. When Lisa said she wasn't feeling well, Brad tried to escape, but she had goons stationed at the door who stopped him, and he was relegated to the cage once again. Brad became seriously ill, and though Lisa refused to take him to the hospital, she did call 911, and had a prescription filled for him.

While she was at the drugstore, Lauren, accompanying Jack on his ski trip, spotted Lisa and decided to follow her back to the lodge. When Lisa opened the door, Lauren pushed her way in and found Brad, but wound up locked in the cage with him. Lisa turned on the gas and left them to die, bumping into Jack on the way out. She pulled a gun on him. He got it away from her and broke down the door to rescue Brad and Lauren. Lisa took off.

The trio returned to Genoa City, where Brad quickly apprised Traci of his return. But he was so weak, he collapsed at Traci's feet. He awakened in the hospital to learn he was no longer a married man.

While Traci was making plans to marry Tim, Brad, desperate to win her back, came up with a proposal: spend two months with him to see if they could resurrect their marriage. If it didn't work out, Brad pointed out, he'd grant Traci her divorce. But if Traci refused to go along with his plan, Brad said he would contest the divorce. He'd see to it that Tim and Traci could not wed for a long time.

Traci reluctantly went along with the plan, and Brad went to work trying to win her over. Ashley played along with him, getting "friendly" to make her sister jealous. Traci took notice. While Tim went to New York to talk with a publisher on Traci's behalf, Traci halted divorce proceedings. She was seriously reconsidering her relationship with Brad. But unfortunately for Traci, Brad was beginning to enjoy Ashley's company, perhaps a little too much. Soon enough, Brad and Traci were divorced.

Professor Tim Sullivan was the "model" professor for every coed who went to college hoping to meet the man of their dreams.

Nina and Phillip were radiant at their delayed wedding reception.

When Victor discovered that Leanna was the author of *Ruthless*, he threw her out. Then he turned his attention to Jack, whom he'd learned was instrumental in getting the book published. For a while, Victor had been secretly buying up privately held Jabot stock in the midst of the Abbotts' plans to take the company public. Victor revealed that he'd successfully completed the buyout and that Jabot now belonged to him!

Victor couldn't wait to show Jack just how "ruthless" he could be! He told Ashley about Jack's role in the book, which turned Ashley against her brother. She'd never forgive Jack for costing her the two things that meant more to her than anything else: Victor and Jabot. Victor then told the banks to refuse any and all loans to the Abbotts, threatening to pull his money out if they didn't obey him. Finally, he asked Brad to head Jabot, which would mean Jack would be forced to report to the one man he hated almost as much as he hated Victor Newman.

Over in another part of town, Nina's transformation was complete and it was now time to put her to the test. Cricket agreed to go on a date with Phillip, but sent Nina in her place. After a rocky start, the young couple had a good time. Later, Cricket told Phillip they had no future and he should spend more time with his son. He did, and also spent more time with Nina. Happy with the changes Nina had made in her life, Phillip asked her to marry him. Chase made one last-ditch effort to win her from Phillip, attempting to seduce her even as the guests were gathering for her wedding. Nina stopped him. Half-dazed from a car accident she and Chase had gotten into on the way to the church, she went through with the ceremony.

Furious she'd just inherited Nina Webster as a daughter-in-law, Jill vowed to keep Nina from Phillip's money, with Katherine's help. But Nina and Phillip Chancellor's happiness ended all too soon when, tragically, Phillip was killed in an automobile accident. He'd had too much to drink at an office party.

While Scott Grainger was on rounds one evening, Cricket looked through a photo album in his hospital quarters and came across a photo of a man who resembled her father. It was actually a picture of Scott's dad, Jim Grainger. Scott was happy that his new love, Cricket, would be able to meet his father when he came through town. But Scott was in for the shock of his life when Cricket's hunch turned out to be correct. Jim admitted to Jessica that he was the boy she'd made love to all those years ago, and explained that he had planned to propose. But he left her alone when she returned all his letters and wrote him to forget about her.

Cricket and Scott were happy and in love before Jim Grainger came into the picture.

Jessica was really confused. She didn't know what letters he was talking about. She had never written to him. Jim had saved the letters, and he showed one to Jessica. She recognized her mother's handwriting, and realized that her meddling mother had kept them apart!

So Jim really was Cricket's father—and Scott's! And Scott had just proposed to her! Heartbroken, they agreed to remain close as brother and sister. In an effort to get on with his life, Scott began seeing Lauren. He accepted a position on the Fenmore board.

John Abbott was shocked that Jessica had never told him the truth. When Jim wanted to marry her, she first said she couldn't hurt John, not after all he'd meant to her. But Jessica was torn by Cricket's desperate wish that her family finally be together.

Jack knew how much Jessica meant to John, so he thought it would be wise to find

Jim a new love. He introduced Jim to Nikki, who was all too tickled that Jim made Victor jealous. The former Mrs. Newman was quick to remind Victor that she was a single woman now. It wasn't long before Nikki told Jim she hoped to have a future with him, but it was obvious to Jim that he could never fill the place Victor still occupied in Nikki's heart. In the meantime, John nobly agreed to dissolve his marriage so that Jessica, Jim, and Cricket could unite as a family.

When Jack hired Chase to work for him, Derek Stuart filled the position Chase vacated as associate director of advertising at Jabot. Derek showed an immediate interest in Cricket and impressed her with his ambition, sincerity, and kindness. One night, Derek went to Cricket's for Chinese takeout. They danced, but when he started to take things too far, Cricket tried to stop him. Derek overpowered her and raped her. Cricket threw him out. Nina showed up and took Cricket to the hospital, where a rape counselor urged Cricket to go to the police.

Derek maintained that Cricket was a willing participant who, feeling guilty about losing her virgin-

Despite Cricket's fierce attempts to fight Derek off, he was simply too strong and powerful for the virginal young woman.

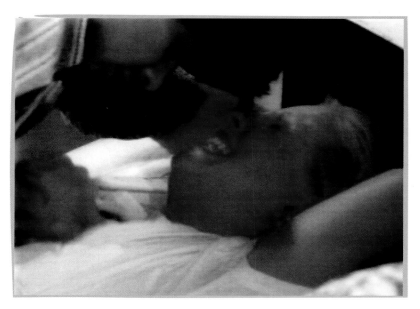

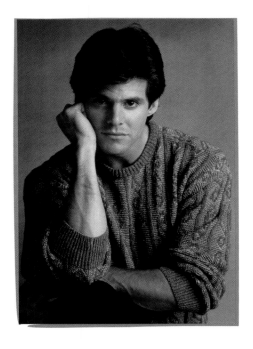

There was no reason to suspect that the handsome Derek Stuart was anything but a personable, ambitious young man with a healthy respect for womanhood!

ity, "cried rape." His lawyer, John Silva, tried to get the case dismissed by discrediting Cricket. As the jury deliberated, Scott and Chase brought in an 11th-hour witness who'd been raped by Derek at school three years earlier. She didn't press charges at the time because the school encouraged her not to. Derek was found guilty, but he insisted he'd prove his innocence. He wasn't about to let Cricket ruin his life. John Silva soon realized he'd defended a guilty man. He called the prosecutor, but Derek had already gotten away.

Derek deliberately secured a job at the Genoa City Hotel where Cricket, Jessica, and Jim were living. He waited until Cricket was alone. He entered their suite, and ordered Cricket to reverse her accusations. Jim and Scott arrived home to find Derek with a gun to Cricket's head. Derek shot Scott and jumped out the window to his death.

Unnerved by the shooting, Scott decided that life was too short. He wanted to plan a future with Lauren. They moved in together at her lavish suite. Soon after, they wed, each looking forward to building a new life together.

Jessica was grateful to John for allowing her

to live her dream for what little time she had left. She wrote him a letter asking him to let her die in a dignified manner, knowing he would ensure her last wish would be honored. Jessica died peacefully.

Jim was comforted in his loss by the thought that he'd gotten to know Jessica, if ever so briefly. And he had a beautiful daughter in Cricket. Jim would move on and reestablish a relationship with Nikki, a relationship neither Jack (who had by now taken an interest in her) nor Victor wanted Nikki to pursue.

Rex couldn't stand the idea of Gina getting involved with a no-good like Clint Raddison. He told Clint he would pay any amount of money to get him out of town and away from his daughter, but it was too late. Gina married Clint before Rex had a chance to tell her who Clint really was. When Gina found out that Clint and Rex had met in prison, she was quick to remind Rex that Katherine had given him a second chance. Didn't Clint deserve a second chance, too?

Marge was in her element at the diner on the edge of town, until fast-talking Clint Raddison propositioned her and took her away.

In the meantime, Nina carefully wooed Esther away from Katherine, incurring Katherine's wrath. Esther loved little Phillip so, and her new job would allow her to take care of him. Nina had also promised to help Esther meet new people—men in particular. Furthermore, Esther would no longer have to wear that silly little uniform that Katherine always insisted she wear!

Clint sent con artists Robert and Shirley Haskell to interview as Esther's replacements, and Katherine hired them just before Esther, realizing she had made a mistake, came back hoping to get her old job back. Nina had gone back on her promises—Esther wasn't meeting any men; she never got any time off; and she had to wear her uniform all over again! Esther's only satisfaction came from the fact that Katherine had to hire two people to replace her.

Clint hung out at an out-of-the-way diner where he met Marge Cotrooke, a feisty redheaded waitress. Though she said she had no relatives in Genoa City, she could've passed for Katherine Chancellor's twin! Clint hatched a diabolical scheme to steal the Chancellor fortune without anyone suspecting a thing. Marge would simply become Katherine! Her hair was dyed blonde, her gold tooth was replaced, and she learned the walk and talk of Mrs. Chancellor. Marge wondered if she was in over her head. The sacrifices were great—after all, she had to give up her smokes and her beer. But then, "Sexy Rexy" was motivation enough to stick with the plan!

Robert's first attempt to chloroform Katherine and make the switch was interrupted when Katherine had an attack of appendicitis. Marge then had to have her appendix out, too! The second attempt was more successful, but Esther, in the wrong place at the wrong time, was kidnapped along with Katherine. Gina, Rex, and Jill became concerned about Katherine, who seemed to be reverting to her old ways: they spied her with a younger man (Clint) and witnessed her drinking. "Katherine" was hurt that Rex could question her about such behavior. She didn't know what he was talking about! The real Katherine and Esther, meanwhile, were taken to a deserted cabin and became the charges of Morey and Lil, who also worked for Clint.

Skip and Carole were happy when the doctors said her disability wouldn't pose a problem if she wanted to have a baby. Unfortunately, the couple had trouble conceiving, and they soon learned that Skip couldn't father a child. Carole assured her husband that she loved him, and she suggested adoption. Adoption agencies, however, deemed them unsuitable parents because of her disability, so Carole and Skip placed an ad in the newspaper, seeking an expectant mother looking for a good home for her baby. Nan, a young, pregnant college student, responded. She eventually moved in with Carole and Skip, who anxiously awaited the baby's birth.

Michael Crawford was reluctant to pick up again with Jill because she'd dumped him once before and he didn't want to get burned again. As a way to revive Michael's interest in her, Jill arranged for him to handle legal matters for Jabot. Jack went along with it on the condition that Jill resign her position upon her marriage to Crawford. That union never came to pass. In the meantime, David Kimble, Jill's hunky assistant at Jabot, didn't take kindly to being left out in the cold after having romanced the boss lady for the last couple of months. He aligned with Jack and spied on Jill for him.

Leanna, having been thrown out by Victor, took a temporary job filling in for Michael's secretary. They began dating as Jill's relationship with Michael was falling apart. Leanna then landed her next job—writing a newspaper advice column for the lovelorn. Readers reacted favorably to her new column, but this was only the beginning for the beguiling "Leanna Love."

David wasn't about to sit around after Jill gave him the cold shoulder. He started dating Nina, and didn't waste any time proposing. Cricket and Danny warned Nina that her new beau might just want to get his hands on Phillip's inheritance. Even Nina wasn't quite sure she could trust her fiancé.

David serenaded Jill, until Nina Chancellor, one of the heirs to the Chancellor fortune, came into the picture.

There was something about him. . . . At first Jill was furious when she discovered that Nina and David were an item, but she cooled down when she realized that if David got closer to Nina, she might have easier access to her grandson. Nina had always preferred that Jill keep her distance and had limited her visitation time with Phillip.

In an attempt to reopen the Rawlins murder case, Carl Williams showed Captain Reardon a photo of Cassandra wearing the very same earrings she'd alleged were stolen the night of George's murder. But the officials insisted the case was closed. Paul knew the only way he'd ever be free was if Cassandra confessed, so he decided to scare Cassandra into telling the truth. He dreamed up all kinds of schemes to break her down: he spoke to her from the grave, then appeared and disappeared in the hallways. This left Cassandra on the verge of collapsing.

Victor, meanwhile, romanced Nikki and spent the night with her. He wanted her to forget about Jim Grainger once and for all.

As the year began, the battle of the titans was still raging, though it had become clear that Victor Newman had attained the upper hand in the business John Abbott had spent his entire life building. The two clashed over everything, but Victor backed off when John was felled by a heart attack suffered during a particularly bitter board meeting. Victor had the deepest respect for John Abbott and found little joy in John's collapse. Fortunately, John's setback would only be temporary; he would be back to do battle with Victor Newman another day.

Meanwhile, Nikki was about to wed Jim Grainger, but neither Victor nor Jack approved of the union. Victor, naturally, thought Nikki was made for him alone. But after upsetting her at Lauren and Scott's wedding by kissing her as they danced to their song, "Through the Eyes of Love," Victor agreed to let her go only if she truly loved Jim. Jack, partly because he'd do anything to best Victor and partly because he loved the chase, lavished Nikki with gifts and attention, promising her a life beyond her wildest dreams.

So as Victor was having the ranch decorated for his wedding to Nikki, anticipating she'd accept his proposal, Jack Abbott, knowing his father was on the road to recovery after his heart attack, lost no time marrying Nikki. Victor was furious at Jack for beating him to the punch. But Victor offered him a deal: Nikki for Jabot!

Nikki and Jack beamed their happiness while Victor fretted over the girl that got away.

Because of his role in the *Ruthless* debacle, Jack felt responsible for John's loss, and saw this as an opportunity to redeem himself in his father's eyes. He instructed Victor to draw up the papers of agreement. When Nikki learned she was the pawn in this outrageous show of one-upmanship, she threw her husband out. Unfortunately, Jack lost twice: for not only did he lose Nikki, he lost Jabot for not signing the agreement before the deadline! A short time later, however, Jack rescued Victoria from drowning in the family pool; he earned Victor's heartfelt gratitude, and Nikki welcomed Jack back into her life.

Meanwhile, Paul managed to spook out Cassandra by having her find him "dead" in her bed in Bermuda. Then Carl moved in for the kill and placed her under house arrest for George's murder! Cassandra tried to explain things away to a living, breathing Paul, who had, by now, learned that Adrian was a hired killer.

Cassandra was indicted. Desperate to prove Adrian was George's murderer, she accepted Adrian's marriage proposal, certain he'd soon attempt to do away with her. No sooner were they wed than Adrian worked out his diabolical scheme. He purchased an untraceable gun and had it rigged to fire automatically. Then, he hired a Cassandra look-alike, Diedre, as a decoy. After cutting the phone lines, Adrian administered drugs to Cassandra that paralyzed her but left her remaining mentally alert. Next, he propped his terrified wife up in a chair, with the loaded gun mounted on a block of dry ice and aimed straight at her temple! When the ice would sublime, Cassandra would be dead—an apparent suicide.

Adrian and Diedre, disguised as Cassandra, then led Carl and fellow officer Salena Wiley on a wild-goose chase, until finally Adrian dropped Diedre off at the hairdresser's, where the detectives figured out they had been suckered.

In the meantime, Victor was trying to reach Cassandra by phone. He finally figured out that something must have gone terribly wrong and he raced over to the Rawlins's home. He got there not a moment too soon, as he yanked Cassandra away from the line of fire a split second before the gun discharged.

When Adrian returned home, he found Cassandra's blood-soaked body lying on the floor! But, was he losing his mind? Did he see her move? Panicking, he emptied the gun into her body, only to realize the bullets he fired were blanks, and the blood was stage blood! Victor, Carl, and Salena came out of the shadows, where they had been hiding. They had baited Adrian, and he'd fallen into their trap! Adrian was arrested.

Meanwhile, young Victoria Newman was stressed out over the realization her parents wouldn't be reconciling anytime soon, if ever. The thought of Jack Abbott as her stepdad left her cold; there was no one who could replace her father! She pouted, sulked, and carried on over what was and was not happening. Victor couldn't stand to see his precious little princess so unhappy, so he thought enrolling Victoria in a boarding school in Switzerland at this time made perfectly good sense. He'd take her there and make their time together a little vacation the two of them would enjoy.

On another front, despite all of the grief Cassandra had caused him, Paul couldn't get her out of his system. But Cassandra discovered that she and Victor had so much in common after they'd exchanged confidences about their trauma-filled childhoods, and she focused her efforts on going after him. Thus, when

Victor disclosed that he was leaving for the continent with Victoria, Cassandra suggested she'd go along, too. She was crushed when he informed her he wasn't ready to enter into a new relationship.

Victor appointed Brad to fill in for him as temporary CEO for Ra-Tech, and also gave him a vice presidency at Newman Enterprises. Stinging from Victor's rejection, Cassandra would later offer Brad a permanent position at Ra-Tech.

While Victor and Victoria were away, Nikki faced up to the fact she could never love Jack the way she loved Victor. She was aching to tell Victor how she felt and planned to deal with it upon his return. But when Nikki discovered she was pregnant with Jack's baby, she knew she had to put any thought of reconciling with Victor out of her mind. For she knew how desperately Jack yearned to have a child of his very own. Nikki couldn't pull out of her marriage now; she felt she owed it to Jack to stay with him.

Meanwhile, there were other romantic liaisons on the home front that were becoming more complicated. While Cassandra was already looking for new conquests and had decided to turn her sights on Brad Carlton, Traci Abbott made up her mind to win back her ex-husband, who'd moved on to Traci's sister, Ashley. He proposed and was waiting for her answer, which Ashley promised him would be forthcoming within a matter of days. The Abbott family, noting Brad and Ashley's closeness, worried as to how Traci would react. Traci didn't take it well at all; she felt her sister had betrayed her. She became all the more determined to fight Ashley tooth and nail for her man!

Ashley was confused. She loved Brad and she loved her sister. Throw into the mix the complicated

Victor Newman! Ashley decided to go to the cabin to mull things over. At the same time, Victor, who had returned from Europe, received the news that Brad and Ashley were going to marry, and he was devastated. He, too, decided to go to the cabin to clear his head. Both Ashley and Victor, overjoyed over their reunion, were convinced that fate had brought them together. Without wasting any time, Victor summoned a justice of the peace to marry them on the spot. John Abbott wasn't at all happy over the sudden nuptials, but Victor assured him he loved Ashley and that he'd never hurt her again. As for Brad, he was furious when Ashley broke the news to him.

Unaware of the developments between Victor and Ashley, Nikki was still uncertain about her relationship to Jack when weighed against her overwhelming desire to make things work with Victor. She, too, had to clear her head. She went horseback riding and took a terrible spill. She was rushed to the hospital, where she came to just long enough to ask about her baby, as Jack stood by her side, stunned. He didn't know until that moment that she had been expecting! She lost the baby and she and Jack mourned over what might have been.

Nikki suffered excruciating back pain from her accident. Jack blamed Victor for the loss of his son and for Nikki's debilitating condition. Though surgery was an option, Nikki feared paralysis and opted for painkillers, upon which she'd soon become dependent. Far from well, she went home, and then suffered a tremendous setback when she learned of Victor and Ashley's marriage.

At the Chancellor mansion, Marge Cotrooke had taken Katherine's place and immediately scored with Rex in the bedroom. It didn't take long for Mitchell Sherman, Rex, Brock, and Jill to notice several subtle behavioral changes in "Katherine"—at first, they feared she might be drinking again. "Katherine" had memory lapses, sold Chancellor Industries to the first bidder, put the estate on the market, and spent a lot of time with Clint. Marge didn't enjoy the scrutiny she was attracting, so she moved out of Rex's bed. When Rex caught her partying with Robert and Shirley Haskell, he said she'd obviously chosen beer and cigarettes over love. He left.

Rex went to Jill for comfort and he filed for divorce. Jill now found herself in the complicated position of being involved with both Rex and John. She was perturbed that Rex had signed a prenuptial agreement for Katherine, but accepted his proposal anyway.

Back at the cabin, Esther learned she was pregnant, from the night she'd spent with Tiny, the plumber, while in Nina's employ. Lil took her to the hospital when she had stomach pains. Luckily, Esther ran into Brock and managed to whisper in his ear that Katherine was in trouble. By this time,

Jill drew men to her like a magnet.

Katherine and Esther were wise to the fact that someone was impersonating Katherine.

Brock got Marge to confess, and convinced her to go along with a plan he devised. True to her promise, Marge went to the cabin, got into a "brawl" with Katherine, and switched clothes with her so Katherine could escape. Katherine was shocked to learn that Clint was behind the plot, but her first order of business was to find Rex and reunite with him. She tracked him to Colorado, where she found herself interrupting his and Jill's wedding night. Mitchell Sherman informed Katherine that Marge's acts were not legal, so both her marriage and business

Clint, Morey, and Lil were the conspiratorial trio who made Katherine and Esther's lives miserable. They planned for the day the Chancellor fortune would be theirs.

were intact. Katherine would bide her time before telling Rex and Jill that their marriage was invalid.

Brad suggested to Jabot's board of directors that they capitalize on the popularity of Leanna's newspaper column and bring her to television with an advice column of the airwaves that would feature Jabot products. The show was an instant success. However, when Leanna did her I HATE MEN! show and marched through the streets of Genoa City, Jabot was upset over what they were certain would be negative publicity. Thus they planned to replace Leanna. But the show was so popular with viewers that Leanna stayed on, while Jabot's sales skyrocketed.

Meanwhile, Rex and Jill hatched a plot to end Leanna's reign as queen of daytime TV talk shows. They'd try to prove her I HATE MEN! campaign was a scam. Rex posed as Roger Bingham, guested on Leanna's show, and had his picture taken kissing her. It was plastered all over the tabloids, but the audience wasn't fazed, and the plot backfired. Rex continued to see Leanna, still posing as Roger. At the same time, he turned his attention to comforting Gina, hoping she'd get over Clint, but the more time Rex spent with his daughter and Leanna, the more time Jill spent with John, hoping he would soon propose.

Rex promised Katherine he'd tell Leanna the truth. Katherine then came up with her own plan to get her sweet revenge on Jill. As far as Rex and Jill were concerned, they were still technically betrothed, so Katherine decided to host a surprise "engagement party" for them. When Leanna, Rex, John, and Jill were together and John publicly proposed to Jill, Jill tried out of the door with the expla- ad a little too much to drink. If

John ever found out she'd been living with Rex for the past many months, he'd hit the roof. Just as she feared, John and Rex saw that Jill had deceived both of them. John stormed out and refused to reconcile with her, but the resourceful Jill still saw a glimmer of hope. Katherine gleefully watched it all happen, and now would try her best to win Rex back.

With Danny's return from his recent concert tour, he and Cricket grew closer than ever. They were the best of friends; neither could imagine life without the other. The young lovers started to make plans to spend the rest of their lives together.

When Nina accepted David's proposal, David told her roommate Cricket to mind her own business and move out . . . or else. Cricket didn't take David's threat lightly, and she went to Jill with her concerns for Phillip's safety. Jill told David to break up with Nina, but he dismissed her admonitions. In an effort to try to convince everyone of his true love for Nina, David signed a prenuptial agreement, but after they married, Nina wrote up a new will naming David as a major heir to the Chancellor fortune. Since Jill had fired David, Nina also set up her new hubby in a (bogus) business.

David lost no time getting involved with Diane, an attractive mailroom attendant who thought David was the spitting image of Tom Harper, a man she'd read about in the newspaper who had been accused of murdering his wife.

By an uncanny coincidence, a brooch David had given Nina appeared to be the very same one Tom's wife, Rebecca, was wearing in the newspaper photo. David dismissed Diane's suspicions out of hand, but he had indeed been the one who ripped the brooch from Rebecca's dress before burying her. Rebecca's friend, Vivian, hoped to prove David killed Rebecca, but she was killed before she had a chance. Now David had to get that brooch away from Nina. He snatched it, told her it must've been stolen, and then tossed it in the lake. In the meantime, he was playing the part of the loving husband and devoted father. But he couldn't stand Cricket and Danny constantly breathing down his neck, so he planted drugs in Danny's dressing room and sicced the cops on him. Danny's arrest forced him to cancel the next leg of his concert tour and put his plans to marry Cricket on hold.

The charges against Danny were dropped on a technicality (the police had searched his dressing room without a warrant), but Danny wanted to fight to clear his name. He risked a prison term to do it. The judge reopened the case when Cricket remembered flowers being delivered the night of Danny's concert. Someone would've had time to plant the evidence. The authorities later found a guard's uniform in an air-conditioning vent and concluded Danny had been framed. Danny's name was officially cleared.

Danny and Cricket's dream would finally come true. They flew immediately to Hawaii and were married in an idyllic paradise setting, with Rex as Danny's best man and Cricket's longtime friend, Nina, as matron of honor. Cricket's half brother, Scott

Being married to the girl of his dreams was Danny's idea of paradise.

Grainger, gave her away. The newlyweds honeymooned on a secluded beach.

Meanwhile, David's lover, Diane, showed up in Hawaii, compelling David to juggle his time between her and Nina. David then told Diane to pursue Chase, as he attempted to do damage repair to his relationship with Nina. He had a fit when the police recovered Nina's brooch after the lake was drained because of pollution. Nina, still unsuspecting, was convinced David was good for her and threatened to leave Genoa City with him and her son if Jill and Katherine didn't stop their bickering over David's desire to adopt little Phillip.

Skip and Carole were thrilled to finally be parents, but they couldn't help but be concerned that Nan might develop a bond with the baby. They asked her to move out. Nan bumped into her old boyfriend, Jeff, and for the first time, she told him the real reason she dropped out of school was because she was pregnant. Nan consulted Cricket as to her legal rights to the baby. She ordered a blood test that proved Jeff was the father.

Baby Skylar's christening was a happy event for her proud parents, Skip and Carole.

Jeff admitted he loved Nan, and he supported her decision to get the baby back. But the young couple soon found that being full-time parents was too much for them to handle. They returned baby Skylar to Skip and Carole, certain she would grow up in a loving home.

Lynne was hopeful about her relationship with Paul when he started paying more attention to her. Lauren, torn between Scott and Paul, told Sheila Carter, a nurse who worked long hours in the lab with Scott, to forget any thoughts of pursuing him. When Scott caught his wife with Paul, he went to his quarters at the hospital, where Sheila plied him with a pitcher of martinis and seduced him. Paul urged Lauren to repair her troubled marriage to Scott, and Lauren and Scott agreed it was time they try to work things out. Sheila was out in the cold, but only until Scott learned she was expecting. When Lauren planned a romantic evening with Scott to tell him the joyous news she was expecting again (she'd miscarried several months ago), he beat her to the punch and told her Sheila was pregnant with his child. Lauren threw him out. The beleaguered Scott could only hope his marriage could be saved.

A street urchin named Drucilla Barber showed up in Genoa City and picked Nathan Hastings's pocket. But her luck had run out on her—she found no money. Destitute, she finally broke down and called her Aunt Mamie, who lived with and worked for the Abbotts. She'd run away from her family seven years before and racked up a police record. Mamie was happy Drucilla was safe, and John Abbott agreed to allow her to live with them, provided she tow the line. She didn't fit in well, and the Abbotts weren't entirely sure they could trust her.

Then Drucilla was caught shoplifting at Fenmore's. When Nathan discovered she couldn't read or write, he got the court to release her into his custody. It was now Nathan's turn to pass along the gift of literacy and help Drucilla turn her life around, just as Amy had helped him several years before. Drucilla was unhappy cooped up in Nathan's apartment, but decided to stick it out when she realized what a good catch Nathan was.

Drucilla's older sister, Olivia, was in Genoa City for a medical internship, and Olivia and Nathan were romantically involved. Olivia was thrilled to see her sister safe and sound after all these years. But Drucilla didn't share her enthusiasm. When they were growing up, Olivia was always prettier, smarter, better, and Dru could never live up to those standards in her parents' eyes. Drucilla knew of Olivia and Nathan's plans to get married, but that didn't stop her. She first tried to win Nathan over with her womanly ways, and when that didn't work, she swore she'd win him fair and square. Olivia might be smarter, but Drucilla could dance! Mamie gave her niece money for dance lessons, and John Abbott offered her a part-time job in the mailroom at Jabot. Things were looking up. But when Drucilla and Olivia's parents came

Drucilla coveted her sister's man, Nathan, and tried her hardest to win him away from the more comely, better educated, more successful Olivia.

to Genoa City, happy that their youngest daughter was alive and well, Drucilla made it clear she didn't want them in her life. Sadly, they returned home.

In other matters, Brock told Katherine to have Tiny over for dinner for Esther's sake. But Tiny bolted when he saw Esther was pregnant. Brock tracked him down at a local bar and told him he had responsibilities to own up to. Tiny wasn't interested. Katherine helped deliver the baby during a terrible storm, and was touched when Esther named the baby after her: Kate, for short. Esther took Brock's advice and made the first move to get Tiny back. She clogged the plumbing and when he came over to fix it, she made sure he would see his daughter. Esther was crushed when Tiny made it clear that he had no desire to become a husband or a father.

On the whole, the holiday season failed to bring joy to the Newman family this year. Nikki was

Ashley and Victor Newman were happy to be spending their first Christmas together, although their married state troubled other family members.

battling her back pain with a combination of painkillers and alcohol. Victor wasn't about to forgive Jack for making a business deal behind his back, or for marrying Nikki. Though Victor and Ashley were happy to be spending their first Christmas together as husband and wife, Victoria, upset over their marriage, decided to stay at school, which made little Nicholas sad.

The end of the year brought big changes for Brad. Victor ordered him to adopt a better attitude at work or find a new job. Jack proceeded with Victor's orders to replace Brad, while Cassandra looked for a place for Brad at Ra-Tech, perhaps as the permanent CEO. She convinced him to go skiing with her to Aspen. On the way, she drugged him and flew to Vegas for a quickie wedding. Brad woke up in Cassandra's bed the next morning, with no recollection of the marriage, which she told him he willingly participated in. Brad was concerned he would miss a date he'd made with Traci when he couldn't get a flight out because of the snowstorm. Paul was still stinging over Cassandra, and Lauren filed for divorce despite Scott's wish that they try to work things out. Neither of them knew Sheila was about to turn their lives into a living hell.

With healthy doses of intrigue and deception thrown into the mix, emotions would reach unparalleled highs and lows this year in Genoa City. But most Genoians met their problems head-on and were able to bounce back with resiliency.

Clint broke out of jail and headed straight for Gina's. He begged, cajoled, and groveled, throwing himself on Gina's mercy until she had no choice but to cave in. She agreed to hide him from the cops. Katherine was beside herself. How could any self-respecting, modern woman allow herself to be used in that way? Especially after what he had done to her. But Gina was leading with her heart. She prostrated herself at Katherine's feet: keep this quiet. Help her. She loved him more than life itself. She needed to protect him.

Brock went over to talk some sense into Gina, and when he left, he was gunned down in the alleyway. Clint flew downstairs to check on him and got in the way of another bullet meant for Brock. Katherine was grateful to Clint for saving Brock's life. Gina put the restaurant on the market and planned to leave town with Clint, but Clint knew he'd caused Gina enough pain and turned himself in to the police. He couldn't let Gina ruin her life for a no-good like him.

David's stories were wearing thin with Nina, and when she found out he'd been spying on her for months, she bought a gun, and then checked out his office. No files, no papers, no phone—no business! It was all a sham! While Nina was snooping, David showed up with Diane, and Nina hid in the closet. Nina couldn't believe what she heard: Not only did David plan to kill her and skip town with her money and Diane, but he also talked about how he'd engineered Danny's drug bust!

Nina went home and waited for her husband. When he showed up, she greeted him by pumping five bullets into him. David survived. He feigned paralysis, and Nina was arrested for attempted murder. Foolishly, she jumped bail and left town with little Phillip. Nina showed up on her mother's doorstep. Flo hadn't changed one whit since Nina had last seen her. She was still a prostitute. She still drank.

At her wits' end, feeling trapped and exposed, Nina determined she'd flee to Mexico. But Cricket talked her out of it. As it was, she was already in a heap of trouble, having jumped bail. Why risk more? Nina returned to Genoa City and stood trial. Things didn't appear to be going her way at all, but when all was said and done, Nina was found not guilty.

David, meanwhile, still hospitalized, plotted to get even with Cricket and Nina. He grabbed a body

It didn't take long for "Jim Adams" to charm Nina's mother, Flo, into marrying him.

from the hospital morgue and planted it in his bed. Then he set the room on fire. The police assumed the charred remains were David's, and Nina could only be thankful that her nightmare was finally over. But it was not to be. David and Diane went to a plastic surgeon to have his face reconstructed ("Could you make me look like David Hasselhoff?" he asked), but the savvy surgeon emblazoned the word KILLER on his forehead instead. David then came up with a new plan. He made himself up as Jim Adams, and started to romance Nina's mother, who had come to Genoa City to sponge off Nina's money. Flo fell for "Jim," hook, line, and sinker. David/Jim then dumped Diane and married Flo.

Jill, meantime, decided it was time for a new approach with John. She'd try to win John's trust, rather than just a place in his bed. They celebrated what would've been their 10th anniversary with a romantic evening. Jack warned his father to be careful; he could see that Jill was up to her old tricks

again. But John assured Jack there was nothing to worry about. He'd be on guard. He wasn't about to forgive Jill her past indiscretions and had absolutely no intentions of getting involved with his ex-wife again.

Leanna, meanwhile, wanted to have a baby, and since she wasn't about to "do the nasty," she decided artificial insemination was the way to go. Rex protested: it was all so clinical, so unnatural, so ersatz. But he finally gave in and made a "deposit." Knowing Rex had no interest in raising a child, Leanna scouted for prospects to be the baby's father. Paul, Brad, John, and Brock all seemed like good candidates, she thought. But it was John who stood out from the pack. He'd always been so kind to her, and she credited him with her success. What a good father he'd be!

Jill and Katherine then made a pact: Jill would help Katherine get Rex back if Katherine would return the favor and help her get John. But Rex and John were suspicious when Jill and Katherine, forever rivals, started touting each other's good qualities.

Drucilla was doing her best to win Nathan from Olivia, who remained skeptical of the boyfriend Drucilla talked about and asked Dru to introduce him to her. Now Drucilla had to produce a boyfriend. But how? She literally bumped into Neil Winters, an up-and-coming Newman executive, and begged him to help her out. He agreed to play along. Dru's plan worked better than she'd hoped when Neil fell in love with Olivia, but she was crushed when Olivia, afraid

Drucilla was closing in on Nathan, moved up her wedding day. The sisters finally reconciled when their father was taken ill. Nathan and Olivia married, while Neil and Drucilla commiserated with each other, and realized how much they had in common. They fell in love. Neil encouraged Dru to continue her dance lessons, but she became smitten with another profession: modeling.

Lauren kept her pregnancy a secret from Scott, and although they were estranged, she hated the idea of Scott spending time with Sheila, who was also carrying his child. Sheila knew the baby was the key to her winning Scott, so when her baby was stillborn, she wore a pregnancy pad, and left Genoa City to visit her mother a few days before she was to "deliver." Then she arranged to have a baby broker get her a boy, since she'd learned Lauren was going to have a boy. She switched the brokered baby with Lauren's and changed the birth records. When

Propinquity brought Neil and Dru together, though each of them had their hearts set on someone else.

Lauren questioned the nurse about a birthmark on her newborn that had mysteriously disappeared, the nurse summarily dismissed Lauren's concerns, saying birthmarks frequently disappeared. Lauren left town, determined to keep her son Dylan's paternity a secret from Scott. Later, she was to learn that Scott and Sheila had married. Scott, meanwhile, assuming Paul to be the father of Lauren's baby, eagerly looked forward to starting a new life with Sheila and Scotty, whom he believed was his son.

Victoria returned home with a plan in mind to bring her parents back together. She moved in with Victor and Ashley (which allowed Nikki to hide her drinking from her daughter), and Victoria tried to make it look as if Ashley were having an affair with Brad. Victor didn't buy it, and Ashley decided Victoria needed some diversion in her life—maybe a

The unsuspecting Scott fell for his nurse, Sheila, who cunningly entrapped him.

Nikki hid the pain in her back and the pain in her heart by drinking whatever she could get her hands on.

boyfriend. Victoria started to date Ryan McNeil, a wily, handsome Jabot executive, several years her senior. When Victor objected, she told him she was merely doing what Ashley wanted her to do. Ashley, upset with Victoria's manipulations, moved out. When Nikki caught on to Victoria's plot and explained it to Victor, he apologized to Ashley and she reconciled with him, albeit cautiously.

Jack warned Nikki that it was dangerous to combine her painkillers with alcohol. Nikki emptied the liquor cabinet and managed, at least for a while, to convince Jack she had given up drinking. But Nikki had a hidden stash upstairs, and after Jack found her passed out drunk on more than one occasion, he convinced her to enter a rehabilitation program in New York. Not knowing the true reason for Nikki's trip, Victor suspected her marriage to Jack was on the skids.

Brad and Cassandra returned to Genoa City as husband and wife. Brad was now CEO of Ra-Tech, but he was also holding on to his position at Jabot out of loyalty to John Abbott. However, his marriage to Cassandra was over as soon as he learned she'd set him up. Paul was furious that Brad would treat marriage to Cassandra so cavalierly, and they came to blows over her honor. Cassandra, knowing Paul would always be there to rescue her, rekindled their romance. Lauren and Lynne were upset that Paul was so blind he couldn't see Cassandra's true colors. Brad and Cassandra amicably settled their divorce, and when Cassandra rushed

to see Paul after signing the papers, she was hit by a truck. She was instantly killed.

Paul was shocked to learn he was the sole heir to her fortune. Jack and Jill pounced on Paul to sell them Ra-Tech, but Paul held off. He had more immediate plans: a new wardrobe for Lynne and a new house for his parents. Paul then learned that the judge died before he could sign Brad and Cassandra's divorce papers so, as it turned out, Brad was the one to inherit the estate.

Traci and Brad became close again, but when Traci learned she was expecting, she made John promise to keep her secret. She hoped Brad would marry her because he truly loved her—not because of the baby. Ashley turned to Brad for a shoulder to cry on when things weren't working out with Victor, and she and Traci were again pitted against one another over Brad. Brad was about to tell Traci they had no future together when Traci insisted on telling him her news first. Brad was shocked, but Traci assured him she was prepared to raise their child alone.

The masquerade ball was the charity event of the year in Genoa City, and it turned out to be a pivotal night in the lives of many Genoa City residents. David, dressed in a wolf costume to match Danny's, shot Danny, Cricket, and Nina, but the bullets in his gun had been replaced with blanks—Paul and the police had been onto him. Later, David would meet his demise when he jumped unwittingly into a garbage chute and was compacted.

Meanwhile, Leanna convinced John to be her escort to the ball, much to Jill's dismay. Jack confessed to a phantom how much he loved his wife; the phantom turned out to be Nikki, and she agreed to reenter her rehabilitation program. Victoria dumped the boy Victor had set her up with and secretly went to the ball with Ryan. An under-the-weather Traci feared for her unborn baby's life and left the ball early. Brad followed, and they were both relieved the baby would be all right. Brad then proposed, and they planned a November wedding. Katherine and Rex, hosts of the ball, were enjoying each other's company again.

That is, until Rex's feelings were hurt when Katherine seemed to be spending more and more time with her new beau, Edward. But when Rex discovered Edward was an actor Katherine hired to make him jealous, he decided to have some fun of his own at Katherine's expense. Katherine found herself standing vigil at Rex's hospital bed after he supposedly had suffered chest pains. Jill discovered Rex's ruse. Katherine didn't appreciate Rex's little joke, but she soon got over her anger and she and Rex reaffirmed their love for one another.

John was amused that Jill was jealous of Leanna, and he told Jack he planned to be married again soon. But he wasn't sure to whom. Jill had to vie with Leanna for John's attention, but Leanna was not intimidated. After all, Jill was the same woman John had divorced years ago. When Leanna found out she wasn't pregnant, she convinced herself she and John would make a baby the old-fashioned way. Things got even more complicated when Dina showed up and played mother of the bride at Traci's wedding. John was so moved by Dina's tale of her brush with death after being ill for nearly two years that they became closer and he asked her to marry him. Jack was pleased, and tried to get Traci and Ashley to share his joy, but they couldn't forgive Dina for deserting them. John sent Dina packing and apologized to Jill when Jill uncovered the truth: Dina had concocted the whole story! Jill and Leanna each renewed their hopes of getting John.

Nikki returned home to confront the fact that her rehabilitation had failed. Terrified about the prospect of surgery, she was self-destructing. Victor

Fairy tales didn't come true with a big bad wolf preying among a pair of innocent young ladies.

Although Molly greatly disapproved of Sheila's manipulative and unethical behavior, her love for her daughter challenged her sense of duty.

finally realized Nikki had a drinking problem and was convinced that Nikki's unhappy marriage was the cause. As Victor dumped Nikki's stash, bottle by bottle, down the drain, Nikki sobbed that Victor was to blame for her drinking, not Jack. She explained she went riding that fateful day because she was so confused over her feelings for Victor. The fall from her horse caused her back pain, and it was only through the combination of painkillers and alcohol that she could get any relief at all. Jack finally managed to convince Nikki that she had no choice but to enter a detox program if she ever wanted to get her life back on track.

At the Newmans' holiday party, Ryan took Victoria aside and gave her an engagement ring. The teen was thrilled, but she and Ryan had to keep their

Victoria and Ryan agreed to keep their engagement a secret from Victoria's battling parents.

plans a secret, so she agreed to wear her ring only when they were alone. When Victoria confided in Ashley that she'd made love with Ryan, Ashley took her for pregnancy and AIDS testing. The doctor lectured her on the dangers of casual, unprotected sex. Victoria was petrified when she was told it would be a year before she could be confident she wasn't infected with HIV. She was furious with Ryan, who begged for a chance to make it up to her.

Sheila was worried when her mother, Molly, came to Genoa City, because Molly knew about the baby switching. When Lauren returned to Genoa City and she and Paul began dating again, Sheila also became concerned that Scott might not be the father of the baby she stole. It terrified her to think that Paul might be the father.

Molly collapsed with a stroke when she was on her way to tell Lauren the truth about the babies. Sheila insisted Molly come to live with her and Scott.

Then, after Molly was learning to speak again, Sheila halted Molly's speech therapy. It was obviously to her benefit if Molly didn't regain her speech. Sheila later had Molly institutionalized, where she began working with a therapist without Sheila's knowledge.

Lauren's little boy, Dylan, died suddenly and Lauren was devastated. Scott consoled Lauren as his marriage to Sheila was crumbling. Sheila, meanwhile, was beside herself when Molly was able to say "baby." What if the truth ever came out? She decided it would be best to get Molly out of the picture, so she shipped her back to the farmhouse in Michigan, where Molly's friend Naomi, a retired speech therapist, continued working with Molly to help her regain her speech. Grieving over the loss of her son, Lauren seduced Paul in the hopes of conceiving again, and unhappily learned her plan didn't work.

On the business front, Brad convinced Victor to merge Ra-Tech and Newman Enterprises. That left no need to fill his job, and Jack, who was eyeing the position, felt like he'd been had. Brad eventually resigned from Newman Enterprises when the demands of Ra-Tech became too great. Victor then gave Jack a chance, hiring him to replace Brad. Jack's first order of business was to draw up a codicil to Victor's will stating that upon his death, Jabot would revert to the Abbotts. Victor signed it. Ashley and Brad found themselves talking business quite frequently, and Traci's never-ending jealousy over her beautiful sister's relationship with Brad became an issue in Traci and Brad's second marriage. Brad and Ashley both tried to tell Traci they were just friends, but Traci was still too insecure to believe it.

Cricket was now working at Legal Aid. One of her clients was a young runaway teen named Julie Sanderson, who claimed she was fired from her job because she was pregnant. Cricket investigated and learned the real reason was because of Julie's drug habit. She wanted to help, but Danny and John Silva warned her it might be dangerous. When Danny and Cricket took Julie to the hospital where she could see firsthand the tragedy of crack babies, Julie decided she'd enter rehabilitation in an effort to save herself and her baby. Cricket nursed Julie through her withdrawal. Then, Julie considered an abortion when her boyfriend, Andrew, said he wasn't interested in a baby, and bolted. But with Cricket's encouragement, Julie decided to go back to school, return to her job, and try to put her past behind her. Sadly, she lost her baby. In the end, Julie decided to go home to be with her parents.

As the year wound down, a reputed lawyer named Michael Baldwin urged Cricket to join his firm. She wasn't certain she wanted to give up her position at Legal Aid, but she ultimately accepted the offer—a move she'd soon come to regret. Cricket and Danny were happy that Nina was finally able to put David behind her. She began dating John Silva and they spent the holidays together. Jill, hoping to work her way back into John Abbott's life permanently, spent the holidays with him and wrangled an invitation to stay on at the Abbott house, long-term, much to Jack and Ashley's objections. Major changes were on the way for Jill.

Storyline
1992

The new year began happily enough for Cricket, whose career was starting to take off. She quickly impressed her new boss, Michael Baldwin, with her work, and Michael went out of his way to show Cricket the ropes. Katherine and Rex were also glad to ring in 1992 and set about making plans to remarry.

Michael Baldwin was a young attorney on the move and he wanted to have Cricket move along with him.

Nikki's life, however, was steeped in misery. Victor, knowing his ex-wife couldn't continue long in her present condition, insisted she have back surgery, after which he hoped she'd consider undergoing rehabilitation for her alcohol and drug dependency. He threatened that if she refused, he'd take custody of the children. Distraught over the possibility of losing her precious Nicholas and Victoria, Nikki swallowed more pills and took another drink. Then, she went for a walk. A horrified Nicholas discovered his mother face down in the snow. Jack rushed Nikki over to the

Jack and Victor listened carefully to the doctor's findings with regard to Nikki's need for back surgery.

hospital, where he and Victor created a ruckus, each blaming the other for causing Nikki's problems.

While Victor was spending all of his time at Nikki's bedside, his wife, Ashley, was finding comfort in Brad's company, much to Traci's chagrin. Ashley questioned Victor about his involvement with Nikki and Victor curtly replied he'd always be involved with Nikki because she was the mother of his children. Besides, in Victor's eyes, Jack wasn't capable of handling the situation.

But Victor and Jack finally put their differences aside and teamed up to convince Nikki to have the risky surgery. Fortunately, the operation was a success. When Nikki was recovering, she and Victor tried to explain to a shocked and disappointed Victoria that they wouldn't be reconciling. Their daughter had seen Victor's vigil at Nikki's bedside as a sign that they would remarry. When Jack expressed his concern to Ashley over Victor's overbearing interest in Nikki, Ashley assured him her own marriage to Victor was on solid ground. But unbeknownst to Ashley, Nikki and Victor were growing closer; they constantly reminisced while she recovered, and when they shared a kiss, a lot of old emotions came rushing back.

The birth of their baby, Colleen, should have brought Brad and Traci closer together, but it didn't work out that way. A large part of the problem was that Traci still saw Ashley as an ever-present threat to her fragile marriage, even though Ashley was married to Victor. When Traci's publisher, Steve

Steve Connelly and Traci worked late into the night, exchanging ideas as to the direction the heroine in her novel would take.

Connelly, came to Genoa City to work through some of the problems she was having with her novel, they instantly bonded. It was as if they had known each other a hundred lifetimes; each seemed to be able to read the other's mind (and heart and soul!), without having to utter a single word. Brad saw it and felt bitter pangs of jealousy. He couldn't understand how Traci could prefer another man. It was only after Brad read Traci's manuscript that he truly understood where her heart was. It pained him, too, to realize how much Steve not only loved Traci but Colleen. And Brad felt he could not deny Traci her happiness. Before either one of them would change their minds, Traci packed her belongings and moved to New York with Colleen to be with Steve. Brad turned first to Lauren, then to Ashley for comfort, as Traci served him with divorce papers.

Scott was growing weary of his marriage to Sheila, and did his best, along with Paul, to try to raise Lauren's spirits. Paul persuaded Lauren to seek professional counseling to deal with her grief over losing Dylan, and before long she turned to Scott for solace. Although Scott continued to spend more time with his son at Sheila's, he soon fell in love again with Lauren. Meanwhile, Sheila was up to her old devices,

and threatened to have Molly committed when she showed progress in regaining her speech. Then, when Molly noticed Scott Jr.'s birthmark, Sheila quickly hired a plastic surgeon to remove it. When Scott brought up the topic of divorce, Sheila threatened to leave town with Scotty, putting Scott in the untenable position of choosing between Lauren and his son.

Katherine and Jill made a pact to bury the past, and Katherine agreed to have Jill as her matron of honor. This was the first step in Jill's plan to get John to the altar again. She hid a marriage license in a pile of papers John had to sign, took care of the blood test and rings, and bribed the minister at Katherine and Rex's wedding to make it a double ceremony. However, despite Jill's admission of deep love for John, he refused to be roped into her scheme, so Katherine and Rex became the only newlyweds that day.

In the hopes of ensuring a long and happy life together, Katherine insisted she and Rex get checkups. She didn't expect, however, to have her doctor discover a lump in her breast. Although she kept the news from Rex, Katherine turned to Jill for support. Jill felt she owed it to Rex to reveal Katherine's secret. Katherine was furious at Jill, but at the same time she was relieved and grateful. Fortunately, Katherine's operation was successful. If Katherine's cancer scare

accomplished anything, it made the two women realize that they loved to hate each other so much that neither of them could imagine life without the other!

Although the double wedding idea didn't work, Jill wasn't about to give up in her pursuit of John. Her brief dalliance with a talented photographer named Blade served its purpose: to make John jealous. She moved out of the Abbott house again in the hopes that John would long for her. But when Jill soon found herself working very closely with Victor, business turned to pleasure and they made love. Although Jack had his heart set on Jill being out of John's life forever now that Jill apparently had a new beau, it was not to be. Victor, still married to Ashley and somewhat preoccupied with Nikki, let Jill down easy, and she turned her attentions back to John.

Despite Lauren's protests over Paul's discovery that Dylan was not Scott's biological son, Paul investigated the possibility of a baby-switch. Adding fuel to the fire was the fact that another OB/GYN Scott hired to work in the lab with him recognized Sheila as the same woman he had treated for a miscarriage a year ago. Scott insisted the doctor was mistaken, and Sheila insisted the doctor take a hike.

Then, confident that Sheila was acting more rational and would be able to handle it, Scott told her he planned to file for divorce. Sheila didn't take the news well, and forced Lauren to drive to Michigan, where she held Lauren and Molly hostage in her mother's farmhouse. When a fire erupted, Lynne and

After her supposed demise, Sheila returned to Genoa City to stir things up again.

Paul managed to rescue Lauren and Molly, but authorities discovered a body. It was assumed that Sheila had perished, but, in fact, she was on her way to Los Angeles, where she found work as nursemaid to Eric Forrester's son.

Lauren and Scott each feared the other would gain custody of little Scotty, so they decided to marry and raise their son together. Neither one of them was happy in the marriage, and Lauren was soon seeking comfort in Brad's arms. Little did Scott or Lauren know that they would soon share Molly's shock upon Sheila's return to Genoa City.

Although he was at first pleased that his wife and her new boss were getting along so well, Danny soon became suspicious of Michael Baldwin's behavior, and was concerned that Cricket seemed to be spending more and more time at the office. Cricket was in awe of Michael's brilliance in the courtroom, and became angry when Danny questioned whether her job was becoming more important to her than their marriage. Cricket told Danny he was off base when he suggested Michael might have more on his mind than fighting legal battles. But when Michael kissed her following a favorable verdict, Cricket, too, began to wonder about Michael's motives.

Michael told Cricket she could ensure a stellar career provided she "cooperated" with him. He insisted her professional life would only be enhanced by establishing a personal relationship with him. Cricket lost no time seeking John Silva's confirmation that Michael's comments smacked of sexual harassment. She soon discovered that the permanent job offer at the firm was rescinded, and brought charges against Michael. Michael, of course, denied Cricket's allegations, and the firm's senior partner, Calvin Wesley, suggested to Cricket that she consider dropping the charges. After all, the negative publicity such a case would bring could damage not only her budding career, but also that of her rock-star husband.

Danny agreed to support Cricket in her decision to fight the case. The suit against Michael was bolstered when Cricket found out that Michael had sexually harassed other women, including her next-door neighbor Hilary. These women, however, had never filed charges against him. Michael vehemently denied Cricket's claims, and quickly reestablished a relationship with Hilary, who was stunned to get a marriage proposal from him.

Cricket stayed on at the firm working for another attorney, hoping to get the evidence she needed to pursue her case. As part of her plan, Cricket and Danny staged a public breakup. Michael seized the opportunity and invited Cricket to work with him on a big case. Michael took Cricket to Los Angeles on "business" and didn't waste any time getting friendly with his protégée. But Cricket got it all on tape.

Drucilla was a talented ballerina but her heart was in modeling.

Michael was fired, and Hilary finally realized what a louse Michael was. Although Michael landed on his feet again with a job at a prestigious, family-oriented law firm, his luck soon ran out as the disciplinary committee agreed to hear Cricket's case against him.

Starry-eyed Drucilla saw fame and fortune within her grasp and signed up with photographer Vinnie Russo, who promised her not only a modeling gig, but a career in films as well. Fortunately, Nathan and Paul exposed Vinnie's porno business before Dru got in over her head.

It wasn't long before Dru met fashion photographer Blade, and turned down the opportunity of a lifetime dancing the lead in *Giselle* to become a legitimate model. She and Blade both accepted job offers at Jabot. Blade was attracted to Ashley as much as he was the job, while Jill wasn't convinced that Dru was right for Jabot. Never one to pass up an opportunity, Drucilla also signed a centerfold deal with *Sensuality* magazine. When Jill, on hand to oversee Blade's shoot for the magazine, discovered Drucilla was the subject, she hit the roof and destroyed the film. Neil, oblivious to Drucilla's transgression, gave Dru an engagement ring. Her elation was short-lived, however, when her centerfold hit the newsstands. The magazine had published her test shots! Devastated, Drucilla returned Neil's ring and left town.

Meanwhile, Olivia's happiness over her pregnancy was tempered by word that she was suffering from a severe medical condition. Vowing to see the pregnancy through because her doctors said it might be her only chance to conceive, she kept this to herself, hoping to save her family from worry. Eventually Mamie found out, as did Nathan, who promised to be strong for her through the critical time ahead.

Neil and Nathan found Drucilla and brought her home before she got into too much trouble again with the wrong crowd. The stress Drucilla was causing Olivia became too much for her, and Olivia was taken to the hospital. Rushing to Olivia's side, their mother, Lillie Belle, made it painfully clear that her eldest was still the favored daughter. The doctors induced labor in an effort to save Olivia and Nathan's baby. After the crisis passed, Olivia and Nathan brought their baby boy home; they named him Nate. Drucilla, hoping to turn her life in a more positive direction, resumed her ballet lessons.

Nina began to appreciate her relationship with John Silva. John helped her to broaden her horizons and take a greater interest in the world around her. Through him, she gained more self-confidence. Unfortunately for John, though, Nina soon turned her attention and affection toward someone else.

Victoria had no interest in responding to Ryan's advances, but Nina was ready, willing, and able. They spent the night together on their first date. Flo chastised her daughter for not considering her budding relationship with John Silva, but no matter how respectable and stable John Silva might be, Nina and Ryan just couldn't seem to keep themselves out of the bedroom. In a show of defiance, Victoria resolved to see Ryan against her parents' wishes. Ryan soon found himself juggling relationships with both women at the same time.

With promises that Ryan would be the next head of Newman Enterprises, Victoria told him they should make plans to marry as soon as she turned 18. Ryan now saw more clearly than ever the advantages of committing to the young Ms. Newman, and had every intention of ending his relationship with Nina—until he

Nina had her heart set on winning Ryan McNeil from Victoria; Ryan responded to both women.

saw the sleek red convertible Nina bought him as a graduation present. After all, Nina was part Chancellor, and that, Ryan knew, had its advantages, as well. While Ryan and Nina were out celebrating his graduation, Victoria decided to wait for Ryan at his apartment. She was forced to hide in the closet when Ryan and Nina came home, and managed to sneak out only after Ryan and Nina fell asleep after their lovemaking.

Ashley wondered whether her future would indeed be with Victor when she heard Nikki profess her love for him. But Victor surprised Ashley. He buoyed her spirits and her hopes by planning the honeymoon they'd never had. Meanwhile, Jack, feeling more confident in his marriage to Nikki, demanded that Victor stay away from the ranch. Nikki found herself torn between the commitment she felt to her devoted husband, Jack, and the passion she would always feel for Victor. But she resolved to stay with Jack and make their marriage work. Nikki, almost fully recovered from her back surgery by now, unfortunately hadn't kicked her addiction to alcohol. Katherine paid her a visit at just the right time. She stopped Nikki from taking a drink, adding that she'd better be true to her own feelings or Nikki would never find the road to recovery.

With the merger between Newman Enterprises and Ra-Tech finalized, Brad and Jack asserted they would be making the decisions now, inasmuch as Victor was so preoccupied with his personal life. The two joined forces against Victor to take over Newman Enterprises. When Victor discovered their collusion, his fury only strengthened their resolve to gain control of his business. Victor bugged Jack's office, and when he had the evidence in hand of Brad and Jack's takeover plot, Victor and Jack faced off in a fierce battle. Victor collapsed, and for a brief moment, Jack wavered. Then he caught himself. He resolutely stepped over Victor's body, and strode from the room, leaving Victor gasping for breath, lying there on the floor, dying.

But Jack's conscience got the better of him and he interrupted his dinner with Nikki to call the paramedics. Then he told Ashley and Nikki about Victor's collapse. Nikki was haunted by the thought that Jack might have had something to do with it. With Victor recovering in the hospital, Brad suggested Jack tell him the truth: that he sought the takeover because Victor was trying to steal Nikki away from him.

Jack admitted to Nikki that her betrayal set him on his plot to destroy Victor. He promptly moved out of the ranch, saying he'd not return until Nikki could profess her undying love for him, and not for Victor.

Victor, faced with his own mortality, determined that his future was with Nikki rather than Ashley. He proposed, and Nikki asked for time to break the news to Jack. Jack, preoccupied with thoughts of Nikki and young Nicholas, became involved in a minor car accident. Nikki rushed to the hospital to be by Jack's side, and bumped into her own doctor, who congratulated her on her pregnancy! Knowing how desperate Jack was to be a father, Nikki turned down Victor's proposal. Victoria was distressed that her parents were not reconciling, while Victor was incensed over losing Nikki once again to Jack Abbott.

Realizing that Jack ultimately saved his life, Victor assigned Jack to Jabot, warning him not to cross him again, and offered Ashley Jack's old position as heir apparent to the Newman dynasty. Tired of Victor's manipulations and the emotional roller coaster she'd been on, Ashley decided to reject

Victor's offer, much to her brother's satisfaction, and sought a divorce.

Victoria wasn't about to let Nina have Ryan. She tried to entice Ryan to make love to her, but he wouldn't give in. Victoria then told Ryan she no longer wanted to wait to get married, and confessed that she'd spied him with Nina on the night of his graduation. Sorry that he hurt her, Ryan wanted to prove to Victoria that he loved her. She reminded him of all he had to gain as the husband of Victor Newman's daughter, and set her plan in motion. She got Victor's permission to visit a college in Chicago with Brandon, the young man Victor had chosen as an acceptable suitor for his daughter. Ryan then met up with Victoria and traded places with Brandon. Using a fake ID, Victoria and Ryan tied the knot.

Nina was floating on air, under the mistaken impression she and Ryan would soon be husband and wife. Jill even checked out Ryan as a prospective father to Phillip and gave her approval. Ryan finally mustered the courage to tell Nina that he was breaking up with her once and for all, explaining that he was a newly married man. Nina figured out it was Victoria whom Ryan had wed, and she didn't waste any time telling Victoria she could easily blow her world apart by telling Victor about the marriage.

Knowing her own sexual inhibitions were making things difficult on Ryan, Victoria told him he was free to go. Much to her surprise, and relief, Ryan insisted he wanted to stay married to her. But Ryan insisted that she see a sex therapist so that they could have a fulfilling relationship as husband and wife. Still not completely convinced that Ryan was out of his daughter's life, Victor hired Paul to trail her, only to have his worst fears confirmed. Victor then had Ryan

Despite Victoria's sexual hang-ups, Ryan patiently remained by her side and offered her the comfort of letting her know he cared.

arrested on criminal sexual assault charges, which forced Victoria to confess that she and Ryan were secretly wed. Victor offered Ryan a blank check to get out of Victoria's life forever. Ryan started to make the check out for $1 million . . . then tore it up, telling Victor he truly loved Victoria. The couple moved in together to begin their new life as husband and wife, as Victor and Nina conspired to break them up.

Victor, enraged when he discovered Victoria was seeing a sex therapist, spent New Year's Eve comforting Nikki over their daughter's troubles, much to Jack's dismay. Ashley, meanwhile, newly divorced from Victor, was comforted by Brad, who was still involved with Lauren. But it was painfully obvious to both Ashley and Victor that they still cared deeply for each other.

Michael Baldwin, meanwhile, was gathering "evidence" to support his case. He claimed Cricket entrapped him by staying on at the firm; then he paid off some female witnesses to testify in support of his gentlemanly nature. Next, he arranged for a "fan" of Danny's to drug the singer's tea, put him in a compromising position with another woman, and record

it on film. Michael planned to use the pictures to prove Danny and Cricket's marriage wasn't the blissful union they claimed it to be. He was counting on this revelation to help get him off the hook.

Lynne, forever pining over Paul, was thrilled when he offered to take her on a ski trip to Aspen. Lynne's hopes for a romantic getaway were dashed, however, when she took a spill and nursed a broken ankle. Not long after, Paul seemed distracted at work with the realization that it was his daughter Heather's birthday. When April paid a visit to Genoa City, Mary did her best to get her together with Paul, but Paul said he didn't want to complicate Heather's life. Seeing no point in staying in Genoa City, April dodged Mary's questions about her marriage to a Dr. Lynch.

By year's end, Olivia convinced Neil to give Dru a second chance, and Nina hired Paul to locate her long-lost father. Flo could provide little help—there had been so many men, she lamented. At the Abbott household, John asked Jill to move back into the family's home. Jill was touched by his kindness, while Jack seethed.

Despite all of Michael Baldwin's attempts to throw the disciplinary committee off track, he was found guilty of sexual harassment, which cost him his job. He was also censured by the State of Wisconsin Supreme Court. Michael put on a seemingly repentant face. He apologized to Cricket for putting her through hell and said he was leaving Genoa City. Privately, he vowed revenge.

Danny, concerned for Cricket's safety, hired Paul to keep an eye on her when he left for Los Angeles to star in the title role in Andrew Lloyd Webber's *Joseph and the Amazing Technicolor Dreamcoat*. With aching hearts, Danny and Cricket bade each other a tearful good-bye.

Michael, of course, never left Genoa City. With Hilary out of town, he wormed his way past the doorman and gained access to her apartment, which was next door to Cricket's. He chiseled his way through a common wall between the two apartments, and then hid out in Cricket's closet, waiting for the right time to get his revenge. When Cricket came home one night, he attacked her. Luckily, Paul figured it out—Michael had been using Hilary's place as a hideout. Paul rescued Cricket and shot Michael, wounding him. Danny immediately flew home to comfort Cricket. Not telling her of his plans, he went to the hospital to confront her

assailant. Danny had to be forcibly removed from Michael's room when he lost his cool and attacked Michael. Later, Michael was transferred to jail. Cricket, despite all warnings to the contrary, went to visit Michael in prison, to upbraid him. He deftly took the play away from her by handing her a letter apologizing again for his actions. He claimed he had no recollection of the assault.

Michael's plan was to defend himself, and plead temporary insanity. So he started to play the part of the certifiably insane inmate, serving up dead rats to his prison guards and creating other mayhem. Cricket, for her part, embraced the challenge to convict Michael.

Mary Williams, forever meddling in her son's affairs of the heart, convinced Paul he should go to New York to check on April and his daughter—she was concerned about them. Paul was disturbed to see April's bruised face and wasn't entirely convinced of the explanation she gave him (that she'd been in a car accident) or that Robert Lynch was a good husband and father. When she admitted that Robert occasionally resorted to violence if she displeased him, Paul was outraged!

Jill's dream came true when she remarried John in an intimate ceremony in the Abbott living room. Jack was able to tolerate the union, only because he believed Jill had signed a prenuptial agreement. While there was no love lost between Jack and his stepmother, at least she wouldn't be able to steal the Abbott fortune.

Jill had other things on her mind, however—primarily, that she and John produce a baby. At this stage in his life, John was looking forward to grandfathering rather than fathering a child, and, tipped off to Jill's desires by Jack, he scheduled a vasectomy. But the night before his appointment, Jill mixed a pitcher of martinis and seduced him. John went through with the vasectomy and later apologized to Jill, who was not only furious with him, but depressed over the prospect of missing out on what could be her last chance at motherhood. But her spirits took a decided lift when she discovered she was pregnant!

John insisted Jill "take care of her condition." She made an appointment at the family planning clinic, but couldn't bear the thought of terminating her preg-

Jill's plan to seduce John was a success. She soon announced she was expecting his child.

nancy. Jill drew up a document relieving John of all emotional and financial responsibilities to the child. John became more accepting of Jill's pregnancy, until he found out the document was not legally binding.

Afraid that Victoria would make good on her threat to run away with Ryan, Victor withdrew his petition in court to have their marriage dissolved and eased up on the young couple. Nina, with as much interest in seeing the marriage end as Victor, was sorry Victor backed off, but sensed Ryan wanted out. He was tiring of his sexless union, and Victoria, at a loss for what else to do, moved back home. Knowing his daughter was at the ranch, Victor rushed over to talk some sense into her. As Nikki tried to keep him from going upstairs to interfere, she took a tumble. She was admitted to the hospital with abdominal pains. Tragically, Nikki and Jack's baby boy was stillborn. In their grief, they were comforted from knowing that their decision to donate their baby's organs would help save the life of another child. Later, in a heartrending moment, Jack would hold in his arms

the little boy who had received the heart of his and Nikki's son.

Victor rushed to apologize to Nikki for causing her fall. She assured him he wasn't to blame, but was also strong in her conviction that she had every intention of continuing to build a life as Mrs. Jack Abbott.

When Eve Howard returned to Genoa City, Victor was reintroduced to her son, Cole, now a fledgling novelist. Although Cole took an immediate dislike to Victor, he accepted an offer to work at the ranch in exchange for a tranquil place to write.

Meanwhile, Ryan filed for divorce. Victoria accepted it as the only solution, and soon directed her attention to Cole, who advised her to try again when she turned 18. Nina awaited a proposal from Ryan, who had no intention of becoming a married man again anytime soon.

Lauren, seemingly content with Scott and raising little Scotty, continued her affair with Brad, while Jack tried to get Traci to see Brad's true colors. During one of Lauren and Brad's trysts, Sheila, secretly back in Genoa City and still banking on a future with Eric Forrester, snapped a photo of the lovers in bed. She had it made into a puzzle, and began sending it piece by piece to Lauren to blackmail her and regain custody of Scotty. Lauren dismissed the puzzle as some sort of ad campaign and decided it was time to give her full attention to repairing her marriage to Scott. Brad made one last-ditch effort to get Traci back, but it was painfully obvious to him that Traci and Colleen's new life was

now with Steve in New York City. Lauren was thunderstruck when Sheila revealed she was alive and well. The conniving Ms. Carter warned Lauren to keep her past indiscretions a secret lest the incriminating photos wind up in the hands of a family court judge. Lauren's suspicions that Sheila was involved with a new man proved to be true, but Lauren was shocked to learn that that man was her good friend, the unsuspecting Eric Forrester. Sheila planned to marry him. Lauren did her best to prevent the wedding, while keeping Scott in the dark regarding Sheila's return from the dead. But despite Lauren's efforts, Eric and Sheila wed. Straight shooter John Silva urged Lauren to tell Scott of Sheila's return.

Meanwhile, Drucilla and Neil tied the knot at the Chancellor mansion. Soon after, Drucilla learned the truth regarding the animosity she always felt from her mother. Walter Barber had come home drunk one night and forced himself on Lillie Belle when she had insisted she didn't want another child. Despite her mother's explanation for hurting Dru, Olivia ordered

Olivia and Drucilla's mother, Lillie Belle, loved her grandson, Nate, but caused major problems in her daughters' lives.

Nikki was inconsolable when she heard of Victor's tragic death.

Lillie Belle out of their lives. Later, Olivia relented and brought a despondent Lillie Belle back to Genoa City where she could care for her. Before too long, Lillie Belle's manipulations drove a wedge between Olivia and Nathan, and Dru was once again hurt when her mother rebuffed Dru and Neil's invitation to stay with them instead of Olivia and Nathan. Dru had wanted her sister and brother-in-law to be given the time and space they needed to repair the damage Lillie Belle had caused to their marriage, but Drucilla deep inside had also wanted to somehow bond with her mother.

When Jack learned that Nikki kept Victor's role in her fall a secret from him, he ordered her out of his life for protecting Victor. It was obvious she would never love him, or anyone else, the way she loved Victor Newman. Victor, meanwhile, feeling shut out by the three most important women in his life—Nikki, Victoria, and Ashley—got in his car and left Genoa City for parts unknown. He was mugged at knifepoint and left on a deserted road in Kansas as his attacker drove off in his Rolls Royce. Victor

approached a farmhouse and rescued its owner, Hope Adams, from an assault by her farmhand. Victor offered to stay with Hope until she recovered from the attack. Back in Genoa City, the authorities informed Victor's family he had perished in a fiery car crash—his ID bracelet and a piece of his driver's license were all they could retrieve from the charred wreckage.

Although family and friends were deeply saddened by Victor's passing, uppermost in Jack's mind was that Jabot would now revert back to John Abbott's control. Even though they learned in court that Victor had revoked the codicil to his will, the judge ruled in favor of the Abbotts. Jack would now run the show. He appointed Neil Winters as his right-hand man after Brad resigned to take a position at Fenmore's, where he could work closely with Lauren.

Victor learned through Douglas, whom he'd contacted, that his loved ones seemed to be getting on with their lives without him. Nikki and Victoria were both comforted in their loss by Cole, and when Nikki proved to be a big help in getting Cole's book published, they celebrated by making love. Victoria urged Jack to work on his marriage to Nikki; she wanted the

Victor met Hope on her farm in Kansas, and began a new life with this incredible woman.

Cole Howard found the Newman ranch a peaceful place to write. He also found the girl of his dreams.

young author to herself. But Nikki was certain her life with Jack was over.

For Victor, it was time to begin life anew. He learned that Hope, blind since birth, had also grown up in an orphanage, and they shared a special bond. As he got to know her, Victor appreciated a spiritual quality in Hope that made her unlike any woman he'd ever known: she had faith, strength, and perspective when it came to the important things in life.

Hope eventually called off her upcoming wedding to her longtime neighbor and friend, Cliff Wilson. Although she still loved Cliff, Victor had a powerful effect on her, for he was unlike any man she'd ever known.

When Victor heard on a radio news report that Jack Abbott had taken the helm at Newman Enterprises, he immediately set a plan in motion to

reclaim what was his. Hope returned with him to Genoa City. Victor sent out anonymous invitations to a "gathering of great significance" to be held at the private dining room at the Colonnade, where he revealed himself to the awestruck guests. Shortly afterwards, he shared a tender reunion with his children. Jack and John could only wonder what Victor Newman might do next.

Victor's number one priority was to fire Jack Abbott. He offered the position to Brad, who turned it down when Lauren wouldn't release him from his contract with Fenmore's. Victor tried unsuccessfully to woo John and Ashley back to the fold, but they advised him that Abbott blood ran thick—as long as Jack wasn't welcome, they weren't interested.

Meanwhile, Ryan asked Nina and little Phillip to move in with him as a sort of "trial" marriage, and

Cole stood dutifully by his mother's bedside, telling her how much he loved her—begging her to get well.

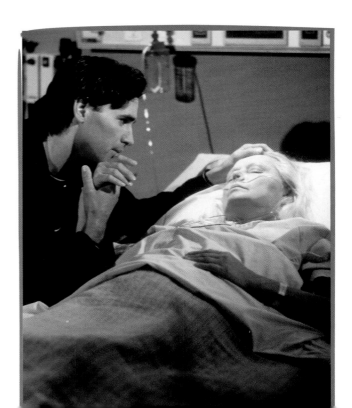

Blade was smitten with Ashley, who responded to his proposal even though his past was something of a mystery.

Jill was pleased Phillip liked his new apartment and his new "daddy" so well.

Elsewhere, Cole told Nikki the fates were giving her a second chance with Victor and that she should take advantage of it. Unbeknownst to Nikki, Cole had written to Eve about the girl he planned to marry—Victoria Newman.

When Eve received Cole's letter, she rushed to Genoa City. She had to stop her son from marrying Victoria, whom she believed to be his half sister. Eve became seriously ill and was hospitalized upon arriving in town. Before she could communicate her fears, Eve passed away, and Cole and Victoria, who had been standing vigil at her bedside assuming she'd come to celebrate their engagement, flew to Las Vegas to be married. Nikki was shocked and hurt that her own daughter had stolen Cole from her. Victor, however, still knew nothing of Cole and Victoria's relationship.

Blade, feeling more and more serious about Ashley, dispelled her concerns that he was hiding something. There was no mystery—he'd simply changed his name in an effort to escape an unhappy past and an evil brother. Blade had been there for Ashley when she

mourned Victor's "death." Their relationship had its share of minor troubles—their respective workloads, for instance, prevented them from sharing quality time together. Blade proposed, and Ashley accepted, though she reminded him that she didn't have the greatest track record when it came to marriage.

Cricket took up the cause of a group of senior citizens who were being victimized by their landlord. Acting on Cricket's legal advice, the seniors staged a rent strike demanding that much-needed repairs be made to their building. The slumlord ignored their request, and then sold the building right out from under them, giving the elderly residents only six weeks to vacate the premises. When Cricket's investigation turned up the fact that Civil War hero Garfield Dandridge Chancellor had drawn up the first Genoa City Charter and hired a world-renowned architect to build what was now the Rainbow Garden Apartments, the building was declared an historical landmark. The seniors were free to stay, and the renovations commenced. Miles and Margaret, the two feisty golden-agers who led the rent strike, wed after their struggle brought them together.

While Paul helped Cricket with her investigative work and saw her through the Rainbow Gardens triumph, Danny was taking his show to Broadway and asked Cricket to join him in New York. The couple deliberated over what would be the best decision for them to make. Finally, Cricket decided she'd go to the Big Apple with Danny, where she could start her professional career anew. But, in the end, Danny realized

April sincerely tried to cope with her abusive husband, but her trusting nature made her a victim of his repeated attacks.

he couldn't ask her to sacrifice her career for the sake of his. Reluctantly and sadly, the couple parted, with Cricket promising Danny she'd visit him as often as possible.

Paul, now fearing for April's safety, convinced her to leave Robert and return with him to Genoa City on the pretext of visiting her mother. In Genoa City, Cricket and Paul introduced April to a domestic violence support group. April attended meetings but, fearing that her husband might become suspicious of her long absence, she returned to New York after assuring Mary and Paul that Robert would never do anything to harm Heather. Even greater trouble was ahead for April, however, because Robert doubted her story that she was visiting her mother. This ordeal brought Cricket and Paul closer together, and Paul admitted he was developing feelings for Cricket.

Lauren made plans to dissolve her marriage to Scott, unaware that he'd recently learned he was dying. Scott was shocked when Sheila showed up in his hospital room, and though she offered to take care of him, he made it clear their time had passed. Lauren was deeply concerned over Scott's worsening condition. Later they went to Catalina where they amicably settled their divorce. Scott passed away peacefully. Lauren grieved, and Brad stepped forward to fill the void in her life and in Scotty's.

Jill gave birth to John's son, whom she named after her father: William Foster Abbott. Jill's mother, Liz, hearing about the baby for the first time when Katherine called to offer her congratulations, returned briefly from London to spend time with her daughter and grandson. Jill explained that she'd kept the pregnancy from her mother because she wanted to spare her the details of her troubled marriage to John. She only hoped Billy's birth would be the catalyst to bring her closer to John again.

As the year was drawing to a close, Hope and Ashley had become friends. Victor and Hope decided to pursue their relationship, much to Nikki and Cliff's displeasure. Nina was on the trail of a man she believed to be her father. John and Ashley reluctantly agreed to return to Jabot, even though Jack was still persona non grata. Paul confessed to Cricket that he was falling in love with her. And Danny told his wife he needed more space to sort out his feelings. Needless to say, the new year was shaping up to be an exciting one.

Storyline
1994

It's said that when one door closes, another opens. Such was the case in Genoa City in a year character-ized by endings and new beginnings. Lillie Belle moved home with Walter after she and Drucilla made peace. Jack and Nikki ended their marriage amicably and would continue to be close friends as Jack's past would come to greet him. Victor and Nikki's son, Nicholas, returned to Genoa City from school overseas. Finally, the appearance of two newcomers—redheaded firecracker Phyllis and a mysterious woman named Mari Jo—would liven things up considerably.

When Cole and Victoria returned from their honeymoon, Victor stopped them cold with the truth: they were brother and sister! This shocking news brought a reconciliation—at least temporarily—between Victoria and her mother, whose hopes of resuming her own relationship with Cole would never be realized. The Howards annulled their marriage and the young lovers tried to get on with their lives, going their separate ways. Determined to learn the truth about Cole's paternity, however, Victor arranged for the exhumation of Eve's body. Happily for Cole and Victoria, blood tests revealed that Cole was not, in fact, Victor's son, so they were free to marry again. But Victoria couldn't forgive Victor for not leveling with her about Cole's questionable paternity in the

Ryan bonded with Nina's son, Phillip, and the McNeils became a family.

first place, and refused to invite him to her wedding. A disconsolate Victor, wanting nothing more than for his daughter to be happy, watched the ceremony from the back of the chapel.

Unfortunately, Victoria's happiness was short-lived. As Cole continued to devote long hours to his novel, and Nina, with Ryan's encouragement, was spending more and more time attending to her college studies, Victoria and Ryan looked to each other for companionship. Although Ryan had planned to break up with Nina, the news that she was carrying his child sent them to the altar instead. Nina could only hope that someday Ryan would love her as much as she loved him. But they worked on their relationship and, with Phillip, coalesced as a family. When Nina miscarried, Ryan dispelled her fears that she'd lose him by insisting he'd always be there for her.

Experiencing a gnawing need to bring her biological family together, Nina renewed her efforts to locate the father she'd never known. Her mother described him as having a distinguishing scar on his neck. When Nina encountered a contractor named Jed Sanders who had such a scar, she was certain she had found her dad at last! She persuaded Jed to join her at Flo's for a home-cooked meal, only to have her hopes dashed when her mother pointed out that the telltale scar was on the wrong side of Jed's neck!

When Victoria learned her mother and Cole had been lovers, she left Cole, feeling heartsick and betrayed. In defiance, she signed a contract with Two Hearts Publications to be *Esprit de Corps* magazine's Miss September. In the meantime, Victor caught wind of this, and bought out Two Hearts. But it was too late. The centerfold had already hit the newsstands. Although Victoria was proud of her work, Cole spurned her. She turned to Ryan, who offered her a shoulder as she contemplated what she would do with the rest of her life.

Concerned over Billy's welfare, John confided in Jill that if anything were to happen to him, he wanted her to remarry. He encouraged his wife to establish a friendship with Jed, who was presently doing some remodeling at the Abbott home, as well as at the Newman ranch.

Not entirely convinced that Nikki had licked her drinking problem, Victor also liked the idea of Jed being around to keep an eye on his ex-wife. Once Nikki got used to the idea of having Jed there, they shared many romantic moments after hours.

Meanwhile, John was suffering from impotence, and Jill longed for male companionship. She turned to Jed, who soon became more than a friend. They became lovers. And how she reveled in their lovemaking, for Jed made her feel deliciously alive and desirable. She was already conjuring up plans in her head to leave John to be with Jed. Mamie lost no time in bringing John up to speed about his wife's affair, and it wasn't long afterward that Jill and John were embroiled in a bitter battle over Billy's custody. As for Nikki, the moment she learned of Jed's involvement with Jill, she sent him packing.

Nikki and Douglas were feeling totally left out of Victor's life as Victor turned his full attention to Hope Adams, with

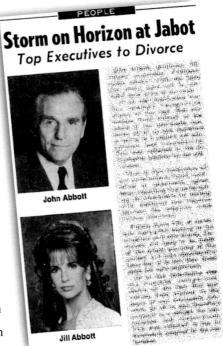

PEOPLE

Storm on Horizon at Jabot
Top Executives to Divorce

John Abbott

Jill Abbott

whom he had fallen in love. But Hope was having serious doubts that Victor would actually commit to her. Could he possibly fall in love with a blind woman?

All Hope's doubts were cast aside by Victor's stunning proposal of marriage. Nikki insisted that Hope would never be able to satisfy Victor. Cliff, on the other hand, knew the kind of woman Victor was getting. There was no other in the whole wide world quite like her, and though Cliff's heart was breaking, he wished Hope nothing but happiness.

When Victor and Hope returned from their honeymoon, Nikki apologized to Hope for crashing her wedding reception and creating a scene. Moreover, she took it upon herself to caution the new Mrs. Newman that Victor didn't take well to babies. But as it turned out, Nikki's warnings, which were entirely unwarranted, were also unnecessary, for Victor had agreed to start a family with his new bride.

When Hope became pregnant, however, Victor was beginning to have serious misgivings. He worried that Hope's blindness might be passed along to their child. Always one to demand perfection in all aspects of his life, he saw no reason to make this an exception. He convinced Hope that it would be unfair

to bring this child into the world under such risky circumstances. But when Hope was involved in a car accident on her way to terminate her pregnancy and she emerged unscathed, she took it as a sign from God that she should see this child to term. A remorseful Victor supported her decision.

Victor was not the only Newman to have some troublesome times that year. Matt Clark had a huge grudge against Victor's son, Nicholas, whom he referred to as Rich Boy, for stealing away his girlfriend, Sharon Collins. Matt swore he'd get even with Nick. Matt couldn't afford to buy Sharon gifts the way Nick could. When he learned that Nick had given her the beautiful coat she was wearing, he ripped it off her back, and then raped her. It was a vicious act that tormented Sharon and would keep playing over and over in her mind. But she was too afraid to say anything about it to either Nicholas or her mother, Doris.

As far as Nikki and Victoria were concerned, Sharon brought Nicholas nothing but trouble and they wished he'd drop her. But Nick loved Sharon. He was prepared to take on the entire world to have her. Victor Newman liked the girl and paid for an operation for her disabled mother, although Sharon asked him to keep his charitable action secret. She promised she'd pay back every cent, but she didn't want to appear a gold digger to Nicholas.

Sharon warned her friend, Amy, who Nicholas used to date, to stay away from Matt, and told her why. But

Hope shared her insecurities with Douglas, who assured her Victor's feelings for her ran deep.

when Amy confronted Matt with Sharon's claim that he had raped her, he insisted it was just sour grapes on Sharon's part because *he* had in fact dumped *her*. Later, when Nick and Sharon beat out Matt and Amy for King and Queen of the freshman ball at GCU, Matt was so outraged he vowed to let Nicholas know his lady was not the innocent he believed her to be.

Knowing from firsthand experience the pain caused by estrangements within a family, Drucilla encouraged Neil to accept his half brother Malcolm, whom he hadn't seen in years. Neil's first impression was that Malcolm wanted to freeload, but when Malcolm, with a little help from Dru, landed a job in Blade's photography studio, their relationship took a positive turn. But that relationship would surely be blown out of the water if Neil ever discovered what had happened while he was away on a business trip. Drucilla—under the weather, overmedicated, and somewhat delirious—made love to Malcolm, mistakenly taking him for her husband.

Shortly afterwards, Neil expressed his desire to start a family, and Dru would soon find herself expecting. But who was the father? When Malcolm admitted to Dru that it was he who had responded to Dru's advances and made love to her that night, Drucilla considered terminating her pregnancy. But at the same time, Dru learned that she suffered from a medical condition that might well prevent her from conceiving again. Then, after seeing the joy Neil derived from playing with their nephew, little Nate, Dru knew she couldn't deprive him of fatherhood. So she put it out of her mind, and with Malcolm's concurrence, the pair decided to keep their rendezvous a secret forever. Meanwhile, Olivia tried to set Malcolm up with Stephanie, a beautiful medical student, but little came of this relationship. Malcolm, unattached, continued to hang out with his brother and his sister-in-law.

Chris was devastated when Danny, out of nowhere, sent her a Dear Chris letter from New York, explaining that he'd moved on with his life and that she should do the same. Paul, always a good friend to Chris, was there to pick up the pieces after the Romalottis' divorce was finalized. Lynne knew Paul was in love with Chris and feared he might be setting himself up to get hurt again. Lynne cared deeply for her boss and always looked out for him. Forever meddling in her son's relationships, Mary thought Christine was not quite right for him—and that perhaps he was moving too fast. She also believed that either April or Lynne would be a much better match for him.

Amy got involved with Matt despite Sharon's warnings. Matt's jealousy of Nicholas was the catalyst for their breakup.

Paul and Chris scoured the streets of Ho Chi Minh City looking for Luan's son, Keemo. They were able to locate him and bring him back to Genoa City, where he reunited with his mother after many years.

Soon after her divorce, Chris befriended Luan Volein, who worked at a restaurant called the Saigon Shack. Luan was mother to a teenage daughter, Mai, fathered by a man she didn't love, but someone who had protected her from the dangers of their war-torn country. Luan also had a son, Keemo, whom she was forced to leave behind when she fled Vietnam. When Luan suffered a gunshot wound in an attempted holdup, Paul and Chris flew to Ho Chi Minh City to find Keemo. Luan explained that Keemo was an outcast in his own country because his father was an American soldier. Chris and Paul persuaded Keemo to return with them. His appearance in Genoa City gave Luan the will to live, and speeded her recovery.

While Luan looked at a photo of a young Jack Abbott, wondering whatever happened to her lover, Jack saw Luan's picture in the newspaper. He was haunted by the uncanny resemblance she bore to Mai Yun, the woman he'd fallen in love with 20 years before in Vietnam.

Meanwhile, Blade and Ashley married. Happy to be sharing their lives together, they were having a new house built. Blade was unnerved, however, when a woman from his past, Marilyn Mason, showed up and began working at Jabot. His ex-lover and his wife working more or less side by side was decidedly *not* a good thing. Marilyn, who now called herself Mari Jo, was still in love with Blade, but

assured him that the secret of their past was safe with her. He made it clear that he'd never forgive her for sleeping with his evil twin brother, Rick. She, on the other hand, reminded him that she was the only eyewitness to Rick's drowning, and was aware that Blade had been on the scene and had ignored his brother's cries for help.

Blade warned her not to get too close to the Abbotts. This was impossible for Mari Jo, as she quickly fell in love with Jack. Jack found Mari Jo to be a good listener, someone to whom he could open up and reveal his innermost thoughts. Mari Jo asked Jack to marry her, and after a few days, he responded with an engagement ring.

When Mari Jo left her wallet behind, Ashley noticed that her name was really Marilyn. She confronted this mystery woman. Mari Jo confessed that she and Blade had been lovers, but assured Ashley it was long over. Mari Jo and Blade then made a pact to bury their past so that each could get on with their lives. Ms. Mason couldn't believe her eyes when Blade's twin, Rick, resurfaced—very much alive—and Ashley, spying them together, assumed that it was Blade that Mari Jo was seeing. Ashley moved into the guest room. Jack was angry that Mari Jo had lied to him about her prior involvement with Blade, but none of that really mattered anymore in view of Jack's reunion with Luan.

Keemo, bitter over what Luan had been forced to endure without his father in their lives, admitted that he hated Americans. Although he was at first reluctant to accept Jack, Keemo came around when Jack showed him the many letters he'd written to Luan. All were marked RETURN TO SENDER. The entire Abbott clan welcomed Keemo into the family, and he was offered a position at Jabot, where he worked in the lab with Ashley. Chris helped Keemo learn American customs and ways, and he mistook her friendship as something more.

Danny, realizing he'd made the biggest mistake of his life, eventually returned to Genoa City. He hoped to reconcile with Chris. He explained that he now had a son, Daniel, by a woman named Phyllis with whom he'd spent one regrettable, drunken night. When Phyllis had threatened to blackmail him by talking to the tabloids, Danny knew that Chris would be a big

part of any story that might hit the press, so he felt compelled to take extreme measures to ensure that wouldn't happen. So he married Phyllis, for whom he felt nothing but contempt, to spare Chris and to help his young son. By the time Danny came back to town to try to right his wrongs, Paul had proposed to Chris, so Danny's road to reconciliation would be much tougher than he'd imagined.

Phyllis's appearance on the scene only made things worse. Phyllis made no bones about blaming Christine for the breakup of her family and bitterly complained to Rex and Gina that Danny had abandoned her and their child. From the moment they met her, Danny's family and friends knew that Phyllis spelled Trouble, with a capital T.

After April took another beating from Robert, she sought refuge in Mary Williams's home. A friend of hers at her spousal abuse support group, fearing that April might decide to return to her abusive husband, gave her a gun for protection. When Robert learned that his wife was in Genoa City, he tracked her down. He'd almost convinced her to return with him to New York when they got into a violent argument, which, unfortunately, was how their discussions usually turned out. This time, however, he went too far and threatened the welfare of her daughter, Heather. April grabbed a letter opener and plunged it into Robert's back, killing him.

When April was arrested, Heather was brought back to Genoa City for the first time since her early childhood. She stayed with Mary, not knowing the kindly woman was her grandmother, or that Paul

Jack found it difficult to forgive Mari Jo for deceiving him about her past relationship with Blade.

To this day, Heather Lynch doesn't know that Paul is her biological father. April took her back to New York after the murder trial.

was her father. April's own heart-wrenching testimony and that of a doctor who treated her for injuries she'd claimed were from a car accident, but which were in fact caused by her husband's brutal beatings, led to a conviction of involuntary manslaughter and a five-year suspended sentence. April would also do community service to heighten the public's awareness of spousal abuse. She and Heather returned to New York to get on with their lives.

Brad had trouble adjusting to the idea of Steve being a father to his daughter, Colleen, and was crushed when she addressed him as "Mr. Carlton." It was some consolation to him that Lauren's son, Scotty, saw him as a father figure, but things got a bit sticky when Traci expressed her displeasure over Brad's relationship with Lauren.

When Brad suffered a heart attack during a particularly steamy encounter with Lauren, he was hospitalized and Traci realized her feelings for him had never really died. She got into a knock-down-drag-out brawl with Lauren when she learned how Brad wound up in the hospital. Realizing how strong her feelings for Brad still were, Traci wondered whether she'd made a big mistake in marrying Steve. Perhaps her future was really meant to be with Brad. Brad, however, insisted they had no future together,

so Traci returned to New York to mend her relationship with Steve, who'd become jealous over Traci's inability to get her ex out of her system.

Brad's hospitalization had ramifications for Newman Enterprises, too, as Jack took his place while he recuperated. Victor actually praised Jack for doing a spectacular job, and assured him his position would be secure, even after Brad got back on his feet.

Esther, forever looking for Mr. Right, answered an ad in the personals placed by a Norman Peterson, who said he was an investment banker. Her heart fluttered when he wanted to meet her. She convinced Rex and Katherine to play the role of house servants to impress her suitor while she passed herself off as the lady of the manor. Katherine didn't trust Norman . . . there was just something about him . . . so she made Esther fess up. But Norman insisted he had to tell Esther something first: he wasn't really a banker, he was just a barber. When Esther confessed her true identity, Norman wanted to dump her, until he learned that she was mentioned in Katherine Chancellor Sterling's will. Instead, he proposed.

The crafty Katherine offered to take care of all the wedding plans and hired an actor to play the role of minister. She couldn't let Esther get suckered in by this con man. After their honeymoon, Norman wanted to start a family right away and told Esther to ask for her inheritance, now, so they could invest it for their children's education. The Sterlings agreed, on

Esther was afraid that as Mrs. Chancellor's maid, she'd never find Mr. Right. She talked Katherine and Rex into playing along with her scheme so she could catch Norman's eye.

the condition the money be in Esther's name only. Norman had a fit and filed for divorce, seeking one half of the inheritance as his settlement. Katherine told him the jig was up; he'd been "married" by an actor and so was entitled to neither a divorce nor a settlement. Esther threw him out. Norman later sneaked back into the house with a gun and rifled through the safe hidden behind a painting in the living room. When Rex caught him in the act, Norman shot Rex and escaped. Katherine was with Rex in the hospital when he died. His last words to Danny were that he should pursue his true love, which moved Danny to seek a divorce from Phyllis.

Mary had finally come to the point of accepting Christine in her son's life, and Paul and Chris planned their wedding. As the guests were waiting at the church, they learned there'd been a terrible accident—on the way to the church, Paul jumped in front of Chris to save her life as a hit-and-run driver raced toward them. What no one knew was that Phyllis was at the wheel! Paul's injuries left him impotent, and he refused to marry Chris.

Jack turned down Mari Jo's invitation to go skiing, and instead planned a Caribbean getaway with Luan. He looked forward to getting reacquainted with his long-lost love, and together they would determine what their future might hold. By this time, Mari Jo was deeply in love with Jack and wasn't about to lose him. She bared her claws, telling Luan that Jack was merely being kind to her out of a sense of obligation. Hurt but grateful for the worldly Mari Jo's advice, Luan backed out of the trip, so a disappointed Jack went alone. Mari Jo soon followed after him—coincidentally to the same destination Blade and Ashley chose to try to rekindle the romance in their troubled marriage. Brad was also on hand—good thing, for he was there to comfort Ashley when she saw "Blade" with Mari Jo.

Evil twin Rick, too, had shown up in St. Thomas, very much alive. Brad and Ashley assumed Ms. Mason and Blade were resuming their affair; Blade, in the meantime, was at a loss to understand Ashley's inability to warm up to him. Rick, up to his old tricks, knocked Blade out, bound him in chains, and assumed his twin brother's identity.

As 1994 was winding down, Jill and John's custody battle over Billy began to heat up. Victoria was content in her new position working on Jabot's junior line, Brash & Sassy, but at home, she was concerned over Cole's relationship to his new editor, Jeri. Nina didn't like the idea of Ryan and Victoria working so closely together and told Ryan that she wanted to expand their family. And Hope reminded Cliff that her life was now with Victor as she and Victor awaited the birth of their baby.

From the beginning of the year to its end, 1995 was marked by several civil, criminal, and domestic disputes. Mainly, Paul, Chris, and Danny had their hands full with Phyllis; Matt and Nick's fight over Sharon had to be settled in the criminal courts; and John and Jill butted heads in a custody/divorce lawsuit.

Paul was adamant—there was absolutely no way he was going to saddle his lovely fiancée, Chris, with a sexually dysfunctional partner! End of discussion! Chris understood where he was coming from when he finally told her what the problem was. She assured him she could live with it, but Paul was too proud and he loved her too much to even consider it.

In other quarters, there were a variety of reactions to the broken engagement. Phyllis, for one, was furious! She had really bungled the job, since her intention was to wipe out Paul and Chris completely, not merely maim them! At least she got to the car rental agency in time to destroy the computer records that would've linked her to the hit-and-run accident. But her ineptness meant that Chris was now available to her ex-husband, Danny, who continued to pine for her—and right at the time when Danny had asked Phyllis for a divorce. Phyllis had managed, however, to twist Danny around her little finger once again, convincing him to stay with her and little Daniel for another four months for a trial marriage. Even though Danny did agree on the proviso that

they maintain separate bedrooms, the important point for Phyllis was that he agreed to stay at all, which would give her time enough, she hoped, to come up with something that would make him want to stay with her forever.

Danny, of course, felt for the heartbroken Chris, but he hoped that once his divorce was final, they'd get together again. Lauren, as would befit her vampish nature, smiled knowingly to herself, as she guessed correctly at the "real" reason for Paul and Chris's broken engagement—and later, much later, when Paul was on the mend, she held him close and thought she detected some response!

A number of other things happened to these two couples over the year. Phyllis had the chutzpah to ask Chris and Paul to be godparents to little Daniel—for her personal gain, of course—hoping this would impress and thus bring her closer to Danny.

And then there was the matter of Danny's trip to New York to meet with a new agent, which innocently coincided with Chris's business trip there. Call it serendipity, but the pair had even managed to select

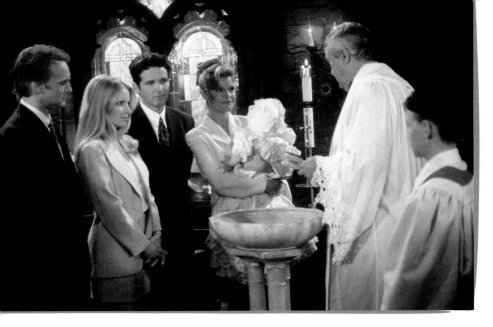

Chris and Paul were happy to be Daniel's godparents for the baby's sake; Phyllis scored some points with Danny by asking them.

the same hotel to stay at, and then ran into each other in the same restaurant! They greeted each other with the same élan that old friends show toward each other when they happen to meet like this in a big city, strictly by accident. Sasha, Phyllis's friend and former coworker, was there, of course, spying on Danny. When Sasha reported to Phyllis that Danny was hanging out with a beautiful blonde, a livid Phyllis added two and two together and came up with six!

Back home, sometime later, Danny stole the paternity report from Phyllis's desk and turned it over to Paul and Chris for evaluation. They advised him that they should check the file in the DMS Lab that did DNA testing in New York (and at which Phyllis used to work!), because Phyllis's report might have been altered. When Paul and Chris went there, they were amazed to find everything in order. This was because Phyllis had followed them and when Sasha refused to change the records to match the paternity report Danny had obtained, Phyllis drugged Sasha and changed the computer records herself, making the two reports match perfectly.

Meanwhile, as Danny's trial marriage was coming to an end, Chris and Paul grew closer and made love, rescheduling their marriage date to coin-

cide with Valentine's Day. Danny grew desperate for his freedom, which would allow him to concentrate on winning Chris back. Phyllis, meanwhile, tried out a new strategy—getting a new boyfriend, an unemployed computer programmer named Peter Garrett, to make Danny jealous. She tried a number of ploys to get under Danny's skin; the only thing that really irked him was the thought of Peter getting closer to Daniel. Danny insisted that he and Phyllis could never be anything more than friends, if that.

Matt Clark and his friend Drake dug around until they located an auto mechanic in Madison named Frank Barrett. Frank was Sharon's high school sweetheart. They got him to admit that he was the father of an out-of-wedlock baby he and Sharon gave up for adoption. Sharon wanted to tell Nicholas about her past, but she was afraid she'd lose him; now Matt, armed with the spicy truth, beat her to the punch. He revealed everything in a letter to Nick, and Nick, infuriated, wanted him to stop lying about his girlfriend. Nick sought Matt out at a college hangout called Crimson Lights, where the two engaged in a violent fistfight, with neither one of them coming out the victor. Sharon was so distraught about causing Nick and his family nothing but pain and trouble that she mailed her engagement ring back to him. After a number of days had passed, Nicholas went back to Sharon and said he still loved her. Sharon then told him everything about her past, and both vowed never to keep any secrets from the other again.

Meanwhile, Amy was tired of Matt's obsessive behavior toward Nick; she wanted to break off with him and get away from Genoa City for the summer. Nicholas found out about Sharon's rape when he tried to make love to her and she couldn't go through with it. He tore over to Matt's place to settle the score, stopping on the way to buy a gun, but without success. Just as he arrived, he saw Sharon's car pulling away, and he found Matt lying face down in a pool of blood. When the police arrived, Nick was wiping the fingerprints off the gun, thinking they were Sharon's. He was indicted for attempted murder.

Soon enough, Matt remembered that it was Amy who shot him after he had raped her. Matt refused to talk, but was worried the police would get the full scoop from Amy.

Amy, meanwhile, lost her memory and was found wandering the streets of Chicago, where she was taken to a shelter. Paul, Chris, and Victor managed to track her down. Back in Genoa City, Sharon was forced to take the stand at Nick's trial and was made to admit that Matt had raped her, but Matt testified that it was consensual. Nick feared the jury would think he had sufficient motivation to shoot Matt, although John Silva tried to convince them that Matt had already been shot before he arrived. The jury found Nick guilty, and he was sentenced to spend 15 years in prison.

As Nick was adjusting to life in prison, his father was literally moving mountains to secure additional evidence to free him. Victor had managed to have Amy transferred to Fairview Sanitarium, which was close by, and got her the best medical care that money could buy. In prison, Nicholas fell into the clutches of "The Wart Man," who made it his personal business to constantly and viciously assault him. Victor realized that, with each passing day, his son's life was in greater danger, and he forced a confrontation between Matt and Amy.

It was only a matter of time before Matt traced Amy to Fairview, where, posing as a doctor, he stole into Amy's room. A confused Amy apologized for shooting him, but when Matt started to get amorous, she remembered he had raped her! Meanwhile, Wart Man initiated an ugly fistfight with Nick, but Victor showed up and

When the police found Nicholas and the gun in Matt's apartment, all the evidence pointed to him as the one who shot Matt. Nicholas's nightmare continued as he was convicted of attempted murder and sentenced to a long prison term.

Drucilla had a difficult labor, but she and Neil were blessed to welcome their daughter, Lily, into the world.

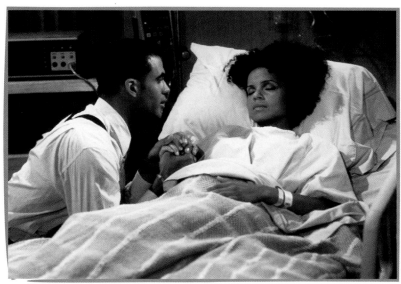

pulverized him. Amy came forth and made a statement to the judge, who then dropped the charges against Nick. Nick proposed again to Sharon.

Elsewhere in town, Nathan found himself deeply involved in a messy affair with Keesha Monroe. Olivia became suspicious when he came home with lipstick on his collar, and when he rejected her advances in the bedroom one time too many. Neil got the shock of his life when he encountered his brother-in-law in a restaurant having an intimate tête-à-tête with this woman. When Neil told Nathan to shape up, Nathan said that at least Keesha had time for him, whereas his workaholic wife spent far too many hours at the hospital. Nathan did try to dump Keesha on various occasions—sometimes out of guilt, sometimes out of fear, sometimes because he realized he still loved Olivia—but either he couldn't give her up or she wouldn't let him go. When Nathan would take Olivia out on a special date, Keesha would pout and threaten to blow their whole affair into the open.

Keesha (using the name Nola) even checked out Olivia in her hospital office, posing as a new patient. It blew her mind that Nathan would have such an attractive wife! Dru, who recently became a new mom, couldn't believe that Nathan would cheat like this on her sister, and she reamed him out, threatening to tell Olivia if he didn't immediately put an end to the affair. As if things weren't complicated enough, the charismatic Malcolm met a forlorn Keesha at Gina's and took an instant liking to her. He became so smitten with her that his unbridled enthusiasm and joie de vivre actually had an effect on Keesha. And that drove Nathan wild with jealousy.

When Malcolm romanced Keesha and fell in love with her, he had no idea she was involved with Nathan.

Olivia wanted to give Nathan another baby, and so the couple, after being sexually distant for a period, began trying to conceive.

Keesha, in the meantime, was falling for Malcolm and refusing to take phone calls from her persistent ex-boyfriend, Stan Jackson. When Keesha told Malcolm the truth about her affair with Nathan, Malcolm was outraged and dropped her. When Keesha eventually tried to get in touch with Stan, she was shocked to learn he had died of AIDS! Shattered, she realized that she might be infected, and that if she were, she may have infected Nathan as well, who had since reconciled with Olivia.

Blade seemed a different man when he returned from St. Thomas with Ashley. He had somehow magically become a most impressive lover. Ashley remarked about this to Mari Jo, who immediately surmised that Rick had traded places with his good twin, the hapless Blade! Rick admitted as much to Mari Jo but refused to reveal how he disposed of Blade. Rick cleverly managed to dupe Ashley's family and friends, and when he told Ashley he wanted her to have his baby, Mari Jo realized that Rick had, in his own way, fallen in love with Ashley. The real Blade, who'd been chained and held captive by hired native hands in the Caribbean, managed to escape, and returned to Genoa City. He confronted his brother, who left town; a perplexed and disappointed Ashley resigned herself to the fact that Blade could not maintain his sexual prowess.

In the meanwhile, Mari Jo was interested in getting back together with Jack. While she was having a rendezvous with Jack's son, Keemo, at the Bartlett Inn, she spied Jack dining there alone. Luan had called to cancel because she wasn't feeling well. So Mari Jo got a hooker to double for her in Keemo's bed. Then she commiserated with Jack over Luan's recently diagnosed terminal illness, which deep down gave her hope that she'd have a future with Jack after all.

Shortly thereafter, Rick had come back to town and, pretending to be Blade, went home with Ashley, who had been waiting for Blade at Gina's. When the real Blade arrived at Gina's, he figured out what happened and dashed home. Mari Jo intervened by calling Rick (who was pretending to be Blade) just as he was about to make love to Ashley. When Mari Jo claimed there had been a fire at the photography studio, Rick had no choice but to check it out or blow the charade. The real Blade then assumed his rightful place in bed with his wife. But several more role reversals occurred, ending with the real Blade being tragically killed in a car–train accident. Rick revealed himself and tried to console the widowed Ashley, but Ashley threw him out. Then she went to Paris to find herself.

Victor, Nina, Katherine, and Mamie all refused Jill's request to testify on her behalf in the divorce/custody suit against John. Jill was forced to take the stand, and made the point that John had a vasectomy without her knowledge to avoid parenthood, thus making the case that he never wanted to be a father to Billy. After they arrived home from court, a remorseful Jill told John she wanted to give their marriage a second chance and she apologized for airing their dirty linen in public. But before he could respond, John collapsed, suffering a massive stroke.

All of the battling Abbotts came together and prayed for John's recovery. Jill, most of all, became the stoic one, professing her undying love for

Mamie fell in love with John Abbott, but Jill found a way to get her out of town.

him. Mamie would steal into his room when she thought no one was around, but Victor came upon her there, holding John's hand. She told Victor she was in love with John. Another time, Jill came upon Mamie kissing John, fired her on the spot, and had her forcibly removed from John's room. Mamie maintained that this was no one-way street; their love was mutual.

When John came out of his coma, he pulled Jill to him and gave her a clinging, ravenous kiss, which left her in a state of shock. But the truth is, as John slipped in and out of consciousness, Jill really didn't know how he felt about her. Sometimes it

When Cliff was in a farming accident, Hope rushed to be by his side. No matter what direction her life might take, she would always love him.

seemed as if he couldn't stand the sight of her, and at others, she was the love of his life!

As for Mamie, no one could keep her from paying a return visit to John's bedside, except for John himself, who inadvertently devastated her when he remembered her only as the housekeeper! When John fully regained his memory, he apologized to Mamie, but said he was unsure about continuing their relationship, even though he did want to divorce Jill and make a life for him and Billy with her.

In the end, after the court battle resumed, Jill suggested they agree on joint custody and call off the divorce. John concurred for Billy's sake and Jill found a way to get rid of Mamie by offering her a staggering sum of money, which she accepted only when John, thinking Mamie's phone call was from an annoying

siness associate, hung up on her. She went on a world cruise with Trent Jordan, a Chancellor Industries executive to whom Kay introduced her.

John and Jill weren't the only couple with marital difficulties. Hope and Victor, despite an abiding love that would transcend time and distance, simply lived in two different worlds. Hope, the blind farm girl from Kansas, and Victor, the world-class entrepreneur, did have a healthy son, Victor Adam Newman Jr.—but they each had different ideas about how and where to raise their child. Victor's namesake was also a minor source of alienation to Victor's other children, who vied for their father's attention, and to Nikki. When things would go badly, Hope would return to her roots and to the love of longtime friend, Cliff Wilson; Victor would go to Nikki for love and understanding. Eventually, Victor would file for divorce, and Hope would consider Cliff's proposal of marriage.

Vicki, Nina, Cole, and Ryan kept getting entangled in each other's lives. Victoria was as brash and sassy as the line of perfume products she marketed for Jabot, and she acted without restraint, both on and off the job. She often defied her father; ran rings around her husband; and in general, she behaved disrespectfully toward family, friends, colleagues, and superiors. Whenever it suited her, she became an outrageous flirt, but she would not brook what she perceived to be "flirtatious" behavior on the part of straight-arrow Cole.

Nina tried her best to keep her husband happy; but she had Ryan's ex-wife, Vicki, and her own former mother-in-law, Jill, to contend with.

Ryan, his nose kept pretty close to the grindstone and ever ready to climb the corporate ladder,

SOCIETY SECTION

Dental Hygienists Announce Awards
Two Students at Fones School Win Scholarships

Genoa City Gossip
BY SY ADAMS

Brad Carlton & Nikki Abbott To Be Married

Nikki Abbott   Brad Carlton

had a serious run-in with his boss, Neil Winters. He was ready to chuck it all when Jill Abbott came to the rescue, promising him nirvana if he accepted a position as her assistant. And so the four would continue living, loving, feuding, and turning things topsy-turvy in Genoa City!

There were several other memorable events that distinguished 1995 as a year of great movement and change. Lauren decided there wasn't much to keep her in Genoa City anymore, so she considered moving to Los Angeles to collaborate on a Forrester/Fenmore line of fashions. As Lauren was making up her mind, Sheila Carter resurfaced in Genoa City in an attempt to stop her from going there. When Traci returned to Genoa City for Jack and Luan's wedding, she told Brad that she and Steve were having marital problems. Meanwhile, Brad and Nikki had paired up and were engaged to be married.

Keesha did just as her primary physician, Olivia, instructed her; she told Nathan straight out that she was HIV positive, and that he should be tested, too. Nathan nearly fell through the floor—not only might he be infected, but so might Olivia! How could he tell her something like this? He picked up the phone and called Olivia, making the excuse that he had to go out of town again on business and that the intimate evening they had planned would simply have to wait.

When Olivia told Dru that Nathan was out of town on business, Dru decided to do a little checking on her own. Paul, Nathan's boss, told her he hadn't given Nathan any such assignment, so Dru did the sisterly thing, and told Olivia that she feared Nathan was cheating on her with Keesha Monroe! Olivia turned on Dru, demanding to know how long it had been going on and why she'd been kept in the dark.

When Nathan confessed, Olivia went berserk! How could he endanger her life like this? How could he betray her? Didn't his marriage vows mean anything at all? She threw him out and ordered him to stay away from her and little Nate. Then Olivia took a pregnancy test and an AIDS test. Thank God, she tested negative. Nathan said he would be tested, too, and later reported that he was negative.

Then he remembered that he and Nate had had a minor accident in the playground in which

Olivia knew she could never forgive Nathan. Dru, Neil, and Malcolm were there to lend support and see her through her most trying times.

both of them had gotten cut. Olivia really lost it! She prepared little Nate to be tested, trying to hide her own anxiety as she told him he had to be a brave little man when the doctor would stick him with a needle.

Little Nate kept asking for his daddy, wondering where he was and when he was coming home. Nathan made attempts to see his little boy, but Olivia kept putting roadblocks in the way. Meanwhile, the compassionate Malcolm was walking a tightrope between Keesha and Olivia. He befriended Keesha, saying he knew about her condition, but wanted her to know he was on hand to help her through the rough days ahead. And he tried to distract Olivia by amusing her, taking her dancing, and generally entertaining little Nate. When Little Nate's first test was negative, Olivia dared to relax a little, but there was Nathan again, making loud noises about his legal rights to see his son.

One day, Nathan picked the lock on Olivia's apartment door and waited for her and Nate to come home. Needless to say, she freaked out. Nathan had long run out of money, so he asked Paul for his old job back. Paul checked with Olivia, who agreed that as long as he didn't cause any trouble, Nathan could go back to work for Paul.

Malcolm, meanwhile, was becoming more concerned over Keesha's deteriorating health. She had developed pneumonia and he sensed that death was imminent. Malcolm felt that more than anything, Keesha craved the nourishment of love for her spirit and her soul, so that her loneliness might be bearable. He asked her to marry him, and in a simple, selfless ceremony gave his heart to her, as they became husband and wife.

Nathan was becoming more and more desperate to experience, in a tangible way, the innocent love a child has for his dad. He kidnapped Nate and lived close to the edge, as he and his son roamed from city to city, keeping just one step ahead of the authorities. Beaten, drained, and broke, he decided to return Nate to his mother. As they approached Olivia's apartment building, Nathan stopped at a flower cart to spend his last two dollars on flowers for his wife.

As Nathan's back was turned, Nate ran across the street, too eager to see his mom to wait for his father. Nathan, not seeing his son at his side, darted into the street to look for him, and was hurtled over the roof of a speeding car. Olivia eventually found little Nate asleep at her door, but she took the small boy to the hospital to see his dad. After good-byes between father and son were said, Olivia thanked Nathan for returning Nate to her. Nathan asked her for forgiveness, then closed his eyes and died.

Now that Nicholas had his freedom, the Newmans celebrated in grand style. The only fly in the ointment from Nikki's point of view was that Nicholas still insisted upon seeing that ragtag fiancée of his, Sharon, even after all the grief she had caused him! Nicholas was eager to get on with his life and looked forward to spending many productive hours at Newman Enterprises, soaking up knowledge and gaining as much experience as possible in his father's business. He also enrolled at Genoa City University as a part-time student to complete work on his degree. Nick had his life, at least for now, all laid out before him: work, school, marriage to the girl of his dreams, and romance and fun in the happy evening hours they'd spend together in the foreman's lodge, which had been newly refurbished, and would become their home after the wedding.

Nikki tried her damnedest to encourage

Sharon was awestruck when Nicholas carried her over the threshold of their new home—the remodeled foreman's house at the Newman ranch.

Sharon to break off with Nicholas by offering her a goodly sum of money to leave town, but Sharon remained steadfast. Nicholas was the man she loved and would spend the rest of her life loving; there simply wasn't money enough to buy her off. The wedding ceremony was beautiful and was carried off without a hitch, despite Nikki's forewarning that she might have to make a scene during the service.

Adjusting to life on the ranch was not without its challenges for Sharon, who was feeling somewhat insecure in the trappings of such wealth. A baby to occupy her attention seemed like the perfect solution, but her mother, Doris, warned her that that was not the way to keep a man. When Sharon's best friend, Grace Turner, showed up from Madison,

Sharon felt she would have someone to relate to. Grace was surprised that Sharon had snagged the son of the wealthy Newmans and thought Nicholas was quite a hunk! (Later, he would even help her land a job in Jabot's research department.)

When Sharon became pregnant, she waited for the right time to tell Nick, only to find there was no right time. He carried on about being too young for fatherhood, and how this put a crimp in all the plans he'd made for them. Sharon was beginning to think that, to save her marriage, abortion was looking more and more like the only viable option. Their relationship became strained, and Sharon didn't want to annoy Nicholas by bringing up the baby subject.

Then, the opportunity came for Nicholas to hurriedly leave on a business trip to Copenhagen with Neil Winters. He begged for a few minutes to pen Sharon a letter on how he felt about the baby, and left it in the "out" box. Grace saw the letter and pocketed it. While Nicholas was away, Sharon spent her time getting the nursery ready. Nick stayed in Copenhagen much longer than either one of them expected, and Sharon fretted over not hearing from him. Her father-in-law even offered to fly her to Denmark, but she declined because the invitation didn't come from Nicholas. At her lowest ebb, she decided to get s⌐ information about abortion from

Sharon couldn't have been ⊦ friend, Grace, relocated from Ma⸤

176

clinic, and learned there was a 48-hour waiting period. She went to see her mother for some tender loving care, and then left, clearly troubled.

When Nicholas returned home, eager to see her, she was nowhere to be found. He waited hours for her to show up. He became worried and began checking with family, friends, folks at the coffeehouse, anyone who might have a clue as to where she could have gone. Then he noticed the phone book was opened to the section on family-planning clinics and he frantically began to search in that direction.

Nicholas located the right clinic and created a disturbance when security tried to eject him, but Sharon said she wanted to speak to him in private. He was furious with her that she would do such a thing without talking to him first, but she wanted to know when he had shown any interest in even broaching the subject. Nick was immensely relieved that she hadn't yet gone through with the procedure, and he promised he'd be a model father.

All kinds of little scenarios were popping up in terms of the *Romalotti* v. *Romalotti* divorce hearing. Prior to the hearing, Phyllis fantasized about making love to Peter Garrett, who was smitten with her, but she chickened out. Danny, on the other hand, confident that he would be granted his divorce, played for Chris his videotapes of their wedding and honeymoon, which got to her, although Chris pretended they didn't. And when each of them received the divorce settlement papers, a shaken Phyllis could not bring herself to sign them, while an elated Danny waved them in front of Chris's face, insisting that they foreshadowed his freedom. Again, this got to Chris and she asked him to leave.

At the hearing, Danny testified that he never loved Phyllis. An injured Phyllis protested that she loved Danny with all her heart and desperately wanted their marriage to work. Danny, she declared, simply wouldn't give it a chance. The judge was persuaded and remanded the couple to seek marriage counseling.

In the meantime, Chris had become somewhat close to Victor Newman during Nicholas's prison debacle. Victor, in fact, offered her a position in the legal department at Newman Enterprises, which she turned down because, as it was, she felt professionally overextended and wanted to be personally available for her fiancé. Victor offered her a sympathetic ear over lunch, as Chris confided in him about her marriage to Danny and her engagement to Paul.

Later, a distraught Danny sought Chris out, wailing that he would now lose her forever. Chris tried to comfort him, and he responded. Soon, things went too far, and they were wrapped in each other's arms, making love. When Paul came by later that evening and saw them together, he turned around and quietly left, his dreams in shambles. Danny thought he had secured Chris's heart, but she insisted she'd marry Paul, and no one else. Their making love had been a huge mistake!

Victor once again was there for Chris, and he counseled her to keep quiet about her night with Danny, unless Paul confronted her. But Paul told Chris what he had seen and said the wedding was off. Then he punched Danny out for good measure, and wept bitter tears of frustration and regret afterward. Victor assured Chris that Paul would come around in time, but since she'd now have extra time on her hands, why not accept the position he offered her? And, call him "Victor," he smiled.

Mary, in the meantime, not understanding

what had really transpired, urged her son to repair things with Chris. Chris gave Paul the birthday gift she hadn't gotten around to giving him—a watch. Much later, he got around to wearing it, wondering if he was proceeding too slowly. Chris, he had noticed, was no longer wearing his ring.

Phyllis, a bit unsettled over the Christine/Paul breakup, swore she'd make certain that Danny and Christine were kept apart. When Phyllis and Danny reported to Dr. Tim Reid for counseling, Danny came off as being an angry and unreasonable lout, while Phyllis was genuine and cooperative. That is, until Danny brought out into the open the whole nine yards: how Phyllis entrapped him by drugging him the night Daniel was conceived. But Phyllis stuck to her guns,

Poor, naïve Tim Reid! He was entirely out of his league with Phyllis the temptress.

maintaining she was completely innocent of any such behavior. Why would she do something like that?

Phyllis was now choreographing two parallel dances: one in which Peter Garrett would get close to Daniel, as if they were father and son; the other in which she would work her wiles on Dr. Reid, who clearly had never dealt this intimately with a woman. Dr. Reid knew it was unethical but he couldn't help himself. Phyllis seduced him, not once but twice; and the second time she recorded the seduction on videotape! She said she'd show it to the judge if Tim didn't recommend against the divorce. But Dr. Reid's code of ethics got the best of him—he confessed everything, and the judge granted Danny's divorce!

One evening, Victor was talking to Christine in his office when a gunshot tore through his body! Victor fell to the floor and lay in a pool of blood. Christine screamed, saw the elevator doors close, and called the paramedics, who rushed Victor to the hospital. Nikki and Brad were at the altar ready to exchange vows when the telephone call about Victor's shooting came. Nikki rushed to the hospital,

Christine called the paramedics and they frantically worked to save Victor's life.

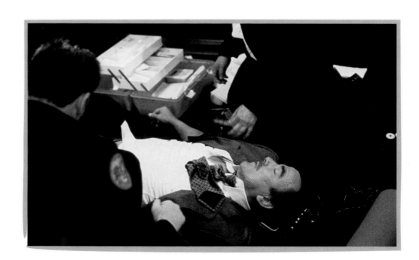

too distraught to complete the recitation of her vows. For hours Nikki and her children waited for word as to whether Victor's life might be saved. Nicholas was inconsolable and screamed for justice as members of his family tried to calm him down.

As the days passed, and Victor was steadily recovering, he insisted upon conducting his own investigation. There were three principal suspects: Brad Carlton, Jill Abbott, and Mari Jo Mason.

At first Brad was thought to be the number one suspect. He had a mile-long string of motives for wanting to do Victor in. Recently, Victor had expressed dissatisfaction with Brad's job performance, and passed him over for a promotion that he gave to Jack Abbott. Then he fired Brad on the day of his wedding to Nikki.

The second suspect was Jill Abbott, who resented Victor's interference in her custody and divorce battle against her husband, John. Victor had issued an ultimatum that if Jill did anything to hurt John, there'd be hell to pay as far as her job at Jabot was concerned! Jill was heard to issue a warning of her own for Victor

to stay out of her life or he'd regret it. Furthermore, Jill had a gun that she was good at firing, and ballistics had identified it as the gun used in the shooting!

And finally, there was the third suspect, Mari Jo Mason. She had been trying to prevent Victor from showing Jack a fax from Keemo—filled with the details of her underhanded schemes.

Brad was soon dropped as a suspect as his gun was not a match for the one that was used in the shooting. Victor knew it wasn't Jill, even though she had been arrested. When Mari Jo reluctantly came forward with a statement that she had seen Jill in her office at the time of the shooting, the case against Jill was dismissed.

Victor suspected Mari Jo, and told her he had the imaging roll to reproduce Keemo's incriminating fax (Mari Jo had stolen the original from Victor's office). He told her he had put it in the hands of an associate (Christine) just in case something should happen to him.

After leaving Genoa City, Victor went to see Hope in Kansas to tell her about the shooting and to renew himself spiritually. Nikki was piqued that Victor refused her invitation for him to recuperate at the ranch and have his Genoa City family take care of him.

When Victor did return, he was on his way to Nikki's to propose to her, because his brush with death made him realize how much he truly loved her and how much Victoria and Nicholas wanted them to be together. He had even bought the ring. And he'd told Nikki he had something special to ask her. But before he could get to Nikki's, he received a call that

There was no love lost between Jill Abbott and Victor Newman, but she was shocked to learn she was a primary suspect in his shooting.

The dangerous and deranged Mari Jo went to extreme measures to keep her long trail of lies a secret from Jack.

Chris's life was in jeopardy until Victor and Paul came to her rescue.

Cliff had been critically injured by a drunk driver, and he hurried back to Hope. Cliff soon would die.

When Nikki heard that Victor had returned to Kansas, she mistakenly thought his reason was to bed Hope. Nikki blew her chance to get what she so desperately wanted all of these years, and jumped immediately into an impetuous marriage with Dr. Joshua Landers in Las Vegas—a marriage that Nicholas tipped Victor off to, and which they both tried to head off.

Victor resumed his investigation of his shooting. By this time, Mari Jo had suspected that Christine was the business associate to whom Victor had entrusted the evidence. She drugged Chris and injected her with truth serum, hoping she'd talk. Mari Jo kept Chris a prisoner in a little-used sound-proof storeroom at Jabot. Paul and Victor saved Chris through a tracking device they'd planted on Mari Jo that led them to the two women. Mari Jo pumped blank bullets into Chris, saying she did it all for Jack. She was committed to a mental institution.

Ryan, Nina, Cole, and Victoria became entangled in a romantic quadrangle. Nina and Vicki had been rivals for some time now, having both competed for Ryan's attention. But Victoria's rocky marriage to Ryan years ago was now remembered in the happiest light; it was inevitable that their proximity at Jabot should throw them together in any number

of professional and personal situations. Vicki's marriage to Cole didn't inhibit her Ryan-chasing activities in any way, and Nina, as Ryan's wife, was thrust into a close and mutually satisfying relationship with Cole when Ryan suggested that Cole might give Nina some constructive criticism on her writing. Cole was so impressed with Nina that he hired her as his research assistant. The four continued to fight, make up, and change partners all year long.

Finally, there were many other happenings throughout the year that were worthy of note. Ashley was attacked by muggers and was saved by a Kurt Costner, who was also badly assaulted. Diane Jenkins came back into Jack's life and became convinced he had changed. Jack pursued the acquisition of Dennison-Vanguard against Victor's orders. Keith

Phyllis followed Chris and Paul to Nevis, intent on spoiling the lovers' romantic getaway. In the bag? An octopus that she would plant in the newlyweds' bed!

Ryan, Nina, Cole, and Victoria all wondered whether their marriages would be able to withstand the strong feelings each held for the other's mate.

Dennison and Jill became lovers. The love of Jack's life, the gentle Luan, died. Dina reluctantly came back to Genoa City to reconcile with John. After John proposed, she returned to France, still single. Tony Viscardi came to town to be near Grace. Sharon frequently thought of the baby she gave up for adoption, but Grace told her to concentrate on the good life she was now living. Drucilla signed a modeling contract with Kellum and Rogers against Neil's wishes. Phyllis and Danny grew closer after Daniel nearly died of meningitis. Paul and Chris married and honeymooned in Nevis, where Phyllis carried out her hijinks, while Tim Reid looked on in nervous embarrassment.

Storyline
1997

The clock struck 12, ushering in the New Year. Crashing a party at Nick and Sharon's, Tony found himself looking at the snooty Victoria Newman in a new light ever since he discovered that she was the daughter of Victor Newman! Meanwhile, at another party, Danny had just proposed to his unstoppable ex-wife, Phyllis, who joyously accepted, and they married shortly afterward.

Tony continued to flirt with Victoria. She was feeling unfulfilled in her marriage to the straitlaced Cole, who was always chained to his computer. Not only was Cole preoccupied with the lives of his fictional characters, but he was trying to lift his good friend and newly rehired research assistant, Nina McNeil, out of her own funk, which was caused by her marital woes with her husband (and Vicki's ex), Ryan. When Cole informed Victoria that the McNeils were going to take a stab at getting back on track, Vicki went straight to her former husband to express her hurt and displeasure. She then headed for the coffeehouse, where Cole found her dancing seductively with Tony. Cole confronted them and ended up in a fistfight with Tony. Vicki told Cole she wanted more excitement in her life, whereupon she packed her bags and left Genoa City to try to sort things out.

Perhaps it was something in the genes of the Newman kids, for Nicholas Newman was also experiencing the same feelings of dissatisfaction and anomie as his sister. The source of Nick's problem rested squarely with his father. With Victor venting his rage over the Dennison-Vanguard acquisition—a sound business deal orchestrated by Jack, Jill, and Nick without Victor's authorization—Nick couldn't help feeling he was in a no-win situation. So he made up his mind: as soon as his baby was born, he intended to leave Genoa City with his family. He was already looking for employment out of state, which caused Nikki to come down really hard on her daughter-in-law to do *something* to stop him!

When Sharon ventured out into blizzard-like conditions to pay Nikki a visit, the pregnant, fragile mother-to-be slipped and fell, only to remain partially buried and completely unconscious in the swirling snow for hours until Nick found her. For many days, Sharon's condition (and that of her unborn child) was unstable, but she was in the capable hands of Dr. Joshua Landers and appeared to be on the upswing. Then something went terribly wrong. Sharon doubled up in pain, bleeding. Immediate surgery was necessary—risky surgery that might cost Sharon her life.

The mysterious and kind Kurt Costner wandered into Genoa City and soon occupied a special place in Ashley's heart.

Linda Costner
131 GREENBRIAR STREET
YARMOUTH, CAPE COD, MA 02675

Dear Kurt:
This is the hardest letter I've ever had to write. I know this will come as a terrible shock to you. I have done everything I could to keep you from learning how much my feelings have changed. But I can't keep it from you any longer. There's someone else I'm desperately in love with. It's not your fault. It's nothing you've done or haven't done. It's me. I've changed. It's been happening for a long time. I've fought it, tried to keep my feelings for you alive. But now, I can't deny it any longer.

Joshua noticed that Victor's presence was causing so much tension that he had to ask him to leave. Much later, when Joshua went home to find Nikki and Victor kissing, he asked Victor to leave again. Then he issued an ultimatum to his wife: It was Victor or him. Victor was no longer welcome in their home!

Hope had a way about her that encouraged people to open up to her. It wasn't too long before the mysterious Kurt Costner was confiding in her, and told her that his wife and daughter had died in a senseless automobile accident back home in Cape Cod. Hope shared this with Ashley; both women had a slowly simmering attraction to Kurt. A low-key rivalry for his attentions ensued.

To help Kurt confront his past (and hopefully move on to a productive future), Ashley purchased two plane tickets to Cape Cod. Once there, Ashley found and pocketed a sealed letter from Linda, Kurt's deceased wife. At his insistence, Ashley returned to Genoa City without him. Ashley opened the letter on the plane and read that Linda had been planning to leave Kurt for another man. Linda had died before she could tell him. Ashley's quandary: should she tell Kurt the truth or let him remember his wife his way?

Kurt returned quietly to Genoa City. He asked Katherine for room and board in exchange for work on her estate. Katherine and Esther were both fond of him and loved having a man around the house again. But, at some point, Katherine just couldn't stand Kurt's brooding any longer, so she played the matchmaker and invited Ashley to come to the estate for dinner. This angered Kurt and he quarreled with Ashley. Finally, realizing that both women were only trying to reach out and do what they thought was best for him, Kurt reconciled with Ashley, and then returned to the Cape with the intention of putting his house on the market. Ashley followed him there.

Widower Keith Dennison raised his two daughters to be considerate and respectful young ladies. The trio was close, though he didn't approve of Tricia's new beau.

While there, Kurt discovered a cache of incriminating photos of Linda, and realized his wife had been having an affair. Ashley showed Kurt the letter his wife had written, hoping he'd realize that Linda *had* intended to tell him everything. Then, when Grant, Linda's lover, appeared, posing as a prospective home buyer but really wanting to gain access to the house to remove the pictures, a raging Kurt held a gun on him. Luckily for Grant, his wife showed up and pleaded for her husband's life. Kurt let Grant go and burned the photos and the letter. He was finally ready to start a new chapter in his life.

Kurt's background as a medical doctor surfaced one night when he performed a cricothyrotomy on Hope, who was choking over dinner. Victor felt deep gratitude toward Kurt for coming first to Ashley's rescue and then Hope's, and he tried to use his influence to secure Kurt a top position in Genoa City's medical community. Kurt didn't want Victor's help; he didn't even know if he wanted to resume practicing medicine. But Kurt eventually opened a clinic in one of the poorer parts of town, where he could provide free or affordable health care to the needy. Hope worked for him as a volunteer.

Ultimately, Kurt didn't wish to get further involved with Hope or Ashley, and left town. Hope returned to Kansas, taking Victor Jr. with her.

Meanwhile, Neil Winters was undergoing his own brand of pain, as Dru continued to accept modeling gigs that would take her away from home for extended periods. Imbued with a strong sense of family, Neil found himself turning to Dru's sister, Olivia, for companionship and understanding. Finally, unable to deal with his wife's absences any longer, Neil phoned Sid, Dru's agent, and made it appear that Dru was in agreement with his desire for her to scale down her assignments. After Drucilla learned from Sid of Neil's ploy, she furiously chewed her husband out for interfering in her career.

Jack Abbott, however, was walking on cloud nine, as far as his personal life was concerned. Diane Jenkins had accepted his marriage proposal, and things would be perfect were Victor not making his professional life so miserable over the Dennison-Vanguard venture. Diane earnestly tried to explain Jack to Victor so that he might better understand her fiancé, but Victor invited her to dinner so that Diane would get to know and understand *Victor Newman* better!

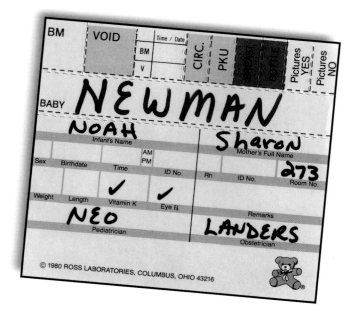

BM	VOID		Time / Date	CIRC.	PKU	BREAST	BOTTLE	Pictures YES	Pictures NO
		BM							
		V							

BABY NEWMAN

NOAH — Infant's Name

Sharon — Mother's Full Name

Sex	Birthdate	Time	AM PM	ID No.	Rh	ID No.	Room No. 273

Weight	Length	Vitamin K ✔	Eye ℞ ✔	Remarks

NEO — Pediatrician

LANDERS — Obstetrician

© 1980 ROSS LABORATORIES, COLUMBUS, OHIO 43216

When John Abbott saw Jill kissing Keith Dennison, he realized that Jill was becoming more than just a little interested in her new business associate. Keith arranged for Jill to meet his two daughters, Megan and Tricia, unaware that they were not particularly thrilled about the new woman in his life.

By this time, Sharon had given birth to a premature baby boy whose chances for survival were practically nil. Grace, distraught that her best friend was in such physical and emotional distress, and believing that Sharon's newborn wouldn't survive, decided to search for the child Sharon had years ago given up for adoption. She wanted to do something positive—to bring some happiness back into Sharon's life. Tony, thinking this was not such a hot idea, went along with it, anyway. There was no way he'd have Grace go off by herself.

They began their search in Madison, Wisconsin, where they contacted Frank Barritt, the baby's father. Grace persuaded him to produce the legal papers he had signed giving up all rights to his and Sharon's child. The papers led them to a prison where the lawyer who had handled the adoption was serving time for an unrelated matter. He was old and

sick, and at first had no interest in helping Grace and Tony. But later, he thought better of it and, on his deathbed, left them a note directing them to an Alice Johnson, who didn't reside at the address they were given. Instead, they found a tired, old woman named Mildred living there. She told them next to nothing. As Grace and Tony turned to leave, disconsolate, a school bus stopped in front of the house, and an appealing, wistful little girl of about six got off and went into the house. She turned out to be Cassie, Sharon's little girl.

Sharon and Nick's baby was barely hanging on to life when Sharon said she wanted her son to be baptized. The ceremony was carried out in the hospital and the baby was named Noah. Miraculously, the infant almost immediately began to improve; but when Grace called from out of town, a hospital staffer led Grace to believe that the baby had died. Grace begged Mildred to allow her and Tony to reunite Cassie with her biological mother. Mildred, whose own daughter had adopted Cassie only to abandon her, finally agreed to Grace's pleas. Grace rushed to the hospital, aching to tell Sharon she had a surprise for her that would blow her away. When a nurse entered carrying little Noah, a stunned Grace made an on-the-spot decision that this would be too great of an emotional strain for Sharon to handle. She'd tell her friend another time.

One night, when Grace offered to baby-sit for Sharon, she fell asleep in the spare bed in the nursery. Nicholas came home drunk, stopped to check in on his son, and slept with Grace, thinking she was Sharon. Grace did nothing to stop him, so her heretofore innocent crush on her best friend's husband would begin to make her life more and more unmanageable. It made

Dear Santa,
I don't want any
gifts for Christmas
this year. All I want
is for my mommy and
DaDDy to get married
and make us a real
family. That would
be The best present
of all. You don't
have to bring me
anything else.
Thank You!
Love Cassie.

Sharon got it into her head to play match-maker between Grace and Tony. He liked the idea; so did Cassie, who prayed that the three of them would become a family. That Mommy (Grace) would marry Tony was all she asked of Santa at Christmas. Tony frowned on all of this, though he loved both Grace and Cassie dearly. He constantly nagged Grace to return Cassie to her rightful mother (Sharon), but Grace proposed marriage to him, hinting they could leave Genoa City and become the family Cassie wanted. The longer she withheld the truth from Sharon, the stronger her bond to Cassie became. Grace couldn't bear to give the girl up!

Neil and Dru continued to disagree over Dru's commitment to her career, and in the wake of Sid's canceling one of Dru's contracts, Dru pleaded with Neil to reconsider. Later, when Dru was asked on a TV talk show to name the person she would give the most credit to for her successful modeling career, Dru replied, with all her heart, that the credit would have to go to her understanding and supportive husband, Neil. Touched by her sincerity, Neil romanced Dru and told her he wanted them to have another baby! What no one would know was that although Dru told Neil she was ready to have a second child, she secretly continued to take her birth control pills.

In the meantime, romance began to thrive for Neil's brother, Malcolm, and Dru's sister, Olivia. Little Nate was continuously expressing his longing for Malcolm to become his daddy, and when Malcolm proposed to Olivia on bended knee, Nate was in seventh heaven!

no sense to Nick when he later went to the master bedroom that Sharon was there, fast asleep. He put two and two together, but said nothing to Sharon. It became a secret that Nick shared only with Cole—and Grace, of course. To compound his discomfort, Nick and Grace would become a team at Newman Enterprises working side by side under the watchful eye of Jack Abbott.

Grace waited too long to reveal the truth about Cassie. The young girl began to call Grace "Mommy," and Grace began to love her as if she were her own daughter.

Neil's happiness was short-lived, because after months of trying to conceive, he accidentally discovered the birth control pills in Dru's purse. He realized that she had been deceiving him all along, and he moved out.

On other fronts, other Genoians were experiencing personal problems of their own. John Abbott became increasingly distressed by Jill's alliance with Keith Dennison, which led him to propose that he be given custody of little Billy. Jill challenged him to go ahead and try!

Nina and Ryan McNeil felt their lives were starting to unravel when a depressed Nina couldn't precisely define the reason for her dissatisfaction with life in general. Later, of course, Tricia Dennison became a major player in their lives, making the schism between Ryan and Nina appear to be unbridgeable.

As for Cole, he had just gotten used to being without Victoria when she returned unexpectedly from her European trip, saying that saving her marriage was her number one priority! In addition to learning that she lost her position as director of Brash & Sassy to Ryan, she learned that Ashley Abbott had become a serious competitor for Cole's affections!

Non-Genoians also made their presence known. For one, Joshua's first wife, Veronica Landers—whom he had presumed dead—recognized a photo of Joshua in a newspaper, which kindled her desire to be reunited with him. She escaped from a mental institution; got run over by a car, which left her face disfigured; and went through reconstructive surgery, which made her look like an entirely different person. She secured a position as a maid for the Landers, where, as "Sarah," she'd bide her time before making her next move.

And then there was Sasha, who began making moves to blackmail Phyllis, demanding a substantial sum of money to keep from exposing her to Danny—or it was off to the tabloids she'd go!

Finally, Michael Baldwin was paroled, and landed a position as a paralegal in Genoa City.

Jack Abbott found he was no match for Victor Newman when it came to sweeping Diane off her feet. Victor not only offered Diane a top-secret assignment any architect would die for (designing the new Newman Towers), but he completely mesmerized her with impetuous and extravagant gifts. On a business trip during which they were to discuss the project, he proposed to Diane on the Newman jet, married her in Nevada, and honeymooned with her in Greece. After Jack got over the shock of losing Diane to his archrival, he decided to remain Diane's close friend and confidant.

What Diane didn't realize was that when she married Victor, his former wife Nikki and their grown children became part of the package! Every cause for celebration—be it holiday, birthday, or special occasion—seemed to take place at the ranch, hosted by Nikki, in the spirit of upholding cherished Newman traditions. This left no room for Victor and Diane to begin establishing their own traditions.

But the icing on the cake: when Nikki suggested that Victor get a vasectomy, he *did*, effectively denying Diane what she wanted more than anything else in this world—to have Victor's child! The two women took a profound dislike for each other.

Although Ryan had informed Tricia early on in their relationship that he was a married man and had a young son, Tricia just couldn't stay away from him. When Nina and Ryan agreed on a 30-day trial

reconciliation period, no one could have been more ecstatic than Nina, nor more sincere in his resolve to make things work than Ryan. But Tricia deliberately set out to make Ryan jealous by cozying up to her pal, Alec, and incurred Nina's wrath to such a point that Nina lost her cool and threatened Tricia, to which Ryan took exception. Nina's subsequent attempts to seduce Ryan were failures, and her misrepresentation of these attempts to Jill drove Ryan wild, prompting him to tell Nina their marriage was over. He moved out.

By this time, Ryan was half crazed with jealousy over Tricia's continuing "interest" in Alec, so he decided to divorce Nina. But he failed to consider the devastating effect it would have on his son, Phillip. Then, when Nina disappeared and Ryan had reason to believe the worst, Tricia was by his side, comforting him. But a despondent Nina resurfaced, armed with a pistol, and threatened to shoot herself in Ryan's pres-

ence. In an effort to save Nina, Ryan struggled with her, and the gun went off. Nina fell to the floor, critically wounded. As Ryan was arrested for attempted murder, Nina hovered between life and death. She recovered slowly, and for a time she couldn't remember a thing about the shooting. Once things were straightened out, however, Nina resolved to put her life back together—*without* Ryan. It was she who instituted the divorce proceedings, and though he was deeply saddened by what was happening to their family, Phillip supported his mother, and wanted nothing more to do with Ryan.

Ryan grieved because his love for Phillip was genuine, but he was also relieved that Nina had freed him to pursue his relationship with Tricia. Nina promised not to drag Tricia through the mud in the divorce proceedings, much to Ryan's relief—and Jill's.

After Phyllis had more than proven what a fit mother she was to Daniel after his life-threatening bout with meningitis, and Danny resigned himself to the fact that Chris was indeed happy in her new life with Paul, Danny realized that he and Phyllis and Daniel *did* share something special. He remarried her—to everyone's disbelief!—but things started to go wrong when Sasha reappeared shortly thereafter. Phyllis successfully intercepted Sasha's package to Danny, which contained the incriminating manuscript detailing how Phyllis had the original paternity test doctored in the New York lab. But a crazed and anxious Phyllis, worried that Sasha would ruin her marriage by revealing the truth, became easy prey for Sasha's blackmail scheme. Then Sasha died fire, and Phyllis moved heaven and earth to track down the telltale manuscripts, which Sasha said she had liberally distributed in case something were to happen to her.

When Danny insisted that a second paternity test be taken to dispel any question he was Daniel's father, it was Michael Baldwin who suggested that Phyllis get a blood sample from Daniel's real father, Brian Hamilton. She invited Brian to Genoa City, drugged him, and then substituted *his* blood for Danny's. Once again, it appeared that Phyllis had won, for the test confirmed that the donor of the blood sample was indeed Daniel's father. But Danny, unbeknownst to Phyllis, had had a second sample taken, and it revealed that he was not Daniel's father. Phyllis finally admitted to a furious Danny that she had doctored the tests but, in a desperate effort to hold her family together, insisted that she did it out of love. Danny immediately sued for divorce and custody of Daniel. He asked Christine to represent him.

The trial dragged on, with its highs and its lows, at times giving Chris and Danny hope and at other times plunging them into the depths of despair. When a recess was called over the holidays, Chris and Paul holed up in their apartment, shutting out the world, and leading everyone to believe they had gone to some far-off vacation spot. It was a time for love and renewal for both, which they sorely missed and badly needed. For Christine's renewed involvement in her ex-husband's life had been taking its toll on her marriage to Paul.

As the year came to a close, life was about to change for a number of Genoa City's children: on Christmas day, Lily missed Neil, who was stubborn in his resolve to stay away from Dru; Cassie sensed the tension as Tony prodded Grace about Sharon's right to know that Cassie was her daughter; and Daniel was saddened by his parents' ongoing feud. On a more celebratory note, Jack hosted a New Year's Eve party at Gina's for his friends: Katherine (who was radiant with her facial rejuvenation), Jill, Nina, Lynne, Victoria, Neil, Olivia, and Malcolm. Jack asked each of them to share their fondest dreams for the new year. Then they lifted their glasses.

For a short while, the Romalottis were the picture of happiness and contentment—to the astonishment of their family and friends. But it all came crashing down when little Daniel's true paternity came to light.

The year began on a note of complex interpersonal relationships centering around family, love and romance, careers, and matters of conscience.

Grace prayed for guidance as to how to deal with her terrible bind—loving someone else's child as if she were her own and having that child love and trust her in return. With Tony's admonition ringing in her ears, she told Sharon everything but pleaded for time to salve the hurt she thought might occur. Sharon, in return, was ecstatic—so much so that Nicholas suspected she was pregnant. When she assured him she wasn't, Nick told her he was glad because the time just wasn't right to expand their family.

The divorce and custody trial between Danny and Phyllis

Tony and Grace made a handsome couple, but they didn't always see eye to eye.

planted seeds of doubt in Paul's mind about the stability of his marriage to Christine, as did his mother, and his insecurity only grew as Chris told him she wasn't ready to start a family.

Dru and Neil remained estranged as the year began. But after months of soul-searching, Neil started to forgive her and both decided to give their marriage a second chance. Perhaps in vitro fertilization was the answer.

Right after the new year, Tricia and Ryan returned from their ski trip. It was the first time Tricia had ever made love, and although Ryan was a tender, sensitive lover, the experience stirred up a lot of emotions. Keith had acted as mother and father for so long, but he was so opposed to her relationship with Ryan that she just couldn't talk to him about her intense feelings. She did confide in Jill and Megan her thoughts about becoming a woman. But mostly, she missed her mother. She also began to display a more subtle possessiveness toward Ryan, and was impatient for him to divorce Nina. Neil, who'd been staying with Ryan, moved back in

resumed after a holiday recess, with Danny in the end winning on both counts, and Phyllis reacting as if "someone had shoved a corkscrew through her heart." Sasha's manuscript had turned up, and apparently turned the tide in Danny's favor. Danny was deliriously happy, but he needed someone to help him raise Daniel. Even though Joani, Daniel's longtime nanny, was an obvious short-term solution, Christine was the woman Danny wanted, and he vowed to win her back. Katherine repeatedly encouraged Danny to pursue Christine if he thought there was any possibility that he could win her back. An on-the-edge Phyllis

Sarah had an uncanny way of knowing Joshua's likes and dislikes. How long would she conceal the fact that she was his first wife, Veronica?

When it came to matters of family, the Winters boys and the Barber girls were of one mind and one heart.

Victoria wondered if dating Tony or Ryan might arouse her husband's jealousy. Alec got a job at Jabot, where he got off on the wrong foot with Victoria. Tony packed up and moved out after all, because of Grace's reluctance to truly let go of Cassie.

Sharon experienced great mood swings as she grew closer to Cassie. With Grace working hard at Newman Enterprises, Cassie began to spend more and more time at the ranch, to Sharon's great pleasure. But Sharon grew paranoid about Grace and Tony, and asked Paul Williams to investigate and keep an eye on them. Victor and Nikki sensed the change in Sharon: Victor suspected she was involved with another man, and went so far as to accuse Tony. Nikki, on the other hand, thought Sharon was obsessed with Cassie (as did Nicholas), and tried to eke whatever information she could out of Doris, who kept her daughter's confidence.

What none of them knew was that Cassie's adoptive mother, Alice Johnson, was furious with Mildred for giving Cassie up, and was hell-bent on finding the girl at any cost.

with his wife and daughter, and Tricia was set on becoming Ryan's new roommate.

Veronica began to fantasize about revealing herself to Joshua, determined that Nikki should not have him. She ran out of the medication she'd been taking since she left the mental institution, spied on Nikki, and began to thwart Miguel's interest in her. Joshua, meanwhile, asked Nikki to consider having a child with him.

A lot of other changes were going on in Genoa City. John Abbott wanted Billy back home where he belonged, instead of in a boarding school, and asked John Silva to explore a custody suit on his behalf. Nina was experiencing the joys of authorship, with the acceptance of her first manuscript. Cole wanted to end his marriage to Victoria (who'd recently been appointed president of Brash & Sassy);

To be continued . . .

Family Trees

THE BROOKSES

The blue-blooded Brooks family was headed by newspaper publisher Stuart Brooks and his socialite wife, Jennifer. Stuart owned and operated the *Chronicle,* Genoa City's only newspaper. Together, Stuart and Jennifer had three beautiful daughters—Leslie, Chris, and Peggy—and raised their fourth, Lorie, an enigmatic whirlwind of a girl, who was so unlike the other three that it caused them to wonder how that could be. Stuart eventually learned that Lorie had been fathered by his best friend, Dr. Mark Henderson.

Stuart Brooks

Stuart was a caring, disciplined, old-fashioned father who, totally involved in the lives of his brood, held them accountable for meeting the high standards of moral behavior he set for them. He was devoted to his wife, and though she had transgressed during the course of their marriage, he stuck by her, forgave her, and loved her with all his heart. Later, after Jennifer died, Stuart briefly married Jill Foster, who he believed was carrying his child (she wasn't). Then he married his onetime mother-in-law, Liz Foster, for whom he had genuine feelings.

Jennifer Brooks

Jennifer had a certain delicate poignancy about her. Though she had everything she could want in terms of money and loving family, she was beset by the feeling that life was passing her by. She felt compelled to reach out for the brass ring on pain of forever regretting it if she didn't. At one point in their marriage, she so shocked and angered Stuart by revealing she had had an extramarital affair (one which she wanted to renew!); as a result, he suffered a cardiac arrest.

Leslie Brooks

She spent the rest of her life trying to make up for it. She also made soap opera history by having a mastectomy when only women in real life had such operations.

Of the Brooks girls, Leslie was the introverted one, but she was multi-talented as a concert pianist and cabaret singer. Her marriage to Brad Eliot marked her triumph over her manipulative sister Lorie, whereas the memorable evening she shared with Lance Prentiss, after the two had suppressed years of desire and longing, changed their lives forever. Her close relationships to her mentor, Maestro Fautsch; to Lance's brother, Lucas; and to her son, Brooks, whom Lance had fathered, were deep and sincere.

Peggy Brooks

Lauralee "Lorie" Brooks

Lorie, the catalyst for so many of the explosive disruptions in the Brooks household, was a successful novelist who unfortunately gained more happiness out of "making believe" than out of real life. Though she had many lovers, the one true love of her life turned out to be her half brother, Mark Henderson!

Chris Brooks was a social worker and journalist. Her love for Snapper Foster put everything she was or would ever want to be in perspective.

Finally, the fourth and youngest Brooks child, Peggy, was a college co-ed who, unfortunately, experienced rape of both body and soul. But she had the courage and the physical and moral fortitude to survive the bad times, and learned to be true to herself and to those for whom she cared.

Brooks Prentiss

Chris Brooks

Family Trees
THE FOSTERS

Though the blue-collar Fosters came from humble beginnings, as in many American families, the next generation of children was upwardly mobile. The family matriarch, Liz Foster, struggled to raise her three children as a single mother, attempting to instill in them high moral values. Her husband, William Foster Sr.—the father of her children—had abandoned the family many years before, forcing Liz to work at her factory job for Chancellor Industries to put food on the table. Her eldest son, William Foster Jr. (Snapper), became a doctor. The middle child, Greg, became a lawyer. The youngest, Jill, pursued a different career path, taking on a job as a beautician to help put her brothers through school. Jill, however, eventually married her way into Genoa City's high society and became a prominent businesswoman.

William Foster Sr.

When Liz's terminally ill husband returned home to die, Liz not only welcomed him back with open arms, but also renewed her marriage vows with him. Unable to bear his suffering, however, she pulled the plug on his respirator, and then promptly erased any memory of having done so. Several years later, she married her longtime friend,

Liz Foster

William "Snapper" Foster Jr.

Greg Foster

newspaper publisher Stuart Brooks, and left Genoa City with him in 1982 to start life anew. The last time Liz returned was in 1994 when her grandson, William Foster Abbott (Billy), was born.

Snapper fell in love with the beautiful Chris Brooks, but before he married her, he had an affair with Sally McGuire, who bore his son, Chuckie. On the wedding day of Snapper's mother and Chris's father, the young couple graced their parents with a new granddaughter, Jennifer Elizabeth Foster.

Jill Foster

Greg was best man at Snapper and Chris's wedding.

After Greg graduated from Yale Law School, he met and married Nikki Reed, who desperately wanted to be a model. They divorced after a brief, troublesome marriage. He met and loved other women after that, but none as passionately as Nikki. He, too, left Genoa City.

Snapper's son, Chuckie

Family Trees
THE CHANCELLORS

The history of the Chancellor family is deeply rooted in the history of Genoa City, which was founded by Civil War hero Garfield Dandridge Chancellor. In 1973, Garfield's great-great-grandson, Phillip Chancellor II, was running Chancellor Industries. He resided in the Chancellor mansion with his alcoholic and promiscuous wife, Katherine (Kay). The two barely communicated with each other as husband and wife, and the lonely Phillip, driven to distraction by Katherine's obsessive behavior, sought refuge in the company of Katherine's young and beautiful paid companion, Jill Foster. Phillip and Jill fell in love, Jill got pregnant, and Phillip demanded a divorce—setting off a long and bitter feud between the two women. But Katherine got her revenge by driving Phillip over a cliff, killing him.

Phillip Chancellor

Katherine had an adult son, Brock Reynolds, from a previous marriage. Brock, who was a "sometimes" minister, a "sometimes" lawyer, and a "sometimes" entertainer, tried his best to keep his mother from obsessing. Sometimes he succeeded and sometimes he failed. But there was no question that mother and son loved each other dearly. At one point, before

Katherine Chancellor

Brock Reynolds

Phillip's death, Katherine even managed to convince Brock to marry Jill himself so that she might effect a reconciliation with Phillip. Brock performed the ceremony.

Jill and Phillip's son, Phillip III, became yet another point of conflict between the two women, who were to do battle over his custody and name change (to "Chancellor") for years to come. While in his late teens, Phillip III married Nina Webster, which displeased both Jill and Katherine, who considered Nina to be beneath them. But Phillip and Nina shared some happy times, and they had a son—Phillip IV. Unfortunately, Phillip III, a young alcoholic, died in a DWI accident in 1989.

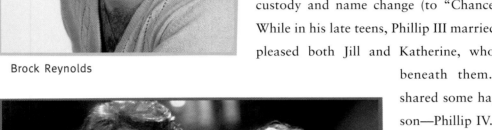

Phillip III, Phillip IV, and Nina

Katherine herself was a recovering alcoholic. A lonely woman, with only her longtime maid, Esther Valentine, to keep her company, Katherine was ready for a serious relationship. Jill played a joke on her, arranging for her to meet a madeover bum and ex-convict, whom Jill dubbed "Rex Sterling." But Katherine and Rex fell in love and they married for the first time in 1988, and then again in 1992 after a misunderstanding had briefly separated them. Rex had two grown children in Genoa City—restaurateur Gina Roma and rock star Danny Romalotti—with whom they were close. Esther would later give birth to a daughter whom she named "Kate," for Katherine. Both Katherine and Rex truly lived life to the fullest until Rex's untimely death at the hands of an intruder (Esther's charlatan "husband") in 1994.

Gina, Katherine, Rex, and Danny

Family Trees

THE ABBOTTS

Having achieved their wealth through hard work, the socially prominent Abbotts are nonetheless a remarkably down-to-earth clan. From the oldest to the youngest, they openly show their love and affection for one another, and still have enough warmth and caring left over to pass around to a wide circle of friends, old and new.

While building Jabot Cosmetics, the family business, John Abbott, the doting father, struggled to hold the family together after his wife, Dina, deserted them during their children's adolescent years. The fact is that the family's loyal maid, Mamie Johnson, came to be regarded by the children as more of a substitute mother than a servant. Grateful for that, John and Mamie became close companions; that is, until Jill Foster, jealous wife No. 2 and No. 3, drove Mamie away. Out of John and Jill's second marriage in 1993 came William Foster Abbott ("Billy"). The two oldest children, Jack and Ashley, not only work in the family business, but still reside at home. Only Traci has struck out on her own.

Jack, John's only son from his first marriage, earned a BA from Harvard and an MBA from the Wharton School of Finance. Although he often wears two faces—a no-nonsense one for business dealings and an incredibly soft and cuddly one for his personal dealings—Jack is usually the guy who loses the girl. He is the father of Keemo Nguyen Volien, the son he shared with his Vietnamese angel-wife, Luan, whom he married on Valentine's Day 1995 after a long separation. Jack's first wife, Patty Williams, divorced him after a brief but turbulent marriage. His marriage to Nikki Newman in 1990 also ended in divorce, but the two have remained close friends to this day. Despite the fact that Jack and Victor

John Abbott Sr.

Dina Abbott Mergeron

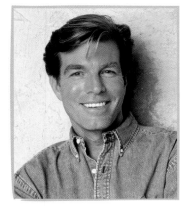

John "Jack" Abbott Jr.

Ashley Suzanne Abbott

Traci Ann Abbott Connelly

Jill, Billy, and John

Newman harbor deep personal resentm[...] each other, Jack holds an executive-level pos[...] at Newman Enterprises and is one of Newman's professional assets.

Ashley Suzanne appears to be her father's favorite, but only John and Traci seem to be unaware that Ashley's biological father was the late Brent Davis, with whom Dina had had an affair. Ashley has a degree in chemistry from the University of Colorado at Boulder, and is a sorority sister of Dr. Olivia Winters. Like many siblings, Ashley is quite close to her brother Jack, although they have a long history of butting heads (for example, he did not exactly support her relationship with Victor Newman, and she pretty much detested Jack's onetime fiancée, Diane Jenkins). Professionally speaking, Ashley is a great success: she runs a lab at Jabot Cosmetics and holds an executive title there as well. Unfortunately, Ashley's personal life has been filled with its share of disappointments. To date, she has been unlucky in love.

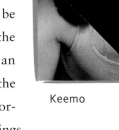

Keemo

Traci Ann, the youngest of John's grown children, has overcome her share of problems as well—most notably, she suffered from low self-esteem and insecurity brought upon by weight problems and eating disorders. Today, Traci is as dignified, well adjusted, and beautiful as her sister, Ashley. Traci, who attended Genoa City University and then went on to Stanford, received her master's in English. An on-again, off-again rivalry between Traci and Ashley over Traci's (twice) former husband, Brad Carlton, rarely rears its ugly head anymore. Sandwiched between her two marriages to Brad Carlton, Traci published two successful novels, *Echoes of the Past* and *Epitaph for a Lover*. Brad and Traci's daughter, Colleen Cecile, is John and Dina's only granddaughter, and lives with her mother and stepfather, editor Steve Connelly, in New York City.

Traci, Colleen, and Steve

~~Fami~~ly Trees
THE WILLIAMSES

...mily. Headed by Genoa City Police Department

...is away on special assignment, and his wife of 46

...on, Steven, is a newspaperman who accepted an

...newspaper in 1981 after Peggy Brooks jilted him and broke his heart. Patty, the

only daughter, also left Genoa City, joining her brother in Washington after her marriage to Jack Abbott

ended in divorce. The youngest member of the Williams nuclear family, Todd, is a priest, who does God's

work in Europe. He rarely comes home for a visit.

With Carl away so often, this leaves only Mary and Paul firmly rooted in Genoa City. To be sure, mother and son are close—sometimes too close to suit Paul. But luckily, Mary is heavily involved in her church work for the Church of the Sacred Heart.

Carl Williams

Mary Williams

Steven Williams

Paul operates his own private detective agency, Paul Williams Investigations. He has a young teenaged daughter, Heather, the product of his failed early marriage to April Stevens. Genoa City lawyer and longtime friend Christine Blair became his bride a few years ago.

Paul's daughter, Heather

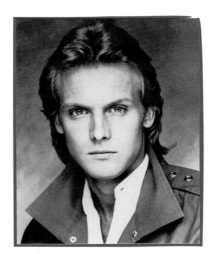

Paul Williams

Chris and Paul

Patty Williams

Family Trees

THE NEWMANS

Although Victor Newman and Nicole (Nikki) Reed, the greatest love of his life, are no longer coupled, the bond they share through their two children, Victoria and Nicholas Christian, will forever keep them involved in each other's lives.

As a boy, Victor, who was named Christian Miller, lived in an orphanage in Buffalo, New York. He was abandoned by his mother, Cora, who couldn't afford to raise him alone. For years, Victor resented her, and vowed he'd never want again. His appearance in Genoa City in 1980 marked the beginning of his phenomenal assent to power. He amassed a fortune, which, by today's standards, places him among the wealthiest men in the entire world. Branded "Ruthless" in a book written by one of his ex-wives, Victor Newman is enigmatically "soft" when it comes to family. His present wife is architect Diane Jenkins.

Victor Newman

Nikki is presently married to gynecologist Dr. Joshua Landers, whom she met in 1996 when she needed to consult with Dr. Laski, whose practice Dr. Landers had assumed. Nikki and Josh live at the ranch, where the hired help also reside: longtime chef, Miguel Rodriguez, makes life easier for them; the same cannot be said for their recent hire, "Sarah."

Victor and Nikki's first-born, Victoria (Vicki) Howard,

Nikki Newman Landers

Victoria Newman Howard

works at Jabot, one of the most successful companies under the Newman Enterprises umbrella. Precocious as a child, Vicki, who is married to Cole, causes both her parents, not to mention her husband, considerable concern over her brash and sassy behavior.

Nicholas Newman, who attended boarding school in Lucerne, recently graduated from Genoa City University. Though his young life has been marred by a series of overwhelming prob-

Sharon and Nicholas with baby Noah

lems, Nick—who resides in the foreman's house on the Newman ranch with his young wife, Sharon, and their infant son, Noah—appears to be on the road to success. He is learning the ropes from his father at Newman Enterprises.

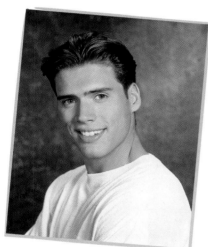

Nicholas Christian Newman

Victor's previous marriage to a blind farm owner, Hope Adams, brought out the less ruthless, more spiritual side of Victor. The two had more than one thing in common. Like Victor, Hope grew up in an orphanage, and they share a precious (and, thankfully, sighted) little boy, Victor Adam Newman Jr.

Vicki and Cole

Hope with Victor Jr.

Family Trees
THE BARBERS/WINTERS

The Barbers and the Winters are a complex African-American family who've had to learn the hard way that honesty and truth were the best ways to surmount the grave problems that threatened the entire family's happiness. The problems, which began with the titular heads of the family—Walter and Lillie Belle Barber—resulted in a serious fallout between their two daughters, Olivia and Drucilla (Dru). Time, marriage, and motherhood have helped both daughters mature, though the contentious nature of their relationship has a way of surfacing from time to time.

Olivia had always been Lillie Belle's favorite. As brilliant as she was beautiful, Olivia became a successful medical doctor. But being "favorite" also had its price. For Lillie Belle fell seriously ill and disrupted Olivia's relationship with her husband, Nathan Hastings, by demanding that Olivia choose between the two of them! As far as Lillie Belle was concerned, the resentment she harbored toward her own husband, Walter, for taking advantage of her in their marriage bed years ago, made going home an option that she couldn't even consider.

Drucilla, meanwhile, reacted to the favoritism shown

Walter Barber

Lillie Belle Barber

Olivia Barber Winters

Neil, Malcolm, and baby Lily

to her older sister all those years by feeling insecure and unworthy. In stark contrast to her sister's success, Dru was an illiterate high school dropout, living on the streets until her Aunt Mamie and Olivia's husband-to-be, Nathan, came to her rescue. Dru overcame her illiteracy, studied ballet, and embarked upon a successful modeling career.

In 1992, Olivia and Nathan had a child, Nathan Oliver (little Nate), and the next year Dru married Neil Winters. By this time, the sisters had reconciled, and Drucilla's mother had made peace with her as well. It wasn't too long before Neil's brother, Malcolm, entered their lives and became an uncle and godfather to Neil and Dru's baby, whom they named Lily Amanda after her maternal grandmother. When Olivia's husband was fatally run down by an automobile in 1996, the entire family, especially Malcolm, rallied around Olivia and little Nate with love and understanding. Malcolm, a successful photographer, recently married Olivia, much to little Nate's wholehearted approval. Now, with two brothers married to two sisters, their problems have yet to disappear. But it might be said that the Winters and the Winters have reached a new ground in having open and honest communication in trying to deal with their disagreements.

Mamie Johnson

Olivia and Nate

Drucilla Barber Winters

Lily

Romance in Genoa City
THE WEDDING ALBUM

Sally McGuire & Pierre Roulland

1973. Pierre had grown to care about waitress Sally McGuire, so when she broke down and admitted to him that she was expecting Snapper's baby, he did the noble thing and asked her to marry him. He wanted to ensure that the child would have a name, and, more importantly, a father. Pierre's sister, Marianne, thought he was making a big mistake. But Pierre knew he was doing the right thing, and he and Sally said their vows in a private ceremony and became husband and wife.

Chris Brooks & Snapper Foster

1974. She was an idealistic college student, whose family was comfortably well-off. He was a struggling medical student, whose family could barely make ends meet. Chris Brooks loved Snapper Foster from the moment she laid eyes on him, and knew that he was the man she'd one day marry. Snapper loved her, too, but the two young people had different ideas about premarital sex. Chris wanted to wait until they were wed, so Snapper turned to Sally McGuire for gratification. Then Chris was brutally raped by a mysterious intruder, and Snapper was there for her, wanting nothing more than to protect and shield her with his love. In time, Chris accepted his proposal of marriage, and in the presence of God, loving family, and close friends, they recited their vows.

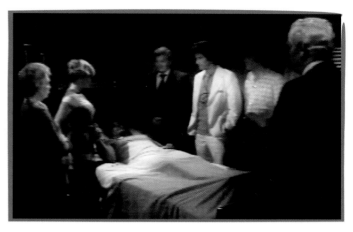

Leslie Brooks & Brad Eliot

1975. Introverted Leslie Brooks was an aspiring concert pianist when the mysterious stranger, Brad Eliot, walked into her life. It wasn't long before he became her best friend and greatest booster, encouraging Leslie to become everything she was capable of being. The two fell in love. Leslie's jealous sister, Lorie, would play the role of spoiler, wanting what was rightfully Leslie's—Brad—just because Leslie wanted him. Eventually, Brad realized just what kind of woman Lorie was and went back to Leslie. The couple wed and was happy at last.

Jill Foster & Phillip Chancellor

1975. It just happened: Phillip Chancellor's sudden realization of how much the young, beautiful, and vulnerable Jill Foster had come to mean to him, after all of those quiet times when they just sat around and talked. He had fallen in love with her! Jill, too, had never expected this to happen, but she responded to Phillip's love. When Katherine caught wise that she was in danger of losing her husband, she schemed to win Phillip back. She convinced her son, Brock, to marry Jill, and Brock performed the ceremony himself. When Jill realized she was pregnant, she knew Phillip had to be the father. She told Phillip that

her relationship with Brock was platonic and that their marriage wasn't legally binding. Overjoyed, Phillip flew to the Dominican Republic for a quickie divorce. Upon his return, Katherine drove their car over a cliff, badly injuring the two of them. In the presence of Jill's family, as he lay dying in his hospital bed, Phillip insisted upon marrying Jill to legitimize their baby.

Liz & Bill Foster

1976. It was Liz Foster's deep religious beliefs that sustained her during the years of struggle and hardship after her husband, Bill, deserted her. For nearly a decade, she wouldn't allow herself to entertain the thought that any other man could take her husband's place, and she steadfastly refused to declare him legally dead. When Bill walked back into her life a sick and broken man, asking that he be allowed to spend his remaining days surrounded by family, Liz's heart went out to him. The two renewed their marriage vows in the presence of their children and a few close friends.

Nikki Reed & Greg Foster

1979. Although Greg Foster's mother, Liz, at first thought Greg might be making the biggest mistake of his life, she came to accept Nikki Reed as the woman with whom her younger son would spend the rest of his life, and gave Greg her mother's ring to present to his bride-to-be. Nikki's dream was finally coming true as she and Greg made plans to marry. Nikki made a beautiful bride in the wedding gown her sister-in-law Chris had worn when she married Greg's brother, Snapper. Things wouldn't be easy for the young couple—after all, Greg was just starting his law practice. But it was Greg's love and support that gave Nikki the strength to put her past behind her and find a new direction in her own life.

Liz Foster & Stuart Brooks

1980. They came from two very different worlds. His success as the publisher of the *Genoa City Chronicle* was in stark contrast to the day-to-day struggle she faced to provide for her children. But Liz Foster and Stuart Brooks shared a unique bond based on mutual respect, commitment to family, trust, and mature love. It was the strength of that love that allowed them to put his relationship with (and short marriage to) Liz's daughter, Jill, behind them and look toward the future. Though Liz still had doubts that she

would fit in among Stuart's wealthy friends and business associates, she accepted his proposal. Stuart and Liz were treated to a double dose of happiness on their wedding day when they became not only husband and wife, but grandparents, as well, as Chris and Snapper's daughter, Jennifer Elizabeth Foster, entered the world!

Patty Williams & Jack Abbott

1982. For Jack Abbott, settling down and getting married to Patty Williams meant he would become president of Jabot—his father's wedding gift to him. For Patty, Jack was everything she could ever hope for in a husband. He was kind, generous to a fault, and wanted her to be happy. He even promised her a modeling career at Jabot! Though Patty's mother and father weren't certain he was the right man for her, they gave her their blessing. Carl and Mary wanted the

day to be special for their only daughter. John Abbott had offered to help with the expenses, but Carl's pride wouldn't allow it. They managed to plan a beautiful wedding within their means. Even Patty's brother, Paul, got involved. He purchased a gown for Patty that was more beautiful (and more expensive) than the one she'd chosen for herself. She couldn't have been happier! Patty asked Ashley to be her maid of honor, and Jack's younger sister Traci to be her bridesmaid. She hoped they would forge a lasting friendship. And Paul agreed to substitute as Jack's best man when Jack's best friend was unable to attend the ceremony. But Jack's sincerity had to be questioned. Poor, innocent Patty had no idea that her husband-to-be had spent his last night as a bachelor with the wily and beautiful Diane Jenkins. When Ashley discovered them together, she quickly sobered up Jack and threw Diane out. Ashley also promised Jack that if he ever hurt Patty, she would see to it that he would lose his newly acquired position of power at Jabot. Much to Jack's relief and Patty's delight, their wedding came off without a hitch!

Jill Foster & John Abbott

1982. Jill Foster and John Abbott took an immediate liking to each other when she went to work for him at Jabot. Though Jill had been seeing John's son, Jack, it was the kind and compassionate John with whom Jill could picture herself spending the rest of her life. Jill, considerably younger than John, brought excitement into John's life, and he soon realized he'd fallen in love with her. Jill happily accepted John's proposal and the two married in the Abbott home. Jack, still convinced John was making a mistake, agreed to be his father's best man, and Liz was

her daughter's matron of honor. After the ceremony, John and Jill jetted off to Paris for their honeymoon.

Nikki Reed & Victor Newman

1984. When business tycoon Victor Newman married the young and lovely Nikki Reed, he transported his bride into a magical world that only great love and great wealth, combined, could provide. Victor befitted Nikki in a wedding gown that was designed by one of Genoa City's top fashion houses and she was truly a vision in imported French silk-faced satin and organza, with a 10-foot train. Her headpiece was a royal crown, hand-beaded with over 20,000 small beads and pearls. The wedding was one of the most lavish Genoa City had ever seen, attracting guests that included family and close friends, as well as sheiks and oil barons from far and wide.

Eric Garrison, Ashley Abbott, & Marc Mergeron

1984. Ashley Abbott had fallen deeply in love with Eric Garrison, who proposed marriage to her. But when Ashley learned that Eric had had an affair with her mother, Dina Abbott (aka Mme. Mergeron), she fled to Rome to clear her head. There she shared a romantic evening with a handsome stranger, Marc, not knowing at the time that he was Marc Mergeron, her mother's stepson! When Ashley returned home with her mind made up to marry Eric, she was unaware that Marc had followed her to Genoa City. After selecting her wedding gown, Ashley had a dream that night that she, eyes closed, was dancing with Eric, only to open her eyes, still dreaming, to find herself in Marc's arms. She also dreamed that the two men fought a duel over her, which totally confused her. Then, completely wide awake, she called off her wedding to Eric, but, unfortunately, not until the last possible moment when their guests were assembled at the church!

Alana Anthony & Tyrone Jackson

1985. Tyrone Jackson, a young black law student from New York City, became Robert Tyrone, a white undercover agent, when he was assigned to infiltrate Joseph Anthony's mob in Genoa City. What he didn't count on was falling in love with Mr. Anthony's beauteous, peaches-and-cream daughter, Alana. When Mr. Anthony saw how deeply the two young people loved each other, he arranged for them to marry. It became a wedding day to remember for both the young bride and groom. Not only was Mr. Anthony shot and killed in a shoot-out shortly after the wedding ceremony (as Mr. Anthony lay dying, he asked Robert to take care of Alana), but Robert had to reveal his true identity to his new bride on their wedding night.

Faren Connor & Andy Richards

1986. Andy Richards and Faren Connor had both been married before they met each other. Divorced from Diane Jenkins, Andy found Faren, a songstress at the Rendezvous, to be the girl of his dreams. But they faced a serious problem. Faren had

been in a serious automobile accident and she didn't know who she was or why she was in Genoa City. Unable to find out anything at all about her past, Faren (aka Michelle Sanderson) was advised to forget her past, get on with her life, and live for the future. She married Andy, and the newlyweds' dreams of raising a family and buying a home of their own appeared to be coming true at last.

Traci Abbott & Brad Carlton

1986. Handsome hunk Brad Carlton was the Abbotts' live-in groundskeeper who had ambitions of climbing the Jabot corporate ladder. Traci Abbott, the youngest of the Abbott clan, always seemed to get lost in the shuffle. Her older siblings, Jack and Ashley, easily outshone her. Jack took an immediate dislike to Brad, believing him to be little more than a flagrant opportunist, while Ashley liked him perhaps a little too much. Ready to declare that she was her own person, Traci stepped onto center stage and married Brad, which prompted John Abbott to offer Brad a challenging position at Jabot.

Mr. John Abbott
Mrs. Dina Mergeron
request the honour of your presence
at the marriage of their daughter
Traci Ann
to
Mr. Bradley Carlton
on Friday, the twentieth of June
Nineteen hundred and eighty-six
at half after five o'clock
Saint James Chapel
Genoa City, Wisconsin

Ashley Abbott & Steven Lassiter

1988. Ashley gazed into Steven's eyes and knew she'd made the right decision. This was the man who had helped her regain her physical and emotional well-being; the man who would shelter her from harm and provide the security and stability she so desperately needed; the man who was so deeply in love with her that no other man would ever pose a threat to their vows. Their wedding took place in the familiar surroundings of the Abbott family home, and no one was happier than John, who believed that his new son-in-law would bring Ashley the happiness he'd always wished for his eldest daughter.

Leanna Randolph & Victor Newman

1988. Fearing the news that his marriage to Nikki was over would send the press scurrying to discover a reconciliation between himself and Ashley, Victor Newman did what he had to do to protect Ashley. He proposed to Leanna, whom he'd gotten to know as she, with his blessing, penned his autobiography. Leanna accepted Victor's proposal, although she really didn't like men to begin with. They jetted off to Vegas and said their I Do's. Their wedding night proved to be rather unusual as Leanna refused to consummate her vows—not now, not *ever*—and a perplexed Victor shared his bed with Douglas, his best man!

Katherine Chancellor & Rex Sterling

1988. Their road to the altar had its share of bumps, but Rex Sterling truly did love Katherine, and she loved him right back. Phillip Chancellor III and his fiancée, Cricket Blair, were on hand for the ceremony. As if a wedding weren't enough excitement for one day, Nina Webster went into labor, about to deliver the next-generation Chancellor. Katherine and Rex postponed their honeymoon and instead spent their wedding night at the hospital. Nina soon introduced Katherine and Rex to a very special wedding gift—Phillip Chancellor IV.

Carole Robbins & Skip Evans

1988. Carole Robbins and Skip Evans were cautious not to move too quickly in their relationship, but what grew from that caution was a very special love they both knew would last forever. Accustomed to the simple things in life, Skip and Carole had each envisioned a modest ceremony to match their means. But John Abbott always considered Jabot's loyal receptionist and talented photographer to be members of the family, and he had other plans for this special young couple. He made sure Carole and Skip had a fairy-tale wedding that neither of them could have ever imagined! John gave the bride away, and Jack and Ashley stood up for their friends.

Jessica Blair & John Abbott

1988. Jessica and John shared a very special love for one another. When John proposed the first time, Jessica wasn't sure it would be fair to him to accept, for she hadn't told him she was suffering from AIDS. John couldn't have been happier when Jessica said yes. But when her condition worsened, Jessica broke their engagement—and, at the same time, John's heart. When John learned of Jessica's illness, he was shattered. After much soul-searching and prayer, John realized how deep his love for Jessica was, and asked her once again to be his wife. Jessica couldn't believe what she was hearing. What a

remarkable man! Again, she accepted, and this time they were married. The ceremony took place in the private dining room of the Colonnade, in the presence of the Abbott family and Jessica's daughter, Cricket. Jessica considered herself truly blessed to be a member of such a loving, generous family.

Nina Webster & Phillip Chancellor

1989. Nina Webster had finally become the woman Phillip Chancellor III wanted to marry. But with just a few minutes to spare before heading to the church, Chase Benson, still following Jill Abbott's orders, tried one last time to convince Nina that he—not Phillip—was the man for her. But Nina knew in her heart that her future was with Phillip and their son. A minor car accident on the way to the church left Nina slightly dazed and the gathered guests wondering what might be causing the delay in the bride's arrival. Jill, convinced there would be no wedding, happily left the chapel. But Nina hurried out of the hospital to join Phillip at the altar and recite their vows: " . . . till death do us part."

Jessica Abbott & Jim Grainger

1989. In the presence of Cricket and her half brother Scott, Jessica and Jim vowed to love one another, "in sickness and in health." The union gave Cricket the greatest gift she could ever ask for—the family she'd longed for since she was a little girl. But the most selfless gift of all—the one that made this union possible—was the noble gesture by John Abbott, who gave Jessica her freedom, even though it meant his own heart was breaking.

Lauren Fenmore & Scott Grainger

1989. Lauren and Scott were two people who came into each other's lives at a time when they most needed someone. They dated for a while, and when Scott and Jim Grainger risked their lives to rescue Cricket from a deranged Derek Stuart, Scott realized how precious life was. It was time to live every moment to the fullest. He moved in with Lauren, and soon after, they married, with the hope of spending the rest of their lives together.

Cassandra Rawlins & Adrian Hunter

1990. Love and lifelong commitment were not uppermost in Cassandra Rawlins' mind when she accepted Adrian Hunter's proposal. Rather, it was a matter of self-preservation. Though they had been involved in a passionate affair for some time, she now faced charges of murdering her late husband, George. Intent on proving that Adrian was George's true killer, and fearing she might be his next victim, Cassandra agreed to marry Adrian. She had to be close to him and monitor his every move if she were ever to prove her own innocence.

Jill Abbott & Rex Sterling

1990. In many ways, the marriage between Rex and Jill was one of convenience. Rex had been unhappy for some time now, given the dramatic changes he'd seen in his wife, Katherine, of late. Of course, he had no idea it was Katherine's look-alike, Marge, from whom he'd filed for divorce. He turned to Jill for comfort, and Jill, who'd been getting nowhere with John, accepted Rex's proposal after voicing her disappointment that he'd signed a prenuptial agreement and would therefore receive nothing of Katherine's fortune. On their wedding night, Jill and Rex got the surprise of their lives when the real Katherine interrupted them. The marriage would be declared invalid once it was revealed that Katherine's impersonator's actions weren't legally binding, and Katherine and Rex were, therefore, still technically married!

Cricket Blair & Danny Romalotti

1990. No wedding could have been more perfect for the joining of two hearts—Danny Romalotti and Cricket Blair chose the island of Maui as the idyllic setting, and the two shared their special day with a small gathering of friends and family. Rex was his son's best man, and Nina was Cricket's matron of honor. Cricket's brother, Scott, gave her hand in marriage to the rock star who was, now and forever, her best friend. Danny's sister, Gina, graced the ceremony with a touching rendition of "Starting Here, Starting Now," and afterwards, the newlyweds flew off to a secluded beach for the romantic beginning of their life together as husband and wife.

Olivia Barber & Nathan Hastings

1991. Olivia was anxious to begin her life as Mrs. Nathan Hastings. She was equally anxious to make sure her sister, Drucilla, would keep her distance from Nathan, for it was obvious the younger Barber sister had designs on him. It was for this reason that Olivia moved up her wedding date, thinking it best not to tempt fate. Dru stood up for Olivia, and Paul was his close friend Nathan's best man.

Mr. and Mrs. Walter Barber
request the honour of your presence
at the marriage of their daughter
Olivia
to
Mr. Nathan Hastings
on Friday, the seventh of June
nineteen hundred and ninety-one
at half after five o'clock
Saint James Chapel
Genoa City, Wisconsin

Traci Abbott & Brad Carlton

1991. Traci and Brad's second wedding took place in the presence of the bride's extended family: siblings Jack and Ashley; brother-in-law Victor; father John and his former wife, Jill; and, of course, Mamie. Even her mother, Dina, returned to Genoa City and used the happy occasion to begin reestablishing her relationship with John. But it was Jill who caught the bouquet, hoping she would be the one to rekindle her romance with the senior Mr. Abbott. The bride was radiant as she looked forward to raising the child she and Brad were now expecting.

Katherine and Rex preceded the ceremony with a delightful rendition of Katherine's favorite song, "I'm Gonna Live 'Til I Die." But even though Jill had managed to convince Rex and the minister that a bigger wedding (two brides and two grooms) was better, John wanted nothing to do with this plan. On this day, only one couple would be declared husband and wife: Katherine and Rex were married again, and this time they planned to make it last.

Katherine Chancellor & Rex Sterling

1992. Katherine and Rex knew they were made for each other. It just took them a little time—and a little game-playing—for them both to realize it. By the time of their second wedding, Jill and Katherine had buried the hatchet (for the time being), and Jill was more than happy to serve as matron of honor. She pulled out all the stops to try to line up a double wedding—Katherine to Rex, and she to John.

Lauren Fenmore & Scott Grainger

1992. Lauren and Scott went through a great deal before their second trip to the altar. But regardless of what might've happened, they shared a special bond with Scotty, and, each fearing the other might seek sole custody, they decided they should raise the boy together to provide a stable home for him. They hoped this time their marriage would last.

Marriage Certificate

This certifies, that on the 29 day of July A.D. 19 92 Ryan McNeil and Victoria Newman were joined this day in holy matrimony Cooks County City Hall according to the laws of the State and by the authority of the foregoing license, by Judge Samuel Keller Evelyn Stowes and in the presence of who have hereto attached their signatures as witnesses to said marriage ceremony. In Witness Whereof, the said contracting parties, the said witness and the said Judge Samuel Keller have hereunto set their hands this 29 who solemnized such marriage ceremony Evelyn Stowes day of July A.D. 19 92 Witness Contracting Party Contracting Party Officer, Minister or Person Performing Ceremony

Victoria Newman & Ryan McNeil

1992. A Chicago justice of the peace performed the ceremony uniting an underage Victoria Newman to Ryan McNeil. Ryan was anxious to cash in on the Newman connection—Vicki had promised that as her husband, he would eventually take the helm at Newman Enterprises. Neither Victor nor Nikki knew of Victoria's intentions. In fact, Victor had given his daughter the OK to travel to the Windy City, thinking she was visiting colleges with his hand-picked escort, Brandon Collins. Vicki soon learned—a little too late—that perhaps she wasn't quite ready for marriage.

Jill & John Abbott

1993. Even after Jill's first marriage to John fell apart, Jill was right in there pitching at Jabot, taking on everyone in sight, but sticking to her guns in terms of protecting her turf. Yet there was something seriously lacking in her life: and that something was John Abbott, whom she'd never stopped loving. But John was playing "hard to get," remembering all too well the battles they fought the first time around. Ever resourceful, Jill kept plugging away at the office, impressing him and making herself indispensable. To make him jealous, she dallied with other men—Rex, Blade, then Victor. But when Victor cast her aside, humiliating her after she'd made it public that they would marry, John melted, and invited her to move back into the Abbott household. To his family's great chagrin, he remarried Jill shortly afterwards right in the Abbotts' own living room.

Drucilla Barber & Neil Winters

1993. At first, if each of them were to have their way, they would have chosen a different partner.

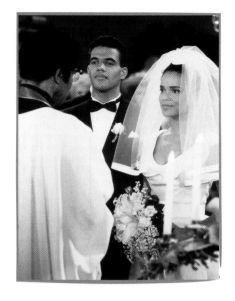

Neil was attracted to Drucilla's sister, Olivia, while Drucilla yearned for her sister's beau, Nathan. But after Olivia and Nathan married, Neil and Dru began to notice each other. What really sold Neil on Dru was her extraordinary talent as a ballerina; she amazed him. He gave her a diamond engagement ring, which he teased was not an engagement ring at all. Then he proposed and she accepted. The couple had a small wedding in Katherine Chancellor's mansion, with Olivia as her sister's matron of honor and Neil's colleague, Brad Carlton, as his best man. The couple honeymooned on the romantic Caribbean island of Antigua.

Victoria Newman & Cole Howard

1993. Cole had written his mother to tell her he'd met the girl of his dreams—the woman with whom he would spend the rest of his life. The woman who would be the mother of his children. Eve was shocked to learn this girl was Victoria Newman—Cole's half sister! Saddened by Eve's death, Cole and Victoria flew to Las Vegas for a quick wed-

ding. Upon returning from their honeymoon, Cole and Victoria were devastated when they learned "the truth," and the marriage was immediately annulled, leaving Cole and Victoria to forge ahead—with broken hearts.

Margaret Anderson & Miles Dugan

1993. A touch eccentric, feisty, and alternately sweet or just plain ornery, Margaret Anderson had racked up no less than six offenses for shoplifting. Still, she managed to dupe Cricket into going to bat for her. But when Miles and her other neighbors in the apartment building where they lived conned Cricket into giving them legal advice in their rent strike against their slumlord, Cricket realized to what extent the elderly were being abused. Cricket even solicited the help of Paul Williams in her efforts to fight for their rights. In the process, Miles fell for Margaret, but he couldn't bring himself to propose to her, hinting instead that two could live as cheaply as one, which Margaret promptly debunked. In the end, Cricket managed, with Paul's and Katherine's help, to get the landlord to shape up. Miles finally proposed, and the two were married, with Paul and Cricket serving as attendants.

Ashley Abbott & Alex "Blade" Bladeson

1994. Maybe this time it would be for keeps, the twice-wed bride-to-be, Ashley Abbott, dared to hope. After all, her fiancé, Blade, a highly successful fashion photographer, had little excess baggage in terms of never having been married before. And, as far as Ashley knew, not one member of his family or even a single friend would be at the wedding! He'd be all hers! Blade was even building a new home for Ashley—her dream house! Blade was so straightforward and honest. Everyone, including John Abbott and even Ashley's brother, Jack, respected him. As for Traci, who was standing up as her sister's matron of honor, the only awkward thing was that she'd have to encounter her ex-husband Brad (Traci was now married to Steve Connolly), who had also been Ashley's ex-beau. Ashley was riding so high she'd invited Brad to the wedding on impulse.

Victoria Newman & Cole Howard

1994. The truth was on their side! Victoria and Cole learned that Cole was not Victor's son after all.

This news paved the way for the young couple to re-marry and have the life they'd planned to share. This time, the wedding took place in Genoa City, with Victor spying from the back of the chapel—an outcast at his own daughter's wedding. It would take some time before Vicki would forgive him for keeping information about Cole's questionable paternity a secret from her.

Nina Chancellor & Ryan McNeil

1994. Nina and Ryan, young as they were, each experienced previous marriages with other partners. Nina was twice-widowed, and Ryan had recently come out of his failed marriage with Victoria Newman. It was during Ryan's marriage to Victoria that Nina had become the good friend who gave him money when Ryan couldn't bring himself to tell his teenaged bride he wasn't working. And it was to Nina that he had turned for other gratifications, as well. When Nina told him

she was pregnant with his child, he proposed. To Ryan's credit, he saw their upcoming nuptials as a new beginning for them—a tabula rasa. He adored Nina's son, little Phillip, who gave his mother away. Neil was Ryan's best man, and Christine was her best friend's matron of honor.

Hope Adams & Victor Newman

1994. What began as a simple friendship when Victor was staying on Hope's farm in Kansas became a moving love story. She was the farm girl, blind since birth, who had a way of making people who were sighted see what was really important in life. And he was the mogul badly in need of a new perspective at a time when he had alienated both family and friends. Hope gave Victor a new lease on life, and after he returned to Genoa City, reenergized to face what he had run away from, she joined him there. She called off her pending marriage to her lifelong friend, Cliff Wilson, who helped her run her farm. Victor and Hope spent many memorable moments together, doing the simple things: Victor, for instance, taught her to dance. He also showered her with all the luxuries that money could buy—fashionable clothes, fine wines, and beau-

tiful jewels. When they realized neither could live without the other, they married, with great expectations for spending a fulfilling life together.

Esther Valentine & Norman Peterson

1994. It all started when Esther answered the personals ad in the *Chronicle* entered by Norman Peterson, who claimed to be an investment banker. He said he'd make the trip to Genoa City, just to see Esther. Esther's heart was aflutter, and so was her head! She talked Kay and Rex into allowing her to entertain Norman as if she were the lady of the house, and they, her servants. She was so sure she had found the man of her dreams! Against their better judgment, Kay and Rex went along with the ruse. Then, Esther came clean and so did Norman, who said he was actually a barber. He said he was glad Esther wasn't rich. Now, Esther was really sure he was Mr. Right, and the couple announced their plans to marry. But Katherine was equally sure he was a crook: her intuition had never steered her wrong. Katherine said she wanted to take care of all the wedding arrangements, and hired an actor to play the role of minister. The couple was married, but the marriage wasn't legal.

Luan Volien & Jack Abbott

1995. Jack was a demoralized 19-year-old American soldier, fighting a war he didn't understand in a strange land far away from home. Luan was his angel of mercy whose presence in his life became a lifeline to sanity and hope. She nurtured his heart and spirit, getting him through the difficult days and the long, dark nights. They fell in love and then fate separated them. A lifetime later, a miracle brought them together in Genoa City! For the first time, Luan told Jack they shared a son, Keemo, whom she had to leave behind in Vietnam. Christine and Paul traveled to Ho Chi Minh City, found Keemo, and reunited him with his mother. Jack proposed to Luan and the couple was wed in a ceremony that combined American and Vietnamese traditions. She wore the conventional Vietnamese red ao dai: a long, mandarin-collared tunic with side slits and symmetrical closure over white pants. She also wore the traditional wrapped gold headpiece. Jack had gifted his bride with a four-carat, pear-shaped diamond ring.

Sharon Collins & Nicholas Newman

1996. No two young lovers could have had a more tumultuous beginning. When they began dating, his mother, Nikki, did all she could to break them up. Then Sharon was raped by Matt Clark, Nick's rival for Sharon's affections. When Matt was shot, Nicholas was arrested as the prime suspect, and he was wrongfully imprisoned. His father, Victor Newman, had to move heaven and earth to gather the needed evidence to free him. When Nick was released from prison, Nikki again tried to prevent the two lovers from being together. On the eve of their wedding, she offered Sharon a substantial sum of money to dump Nick for good and leave town. But Sharon would not be deterred; she refused to accept the bribe. The couple was married in a simple but elegant ceremony at the Newman ranch, in the bosom of family and close friends.

Keesha Monroe & Malcolm Winters

1996. Malcolm had fallen deeply in love with Keesha, long before he knew a storm would soon be brewing over an illicit affair Keesha had been having with Neil's brother-in-law, Nathan Hastings—which Neil and Dru found out about! Once Keesha had succumbed to Malcolm's irresistible charms, she

confessed she had been carrying on with Nathan, even while seeing Malcolm on the side. Sorely wounded, Malcolm stopped seeing her. Then Keesha learned she had AIDS and had possibly infected Nathan. When Malcolm realized that Keesha was alone and was dying, he went to her, offering her nourishment for both her body and soul. More crucial than food was his friendship and unconditional love. To make her waning moments on this earth content, he offered her the gift of marriage—something she dearly wanted.

Nikki Newman & Brad Carlton

1996. Everything was in place for Nikki and Brad's wedding. The Newman ranch never looked more beautiful. The guests—an intimate group of family and friends—had gathered. Victor, of course, had turned down Nikki's invitation to attend. Victoria, who grew to accept her mother's new beau, was matron of honor, and Cole was Brad's best man. The groom arrived late, and seemed edgy, but quickly took his place beside Nikki and the ceremony began. A frantic telephone call, with the news that Victor had been shot, sent everyone into a frenzy. Despite Brad's pleas that they complete their vows, Nikki's only thought at that moment was to get to the hospital to be at Victor's side. The union between Nikki and Brad was never to be.

Christine Blair & Paul Williams

1996. For Chris and Paul, the third time truly was the charm. They'd made plans to wed on two earlier occasions, but circumstances caused both weddings to be called off. These two lovers would finally put the past behind them and become husband and wife. Friends and family gathered to wish them well, and Victor Newman proudly

Miss *Christine Blair*
and
Mr. *Paul Williams*
request that you join them
as they celebrate their marriage
and for the reception
immediately afterward at
Christ Church

gave away the bride. Chris and Paul's respective workloads caused them to briefly postpone their honeymoon. But it was worth the wait, as they escaped to the tropical paradise of Nevis. Much to their dismay, Phyllis followed (with Dr. Reid) to wreak her own brand of havoc on the newlyweds, but it wasn't long before the spoiler and her friend were shipped back to the States, leaving Paul and Chris to enjoy the most romantic getaway ever!

Nikki Newman Abbott
and
Bradley Carlton
invite you to share their joy
as they unite in marriage
on Wednesday, the twenty-second of May
Nineteen hundred and ninety-six
at six o'clock in the evening
Newman Ranch
421 Larkspur Trail
Genoa City, Wisconsin
Celebration following the ceremony

Black tie

Nikki Newman & Joshua Landers

1996. Nikki had been noncommittal as far as setting her wedding date to Joshua Landers: she was expecting a proposal from Victor. He had told her he had something important to ask her, but when she learned he'd gone off to see Hope in Kansas (not knowing it was because Cliff had been gravely injured), Nikki announced to Joshua that today was the day! He was surprised, to say the least, but couldn't wait to make Nikki his bride. They put together an impromptu prenuptial party for family and a few close friends, and then jetted off to Vegas to say their I Do's. Nicholas convinced Victor that they had to try to stop the wedding, but their call, made from the Newman jet, confirmed that they were too late. Nikki had already become Mrs. Joshua Landers. Though the consummation of their vows would have to wait because of Nikki's ovarian cyst, Nikki and Joshua shared a romantic wedding night, exchanging gifts: hers, a diamond necklace; his, an engraved wedding band.

Phyllis Sommers & Danny Romalotti

1997. Danny and Phyllis were brought together and bonded in a way that had never before been possible for them when their son, Daniel, became critically ill. Danny made a pact with God: he promised he would be more understanding of Phyllis, if only Daniel would get well. Even Phyllis gratefully learned the power of prayer when little Daniel recovered. Danny moved back home so his son would have a full-time father, and he and Phyllis planned to take things slowly. It wasn't long, though, before Phyllis got what she always wanted—Danny proposed and the two were married for the second time. Paul was Danny's best man, but Chris declined Danny's request that she serve as Phyllis's matron of honor, although she did reluctantly agree to attend the wedding. Gina stood up in her place.

Olivia Hastings & Malcolm Winters

1997. When Malcolm proposed to Olivia in traditional fashion, on bended knee, she accepted.

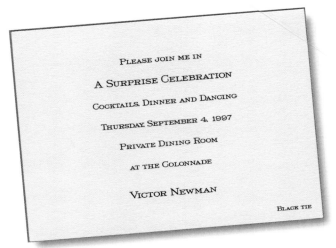

Olivia Barber Hastings
and
Malcolm Winters
invite you to share their joy
as they unite in marriage
on Friday, the eleventh of July,
Nineteen hundred and ninety-seven
at six o'clock in the evening
Chapel of the Good Shepard
Genoa City, Wisconsin

Not only had her friendship with him grown much deeper, but Malcolm filled the big gaping hole left in her son Nate's life when Nathan died. Now, they would be a family, and the wedding, which took place only a month after the couple's engagement, was truly a family affair. Drucilla was her sister's matron of honor, and Neil, his brother's best man—though both thought the couple might be moving a bit too quickly. Lily was the flower girl, and little Nate couldn't have been more proud and overjoyed to be ring bearer. Olivia was even more certain she'd chosen the right mate when, lonely for her son, Malcolm arranged for Nate to join them for the last few days of their honeymoon in Bermuda.

Diane Jenkins & Victor Newman

1997. It was to be a business trip—or so Diane thought. Victor had invited her to join him on his jet so they could discuss the sketches she'd pre- pared for the new Newman Towers complex. Victor's presentation of an engagement ring and his proposal that they marry—immediately—caught Diane off guard. But she was thrilled and quickly accepted. She would be Mrs. Victor Newman! In his typical fashion, Victor had taken care of every detail—the dress; the flowers; and the justice of the peace, an old friend who joined them to perform the ceremony right there on the Newman jet as soon as it touched down in Nevada. Diane's next surprise came in the form of a party at the Colonnade that Victor threw in her honor, where he announced to the gathered guests that he had taken a new bride!

JILL AND HER MEN

Jill Foster. A simple name for a complex woman. She's described as being someone for whom nothing is ever enough, and by her own admission, the doer of some stupid, even evil, things. But infinitely redeemable, she's also a woman with a great heart and a great soul. Impulsive. At times, irrational. Often brilliant. She was once a less-than-ideal mother—selfish, meddling, foolish—but she had the capacity to change and became a good mother. So what drives her? The fear of being poor again? Her insecurity? Her unending search for perfect love? Or just good old-fashioned sex? Hungry for drama in her life, she created it when things became too settled, as she went from one alliance to another, one love to another. She sought older men, in the absence of a father, who'd comfort her. And younger men, who'd excite her. And a slew of in-between men who'd regard her as their equal and give her the respect she craved. This is Jill Foster.

Brock Reynolds. A marriage of convenience, engineered by Katherine Chancellor, to give Jill and Phillip's illegitimate heir-to-be a name. Katherine hoped it would pave the way for her own reconciliation with her estranged husband, Phillip. Brock, a self-styled minister, performed the highly irregular ceremony.

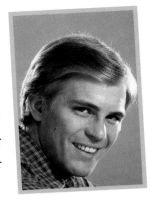

Phillip Chancellor II. The first—perhaps the greatest—love of the young Jill Foster's life. It began innocently, and ended tragically.

Derek Thurston. For the first time since Phillip's death, Jill felt herself drawn to a man. She saw him first and fell in love with him. Katherine stole him away and married him.

Stuart Brooks. Jill needed someone to support her and her son, Phillip. Why not do it in grand style? She went after wealthy widower, Stuart Brooks, in whom her own mother was interested, and tricked him into marrying her.

Andy Richards. She accepted Andy's proposal and wore his ring. Andy would make a good father, but he didn't have the kind of money she was looking for in a man. Furthermore, John Abbott had returned to Genoa City and she hoped they'd resume their relationship. Jill broke off her engagement to Andy.

John Abbott. Jill was sure she truly, deeply loved John. She not only married him once, but she would marry him for a second time 11 years later.

Jack Abbott. After Jill quarreled with John, she rushed out of the house in a blinding snowstorm. Jack rescued her and they spent the night in an abandoned cabin, where they shared a night of passion. It was a huge mistake and both paid dearly for it.

Michael Crawford. In negotiating her divorce settlement against John, Jill hired divorce lawyer Michael Crawford, whom she seduced.

Sven. One of her more foolish involvements was with psychomasseur, Sven. When she resisted his advances, he shot her thrice in the shower. Fortunately, Michael Crawford and Jack Abbott happened along at the right time.

David Kimble. Younger man, older woman! It made Jill feel reborn to have her young office assistant singing love ballads to her. She involved David in her scheme to insinuate the bum, Rex Sterling, into Katherine Chancellor's life!

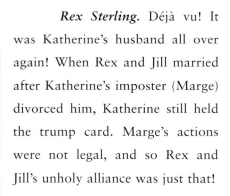

Skip Evans. Turnaround is fair play! Katherine attempted to return the favor by fixing up photographer Skip Evans with Jill. Though he was clearly beneath her status, Jill did try to make the situation work before giving him his walking papers.

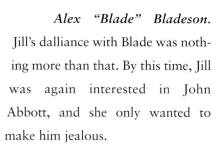

Rex Sterling. Déjà vu! It was Katherine's husband all over again! When Rex and Jill married after Katherine's imposter (Marge) divorced him, Katherine still held the trump card. Marge's actions were not legal, and so Rex and Jill's unholy alliance was just that!

Alex "Blade" Bladeson. Jill's dalliance with Blade was nothing more than that. By this time, Jill was again interested in John Abbott, and she only wanted to make him jealous.

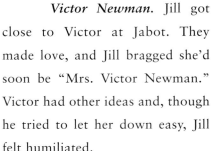
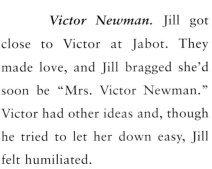

Victor Newman. Jill got close to Victor at Jabot. They made love, and Jill bragged she'd soon be "Mrs. Victor Newman." Victor had other ideas and, though he tried to let her down easy, Jill felt humiliated.

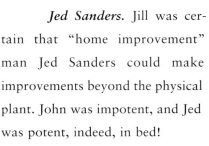

Jed Sanders. Jill was certain that "home improvement" man Jed Sanders could make improvements beyond the physical plant. John was impotent, and Jed was potent, indeed, in bed!

John Silva. Jill had her hands full. Mamie blew the whistle about her affair with Jed Sanders, and she ended up in court battling with John over little Billy's custody! Her attorney, John Silva, succumbed, amorously, to Jill's need for comfort, but he still managed to preserve his lawyerly decorum.

Keith Dennison. Could Jill have found the perfect partner in Keith Dennison? He loves and respects her for her business acumen and for her insight in dealing with family problems. Keith has money and power, he loves "family," and they're great partners in bed. At long last, someone has brought out the best in Jill!

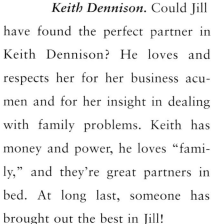

VICTOR AND HIS WOMEN

Powerful, complex, intimidating, intense, and oftentimes described as a ruthless tyrant and control freak, Victor Newman is one of the world's wealthiest men. When it comes to his private life, Victor Newman is both a lover and a family man. The women in his life see him as sexy, dashing, and charming in an "old world" kind of way. Generous to a fault, he's nevertheless unpredictable, at times temperamental, and he's certifiably enigmatic. He approaches each new woman in his life as if he's measuring her against the Newman standard of being a marriage partner. And though he's frequently changed partners, most of his ex-wives have forever remained his dear and loyal friends. It's as if it were a requirement. Only a few of his women have remained outside his inner circle—and Jill Foster is one of them!

Julia Newman. As newcomers to Genoa City, Victor quickly gained a reputation for being a ruthless businessman, while his beautiful wife, Julia, was sought after as a model by Jabot photographer Michael Scott. No one knew better than Julia how loveless her marriage had become, and soon she had entered into a full-blown affair with Michael, who offered a shoulder to cry on. The vengeful Victor went to extraordinary lengths to break up their relationship, and lost Julia in the process. In later years, they became good friends.

Lorie Brooks. Lorie Brooks duped Victor into returning Prentiss Industries to her by promising to marry him. She stole his heart and left him waiting at City Hall, leaving a Dear Victor letter, explaining, "You've betrayed Lance and me and it's come back to haunt you. We've battled, we've fought, we've loved. The circle is complete. Good-bye, Victor." Some years later, she returned briefly as a guest at Victor's wedding to Nikki.

Eve Howard. From time to time, Eve Howard invaded Victor's life, causing him pain and destruction. She claimed he fathered her son, Cole, and wanted revenge. Escaping from a mental institution, she tried to poison Victor and, later, Nikki. Rather than proffer charges against her, Victor again had her carted off to a mental institution.

Nikki Reed. She was and remains the true love of Victor's life, and he, hers. Truly star-crossed lovers, both before and after their marriage, they interfered and continue to interfere outrageously in each other's lives. They've attributed these intrusions to the fact that they share two children. But for Nikki and Victor, as other husbands, other wives, and other lovers come and go, they still look at each other "through the eyes of love."

Ashley Abbott. If Victor considered anyone his intellectual equal, it would have to be the beautiful Ashley Abbott. Their love was passionate and more than enough to separate Victor from his beloved Nikki. By the same token, Ashley loved Victor so

much that she gave him up so he could be with Nikki. They did marry, however, and though they've gone their separate ways, they love and have great respect for each other to this day.

Leanna Randolph. At first Leanna was a foil for Victor to divert the paparazzi from Ashley. He made the supreme sacrifice and married Leanna. But she wanted to remain a virgin and refused to sleep with Victor after their marriage. Then she'd betray him by penning his unauthorized biography, *Ruthless.*

Jill Abbott. He used her and then cast her aside like an old shoe. Of all his women, Victor probably treated her the most shabbily, and even today, the two hold each other at arm's length, the one not trusting the other. But as enemies often do, they have great respect for each other.

Hope Adams. He met her when he was at the lowest point in his life. She was the simple, blind farm girl from Kansas, who taught him to see with his heart. They share an adorable son, Victor Adam

Newman Jr., but it wasn't enough to keep them together, and they divorced.

Christine Romalotti. This young, beautiful lawyer occupied and continues to hold a soft spot in Victor's heart that's all her own. She loved and respected him like a father; he counseled her in her rocky romance with Paul Williams, as if she were his daughter. The difference was, however, that the deference he paid Christine was not anything like his relationship with his own daughter, Victoria, but rather, bordered on romance.

Diane Jenkins. From the moment Victor laid eyes on the captivating architect, Diane (then Jack Abbott's fiancée), he had to make her his. He married her after a whirlwind romance that caught everyone off guard, explaining to family and friends and Jack Abbott, "Diane's not some whim. I really want this to work."

Tour Guide to Genoa City

WELCOME TO WISCONSIN

GENOA CITY, COUNTY OF WALWORTH

ZIP CODES: 53128, 53147

POPULATION: > 500,000

FOUNDED BY: GARFIELD DANDRIDGE CHANCELLOR, CIVIL WAR HERO

This guide was prepared with the intent of helping the visitor taste the flavor and capture the uniqueness of this ever burgeoning, historic, midwestern American city, with the hope of stimulating a spirit of exploration and adventure to go beyond what is representational, and to open eyes and hearts to see what truly lies beyond the obvious. People and places, past and present, will reveal the fabric of the city.

HOTELS

GENOA CITY HOTEL 1100 EAST CHESTNUT

Formal, elegant, established. Desk Clerk Keith Armstrong is a fixture here.

GENOA TOWERS 1500 ASHLAND

A study in contrasts, this hotel is very contemporary. Try it.

The Genoa Grand Hotel is also recommended, but avoid the Croyden and the Delton Hotel at all costs.

RESTAURANTS

COLONNADE ROOM

350 EAST CHESTNUT

For celebrating what is truly memorable. Jacques, the maître d', ensures you will savor every moment in your dining and wining pleasure.

Colonnade Room

THE EMBERS 1100 EAST CHESTNUT

Located in the posh Genoa City Hotel.

GINA'S PLACE 216 SUMMIT

If it's a relaxing, romantic setting you crave, or the best pasta in town (try the Fettuccini Alfredo à la Gina), this is the place.

Shelby's, Top of the Tower, The Lodge, and Franklin's are also recommended for fine dining.

SHOPPING

FENMORE'S 470 EAST CHESTNUT

The Saks Fifth Avenue of Genoa City. Carries Versace, Jennifer Johns, and Forrester Creations. (Try Wiley's Department Store if you favor Spectra Fashions.)

For the man in your life, there are several fine specialty shops, such as Rodney Carson Clothiers. Tip for men: For your best girl, try Easy Teddy's for her lingerie. You might just run into top fashion model Drucilla Winters!

470 Chestnut
Genoa City, WI 53128   555-7842

HOSPITALS AND CLINICS

GENOA CITY MEMORIAL HOSPITAL

308 SOUTH FOURTH STREET

Just as Drs. Snapper Foster, Casey Reed, and Scott Grainger before her, Dr. Olivia Hastings Winters maintains her office at Memorial. Dr. Joshua Landers is also affiliated here.

MARKET STREET CLINIC

81 MARKET STREET

Located on the edge of town, this clinic was gutted and refurbished by Dr. Kurt Costner, who dedicated himself to serving the needy, as other Genoa City doctors before him, Snapper Foster and Mark Henderson, did.

SCHOOLS/COLLEGES

GENOA CITY UNIVERSITY

1200 HYDE PARK

This liberal arts institution attracts most of its students from local high schools and community colleges. Boasts a high

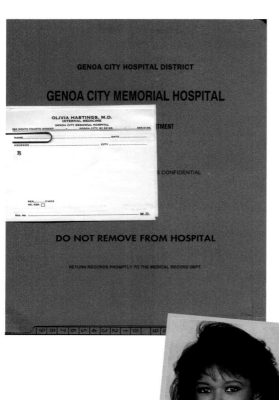

placement ratio for its graduates, which include Chris and Peggy Brooks, Phillip Chancellor III, Traci Abbott, Lauren Fenmore, Christine Williams, Ryan and Nina McNeil, and, most recently, Nicholas Newman. Professors Tim Sullivan and Jack Curtis served on the faculty.

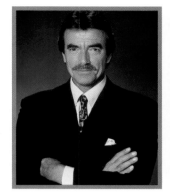

CHURCHES

CHURCH OF THE SACRED HEART

4458 EAST CHESTNUT

Mary Williams's church, where daughter Patty married Jack Abbott.

There are several houses of worship in Genoa City. Ryan and Nina, and Paul and Chris, chose the Chapel of the Good Shepherd for their nuptials, while Cole and Victoria were married at the Founders Chapel. Little Daniel Romalotti was baptized at St. Elmo's Catholic Church.

BUSINESS LISTINGS

NEWMAN ENTERPRISES

7800 MELROSE AVENUE

Overlooking the city in his offices on the 22nd floor of Newman Towers, Chairman of the Board and President Victor Newman keeps close tabs on his worldwide financial empire. His lieutenant, Chief Operating Officer Jack Abbott, is in charge of the day-to-day operations, having won his berth over Brad Carlton, who is no longer with the company. Victor entrusted to Jack the training of his son, Nicholas, in every phase of the business. Grace Turner assists Nick. Neil Winters, vice president, is one of Newman's most trusted associates.

JABOT COSMETICS
304 SOUTH FOURTH STREET

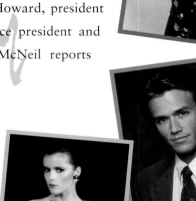

John Abbott, CEO, has his offices on the 12th floor of the Jabot building. He operates the business relatively independently of Newman Enterprises, the parent company. Ashley Abbott serves as president and chief chemist; she is in charge of product development. Jill Abbott continues to serve in an advisory capacity to the men's line, and is director of special projects. Other officers include Victoria Newman Howard, president of Brash & Sassy; and Ryan McNeil, vice president and director of the Jabot Men's Division. McNeil reports directly to Victor Newman.

DENNISON-VANGUARD INDUSTRIES

Keith Dennison continues to run his company, which recently merged with Newman Enterprises. All financial backing is assumed by Newman Enterprises, which holds controlling interest.

CHANCELLOR INDUSTRIES
1000 MARKET STREET

Before his death, Phillip Chancellor II supervised all of the company's holdings, including the factory in Genoa City, where Liz Foster worked. After Phillip's death, Katherine relied on good friend Victor Newman to keep an eye on things, and on Mitchell Sherman for legal advice.

PRENTISS INDUSTRIES
402 N. CLINTON

One of the premier businesses in Genoa City, Prentiss Industries still stands. Vanessa Prentiss owned controlling stock interest; her two sons, Lance and Lucas, battled each other for power and shared the rest of the stock between them.

PAUL WILLIAMS. INVESTIGATIONS

NEWMAN TOWERS
SUITE 1002
7800 MELROSE
GENOA CITY, WISC. 53128
(414) 555-3500

PAUL WILLIAMS

INVESTIGATIONS

NEWMAN TOWERS,

SUITE 1002

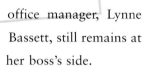

Paul Williams operates his PI firm out of Newman Towers. Partners Andy Richards and Nathan Hastings are no longer with him, but longtime office manager, Lynne Bassett, still remains at her boss's side.

LAWYERS

LEGAL AID

75 MARKET STREET

GENOA CITY LEGAL AID
75 Market, Genoa City, WI 53128

Some of Genoa City's finest labored on behalf of the needy, including Greg Foster, with his aide, Chris Brooks, and Brock Reynolds. Even before she earned her law degree, Christine Williams interned here and devoted her energies to such causes as the rights of seniors, drug addicts, and abused women.

JOHN SILVA

WILTON BUILDING, SUITE 308

Barristers are as plentiful in Genoa City as anywhere else in the nation. John Silva has practiced both criminal and civil law.

Other high profile attorneys in Genoa City are Mitchell Sherman, Michael Crawford, Kevin Andrews, Michael Baldwin (disbarred), and Patrick Baker.

OTHER POINTS OF INTEREST

CHRONICLE SQUARE

One of the more prominent of the city's squares, historically and architecturally. It features the *Chronicle*, Genoa City's only daily newspaper; Transglobal Airlines; the offices of Dr. Timothy Reid, psychotherapist and marriage counselor; and the courthouse.

PRIVATE HOMES AND MANSIONS

No tour of Genoa City would be complete without driving past some of the city's finest residences. Although these homes are not open for public inspection, they represent the finest architecture the city has to offer.

The Abbotts 603 Glenwood Drive

The Brookses 300 Hyde Park

The Chancellor Estate 12 Foothill Road

The Dennisons 715 Hyde Park

The Newman Ranch 421 Larkspur Trail, Hwy B

The Prentiss Estate 3780 Lake Shore, on Lake Geneva

The Rawlins/Carlton Home 1185 Cottage Grove Road

A Day in the Life of
The Young and the Restless

The Writing Team

At the heart of *The Young and the Restless* is William J. Bell and his writing team, who craft the stories and create the scripts for over 250 shows a year. The head writing team (headwriter Bill Bell, co-headwriter Kay Alden, John F. Smith, Jerry Birn, and Trent Jones) "meet" daily by telephone. They spend anywhere from two to five hours per day hammering out the direction of the story, and plotting out the lives of the inhabitants of Genoa City. Though storylines aren't set in stone, the writers project into the future and establish the general direction for stories months in advance. During these daily story confer-ences, the writers also develop "breakdowns." These breakdowns determine how much of the story will be told each week, and then, more specifically, where the story will begin and end each day. By the time the scripts are turned over to *Y&R*'s scriptwriters, they are sometimes nearly 50 percent complete—with much of the dialogue already written. The scriptwrit-ers are then responsible for fleshing out each scene and completing the dialogue. The writing team is scattered throughout various parts of the country, but the telephone, fax, and modem make the process manageable.

The home of The Young and the Restless, CBS Television City in Hollywood, where the show is produced.

As creator and headwriter of The Young and the Restless, it is Bill Bell's vision that has guided the show every day for 25 years.

Co-headwriter Kay Alden (seated) with writers' assistant Natalie Minardi.

Writer Trent Jones is able to transfer files from his home office in New York.

Rex Best makes some notes on a story outline.

Bill Bell confers with writer Jerry Birn on a story in Bill's office at CBS.

Writer John F. Smith in a particularly proud moment.

A common occurrence: writer Eric Freiwald on the phone talking over a script.

Before becoming a member of the show's writing team, James Houghton played Greg Foster.

Writer Janice Ferri works on her assigned script.

Writer Linda Schreiber spreads out and gets to work.

Michael Minnis takes a breather from the never-ending task at hand.

Producing *The Young and the Restless*

Once the words are on paper, it becomes the job of the producers, directors, cast, and crew to bring it all to life. Executive producer Ed Scott calls the shots in the studio, along with producer David Shaughnessy. Getting the show to look the best that it possibly can, day in and day out, is their responsibility. It's a multifaceted role that takes them from the booth, to the stage floor, to music, to editing, and beyond. The production process is an around-the-clock operation, with over 175 people contributing in front of and behind the cameras. The actual taping schedule typically begins at 7:00 A.M. and runs until 6:00 in the evening. On a good day, they might wrap up even earlier. Of course, some of the "big production" shows—weddings or parties, for example, that involve just about every member of the cast—have been known to run into the wee hours of the morning!

Studio 43 at CBS Television City in Hollywood is the morning stage for taping the show. In the afternoon, the action shifts to Studio 41.

Director Sally McDonald and producer David Shaughnessy study a shot as Mark Beruti (left) looks on. The director must "block" the show before taping. They determine how the actors will move on stage and the angles from which the cameras will record the action.

As the show goes to camera, executive producer Ed Scott and producer David Shaughnessy are in the production booth. They make sure they get what they want out of every shot, and keep their eyes and ears tuned to all aspects of the production.

Tommy Persson (right) controls which microphones are open, to ensure that the audio portion of the taping goes smoothly. Ed Scott and director Heather Hill eye up the monitors.

Inside the booth, monitors show the scene as each camera sees it. The director makes the call as to which shot will be used moment by moment to record the scene. Here, director Kathryn Foster and associate director Betty Rothenberg discuss a scene.

Ed Scott scrutinizes the scene as Kathryn Foster directs.

Production supervisors Joan Ellsworth and Andrew Keane are the liaisons between the show and CBS. It's their job to take care of Y&R's "below the line" needs, such as camera operators, equipment, and sets, by working with the appropriate departments at the network.

Tommy Persson (audio), Jim Dray (technical director), Kathryn Foster (director), Heather Hill (director), Eva Marie P. Arquero (production assistant), Betty Rothenberg (associate director), Nora Wade (production associate), and Chris Maddalone (audio) work closely in the studio.

More of the talented people behind the scenes. (Front row) Victor Lopez, Ray Thompson, Bernie Geestman. (Middle row) Mike Bianes, Rudy Hunter, Jason Tait, Dean Lamont, Art Peters, David Shaughnessy, Ed Scott, Luis Godinez, Billy Roberts, Joe Atkinson, John Bromberek, Chico Godinez, Jim Weems, Don Jacobs. (Top row) John Recippio, Dennis Boyle, Herbie Weaver Jr., Mark Beckley, David Wollin, Dennis Whitney.

Scenic Design

Designing the elaborate sets for *The Young and the Restless* is an exciting and challenging responsibility. Production designer Bill Hultstrom reviews each script and generally works two to three weeks ahead of taping to design the various sets that will be needed. For sets that will have considerable on-screen presence or permanence, Bill Hultstrom will talk with executive producer Ed Scott, who conveys to him the wishes of headwriter Bill Bell. Hultstrom will then develop a floor plan, sketch the design of the set, and suggest surfaces, fabrics, colors, or woods appropriate to the set. Once the sets have been approved, the shop at CBS does the actual construction.

A sketch of Nick and Sharon's living room.

Production designer Bill Hultstrom (right) and art director David Hoffmann make modifications to a blueprint of one of the show's sets.

The sketch comes to life as the set is complete.

Set Decoration

Once the sets are designed, it's the role of the set decorators to do just that—decorate! They review each script and identify whatever props are necessary for that particular show. For each new set, they will shop for furniture and accessories, and their decoration must match the vision of the production designer. Beyond the furniture, any props viewers see on the show, from pictures on the walls, to flowers, to food, to animals, are also the responsibility of the set decorators. The attention to detail in decorating the sets is just one of the aspects of *The Young and the Restless* that sets it apart from other soaps. The set decorators have made it their job to include every last detail in all the work they do, especially since they never know where the camera might decide to focus. Every day is different from the last, and even though the hours are grueling (a 12-hour day is nothing out of the ordinary), the set decorators enjoy meeting the challenges as a team. The most challenging prop the team has ever had to produce? Joe Bevacqua and Andrea Joel agree: freeze-dried tarantulas for the Suzanne-Katherine storyline years ago!

Set decorator Joe Bevacqua is the senior member of the department, having started on the show over 18 years ago.

Set decorator Andrea Joel shares the responsibility for, among other things, the hand props, including all of the documents, newspapers, and letters seen on the show.

Set decorator Fred Cooper talks with a vendor to see if they have exactly what he's looking for. When they're out of the office, cell phones and pagers save the decorators a tremendous amount of time.

Props are housed at the CBS studios. The shelves are seemingly endless, but meticulously organized.

Props for various Y&R sets remain in storage until they're needed again.

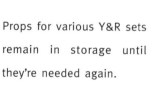

Known for their attention to detail, the set decorators produce driver's licenses, credit cards, and business cards so that characters' wallets are realistically full.

Setting Up in the Studio

"Zelda" helps out at the beginning of each day to color balance the cameras. The show typically shoots with three cameras, though for certain more complicated shows, occasionally a fourth or even a fifth camera will be used.

Furniture is arranged on the set.

Scenic backdrops are raised before the sets are put in place. These backdrops provide realistic outdoor views from set windows.

Walls are put into place on the studio floor.

A chandelier is hoisted into place.

Lighting contributes in a major way to the warm, rich visual look of the show. Lighting director Rudy Hunter (foreground) supervises stagehands.

Set decorator Andrea Joel confers with Jim Crosby on the set of the Newman ranch.

Production associate Jennifer Scott talks over the day's tape schedule with stage manager Randall Hill.

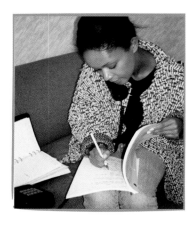

Tonya Lee Williams is on the telephone getting notes as to what dialogue is being cut from her scenes. Occasionally, a show may be running long and such last-minute changes become necessary to keep the show within its time limitations.

Stage manager Don Jacobs checks his script and makes sure everything is set up and ready to tape.

Jeffrey Long works on cue cards, which some of the actors will utilize as a safety net once the cameras begin to roll. Sometimes an actor might have 40 pages of dialogue to memorize overnight!

Scott Reeves studies his script in his dressing room. He keeps his guitar close by, and enjoys playing to relax and pass the time.

For Bob Guzzi, good penmanship is a must! Actors' names and lines are color coded so it's clear which dialogue belongs to whom.

Jennifer Gareis coaches Camryn Grimes as they rehearse their lines together.

Luis Godinez positions the boom microphone as cast and crew are now ready to tape.

Executive producer Ed Scott gives notes to Sabryn Genet. He has an incredible rapport with actors that enables him to communicate exactly what he's looking for in a scene.

Producer David Shaughnessy gives notes to Alex Donnelley. His extensive acting and directing credits prior to joining Y&R make it easy for him to relate to the actors on the show.

Action! Stage manager Randall Hill works his clapboard.

The camera is moved into place for a close-up of Nina in the hospital.

Some members of the production crew. (Front row) Bob Grassi, Billy Roberts, Ray Thompson. (Middle row) Rod Yamane, Victor Lopez, Dennis Whitney, Scha Jani, Brent "Woody" Conner, Sean Nelson, Roberto Bosio. (Back row) Herbie Weaver, Dennis Boyle, Rudy Hunter.

Music has always played a critical role in *The Young and the Restless*, from the earliest days when characters might've broken into song at any moment, to the Danny Romalotti rock concerts, to the background music that underscores the emotion in a scene. *Y&R*'s music coordinators review each script two to three weeks ahead of time; they "hear" the script as they're reading it, and then decide what music should accompany each scene. When the scenes are taped, musical selections accompany the taping, though they're not recorded at this stage. Executive producer Ed Scott reacts to what he hears, may suggest changes, and ultimately approves the music that viewers hear as they watch the show. The show's composers have written a music library, which they supplement every so often with new compositions. This guarantees a fresh, new sound for the show each and every day.

Music coordinator Jay Leslie, Ed Scott, composer and music coordinator Jez Davidson Guito, and composers Jack Allocco and David Kurtz.

Ralph Gertel (left) and Dan Brummett (right) edit videotape to piece together the show, which is shot out of sequence. Early in the morning, producer David Shaughnessy will meet with the editors and run through the notes he made from taping the day before, indicating what takes of which scenes are best. Editing of most shows takes place approximately two to three weeks after the taping. It's the associate director's job to oversee the actual editing process.

Once the show is edited, the music and sound effects are added in postproduction. This process of "audio sweetening" is the domain of (inset) Otto Svoboda; and (left) Don Henderson, Manny Moreno, and Carlos Torres; and (right) Harold "Lanky" Linstrot, Pete Mallard, and Tommy Persson.

Casting

Every job at *The Young and the Restless* is a never-ending one, and casting is no exception. All actors who appear on the screen, from the most prominent players to the extras in the background, are selected by the casting department. Known for its beautiful people, *Y&R* may cast anywhere from five to over 20 actors in any given week, depending on the demands of the storytelling. Executive producer Ed Scott and headwriter Bill Bell are included in the process once the casting department has identified several potential actors for a role. Ultimately, Bill Bell has the final say on casting decisions for contract players. One of the biggest challenges the casting department faces is when they must recast a role. Although physical resemblance is an important consideration, the performance is key, and new actors usually don't take long to make the characters their own.

Casting director Meryl O'Loughlin, C.S.A., looks over the photos and résumés of prospective new cast members.

Associate casting director Gail Camacho's work never ends!

Casting assistant Marnie Saitta talks with an agent about an actor's potential for an upcoming role.

It's the job of the *Y&R* wardrobe department to dress every actor on the show. When costume designer Jennifer Johns gets the unedited script, she first reads it through and makes general notes as to how each character must be attired: business, casual, lingerie, nude . . . whatever the scenes call for. She'll talk over wardrobe decisions with executive producer Ed Scott to get his input. It's the responsibility of wardrobe to shop for new clothes, do fittings with the actors, and make sure not only that the character is dressed properly, but that the actor is comfortable, too. Two days before the show airs, they pull all necessary clothes, shoes, jewelry, and accessories, making sure everything is in good order and ready for use. A member of the wardrobe department will be on the set checking for continuity from day to day during taping, often making use of the many Polaroid photos taken specifically for this purpose.

The talented people who dress the residents of Genoa City: (Front row) Christine Bresler, Kay Wataguchi, Juliette Huerta, Carrie Christine, Paula Flanagan. (Back row) Tommy Puckett, costume designer Jennifer Johns, David Bruce, and Gina Chappa.

Late costume designer Greg York collaborated with the writers and producers to conceptualize the costumes Y&R's characters would wear to the Masquerade Ball. Their goal was to match each character's personality to the costume. Greg sketched out his ideas and presented them to Bill Bell for his approval.

Kay Wataguchi makes an alteration to one of the costumes.

Who wouldn't want a closet like Y&R's? Wardrobe storage is jam-packed with thousands of costumes—old and new. As certain pieces are no longer used, they're moved higher and higher up in storage. After 25 years, the wardrobe for Y&R is nearly to the rafters! Sharon Case has some personal favorites.

Greg's drawing was finalized, and fabric selections were made.

Jeanne Cooper as the Queen of Hearts.

Greg envisioned Rex costumed as the Mad Hatter.

The finished costume comes to life.

Wedding gowns provide both excitement and challenges for Y&R's costume designers. The objective is to create the perfect dress that embodies the character's own style and personality. Jennifer Johns envisioned Christine in a pale blue dress with an embroidered and beaded bodice and taffeta skirt.

Makeup and Hair

One of the first stops the actors make when they come into the studio each day is the makeup and hair department. The process of readying them for the camera usually takes approximately 15 minutes for the men, and about half an hour for the women. Most of the work is done in the department's own space, but at least one member of the makeup and hair teams must also be on the studio floor at all times when the show tapes. Makeup artists and hair stylists often try to work on the same actors each day for efficiency's sake. But they also observe and study each other's work so that they're prepared for any actor who might show up in their chair. A typical day for the makeup and hair staff runs from 6:30 A.M. until 6:30 P.M.

The makeup department. (Seated) Kathy Jones. (Standing) Rhavan Briggs, Ralph Wilcox, Patti Denney, Farah Bunch, Taia Red, Terry Funatsu, and Barry Wittman.

The Y&R makeup artists enjoy the many challenges brought on by such things as Veronica's accident. They pay particular attention to injuries that must "heal" gradually and realistically over a number of days or weeks. Here, Candice Daly studies her new look.

The Y&R hair department. (Inset) Mira Wilder. (Left to right) Hitomi Golba, Annette Jones, Mary Jo Fortin, and Arrick Anderson.

Jess Walton doesn't mind being teased by hair stylist Hitomi Golba.

Like an artist with his palette, Barry Wittman prepares to apply makeup.

Michael Damian clowns around with makeup artist Ralph Wilcox.

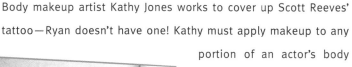

Body makeup artist Kathy Jones works to cover up Scott Reeves' tattoo—Ryan doesn't have one! Kathy must apply makeup to any portion of an actor's body that will be shown on camera—and for some scenes, this means just about everywhere!

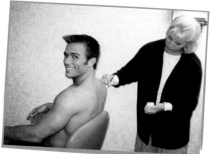

Once actors move down to the set, makeup and hair are always there for last minute touch-ups before tape rolls.

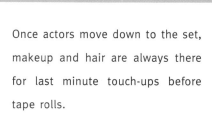

Annette Jones tends to Granville Van Dusen. Whenever an actor is contemplating a change in hairstyle, they must discuss their wishes with the writers and producers of the show.

On-set maintenance is even more intense for big production scenes. Rhavan Briggs takes the shine off Shari Shattuck as Barry Wittman touches up Alex Donnelley at Victor and Diane's party.

Hamming it up for the camera, Shemar Moore fixes Kristoff St. John's makeup.

Occasionally, Y&R recruits its own behind-the-scenes talent to play their role on camera. Here, Patti Denney plays a makeup artist, and assists Veronica in covering the scars from her laser surgery.

Behind-the-Scenes Stars

Lucy Johnson is Senior Vice President of Daytime/Children's Programs and Special Projects for CBS.

CBS's director of Daytime Television, Margot Wain, and Y&R's coordinating producer, Nancy Bradley Wiard, confer on the Y&R 25th Anniversary press kit. In addition to serving as a liaison with the network and coordinating all publicity and promotion for the show, Nancy Wiard's position requires that she oversee all production and postproduction scheduling, plan all location shoots, handle negotiations with talent, and administer the show's budget. The staff, cast, and crew she supervises numbers 175.

CBS promotion director Susan Banks (left) works with promotion writer/producer Michelle Voss Greenberg on one of the on-air promotions viewers will see for Y&R.

Production coordinator Michael Okamura takes each day's script and must break it down into an efficient production schedule. The task is compounded by the fact that the show crosses two studios. It's his job to make sure that the actors' days are manageable—oftentimes actors will work either a morning or an afternoon shift. An actor on the morning shift may be finished for the day by noon. Actors working the afternoon shift aren't expected in until late morning.

Associate production coordinator Christina Knack also breaks down each script into a shooting schedule. She and Michael Okamura then compare notes. Two sets of eyes looking at the same puzzle pieces ultimately makes for the most sensible production schedule.

As assistant to the producers, Joshua S. McCaffrey serves as a liaison between the writing staff and the various aspects of production. He also ensures the continuity of the show's scripts from one day to the next.

Jack-of-all-trades Josh O'Connell assists the Y&R writers and producers. Among his duties are handling the distribution of scripts and schedules, supervising and training interns, assisting with the Y&R web site, and helping with other details around the office.

Production assistant Brenda Garcia contributes to Y&R's global reach by preparing scripts for translation.

Fan club supervisor Victoria Curea plans the biannual fan club luncheons and edits Y&R's official newsletter. She also responds to inquiries fans make to the show. Most actors themselves answer their own fan mail. Y&R's fan club is run by the show to ensure that fans receive the attention Y&R believes they deserve.

Production staff member Trina Gavieres is the friendly voice you'll often hear answering the phones at The Young and the Restless. She also helps with general office duties and keeps the staff apprised of where actors are making personal appearances.

Sometimes the stress of producing over 250 episodes a year gets to the staff, and they just have to let go! That's show publicist Charles Sherman on the far right, getting into the act.

The Cast of Y&R through the Years

1973–1974. (Seated) Brenda Dickson, Julianna McCarthy, Robert Colbert, Dorothy Green, Janice Lynde. (Middle row) James Houghton, William Grey Espy, Trish Stewart, Jaime Lyn Bauer. (Top row) Lee Crawford, Tom Hallick, Donnelly Rhodes, Jeanne Cooper.

Bill Bell created the role of Pierre specifically for actor Robert Clary.

Actor Tom Selleck played Jed Andrews, and went on to a successful television and movie career after leaving the show.

Another famous graduate of the show, David Hasselhoff, played Dr. Snapper Foster.

1976. (Front row) Brenda Dickson, Charles Gray, Trish Stewart, Jeanne Cooper, Dorothy Green, Pamela Peters Solow. (Middle row) K. T. Stevens, John McCook, Jaime Lyn Bauer, Julianna McCarthy, Janice Lynde, Beau Kayzer, Robert Colbert. (Top row) David Hasselhoff, Anthony Herrera, Kay Heberle, Tom Hallick.

1980. (Front row) Joe LaDue, Doug Davidson, Lilibet Stern, David Winn, Roberta Leighton, David Hasselhoff. (Seated, second row) Meg Bennett, Eric Braeden, Margaret Mason, Melinda Cordell, Melody Thomas Scott, K. T. Stevens, Loyita Chapel, Deborah Adair. (Back row) Nick Benedict, Jaime Lyn Bauer, Jerry Lacy, Victoria Mallory, William Wintersole, Bill Long, Terry Lester, Jeanne Cooper, Robert Colbert, Pamela Peters Solow, Tom Ligon, Brett Hadley, Carolyn Conwell, Wings Hauser.

1982. (Front row) Peter Brown, Liz Keifer, DeAnna Robbins, Meg Bennett, Brock Peters. (Second row) Deborah Adair, Julianna McCarthy, Victoria Mallory, Lilibet Stern, Lynn Wood, Kristine DeBell. (Standing, third row) Suzanne Zenor, Michael Damian, Beth Maitland, Jay Kerr, Eileen Davidson, Doug Davidson, Terry Lester, Jeanne Cooper, Michael Evans, Jerry Douglas, Robert Colbert, Brett Hadley, Steven Ford, Mark Tapscott, Ben Hammer, Christopher Holder, Marguerite Ray, Carolyn Conwell, Patty Weaver.

Proud father Bill Bell tended to daughter Lauralee as she began her career as Cricket Blair. John Denos played her cousin, photographer Joe Blair.

1985. (Front row) Christopher Templeton, Jon St. Elwood, Marguerite Ray, Jerry Douglas, Brenda Dickson, Beth Maitland, Eileen Davidson, Terry Lester, Marla Adams, Stephanie E. Williams, Brock Peters. (Second row) Frank Benard, Meg Bennett, Ashley Nicole Millan, Eric Braeden, Melody Thomas Scott, Tracey Bregman-Recht, Doug Davidson, Carolyn Conwell, Brett Hadley, Logan Ramsey. (Third row) Joy Garrett, Phillip Morris, Lauren Koslow, Susan Seaforth Hayes, James Storm, Patty Weaver, Steven Ford. (Top row) John Denos, Brian Matthews, Grant Cramer, Lynwood Boomer, Bert Kramer, Kate Linder, Anthony Peña, Michael Damian.

Brenda Dickson in a signature pose as the original Jill Foster.

Don Diamont played the upwardly mobile Brad Carlton.

In 1987, former President Gerald Ford was greeted on the set by his son and other member of Y&R's cast: Michael Damian, Steven Ford, Todd Curtis, Jeanne Cooper, Jerry Douglas, Brenda Dickson, Tracey Bregman-Recht, Gerald Ford, Tricia Cast, Eileen Davidson, Don Diamont, Lauralee Bell, Michael Corbett, Thom Bierdz.

1987. (First row) Tom Langan, Bill Bell, Lee Phillip Bell, Ed Scott, Nancy Bradley Wiard. (Second row) John Shearin, Colleen Casey, Steven Ford, Susan Seaforth Hayes, Tracey Bregman-Recht, Doug Davidson, Lauralee Bell, Thom Bierdz, Jeanne Cooper, Tricia Cast, Kate Linder. (Third row) Carolyn Conwell, Nathan Purdee, Marguerite Ray, Stephanie E. Williams, Colby Chester, Eileen Davidson, Brenda Dickson, Jerry Douglas, Mich[...] Damian, Beth Maitland, Patty Weaver, Michael Corbett, Todd Cur[...] row) Brett Hadley, Scott Palmer, Michael Evans, Rod [...] Parucha, Melody Thomas Scott, Ashley Nicole [...] Roberta Leighton, Terry Lester, Anthony Peña [...] Templeton, Jennifer Karr.

Nina Arvesen on the rocks in Bermuda—
intoxicating!

Lee and Bill Bell, Melody Thomas Scott, Eric Braeden, Lauralee Bell, and
Kimberlin Brown visited the "real" home of The Young and the Restless,
Genoa City, Wisconsin, in April 1996, and met with gathered fans at the Grand
Geneva resort in Lake Geneva.

259

n, Quinn Redeker, Jeanne Cooper, Eric Braeden, John Nelson-Alden, Melody Thomas
ᶠ St. John, Victoria Rowell, Michael Damian, Lauralee Bell, Doug Davidson, Heather
st. (Top row) Michael Tylo, Laura Bryan Birn, Brenda Epperson, Kate Linder, Don
-Recht, Veronica Redd-Forrest, Peter Barton, Paul Walker, Kimberlin Brown, Anthony

ael
tis. (Back
Arrants, Robert
Millan, Eric Braeden,
, Don Diamond, Christopher

1994. (Front row) Peter Bergman, Melody Thomas Scott, Eric Braeden, Jeanne Cooper, Jerry Douglas, Jess Walton, Doug Davidson, Lauralee Bell. (Second row) J. Eddie Peck, Heather Tom, Signy Coleman, Kristoff St. John, Victoria Rowell, Don Diamont, Tracey Bregman-Recht, Scott Reeves, Tricia Cast. (Third row) Josh Taylor, Beth Maitland, Diana Barton, John Castellanos, Tonya Lee Williams, Veronica Redd-Forrest, Brenda Epperson, Michael Tylo. (Top row) Michael Evans, Patty Weaver, Kate Linder, Sharon Farrell, Carolyn Conwell, Laura Bryan Birn, Anthony Peña.

Jeanne Cooper and Eric Braeden talk with Dick Van Dyke during a break from taping a special episode of Diagnosis Murder which featured the Y&R cast.

Nick Scotti and Josie Davis as Tony and Grace.

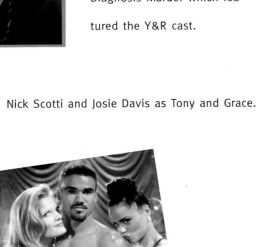

Shemar Moore and Kristoff St. John perform a balancing act.

Michelle Stafford (Phyllis) and Victoria Rowell (Drucilla) with Shemar Moore (Malcolm).

1997. (Front row, seated) Jennifer Scott, Josh McCaffrey, Rouhi Taylor, Tom Puckett, Marnie Saitta, Robin Brady, Don Jacobs, Eva Marie P. Arquero, Michael Okamura, Bryant Jones, Brooke Marie Bridges, Gail Camacho, Camryn Grimes, Barry Wittman, Kathy Jones, Monty Brinton, Meryl O'Loughlin, Victoria Currea, Charles Sherman, Barbara Daly, Sarah Bunch. (Second row) Trina Gavieres, Stacy Caballero, Nora Wade, Frank Tobin, Christina Knack, Kay Wataguchi, Paula Flanagan, Lauralee Bell, Doug Davidson, Melody Thomas Scott, Eric Braeden, Patti Denney, David Shaughnessy, Lee Phillip Bell, Bill Bell, Jeanne Cooper, Nancy Bradley Wiard, Arrick Anderson, Peter Bergman, Mary Jo Fortin, Jess Walton, Ralph Wilcox, Annette Jones, Taia Red, Jerry Douglas, Josh O'Connell, Rhavan Briggs, Linda Dalbeck. (Third row) Jennifer Johns, Carrie Christine, Gina Chapa, Tricia Cast, Michael Damian, Alex Donnelley, Sharon Case, Joshua Morrow, ... Peck, Shari Shattuck, Sandra Nelson. (Fourth row) David Bruce, Peter Helenek, Sabryn Genet, ...habazzi, Ashley Jones, Nick Scotti, Jennifer Gareis, Tonya Lee Williams, Shemar Moore, Victoria ... (Top row) Laura Bryan Birn, Patty Weaver, Granville Van Dusen, Heath Kizzier, Candice Daly, ...y Peña, Kate Linder, Marita De Leon, Jennifer Qualls.

25 Letters from Avid Fans

The Young and the Restless is my second family, my escape, my video recorder's best friend, my day's completion, and my "second most passionate love."

—Carol A. Piper. age: 49
Allentown, PA
tuning in for 24 years

I truly enjoy *Y&R* because, despite our busy schedules, this is the one hour of the day that my wife and I faithfully share together.

—David Look. age: 32
Wisconsin Rapids, WI
tuning in for 8 years

The Young and the Restless is the first daytime soap to put Afro-American characters in nonstereotypical storylines that are "color-blind" and real.

—Johnny L. Finley II.
Springfield, MO

I have loved *Y&R* since day one. I will never forget how a shirtless Snapper stirred a 12-year-old's heart.

—Tammy Hicks. age: 37
Salamanca, NY
tuning in for 25 years

It's my childhood favorites—the kaleidoscope and Viewmaster—rolled into one! A world of colorful personalities and frame-by-frame intrigue! The "masterpiece of soaps."

—Lydia M. Barker. age: 44
Schenectady, NY
tuning in for 25 years

I love *The Young and the Restless* because it is the American dream on the screen—upward mobility from ground floor to glamour.

—Elizabeth K. Copple. age: 28
Mt. Holly, NC
tuning in for 13 years

Begin with heaping portions of creativity and delicious storylines. Fold in romance, intrigue, and adventure. Add the Newmans. Simmer for 25 glorious years! *Y&R* rules.

—Jonathan Weinberg. age: 31
Bethesda, MD
tuning in for 6 years

I have few memories of my deceased grandfather. One of them is being a little girl, curled up on his lap, and watching your show.

—Cindy Simak. age: 17
Houston, TX
tuning in for 12 years

I am neither Young nor Restless, but for 25 years you've allowed me to reap the benefits of pretending to be both. Thank you.

—Fran Smith. age: 68
Hilo, HI
tuning in for 25 years

The show lets us middle-class individuals see how the "other half" lives, but it also reveals that being wealthy doesn't mean living problem free.

—Antoinette Jewel Lott. age: 22
Fort Lauderdale, FL
tuning in for 3 years

Genoa City is both a home and a place far away . . . I love that about *Y&R*. It makes the *everyday* exotic and the exotic *every day*.

—Glenn Cummings. age: 33
Charlottesville, VA
tuning in for 15 years

I love *Y&R* like family—I laugh with them, I cry with them, I defend them, and sometimes I'm ashamed of them.

—Patsy Bullock. age: 49
Bainbridge, GA
tuning in for 25 years

I, Lana, take *Y&R* as my loyally watched soap. I promise to be true through glamour and deceit, "ruthlessness" and happiness. I'll love you always.

—Lana Hampp. age: 26
Maryland Heights, MO
tuning in for 15 years

I love *The Young and the Restless* because I grew up with it. I loved it so much that I hated to start first grade.

—Teresa Blow Gibson. age: 30
Woodbridge, VA
tuning in for 25 years

I love *The Young and the Restless* because of the excellent stories, the superb acting, and the low percentage of turnovers. Great entertainment.

—Evelyn Marr. age: 71
Fremont, NE
tuning in for 25 years

When I was 5 I loved Snapper. When I was 17 I loved Paul. Now I'm 28 and I just still love *Y&R*!

—Michelle Aldridge. age: 28
Clear Lake, WA
tuning in for 23 years

I love *Y&R* because of its sensitive portrayal of real-life issues and . . . Ryan's dimples.

—Annette Taylor. age: 45
Garland, TX
tuning in for 25 years

I love *Y&R* because after having my daughter, who was born with jaundice, the only thing that would calm her was the *Y&R* theme song.

—Tina M. Huff. age: 34
Willet, NY
tuning in for 22 years

It is the most imaginative, refreshing, unpredictable, sensual, exasperating, turbulent, explosive, teasing, compassionate, captivating, bold, original, thought-provoking, and socially conscious daytime drama on television!

—Nicholas Powell. age: 40
Jacksonville, FL
tuning in for 25 years

I can "Romalotti," but feel like a "Newman" when I come home, happy as a "Cricket" to "Sharon" the latest *Y&R* adventure.

—Raylene M. Deck. age: 62
Valley Center, CA
tuning in for 12 years

In Genoa City, men can be sensitive without looking sappy, and women can be powerful professionals without being offensive. That's why I love *Y&R*.

—Linda S. Babcock. age: 34
West Bloomfield, MI
tuning in for 19 years

From the beginning, we grew together. Through motherhood, school, and career, *Y&R* has always been there. You're simply the best—may we grow old together.

—Carolyn Butkier. age: 49
Mohegan Lake, NY
tuning in for 25 years

I wouldn't miss *Y&R* for anything. It gets so exciting I can barely stand it. Please let Peter Bergman know that I'm available for marriage.

—Nancy L. Gooch. age: 40
Upland, CA
tuning in for 9 years of sheer pleasure

It got me through putting a husband through both chiropractic and medical school without a divorce or nervous breakdown.
25-year watcher—25th wedding anniversary 1997.

—Ericka Henderson. age: 50 years young
Davenport, IA
tuning in for 25 years

Jack's wit
Katherine's grit

Malcolm's style
Paul's smile

Nick's cool
Victor's rule

Danny's dreams
Dru's schemes

Victoria's brassiness
Nikki's classiness

Cricket's guts
Phyllis is nuts

—Chris Guthrie. age: 12
Morris, IL
tuning in for 3 years

The Young and the Restless has been such a significant part of my life since my parents created it in 1973 and I began playing 'Cricket' in 1984. From that day on, I've had a wonderful opportunity to learn. I would like to thank everyone in the production staff, crew, and our incredibly talented cast because I have learned something from every one of you.

But this is anniversary time, and it takes two to make a successful marriage. A commitment that is still going strong after 25 years is a major accomplishment. This could not have occurred without the marriage of the creators, Bill and Lee Bell and our viewers.

Since I can give Bill and Lee a "thank you" in person, I'd like to concentrate on our audience. Thank You. Thank you for allowing me to do something that very few actors have had the opportunity to do, that is, literally grow up in front of your eyes. It has been a pleasure to go from a 1 yr. old Cricket to 28 yr. old, married Christine.

Happy 25th Anniversary Y&R. It's been a

What a great ride this has been. I am forever grateful! Love, *Peter Bergman*

The Young and the Restless *Peter Bergman*

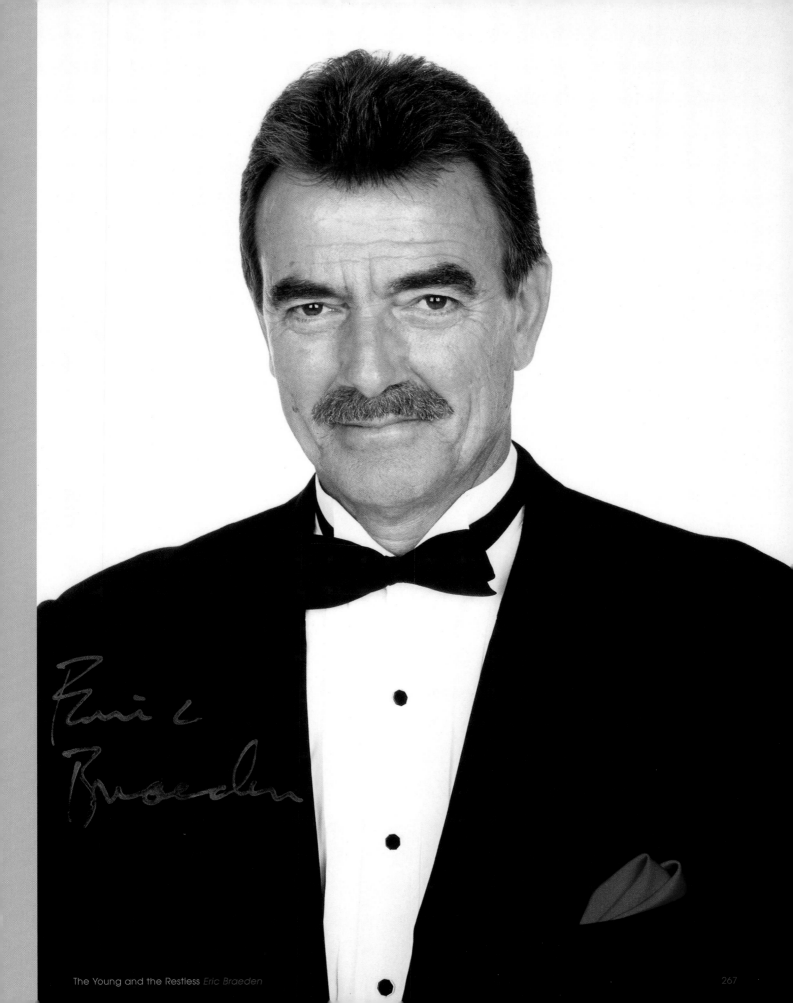

Pictures from my Personal Photo Album

My boyfriend RON

My dog Jack

My best friend Sara

Sunbathing AND READING A GOOD magazine. One of my favorite pastimes.

My family

Sharon's Page

Dear Readers,

What a wonderful opportunity it is to be able to thank you for all your support through the eleven or so years that I've been with this outstanding show. I have spent over a third of my life and over half my career associated with The Young and the Restless, so you might imagine the close connection I have with the people who make the show happen every day. I even married one of them and I am privileged to call many of them my close friends. It is to these people with whom I work that I would like to pay homage. I couldn't possibly do the work that I do without every single one of the cast and crew members and all of the people who work at Television City. They give me such an enormous amount of love and encouragement. Not only am I a better actress because of them, I am also a better person. They are kind, considerate, and a most precious source of strength. Not only are they the nicest people in the world but they are the best at what they do. Each one has my respect and admiration. They're the people who make the show look and sound its best. Some of their names are on the crawl at the end of the show and some are not. However, from the third floor to the ground floor, each and every one of them, without exception, is fundamental to the success of the show. To them I offer my deepest respect and gratitude and ask them to join me in a heartfelt tribute to the man without whom none of this would be—the ever present, inventive, and so endlessly creative Mr. William J. Bell. If it were not for him, I would not have my darling husband, I would not have the wonderfully rich life I have, and I would not have in my life one of my very dearest friends, Lauralee.

I am so lucky to be a working actress. Add to that the good fortune of being able to work for and with the people I do, and I am doubly blessed. Thank you for watching and allowing me into your home on a daily basis. Your patronage keeps us all working and we appreciate you so very very much.

Sincerely,

Tricia Cast

Katherine Chancellor has allowed me to walk by her side for two decades plus four years. The Lady has introduced me to people worldwide . . . people I would never have had the pleasure of knowing had it not been for her. She paid for the college education of my three children. She has given me a weekly allowance, new cars, and a new home. She is so generous to me there is no earthly way to repay her except to be grateful and respectful of her at all times. She is a reasonable and just Lady . . . she is the best friend I have. And I know Jeanne Cooper is the best friend she will ever have. Right, Katherine??!!!

Jeanne Cooper

A LONG TIME AGO IN A FARAWAY GALAXY, THERE WAS A SINGER–VIBE/KEYBOARD PLAYER FROM THE REMOTE PLANET OF BONSALL, CALIFORNIA, POPULATION 498. THANKS TO HIS FAMILY OF 11, THEY CRACKED THE IMPERIAL CODE AND MADE IT TO HOLLYWOOD. AFTER BATTLING JABA THE HUT (AKA AGENTS/MANAGERS) AND TOURING UNSAVORY NIGHTCLUBS AND REMOTE MILITARY BASES, HE WAS SPOTTED ON AMERICAN BANDSTAND AND RECRUITED BY THE BIG KAHUNA, Y&R. THEY GAVE THE ROOKIE SIX MONTHS TO GET ON BASE. AND WHEN WE SAY ROOKIE WE MEAN FOUR DAYS OF ACTING CLASS THE WEEK BEFORE THE SEASON OPENER. LUCKY FOR HIM, THE BALL CLUB OWNER (BILL BELL) GAVE HIM A SHOT AND THE SIX MONTHS TURNED INTO 17 YEARS.

IN MY WILDEST DREAMS, I COULD NEVER HAVE GUESSED THAT MY LIFE WOULD TURN OUT THE WAY IT HAS. WHEN I WAS A KID, ALL I WANTED WAS TO BE A PROFESSIONAL BASEBALL PLAYER. OF COURSE THAT WASN'T MEANT TO BE AND I ENDED UP IN A DIFFERENT FIELD. BUT LUCKY FOR ME, I WAS FORTUNATE ENOUGH TO LAND ON A CHAMPIONSHIP TEAM. THE YOUNG AND THE RESTLESS HAS NEVER BEEN JUST A JOB TO ME; IT HAS BEEN A VERY IMPORTANT PART OF MY LIFE. IN THE PAST 17 YEARS, I HAVE HAD THE PLEASURE OF WORKING WITH SOME AMAZINGLY GIFTED PEOPLE AND THEY HAVE BECOME LIKE FAMILY TO ME. I HAVE BASICALLY GROWN UP ON THE SHOW AND FEEL INCREDIBLY FORTUNATE TO HAVE HAD A CHARACTER CREATED FOR ME THAT I HAVE SO MUCH FUN WITH. I HAVE TO ADMIT THAT THERE ARE TIMES WHEN DANNY ROMALOTTI HAS BECOME SO CLOSE TO ME THAT I FORGET WHERE I END AND HE BEGINS. BUT IT'S A GOOD THING BECAUSE I'VE LEARNED A LOT FROM DANNY, LIKE STEER CLEAR FROM ANY WOMEN THAT HAVE GRADUATED FROM THE UNIVERSITY OF DECEIT AND MANIPULATION WITH A MAJOR IN MICKEY SLIPPING–BLOODTEST SWITCHING AND GOT AN A ON THEIR HIT-AND-RUN DRIVER'S TEST. NOT TO MENTION THE TELLTALE SIGN TO STEER CLEAR IF SHE OWNS A RIDING CROP BUT DOESN'T OWN A HORSE. NEEDLESS TO SAY, THERE IS NEVER A DULL DAY IN GENOA CITY, THANKS TO THE WONDERFUL IMAGINATIONS OF THE WRITERS ON THE SHOW.

OVER THE YEARS I HAVE HAD THE OPPORTUNITY TO MEET A GREAT NUMBER OF THE Y&R AUDIENCE. THEY ALSO HELP OUT AND GIVE ME POINTERS ABOUT WHICH WOMAN TO STEER CLEAR FROM. ACTUALLY, HEARING THEIR DIFFERENT STORIES AND HOW MUCH THE SHOW MEANS TO THEM HAS BROUGHT A GREAT DEAL OF JOY TO MY WORK AND PUSHES ME EVEN HARDER TO TRY TO ALWAYS BETTER MY PERFORMANCE. LET'S FACE IT, TO A LOT OF US, THE YOUNG AND THE RESTLESS IS MORE THAN JUST A SOAP.

IN CELEBRATION OF A QUARTER OF A CENTURY

MAY 15, 1978 WAS MY FIRST DAY ON Y&R. IT
FOREVER CHANGED MY LIFE. IT WAS SHOW
NUMBER 1500 AND SOMETHING. TWO
CONSECUTIVE DECADES FOLLOWED. I GREW
RIGHT ALONG WITH PAUL. EACH OF US
LEARNED FROM THE OTHER'S SUCCESSES AND
FAILURES.

LOOKING BACK I SEE A BOY...
NOW I SEE A MAN.
I WAS SINGLE...
NOW I AM A HUSBAND.
I WAS A KID...
NOW I AM A FATHER.
I WAS A JESTER...
AND NOW...WELL, SOME THINGS NEVER CHANGE.

I FEEL SO BLESSED TO BE A PART OF THE
YOUNG AND THE RESTLESS FAMILY. MY
THANKS TO ALL--FROM THE CREATORS TO THE
VIEWERS AND EVERYONE IN BETWEEN--WHO
HAVE CONTRIBUTED TO MAKING MY "RESTLESS"
YEARS THE BEST YEARS OF MY LIFE. I RAISE
MY GLASS IN ANTICIPATION--TO ALL THE
STORIES YET TO BE TOLD.

Oh, Lucky Me !

And for that,
I'd like to thank
all the wonderful fans
for their generous
support...

And, thankyou to
Lee and Bill Bell
for making me part
of the Y and R family.

Love, Alex
                xox

Alex Donnelley

This is a prayer that I wrote and shared at Hunter's christening. I thought it appropriate to share with our fans.

Dear Lord,

I come to you today and ask for your guidance, your love, and your wisdom . . . with this prayer.

Words cannot express my gratitude for your giving my love, my wife Kymberly, the birth of our son Hunter. We tried for five long years to conceive and it seemed so futile. Kymberly never lost faith. But me, well I'm an old fool that never learns. Your love is so powerful it even embraces me. And I thank you from the bottom of my heart.

Our son Hunter is the reflection of your light. He illuminates and bonds our families into one.

I ask that you guide him with the power of "Your Light" throughout his life. That he always feel you within him as a center of reason, of consideration, of patience, and kindness and love towards his fellow man.

That his work be an honorable expression of his Talent and never overwhelm or control his life.

If he is given special gifts by you, may they be used wisely.

If he has fame and power, may he always remember the Source is you, Dear Lord, and wear them with humility.

And may he always know . . . "The Greatest Thing You'll Ever Learn Is Just to Love and Be Loved in Return."

Love

Jerry

A SPECIAL DEDICATION

To all of the people who have helped me to get this far. Without the love and support I have received I could have never accomplished my successes in life. Thank you to my family who raised me well & taught me the values I carry throughout my life. To my friends who have always been by my side, sharing with me the joy of friendship.

↑(Camryn(Cassie) and me(Grace) and our mom's)↑

To my boyfriend who has showed me the meaning of true romance & true love. To all of the cast & crew who have made my work at Y&R so much fun. To the directors, producers & writers for their wonderful work. And to all of the fans for watching & making "The Young & The Restless" #1

Thanks to all of you !!!

↑(me and my boyfriend, Scott Decker)↑

JOHN PASCHAL/JPI

Best wishes to all that have touched my life. Thank you for your constant love and support !!! Love, Jennifer

(my cute nephew, James, who has touched my heart)
→

↑(my lovely mother & father)↑

Jennifer L. Gareis

To the family and friends of *The Young and the Restless*

When I was offered the opportunity to be a part of this commemorative book, I was delighted and proud to be included. My first instinct was to thank the fans for spending their valuable time each day watching the drama of Genoa City unfold. As I travel, I am truly amazed at the response that is generated around the country by our show and the passions it produces in people. I am honored to be a part of such success!

In much of the mail I receive I am asked quite often what things I like to do while I am not working or spending time with my wife and kids; camping, golf, and woodworking are high on the list of hobbies but the focus of time is used for writing. Whether it's a book, letters, journal writing, or poetry—I simply enjoy the process. I thought perhaps I would contribute a sample of my obsession. THANKS AGAIN FOR WATCHING.

Prologue to an untitled book

Scott Garrison, although now a strong and confident 24-year-old, was nervous and even a little scared about this meeting as he knocked lightly on the long-used screen door. The ancient feelings of a terrified 14-year-old somehow emerging from the depths of his repression, this ranch, he thought as he waited, was the source of a lot of pain . . . would . . . *could* that be changed today? Just as his fear was beginning to overtake him, the main door slowly opened and through the screen mesh Scott barely recognized his father.

The span of 10 years since their last meeting had not been kind to the man; although still large and strong-looking, Dan Garrison slumped a bit at the shoulders which only years ago had been straight and proud. The older man's hand, which held the door glaringly, displayed the many years of sun-beaten ranch work combined with the unmistakable affliction of rheumatoid arthritis, each knuckle swollen, altering the natural fall of the hand into a crippled half-fist. His deep-set eyes had hooded over with a heavy fold of skin and his dark strawberry-red hair, although still thick, was scattered with gray . . . Standing at the door, Scott could only stare at this once-great man.

He could tell that his father sensed a feeling of recognition but under the low, late afternoon autumn light he wasn't able to connect the unexpected visit. "Can I help you?"

Scott's heart jumped. *The voice was the same.* The same deep, Irish-tinted cadence still held the strength and control that Scott remembered from his youth. Emotion rose in his constricted throat, nearly preventing him from speaking; finally, he managed to utter quietly, barely audible, "Dad, it's me."

All of the features in his father's face froze. In any other situation, his reaction would have been comical but for now the stakes were much too high for this exiled son to notice such things. His father just looked at him. Scott tried but couldn't read the thoughts that flashed through the man's eyes. After less than two seconds, he was regretting this moment. *He still hates me . . . Damn it! . . . why would I do this to myself?! Why would I come back? . . . Because you miss your family!!*—That was it and he knew it. He had been thinking of his mother and father for years and he knew that if he waited until one of them died he would never forgive himself . . . *No, I will not run away again . . .*

In disbelief, Dan's head involuntarily tilted to one side, trying to accept the moment. Without leaving Scott's eyes, the older man reached out and inched open the screen door, which Scott side-stepped around. The two men were left facing each other in stillness for what seemed like an eternity to Scott.

The grown boy stood unsure as his dad's eyes began to glisten. *Oh God . . .* A hundred thoughts raced simultaneously through Scott's mind refusing to connect the words that wouldn't come. Finally, at a loss, he reached his arm out for a handshake.

His father looked at the outstretched hand, then back into his son's eyes; with a small shake of his head he allowed many years of debilitating ego to fall away. On the porch of his long-time ranch home, Dan stepped forward and drew his boy into his arms.

The instant Scott felt his father's muscled arms around his shoulders and smelled the familiar mixture of Old Spice and ranch dust, his apprehension faded, turning to heartache and longing. The suffering and pain from long ago was never to replace the love a son feels and needs from his father; it had only been masked with complications. Without a word, the father and son clutched to each other minute after minute, the tears flowing freely as the two silently cried. The feelings of happiness, regret, homecoming, unnecessary loss, sorrow, and rekindled father–child love passed between the two as if handed from one to the other, neither man allowing the moment to end.

"Oh my God . . . !" In shock, almost to herself, Peg gasped. She had walked out of the kitchen to see who the visitor was and saw a 10-year fantasy coming true, her husband and her son—*together*!

The men released their embrace and Scott moved over to her. With a tear-stained face, he stood for a moment trying to remember the collection of words he had rehearsed a thousand times . . . Dazed, the only appropriate words for the moment surfaced . . . "I'm sorry, Mom."

Hearing her boy's voice for the first time in years, Peg's hands covered her face as she erupted into tears. Scott stepped forward and held his overcome mother until she threw her arms around him and held him fiercely against her, making sure he never disappeared again.

Dan watched his wife and son as long as he could withstand, until finally being forced by painful, welling emotion to turn away. The moment of exhilaration and happiness collided with the never-ending, festering guilt created so many years ago. His usually rigid thoughts exploded into fragments and the only thing he could do—the only thing his body would let him do . . . was release them . . . Dan sat on the front step and cried out loud for the first time in 40 years . . . alone.

Heath Kizzier

When I was a little boy, My favorite game was "Play-Pretend". For the last three and a half years, I've had the greatest time of my life "Pretending" to be Malcolm Winters .... I thank my family friends, and definately my fans. All your love and support is what gave me the strength to chase a childhood dream. Thanks for believing in me.... Always believe in you... And Always believe in Dreams !!!!

SHEMAR
"MALCOLM"

Dear YR fans!

I just wanted to thank you for welcoming Nick into your hearts. It truly has been the best three years of my life playing Nick. On my countless PAs (public appearances) that I have done in the United States and Canada—you the fans have shown me how important Nick is to *The Young and the Restless* and that makes me proud. I look forward to being Nick in the future and meeting fans who are so very important to *The Young and the Restless* being the Number 1 show.

Love ya later

John J. Morrow "Nick!"

Joshua Morrow

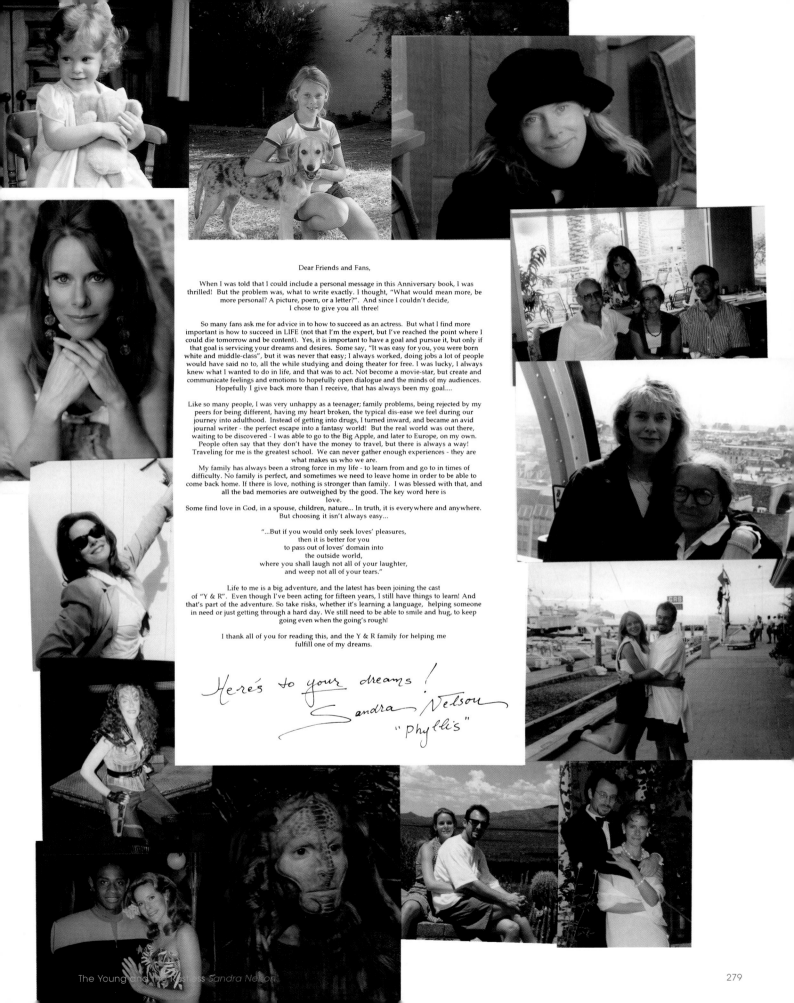

Dear Friends and Fans,

When I was told that I could include a personal message in this Anniversary book, I was thrilled! But the problem was, what to write exactly. I thought, "What would mean more, be more personal? A picture, poem, or a letter?". And since I couldn't decide, I chose to give you all three!

So many fans ask me for advice in to how to succeed as an actress. But what I find more important is how to succeed in LIFE (not that I'm the expert, but I've reached the point where I could die tomorrow and be content). Yes, it is important to have a goal and pursue it, but only if that goal is servicing your dreams and desires. Some say, "It was easy for you, you were born white and middle-class", but it was never that easy; I always worked, doing jobs a lot of people would have said no to, all the while studying and doing theater for free. I was lucky, I always knew what I wanted to do in life, and that was to act. Not become a movie-star, but create and communicate feelings and emotions to hopefully open dialogue and the minds of my audiences. Hopefully I give back more than I receive, that has always been my goal....

Like so many people, I was very unhappy as a teenager; family problems, being rejected by my peers for being different, having my heart broken, the typical dis-ease we feel during our journey into adulthood. Instead of getting into drugs, I turned inward, and became an avid journal writer - the perfect escape into a fantasy world! But the real world was out there, waiting to be discovered - I was able to go to the Big Apple, and later to Europe, on my own. People often say that they don't have the money to travel, but there is always a way! Traveling for me is the greatest school. We can never gather enough experiences - they are what makes us who we are.

My family has always been a strong force in my life - to learn from and go to in times of difficulty. No family is perfect, and sometimes we need to leave home in order to be able to come back home. If there is love, nothing is stronger than family. I was blessed with that, and all the bad memories are outweighed by the good. The key word here is love.

Some find love in God, in a spouse, children, nature... In truth, it is everywhere and anywhere. But choosing it isn't always easy...

"...But if you would only seek loves' pleasures,
then it is better for you
to pass out of loves' domain into
the outside world,
where you shall laugh not all of your laughter,
and weep not all of your tears."

Life to me is a big adventure, and the latest has been joining the cast of "Y & R". Even though I've been acting for fifteen years, I still have things to learn! And that's part of the adventure. So take risks, whether it's learning a language, helping someone in need or just getting through a hard day. We still need to be able to smile and hug, to keep going even when the going's rough!

I thank all of you for reading this, and the Y & R family for helping me fulfill one of my dreams.

Here's to your dreams!
Sandra Nelson
"Phyllis"

J. EDDIE PECK   ``COLE HOWARD``

Five years ago I auditioned for the role of Cole Howard in the office of Executive Producer, Bill Bell. That was the first time we had met and yet his sincerity and professionalism immediately made me feel welcome.

Bill is a creative genius. The elegance, class and ingenuity of this show comes from the man himself. Writing and producing a show everyday for twenty-five years is something that all in the entertainment industry applaud.

Bill Bell, Kay Alden and our staff of writers have created a character in Cole Howard with integrity, intelligence, sinsitivity, and can still get away with wearing a pair of jeans.

Working on The Young and the Restless I seem to have a friend everywhere I go. It's great to be a part of a show where so many viewers include the Y&R family as part of their day. You, our fans, friends and new viewers help make us #1. We do our best for you and I thank you for supporting The Young and the Restless.

Eddie Peck
"Cole Howard"

To all of you who have made this phenomenon possible,

Words can't express my gratitude for the wonderful experience I've had in the years I've been a part of the Y&R team. I can't imagine a more loving + caring group of people to work with. I especially want to express my thanks + appreciation to you, the fans, who support us through thick + thin. Without you, none of this would be possible. It is my wish to give you another 25 years of what you've tasted, and then some. I hope we satisfy your appetites. Happy 25th!!!

Thank you to my beautiful wife + children, for they are the reason I breathe.

Scott
Reev

The Young and the Restless *Scott Reeves*

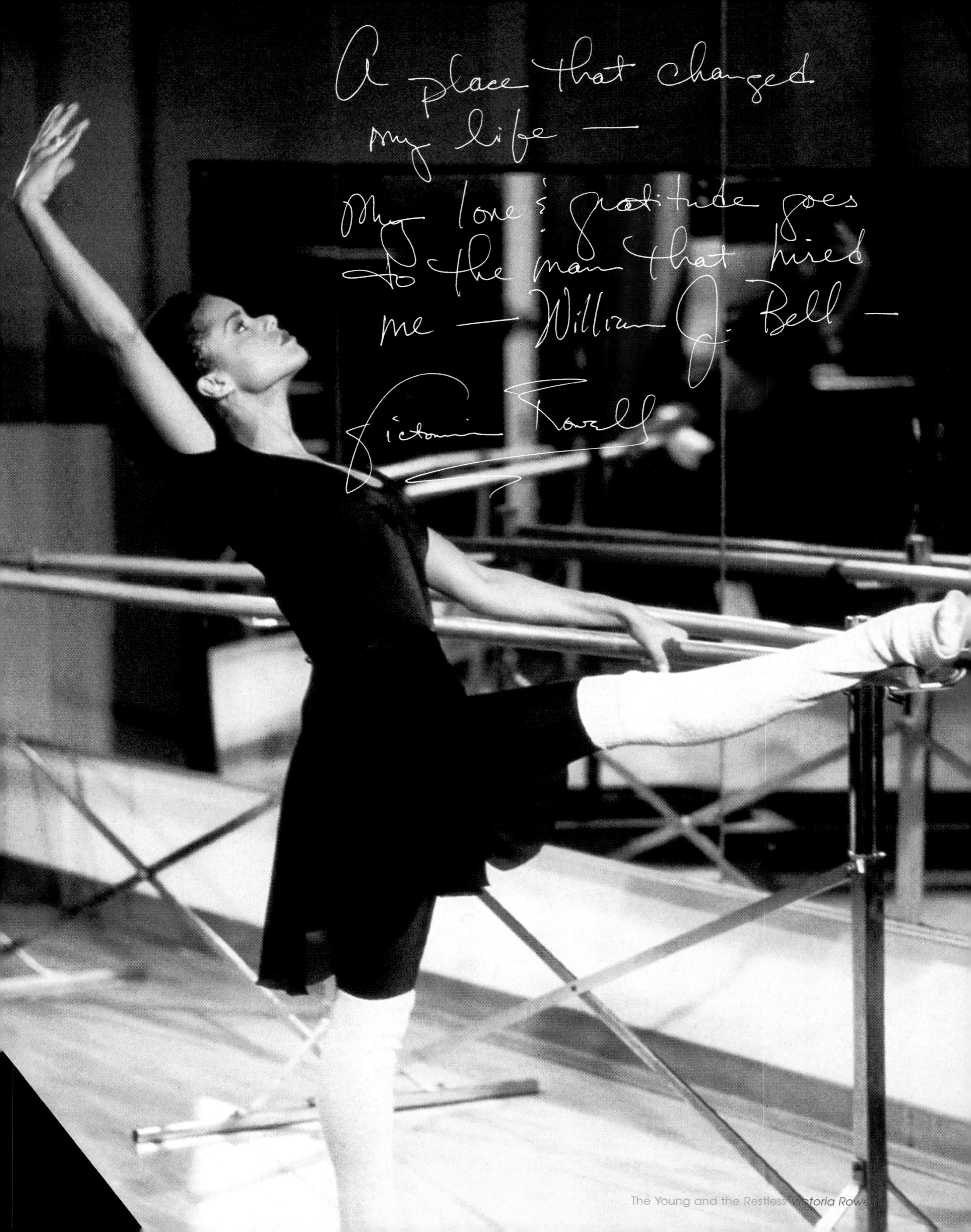

A place that changed
my life —
My love & gratitude goes
to the man that hired
me — William J. Bell —
Victoria Rowell

The Young and the Restless *Victoria Rowell*

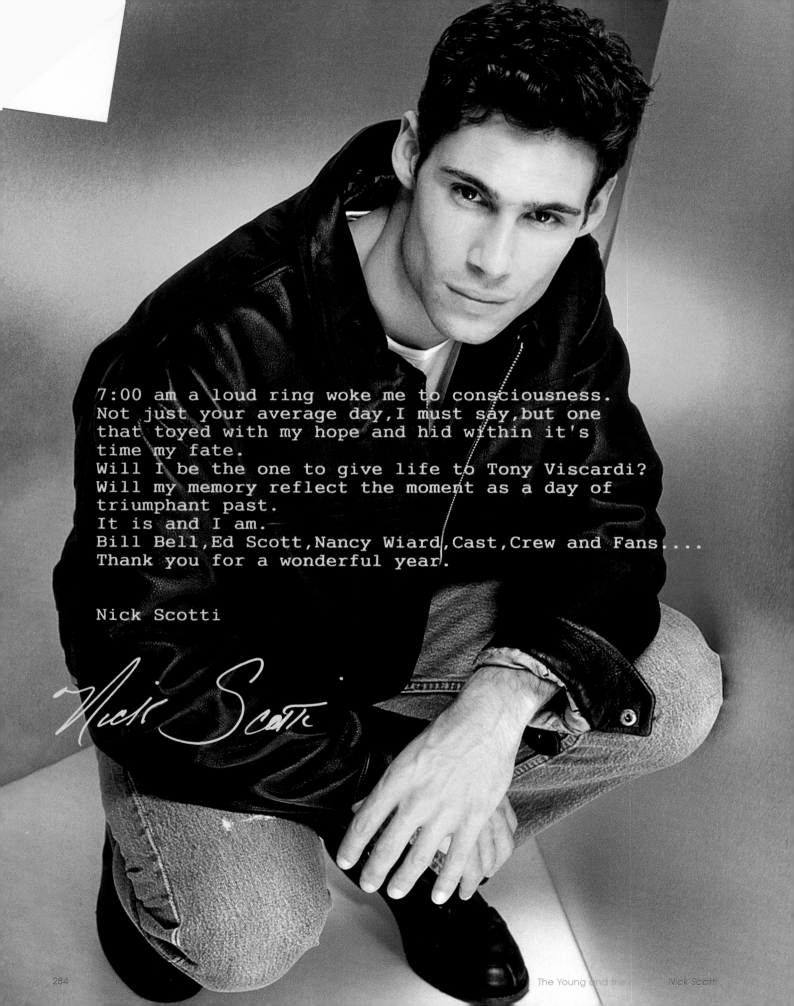

7:00 am a loud ring woke me to consciousness.
Not just your average day,I must say,but one
that toyed with my hope and hid within it's
time my fate.
Will I be the one to give life to Tony Viscardi?
Will my memory reflect the moment as a day of
triumphant past.
It is and I am.
Bill Bell,Ed Scott,Nancy Wiard,Cast,Crew and Fans....
Thank you for a wonderful year.

Nick Scotti

I'm playing a part
that's noble and proud.
She's rich and she's strong,
no pouting's allowed.

Others have played her
before me, I'm told.
(Though I never saw them,
I was tuned into "Bold").

But my husband was paying
attention and so,
when they held auditions,
he told me to "Go!"

I read for some guys,
really nice, Bill and Ed.
And later they called me
"You're Ashley!" they said.

For almost two years now
I've been compared
to two other ladies
in this role we have shared.

"How are you different?"
The press always queried.
I don't really know
except they both got married.

You see, it's the character,
Ashley must stand alone.
Both those ladies were great
but I've made her my own.

So thanks to Bill Bell
and, of course, to Ed Scott
and all of you others
who've helped me a lot!

I see it all clearly
my perception's not blurred.
I'm damn glad to be
Ashley Abbott the third.

IF NOT IMPOSSIBLE, TO CAPSULIZE ON A SINGLE PIECE OF PAPER THE MANY EVENTS THAT HAVE TRANSPIRED OVER ~~EN YEARS FOR ME AS AN ACTOR ON THE YOUNG AND THE RESTLESS. LOVINGLY, I CALL IT THE "FACTORY," A PLACE ~~~~TIVELY AS A TEAM, WE CHURN OUT A POLISHED 40 MINUTES OF QUALITY ENTERTAINMENT EVERY SINGLE WEEKDAY. THE SHOW ~~ TRULY A WILD ROLLER-COASTER RIDE THAT WINDS ITS WAY THROUGH AN INTRICATE MAZE OF DIFFICULT ISSUES. IT'S A HOME WHERE I FIND MYSELF COMPLETELY ABSORBED IN THE MOMENT, LIVING IN THE HECTIC, OFTEN CHAOTIC, WORLD OF THE WINTERS CLAN. MANY TIMES I HAVE CRIED MYSELF BACK TO REALITY AFTER LIVING IN THE EMOTIONAL SURREAL CONFINES OF GENOA CITY, A PLACE WHERE ANYTHING CAN HAPPEN, AND DOES. IT'S AMAZING TO ME THAT LIFE OFTEN IMITATES ART, AND VICE VERSA, UPON WHERE I'VE FOUND MANY PARALLELS BETWEEN MY OWN PERSONAL SOAP OPERA AND THE FANTASY OF THE YOUNG AND THE RESTLESS. THE "FACTORY" HAS BEEN A SAFE HAVEN FOR ME, THE QUIET WITHIN THE STORM, AND I AM EVER SO BLESSED AND GRATEFUL FOR THE INCREDIBLE OPPORTUNITY TO WORK WITH SUCH A TALENTED ARRAY OF UNIQUE INDIVIDUALS.

WHEN I BEGAN MY JOURNEY ON THE SHOW IN 1991, I WAS 24, MARRIED, WITH A YOUNG AND RESTLESS TWO-YEAR-OLD SON NAMED JULIAN, WHO HAS SINCE BEEN JOINED ON THE PLANET EARTH BY HIS SISTER PARIS. AS I WATCH THEM GROW, I AM OVERWHELMED WITH EMOTION, KNOWING THAT MY REAL-LIFE JOB IN LIFE IS TO TEACH AND GUIDE THEM WITH AS MUCH LOVE AND UNDERSTANDING AS I CAN GIVE. MY CHILDREN HAVE BECOME A STRONG SOURCE OF INSPIRATION FOR MY WORK, AND THEY CONTINUE TO GIVE ME THE NECESSARY CONFIDENCE FOR MY DAILY ROUTINE. THEY ARE THE SHINING STARS IN MY FAMILY AND THEIR STARLIGHT GROWS BRIGHTER EVERY DAY. OH, BY THE WAY, IT DELIGHTS ME TO NO END THAT BOTH OF MY CHILDREN COULD CARE LESS ABOUT WATCHING DEAR OLD DAD ON THE TUBE, OPTING INSTEAD FOR THE DISNEY CHANNEL!

THE ROLE OF NEIL WINTERS IS INDEED A SPECIAL ONE FOR ME. I AM PROUD TO PLAY SUCH AN HONORABLE, UPSTANDING MAN, FULL OF CHARACTER, FAMILY VALUES, AND MORALS. I AM PROUD OF BILL BELL, WHO HAS MANAGED TO TRANSCEND THE COLOR BARRIER BY GIVING AN AFRICAN-AMERICAN FAMILY THE SAME HOPES AND DREAMS, DEFEATS AND FAILURES AS ANY OTHER AMERICAN FAMILY. WITH THE STEREOTYPE LONG REMOVED, IT HAS GIVEN ME THE CHANCE TO EXPLORE THE UNIVERSAL ESSENCE OF NEIL, A MAN WHO IS NOT AFRAID TO SHED A TEAR OR LAUGH IN THE FACE OF IMPENDING DOOM. FROM BOARD MEETINGS TO HIS EVER-SO-PRECIOUS COMPUTER, TO HIS HOME AND THE GOODNIGHT KISS THAT HE PLANTS ON BABY LILY AND HIS WIFE DRUCILLA, NEIL IS THE QUINTESSENTIAL MAN! I CAN RECALL SECRETLY WISHING THAT BILL BELL WOULD EXPLORE THE DARK SIDE OF NEIL, BUT AS TIME MARCHES ON, I FEEL CONTENT AND COMFORTABLE WITH DISPLAYING ALL OF NEIL'S GOOD ATTRIBUTES. HOWEVER, I'VE BEEN TOLD BY CERTAIN FAMILY MEMBERS THAT NEIL SHOULD REFRAIN FROM STEPPING ON THE DANCE FLOOR!

THIS SHORT STORY WOULD BE AMISS IF I DIDN'T MENTION A FEW OF THE PEOPLE THAT I HAVE ENCOUNTERED AND HOLD CLOSE TO MY HEART ON THIS REMARKABLE ENSEMBLE SHOW. THE INFECTIOUS LAUGH OF DOUG DAVIDSON; THE WORDS OF WISDOM FROM ERIC BRAEDEN ("LET'S SHOOT THIS SHIT!"); THE HEARTFELT TALKS WITH JESS WALTON; THE GUIDANCE FROM JERRY DOUGLAS; THE ZANY MICHAEL DAMIAN (ROCK ON, BRO!); THE PURE PROFESSIONALISM OF PETER BERGMAN ("HE WHO PRACTICES WILL WIN!"); THE SOFT-SPOKEN WORDS FROM J. EDDIE PECK (HE DRIVES A TRACTOR?); THE COMICAL, LIKABLE, NICEST GUY ON THE PLANET: SCOTT REEVES; THE DEMURE HEATHER TOM (WHO SLEEPWALKS HER WAY THROUGH BLOCKING IN THE A.M.); THE HARDWORKING TALENTS OF TRICIA CAST (YOU'VE COME A LONG WAY SINCE THE BAD NEWS BEARS!); THE REGAL, SOMETIMES GOOFY MELODY THOMAS SCOTT (SHE'S ALWAYS CRYING AT THAT DAMN NEWMAN RANCH!); THE ECCENTRIC QUINN REDEKER; THE BEAUTIFUL SHARON CASE; THE MOTHER OF EVERYONE ON THE SHOW, THE ILLUSTRIOUS JEANNE COOPER; THE "I'M SO PRETTY" DON DIAMONT; THE ARTISTRY OF CHRISTIAN LEBLANC (HE THINKS HE'S BLACK!); THE GENUINE HEART OF LAURALEE BELL (DOESN'T HER DAD DO SOMETHING ON THE SHOW?); THE CRAZED SPORTS FANATIC JOSHUA MORROW (I'VE LOST EVERY BET TO HIM!); THE PAPARAZZI-CHASING KATE LINDER AND SHARON FARRELL (YOU KNOW I LOVE YOU, KATIE AND SHARON!); THE LIBERAL SHARI SHATTUCK (DUAL INCOME—YOU GO, GIRL!); THE LOVABLE, JARGON-FILLED SHEMAR MOORE (THOSE ABS ARE IMPLANTS!); THE BEAUTIFUL, ALWAYS OPTIMISTIC TONYA LEE WILLIAMS (SAY

THE ENGLISH VERSION, NOT THE CANADIAN!); AND LAST BUT NOT LEAST, MISS DIVA HERSELF: THE EXTRAORDINARY, MULTITALENTED VICTORIA ROWELL (PRIME TIME, DAYTIME, MOVIES, COMMERCIALS, CAN YOU SAY "SHOW ME 'DA MONEY"?). THEN THERE'S THE GRUFF BARK OF EDWARD SCOTT (HE'S REALLY A TEDDY BEAR); THE TIRELESS EFFORTS OF EVERYONE'S BEST FRIEND, NANCY WIARD (DOES SHE EVER LEAVE HER OFFICE?); THE CHUMMY DAVID SHAUGHNESSY (I'LL BET HIS ACCENT'S FAKE!); THE WRITING DEVOTION FROM KAY ALDEN; AND, FINALLY, THE CREATORS THEMSELVES—BILL AND LEE PHILLIP BELL, WHO HAVE CREATED A HOME FOR EVERY ONE OF US AND CONTINUE TO PUT OUT THE BEST SHOW ON DAYTIME TELEVISION YEAR AFTER YEAR! ALL OF THESE SPECIAL PEOPLE WILL BE FONDLY REMEMBERED IN THE Y&R CHAPTER OF MY PERSONAL HISTORY BOOK. HERE'S TO ANOTHER 25!

When asked to write a few words about my experience with *The Young and the Restless,* several thoughts came to mind. I could write about the experience of growing in this environment from a struggling adolescent to a more centered, if still struggling, adult. I could talk about the feelings of family that I share with so many members of the cast and crew, or my thoughts about recent departure and ultimate return. But these themes do not seem to capture the essence of what *The Young and the Restless* has meant to me, and what I think it means to so many people.

Shakespeare once said that the stage is an actor's playground, and this notion is certainly true of stages 41 and 43. Every day, for most of seven years, I have walked through the artist entrance at CBS Television City, carrying a script in my hand, with one intention in mind: to play. No matter what was happening in my life at the time, Victoria invariably had something worse to contend with. Slipping into her shoes for a while was always a welcome break from the real world. Her problems were often so much larger than my own, and, for a brief moment, I could forget my own drama and relish in her delicious manipulations, confusions, and passions. The amazing part is, so frequently, Victoria's feelings mirrored my own. Repeatedly, words that I had said in real life would come out of Victoria's mouth, and a more paranoid person would think that Bill Bell was bugging my dressing room! Of course, her experiences were generally much more fantastic than mine, but our basic frustrations, insecurities, and, above all, passions seemed equal to each other. This aspect of passion is, to me, the essence of *The Young and the Restless.* It is how I connect with Victoria, and why I think so many others relate so strongly to the characters of this show.

From the moment I first picked up a script, I was fascinated with the intricacy of each character's passion. So often on television shows, characters' ambitions seem incredibly one-level. They are either all good or all bad, depending on what their intentions are. In real life, however, our motivations change with our wants. Passions flow and evolve. What we wanted when we were 16 years old most often shifts and changes as maturity hones and directs our desires. I would think that it must be very hard to play a character whose wants are constant, or whose motivations are always absolutely good or absolutely evil because that is not real human behavior. The characters on *The Young and the Restless* are so exciting to play because regardless of the situation, their reactions are human and basic to themselves. These characters do not flip-flop and suddenly do a 180 on an issue, but instead evolve and grow like the rest of us—so while their opinions and needs may change with time, these changes are consistent with their emerging passions.

Hopefully, we all have a passion that drives us. No matter where it comes from, the love of a man or a woman, the love of a child or a parent, the ambition that motivates a career or an education, passion stimulates our lives. Passion is not one-level, one-sided, or exclusive to one group of people, but instead it is innate to all of us. So often as actors we are called upon to play characters who are less passionate than ourselves and, consequently, we have to manufacture their passion for them. How lucky are we who have the opportunity to play with characters whose passions run wild! Characters such as Victoria—who acts from her heart, no matter how misguided, because her passion does not give her any other choice. This is why performing in this playground is so much fun. How often can we say we have tackled deception, infidelity, heartbreak, love, and sometimes murder all in a day's work?

Heather Tom

Jess Walton with The Late Great Greg York

For a decade
of joy;

of friendships
past
and present;

of on screen connections with
other actors
that
stopped my heart;

of touching people
in
living rooms I have never seen;

Thank You,

To the Creators, Producers, Writers,
Directors, Cast, Crew and Fans of

The Young and the Restless

Jess Walton

In May of 1990 I booked an acting job. Not unlike many other acting jobs I had booked over the years. Or so I thought. Eight years later I am still at that job, only that job has become my second home and the people there have become my brothers and sisters, aunts and uncles, cousins and the dearest of friends I shall ever know. The Young and The Restless has changed my life. In the beginning I took the character of Olivia, and shaped and molded her into a living person. Somewhere along the way Olivia took me and shaped and molded me into a fuller person. When Olivia got married (both times), when she had her baby, when she was reunited with her sister, my heart filled with joy and happiness. When she fought with her sister, when she confronted her Mother about the past, I wept with her. The hardest and most heart wrenching for me, was to go through Olivia's discovery of her husbands extramarital affair with a woman who was HIV positive. The grueling months as she waited for her test results and those of her son, and the horrible months of a desperate mother searching for her kidnapped son. Yes, Olivia and the wonderful writers of the show, Bill Bell, Lee Bell, Edward Scott, Nancy Wiard, the cast and crew and most importantly you the fans, have given me memories and experiences I shall carry and hold in my heart forever. Y&R will never be, can never be just another acting job!

Thank you all for the journey, I excitedly await the future,

love,

Lauralee Bell (Christine Williams)

Birthplace: Chicago, Illinois / Birthdate: December 22

Lauralee Bell, daughter of *Y&R* creators Bill and Lee Phillip Bell, began her career with the show at the age of 9 as an extra in a nonspeaking part. She made several more such appearances over the next few years, and, at 13, was cast in a speaking role that became a recurring one. Lauralee became a full-time cast member in 1986 while completing her senior year in high school. She's had a pivotal role in storylines addressing such issues as date rape, drug and alcohol abuse, sexual harassment, and spousal abuse. Lauralee is an accomplished model and has appeared in many national publications. She is married to photographer Scott Martin. Her hobbies include playing tennis and needlepoint. Lauralee was voted Favorite Soap Opera Actress by *TEEN Magazine*'s national poll in 1989. She was nominated for a Soap Opera Digest Award as Outstanding Younger Lead Actress in 1996, and in 1997 she received a Soap Opera Update nomination as Outstanding Younger Lead Actress.

Peter Bergman (Jack Abbott)

Birthplace: Guantanamo Bay, Cuba / Birthdate: June 11

Peter joined the cast in 1989. He attended the American Academy of Dramatic Arts in New York, and upon graduation, appeared in regional theater productions and television commercials before joining *All My Children*. His TV film credits include *Kojak*, *Palomino*, and *Pity the Poor Soldier*; he has also appeared on shows such as *The Five Buchanans* and *The Nanny*. Peter also appeared on stage in *Love Letters* with *Y&R* cast member Melody Thomas Scott. He lives in Los Angeles with his wife, Mariellen, and their children, Connor and Clare. He donates his time to several charities, coaches his children's sports teams, serves on their school's board of directors, and enjoys playing the piano. Peter has been nominated for eight consecutive Emmy Awards in the category of Outstanding Lead Actor in a Daytime Drama Series, winning in 1991 and 1992. He was honored with a Soap Opera Digest Award as Outstanding Lead Actor in 1992 and 1993, and received the MVP Award from Soap Opera Update in 1991, 1992, and 1994.

Laura Bryan Birn (Lynne Bassett)

Birthplace: Chicago, Illinois / Birthdate: April 3

Laura joined *Y&R* in 1988, just a year after her father, Jerry Birn, became a staff writer for the show. She appeared in several plays while a student at New Trier High School in Chicago, and attended Northwestern's summer theater program. She received a B.F.A. in drama from the University of Southern California's acting conservatory program. Laura appeared in the feature film *Risky Business* and the made-for-TV movie *Hot Times at Montclair High*. She was a guest host on the fitness show *Bermuda Sunrise*. Her theater credits include regional productions of *A Chorus Line*, *Evita*, *Vanities*, and *Crimes of the Heart*. Laura enjoys all sports, both as a fan and as a participant. She also continues to study voice and dance.

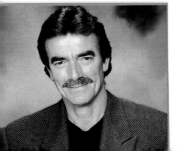

Eric Braeden (Victor Newman)

Birthplace: Kiel, Germany / Birthdate: April 3

Eric joined *Y&R* in 1980. Born Hans Gudagest, he emigrated to the United States in 1959. He lived in Texas for several years and worked in the University of Texas medical school lab before moving to Los Angeles, where he attended Santa Monica College. He joined a local semiprofessional soccer team while launching his acting career. Eric has appeared in over 120 TV series as well as numerous made-for-TV movies, including *The Judge and Mrs. Wyler* with Bette Davis, *Happily Ever After* with Tyne Daly, and the Jackie Collins miniseries, *Lucky*. His film credits include *Escape from the Planet of the Apes* and *Titanic*. He appeared in the Broadway production of *The Great Indoors* with Geraldine Page and Curt Jurgens. In 1989, Eric was chosen as the only actor on the newly formed German American Advisory Board, whose members include Dr. Henry Kissinger, Katherine Graham, Alexander Haig, and Paul Volcher. He continues to play soccer with several teams, including the Maccabees, with whom he won the 1972–73 National Soccer Championship. He and his wife, Dale, live in Los Angeles and have one son, Christian. Eric was honored as Most Popular Daytime Actor at the 1992 People's Choice Awards. He won the Soap Opera Update Award in 1997 as Lead Actor in a Daytime Drama Series, and received Emmy Award nominations as Outstanding Lead Actor in a Daytime Drama Series in 1990 and 1997.

Brooke Marie Bridges (Lily Winters)
Birthplace: West Hills, California / Birthdate: August 5

Brooke joined the cast of *Y&R* in October 1996. She has made appearances in several motion pictures, including *Space Jam*, *Frankie D*, *Nothing to Lose*, and *A Devil Disguised*. Brooke has also appeared in national television commercials. She is currently in the first grade, and enjoys skating, bowling, swimming, and playing basketball and tennis.

Sharon Case (Sharon Newman)
Birthplace: Detroit, Michigan / Birthdate: February 9

Sharon joined *Y&R* in 1994. She grew up in Chatsworth, California, where her family moved shortly after she was born. Prior to joining *Y&R*, she starred in *As the World Turns* and *General Hospital*. Her other television credits include *Silicone Wars* with David Schwimmer, *Cheers*, *Beverly Hills 90210*, *Silk Stalkings*, and *Doogie Howser*. Sharon starred in the feature film *Diplomatic Immunities*. She has also appeared on stage in *Grease* and *The Nutcracker*. Sharon's hobbies include shopping, reading, and traveling. She received Emmy Award nominations in 1996 and 1997 as Outstanding Younger Leading Actress in a Drama Series.

Tricia Cast (Nina McNeil)
Birthplace: Long Island, New York / Birthdate: November 16

Tricia joined *Y&R* in 1986. She attended Saddleback Community College before moving to Los Angeles to pursue her acting career. Tricia's TV credits include *Santa Barbara* and *The Bad News Bears*. She costarred with Michael Corbett in *Love Letters* at the Canon Theater in Beverly Hills. Tricia is married to Jack Allocco, a music composer for *Y&R* and *The Bold and the Beautiful*. She enjoys tennis, traveling, crafts, painting, and drawing, and also donates her time to several environmental organizations. She and her husband have two dogs and two cats. In 1992, Tricia received an Emmy Award as Outstanding Younger Lead Actress. She was also nominated for an Emmy as Best Supporting Actress in 1991.

John Castellanos (John Silva)
Birthplace: La Mesa, California / Birthdate: April 11

John joined *Y&R* in 1989. He attended Grossmont College in San Diego and appeared in the Old Globe Theatre's production of *Poor Murderer*. He studied theater arts at San Diego State University, and was invited to participate in an exchange program at the National Theatre of England. His theater credits include a costarring role opposite Frank Langella in the Los Angeles stage production of *Les Liaisons Dangereuses*, as well as roles in *Cat on a Hot Tin Roof*, *Love's Labor Lost*, *Romeo and Juliet*, and *King Lear*, and other productions of the American Conservatory Theater, the Oregon Shakespearean Theatre, the Berkeley Shakespeare Festival, and the Sunnyvale Repertory Company. Other credits include TV's *Miami Vice*. John lives in Los Angeles with his wife, Rhonda Freedman, an associate producer on *The Bold and the Beautiful*. He enjoys playing tennis and golf, woodworking, writing, and storytelling, and is active in numerous charitable organizations.

Carolyn Conwell (Mary Williams)

Birthplace: Chicago, Illinois / Birthdate: May 16

Carolyn joined *Y&R* in 1980. She earned a B.A. in Theater Arts from Lawrence College, and starred in regional theater productions of *Hamlet*, *Born Yesterday*, *Tea and Sympathy*, *Summer and Smoke*, *The Taming of the Shrew*, *A Streetcar Named Desire*, and *Our Town*. Carolyn has had starring roles in the Los Angeles stage productions of *The World of Ray Bradbury*, *World of Sholom Aleichem*, *Othello*, *Come Blow Your Horn*, and *Once More with Feeling*. She appeared on *General Hospital*, *Knots Landing*, *Little House on the Prairie*, *Lou Grant*, and *Medical Center*, and in the feature films *Torn Curtain*, *The Boston Strangler*, *The Magnificent Seven Ride*, and *Cheech and Chong: The Next Movie*. Carolyn's hobbies include gardening, golf, singing, and reading. She lives in Los Angeles and has three children.

Jeanne Cooper (Katherine Chancellor)

Birthplace: Taft, California / Birthdate: October 25

Jeanne joined *Y&R* in 1973. She attended the College of the Pacific and performed in the Civic Light Opera Company and Revue Theater in Stockton. A graduate of the famed Pasadena Playhouse School, her television career has included guest starring roles in over 400 episodic shows, including *Twilight Zone*, *Perry Mason*, *Maverick*, *Ben Casey*, and *Touched by an Angel*. Her appearance in *LA Law* with her son, actor Corbin Bernsen, earned her an Emmy nomination. She also appeared with him in the TV movie *Beyond Suspicion*. Jeanne's film credits include *The Man from the Alamo*, *The Boston Strangler*, and *Tony Rome*. Her stage credits include *On the Town*, *The Miracle Worker*, *Plaza Suite*, and *Love Letters*. Jeanne founded a national volunteer support network called the Katherine Chancellor Society. She donates her time to numerous charities, hospitals, and organizations, including the Humane Society of Hawaii, Greenpeace, the National Wildlife Association, and the Children's Hospital of Toronto. Jeanne has three children: Caren, Collin, and Corbin, and six grandchildren. She currently lives in Los Angeles with her two grandsons, Weston and Harrison. Jeanne was nominated for the Outstanding Leading Actress Emmy Award four consecutive years (1988–1991). In 1989, she was honored with Soap Opera Digest's Editor's Award as well as their award for Outstanding Leading Actress. She also received Soap Opera Update's MVP Award in 1990, and the Pasadena Playhouse Alumni & Associates "Woman of the Year" award in 1989.

Candice Daly (Veronica Landers/Sarah)

Birthplace: Los Angeles, California / Birthdate: January 4

Candice joined the cast of *Y&R* in 1997. Her film credits include *Where the Truth Lies*; *Steal Big, Steal Little*; *Liquid Dreams*; *Heart of Darkness*; *Girls Just Want To Have Fun*; and *The Return of Winnitou*. Her television credits include *Boys and Girls*, *Captain Power*, and *Hotel*. She has appeared in a number of regional theater productions. Her hobbies include scuba diving, sky diving, snorkeling, and horseback riding. Candice donates her time to AIDS Project L.A., People for the Ethical Treatment of Animals (PETA), and the Children's Cancer Society. She lives in Los Angeles with her four Siberian Huskies.

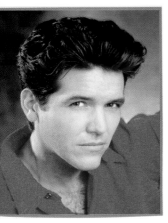

Michael Damian (Danny Romalotti)

Birthplace: San Diego, California / Birthdate: April 26

Michael joined *Y&R* in 1981. Born Michael Damian Weir, youngest son in a family of nine children, he began studying classical piano at the age of 6. He proceeded to learn organ, clarinet, trombone, and vibes, and, at age 11, formed the band The Weirz, along with his brothers and sisters. They toured and released three independent albums before Michael went solo. In 1981, he recorded a remake of Eric Carmen's "She Did it." The success of this song on Billboard's Top 100 chart led to Michael's appearance on *American Bandstand*. The producers of *Y&R* spotted him, and created the role of Danny Romalotti specifically for him. He collaborated with his brothers on the album *Love Is a Mystery* in 1985, and has toured the country to promote numerous solo albums, including *Dreams of Summer*, *Michael Damian*, and *Where Do We Go From Here?*, which produced the gold single "Rock On." He also contributed to the *Y&R* album with other cast members. Other credits include the TV movie *Cold Heart of a Killer* and series *The Facts of Life*.

In 1993, Michael took a break from *Y&R* to star in the touring production and Broadway cast of Andrew Lloyd Webber's musical, *Joseph and the Amazing Technicolor Dreamcoat*. He is writing and will direct two independent feature films, and wrote and directed the short film *Finders Keepers*, which debuted at the Cannes Film Festival. Michael enjoys golf, roller blading, and spending time with his two dogs. He also volunteers for numerous antidrug campaigns. Michael and his fiancée, Janine Best, plan to be married this year.

Doug Davidson (Paul Williams)
Birthplace: Glendale, California / Birthdate: October 24

Doug joined the cast of *Y&R* in 1978. His other TV credits include *Diagnosis Murder* and the Judith Krantz miniseries *I'll Take Manhattan* and *The Initiation of Sarah*. Doug also hosted the nighttime version of *The Price Is Right*, the 1998 Rose Parade, and continues to serve as regular host of CBS's *Coming Up Roses New Year's Special*. He was the master of ceremonies for the Miss California Pageant and hosted the Kenny Rogers Cerebral Palsy Telethon. His film credits include *Mr. Write* with Paul Reiser, *Don't Stop Now*, and *Fraternity Row*. Doug enjoys traveling, camping, and playing the bagpipes, and contributes much of his time to charities, including the YMCA. He and his wife, actress Cindy Fisher, served as National Honorary Chairpersons for WE-TIP, a nonprofit anonymous tip line that aids in crime prevention. The couple has two children, Calyssa and Caden.

Marita De Leon (Joani Garza)
Birthplace: Santa Ana, California / Birthdate: February 18

Marita joined the cast of *Y&R* in 1995. She earned a Bachelor of Arts degree in humanities, with a minor in theater from the University of Southern California. During her childhood summer vacations, she would often visit relatives in Germany. She also toured Europe playing soccer for the American Eagles. Her feature film credits include *Mi Vida Loca*, *Mi Familia*, and *The Big Squeeze*, written and directed by her brother, Marcus De Leon. She has appeared in Los Angeles theater productions of *The Impostor*, *The Savior*, and *Bernabe*. In her free time, Marita enjoys traveling and hiking.

Alex Donnelley (Diane Jenkins Newman)
Birthplace: Frankfurt, Germany / Birthdate: August 13

Alex was first on *Y&R* from 1982 to 1986. After a 10-year hiatus, she returned in 1996. Born in Frankfurt, Germany, Alex later moved with her family and grew up in Lake Forest, Illinois. She attended the University of Denver at age 16 and earned a degree in broadcast journalism from the University of Southern California. Alex's TV credits include *Dallas*, Bob Hope specials, *Simon and Simon*, *Fantasy Island*, and *Matt Houston*. Her feature film credits include *Death Wish II* and *My Girl II*. Alex enjoys running, skiing, and traveling, and spends most of her free time with her two daughters, Kate and Sean.

Jerry Douglas (John Abbott)
Birthplace: Chelsea, Massachusetts / Birthdate: November 12

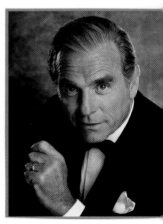

Jerry joined *Y&R* in 1982. He attended Brandeis University on a football scholarship and graduated with a B.S. in economics, then began his acting career, studying with Uta Hagen in New York and Jeff Corey in Los Angeles. Jerry has appeared in over 100 TV series and films, including *The FBI*, *The Rockford Files*, *Police Story*, *The Streets of San Francisco*, *Hill Street Blues*, *Hunter*, *Walton's Mountain*, and *Night Watch*, and such feature films as *Avalanche*, *Mommie Dearest*, and Oliver Stone's *JFK*. Jerry developed and produces a touring variety show, *The Young and the Restless and The Bold and the Beautiful Soap Stars in Concert*, which highlights the musical and comedic talents of *Y&R* costars Scott Reeves and Jeanne Cooper, and *B&B*'s Bobbie Eakes. He also writes and develops projects through his own production company, Jovra Films. Jerry donates his time to charities, including the Variety Clubs and the Salvation Army, and enjoys playing golf, reading, and traveling. He and his wife, Kym Douglas, entertainment host on the Family Channel's *Home and Family Show*, have an infant son, Hunter. Jerry also has two grown children, Jod and Avra, from a previous marriage.

Jennifer Gareis (Grace Turner)

Birthplace: Lancaster, Pennsylvania / Birthdate: August 1

Jennifer joined the cast of *Y&R* in 1997. She majored in accounting at Franklin & Marshall College, where she was an NCAA All American swimmer. She held the titles of Miss New York and Miss Hawaiian Tropic, among others, and has appeared in numerous commercials. Her TV credits include *Guiding Light*, *One Life to Live*, *Baywatch*, *The Cosby Mysteries*, *The Larry Melman Show*, and *The Q2 Fitness Show*, which she hosted. She has also appeared in numerous motion pictures, including *Howard Stern's Private Parts*, *The Mirror Has Two Faces*, and *Weekend at Bernie's II*. Her hobbies include gymnastics, running, hiking, and biking.

Sabryn Genet (Tricia Dennison)

Birthplace: Whittier, California / Birthdate: May 14

Sabryn joined the cast of *Y&R* in 1997. She's guest starred in TV's *Married with Children*, *We Are Angels*, *Courthouse*, and *Exposed*. Her feature film credits include *Swimming With Sharks*, *Smokin' n' Lightnin'*, *Illegal Entry*, and *Did You Miss Me, Hon?* She has also appeared on stage in *Rumplestiltskin*, *Get a Life*, and *Sleeping Beauty*. Sabryn is involved in charitable causes, including Project Angel Food. She enjoys writing poetry, roller blading, and dancing.

Camryn Grimes (Cassie)

Birthplace: Van Nuys, California / Birthdate: January 7

Camryn joined the cast of *Y&R* in 1997. As a newborn, she appeared on *Days of Our Lives*, and has since appeared on *Wide World of Kids* and in national commercials. She learned to swim at the age of six months, and was diving before she was 2. Camryn enjoys drawing, singing, playing soccer, white-water rafting, and swimming and diving. She lives in Studio City, California, with her family, and is in the second grade.

Ashley Jones (Megan Dennison)

Birthplace: Memphis, Tennessee / Birthdate: September 3

Ashley joined the cast of *Y&R* in 1997. She was raised in Houston, Texas, and moved to Los Angeles in 1994. Her credits include the TV movie *Our Son, the Matchmaker* and the series *Dr. Quinn, Medicine Woman*. She received a 1994 Youth in Film nomination for her costarring role in *Fire Next Time*. On the Los Angeles stage, she has starred in *Betrayal*, *The Chalk Garden*, and *The Women*. She also appeared in the Actors Theater of Houston performance of *Brighton Beach Memoirs*. Ashley is currently majoring in television production at Pepperdine University, and plans to graduate in May 1998. She enjoys painting, running, and taking walks, and volunteers at AIDS Project Los Angeles, the Urban Plunge Shelter, and the Pepperdine Volunteer Center.

Bryant Jones (Nate Hastings)

Birthplace: Camarillo, California / Birthdate: July 1

Bryant joined the cast of *Y&R* in 1995. His work has included appearances in national TV commercials, as well as modeling for the Hilton Hotel franchise. He was named Little Mr. Oxnard in a local pageant in 1993. Bryant, who is in the first grade, enjoys playing basketball with his dad and watching videos with his two sisters—a twin named Bethany, and Kayla.

Andre Khabbazi (Alec Moretti)

Birthplace: Sacramento, California / Birthdate: January 15

Andre joined the cast of *Y&R* in 1997. He attended American River College in California where he majored in criminal justice. His other TV credits include *Suddenly Susan* and *Sunset Beach*. Andre is a semiprofessional tennis player and enjoys teaching the sport to his young son, Andre. His other interests include Thai boxing and reading.

Heath Kizzier (Dr. Joshua Landers)

Birthplace: Rapid City, South Dakota / Birthdate: August 3

Heath joined the cast of *Y&R* in 1996. He moved to Los Angeles in 1985 to pursue his acting career. His credits include the TV series *Dr. Quinn, Medicine Woman*; *Murder, She Wrote*; and *Columbo*; and the feature films *The Sons of Trinity*, *Wyatt Earp*, *Rituals of Obsession*, and *Dead Man's Revenge*. He has appeared in regional theater productions of *Danny and the Deep Blue Sea*, *All My Sons*, *Summer Tree*, and *Fantasies at the Frick*. His interests include camping, horseback riding, football, basketball, singing, karate, marksmanship, and woodworking. Heath and his wife and two children live in the San Fernando Valley.

Christian Jules LeBlanc (Michael Baldwin)

Birthplace: Fort Bragg, North Carolina / Birthdate: August 25

Christian joined the cast of *Y&R* in 1991. LeBlanc graduated with honors from Tulane University, where he majored in ancient history and pre-med. After being offered a role in the PBS series *Edit Point*, he decided to pursue an acting career. His TV credits include *Cheers*, *Gabriel's Fire*, *Perry Mason*, *In the Heat of the Night*, and *As the World Turns*. He costarred on stage with Julie Harris in *Ladies in Retirement*, and has also worked as a substitute teacher in the Los Angeles school district. An award-winning artist, Christian is currently writing and illustrating his first children's book. He lives in Los Angeles with his two dogs, and enjoys water skiing, swimming, racquetball, body surfing, and traveling the globe.

Kate Linder (Esther Valentine)

Birthplace: Pasadena, California / Birthdate: November 2

Kate joined *Y&R* in 1985. She earned a B.A. in theater arts from San Francisco State University, and has appeared on television in *Bay City Blues*, *Archie Bunker's Place*, and *Dream Girl*, and in the feature film *Rocky III*. Kate is active with Big Sisters of Los Angeles and Love Is Feeding Everyone, and hosts a celebrity bowling tournament to benefit both organizations. She is a founding member of TV Cares, the AIDS awareness and fund-raising arm of the Academy of Television Arts and Sciences. She was the only daytime actress to be featured in *Portraits of Life, with Love*, a coffee-table book published to raise funds for various AIDS organizations. Kate also works as a United Airlines flight attendant, mostly on weekends. She and her husband, Ronald Linder, a leading expert on drug abuse and president of American Medical Productions, live in Los Angeles.

Shemar Moore (Malcolm Winters)

Birthplace: Oakland, California / Birthdate: April 20

Shemar joined the cast of *Y&R* in 1994. He was raised in Palo Alto, California, and majored in communications at Santa Clara University, where he played varsity baseball. Shemar was a successful print and runway fashion model before launching his acting career. He has appeared in such publications as *Gentleman's Quarterly* and *Mademoiselle*, as well as in fashion layouts for major department store chains. He guest starred in *The Nanny*, *Living Single*, and *Arliss–The Art of the Sports Super Agent*, and recently played the lead role in the HBO movie *Butter*. Shemar has also appeared in national TV commercials. In 1996 and 1997, he was honored with Emmy Award nominations as Outstanding Younger Actor. Photography, sports, traveling, and baking are among his hobbies.

Joshua Morrow (Nicholas Newman)

Birthplace: Juneau, Alaska / Birthdate: February 8

Joshua joined the cast of Y&R in 1994. He was born in Alaska, where his father was stationed in the Coast Guard, and grew up in Oklahoma and New Mexico. Joshua moved to Southern California and majored in communications with a minor in theater at Moorpark College. He starred opposite Rachel Ward in the TV movie *My Stepson, My Lover*. On stage, he has appeared in the Young Artists Ensemble production of *Ordinary People* and regional productions of *Picnic*, *The Rainmaker*, *Road to Ruin*, *The Witching Hour*, *Staring into the Abyss*, and *Dark of the Moon*. He is a founding member of TV Cares, a fund-raising and charity arm of the Academy of Television Arts and Sciences, and plays on celebrity basketball and softball teams to benefit various charities. He enjoys sports, collecting baseball cards, and reading. In 1996, Joshua was honored with the Soap Opera Digest Award for Outstanding Younger Lead Actor, and also received Emmy Award nominations in 1996 and 1997 as Outstanding Younger Actor.

Sandra Nelson (Phyllis Romalotti)

Birthplace: Madison, Wisconsin / Birthdate: December 29

Sandra joined Y&R in 1997. She spent most of her childhood in Tucson, Arizona, and in France. At 16, she moved to NYC to study at the Lee Strasberg Theater Institute and the Actors Studio. She has appeared on television in *Star Trek: Deep Space Nine*, *Star Trek: Voyager*, *Due South*, *The Outer Limits*, and *Highlander*, to name but a few, and played the lead role in the TV movie *Captain's Courageous*. Other movie credits include *A Baby of Their Own*, *Halfback of Notre Dame*, *Voices from Within*, *Dying to Remember*, and *A Child Too Many*. She costarred with Lauren Bacall on Broadway in *Sweet Bird of Youth*, and also appeared on stage in, among others, *The Respectable Whore*, *The Crucible*, *The Three Sisters*, *In the Boom-Boom Room*, *One Flew Over the Cuckoo's Nest*, *Golpes a Mi Puerta*, *Romeo and Juliet*, and *La Zapatera Prodigiosa* (in a role that she performed in English and Spanish on alternate nights). Sandra directed, edited, and appeared in a documentary film, *Sex at Delilah's*, and also appeared in the feature film *The Wedding Project*. She lives in Los Angeles and enjoys traveling, hiking, scuba diving, skiing, and playing the piano and cello; she also shows horses. Sandra volunteers for such charities as The American Cancer Society and the Make a Wish Foundation.

J. Eddie Peck (Cole Howard)

Birthplace: Lynchburg, Virginia / Birthdate: October 10

J. Eddie Peck joined the cast of Y&R in 1992. When he was eight years old, his family moved to Kansas City and later to Joplin, Missouri, where he grew up. He earned a B.A. in marketing from Missouri Southern State University, and paid his tuition by hosting a country-and-western show on KSYN radio in Joplin. Eddie was cohost (with Ivanka Trump) of the *Miss Teen USA Pageant*. His other television credits include *Days of Our Lives*; *Dynasty*; *Dallas*; *Cheers*; *Murder, She Wrote*; *Knight Rider*; *Highway to Heaven*; and the made-for-TV movies *To Grandmother's House We Go* and *Breaking Home Ties*. His feature film credits include *Lambada: Set the Night on Fire*, *Curse II: The Bite*, and *Dangerously Close*. Eddie enjoys basketball, horseback riding, and all sports, and moonlights as a singing/vocal coach. His charitable interests include the Juvenile Diabetes Fund, the AIDS Consortium in Atlanta, and the United Blood Drive. He and his wife, Sonya, have two sons, Austin and Dalton.

Anthony Peña (Miguel Rodriguez)

Birthplace: San Antonio, Texas / Birthdate: February 18

Anthony joined Y&R in 1984. He participated in high school athletics and was scouted by the Cincinnati Reds to play professional baseball. Anthony majored in English and history at the University of Santa Barbara, and obtained the credentials to teach challenged students. He appeared on *General Hospital*, *Hill Street Blues*, *Simon and Simon*, *Highway to Heaven*, *MacGyver*, *Hunter*, *Quantum Leap*, and *Dynasty*. His feature film credits include *Marathon Man*, *Altered States*, *Megaforce*, *Porky's II*, *The Running Man*, *Born on the Fourth of July*, and *Backtrack* with Jodie Foster and Dennis Hopper. He starred on stage in *Zoot Suit* and *Bronze Images*. Anthony was honored in 1996 with a Nosotros Silver

Anniversary Golden Eagle Award for his contributions to daytime television. His hobbies include snow skiing, jet skiing, reading, and traveling. He is actively involved in the Salvation Army, Mother Antonia's Foundation, and several Stay in School programs. Anthony and his wife, Raylene, have two children.

Scott Reeves (Ryan McNeil)
Birthplace: Santa Monica, California / Birthdate: May 16

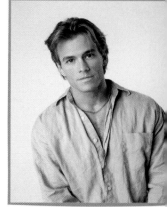

Scott joined the cast of *Y&R* in 1991. He grew up in the San Fernando Valley and attended acting classes at the Beverly Hills Playhouse. Scott's movie credits include *Big Man on Campus* and *Friday the 13th: Jason Takes Manhattan*. His TV credits include *Days of Our Lives*, the TV miniseries *I Know My First Name Is Steven*, and the made-for-TV films *When the Cradle Falls* (with Martha Byrne of *As the World Turns*) and *Hearts Adrift*. He appears in a touring variety show, *The Young and the Restless and The Bold and the Beautiful Soap Stars in Concert*, with costars Jerry Douglas and Jeanne Cooper, and *B&B*'s Bobbie Eakes. Scott received a Soap Opera Digest Award for Outstanding Younger Lead Actor in 1993, and was honored with an Emmy Award nomination in 1997 as Outstanding Supporting Actor. He enjoys sports, backpacking, and playing the guitar. Scott and his wife, Melissa (formerly Jennifer on *Days of Our Lives*), have two children, Emily and Larry.

Victoria Rowell (Drucilla Winters)
Birthplace: Portland, Maine / Birthdate: May 10

Victoria joined *Y&R* in 1990. She grew up in Portland and Boston, and began formal ballet training at the age of 8. By 16, she had received scholarships to the School of American Ballet and the Dance Theater of Harlem. After completing high school, she moved to New York, where she danced professionally with the American Ballet Theater II Company, the Ballet Hispanico of New York, and the Twyla Tharp Workshop. Victoria also enjoyed a successful modeling career. She currently costars in *Diagnosis Murder*, and has appeared in *As the World Turns*, *One Life to Live*, *The Cosby Show*, *The Fresh Prince of Bel Air*, and *Herman's Head*. She starred opposite Mario Van Peebles in the HBO film *Full Eclipse*, and with Lloyd and Beau Bridges in the TV movie *My Father's Son*. In 1990, she formed the Rowell Foster Children's Scholarship Fund, an organization that sponsors foster children studying classical ballet. Her charitable work involves the Massachusetts Department of Social Services, foster care awareness, and the United Way. Victoria teaches ballet at the Portland School of Ballet and the Ballet Company. She lives in Los Angeles with her daughter Mya and son Jasper. In 1993, Victoria received a Soap Opera Digest Award for Outstanding Scene Stealer. In 1994, that magazine nominated her as Hottest Female Star. She has also been honored with four NAACP Image Awards as Outstanding Actress in a Daytime Series.

Melody Thomas Scott (Nikki Newman Landers)
Birthplace: Los Angeles, California / Birthdate: April 18

Melody joined *Y&R* in 1979. She started in show business at the age of 3 under the tutelage of Ethel Meglin, who helped launch the career of Shirley Temple. Melody studied singing, tap dancing, ballet, and jazz, and became one of the "Meglin Kiddies," performing at U.S.O. shows in Southern California. She made her feature film debut at the age of 8 in Alfred Hitchcock's *Marnie*. Melody went on to major in music at the University of Southern California. She has costarred in motion pictures with some of Hollywood's most famous leading men, including *The Shootist* with John Wayne; *Dirty Harry* with Clint Eastwood; and *Posse* and *The Fury*, both with Kirk Douglas. Her TV credits include *The Waltons*, *My Three Sons*, *Ironside*, and the made-for-TV films *Moviola* and *Secrets*. Melody is married to *Y&R* executive producer Edward Scott. In 1989, they co-founded the Save the Earth Foundation, an organization that endeavors to create awareness about environmental issues. The couple has three daughters: Alexandra, Jennifer, and Elizabeth.

Nick Scotti (Tony Viscardi)

Birthplace: Queens, New York / Birthdate: May 31

Nick joined the cast of *Y&R* in 1996. He was raised in New York and began his career at age 18 as a fashion model, working for Valentino, Yves St. Laurent, and Thierry Mugler. He appeared on the cover of *Newsweek* in a story entitled "The Biology of Beauty." An accomplished singer and songwriter, he collaborated with Madonna on "Get Over," on which Nick sings lead vocals and Madonna, background vocals. The song was on the soundtrack for the feature film *Nothing But Trouble*, and soon after its release, Nick was awarded a record deal with Warner/Reprise. In 1993, he released his debut album, *Wake up Everybody*, which climbed to No. 3 on the Billboard charts. In 1994, his success continued with the hit dance single "Wild Planet/Love So Strong." His first TV role was in 1995 in the series *Educating Matt Waters*. He also starred in the critically acclaimed independent film *Kiss Me Guido*. Nick enjoys writing music and poetry and playing racquetball.

Shari Shattuck (Ashley Abbott)

Birthplace: Atlanta, Georgia / Birthdate: November 18

Shari joined *Y&R* in 1996. She was raised in Atlanta and was a competitive ice skater before moving to Los Angeles in 1984 to study acting. Her credits include the made-for-TV movies *Goddess of Love* and *Laker Girls*, and the international miniseries *The Baron*. She has guest starred in the series *Babylon 5*, *Sisters*, and *Life Goes On*. Her film credits include *Spy Hard*, *On Deadly Ground*, *Immortal Sins*, and *The Naked Cage*. Shari's play, *In Progress*, was performed at the Matrix Theater in Los Angeles. She appeared on stage in *How to Catch a Man*, *Rosencrantz and Guildenstern Are Dead*, *Macbeth*, *The Taming of the Shrew*, *Much Ado about Nothing*, *Twelfth Night*, and *The Glass Menagerie*. Shari enjoys writing, cooking, roller blading, and hiking. She and husband Ronn Moss (*B&B*'s Ridge Forrester) donate their time to various charities, including the American Cancer Society. The couple has a daughter, Creason Carbo.

Kristoff St. John (Neil Winters)

Birthplace: New York, New York / Birthdate: July 15

Kristoff joined the cast of *Y&R* in 1991. He studied at the Actor's Studio in Los Angeles, the Virgil Frye Workshop, and the Tony Morina Workshop. Kristoff began his TV career at age 7 with an appearance in the series *That's My Mama*. His other TV credits include *Generations* (for which he earned two Emmy nominations), *Martin*, *The Cosby Show*, *Diagnosis Murder*, *A Different World*, *Jake and the Fatman*, and *Happy Days*. He appeared in the TV movies *The Atlanta Child Murders*, *Roots II: The Next Generation*, and *Finish Line*. His feature film credits include *Avatar* and *The Champ*. Kristoff developed and directed *Soap World*, a television pilot that eventually became *CBS Soap Break*. He wrote a screenplay, *Cafe America*, which will be produced by his own production company, Moonboy. Kristoff earned an Emmy Award in 1992 as Outstanding Younger Lead Actor for his role as Neil Winters, and was nominated again in 1993. He has also been honored with four NAACP Image Awards as Outstanding Actor in a Daytime Drama. Kristoff is a movie buff, enjoys playing the guitar, and volunteers for various child-related causes. He has two children, Julian and Paris.

Heather Tom (Victoria Newman Howard)

Birthplace: Hinsdale, Illinois / Birthdate: November 4

Heather joined *Y&R* in 1991, left the series in April 1997, and returned in October 1997. She grew up in a suburb of Chicago, and then moved to Seattle, where she performed with the Seattle Children's Theatre and the Pacific Northwest Ballet, and studied piano at the Academy of Music and Dance. She also studied at the famed Strasberg Institute and at the Young Actor's Space. Heather starred in the TV films *Deadly Whispers* and *I'll Take Romance*, and guest starred in the series *Who's The Boss*, *Trial by Jury*, *Kids Inc.*, and *Divorce Court*. Her theater credits include a lead role in *Pinocchio II* for Center Stage U.S.A. She co-founded the Creative Outlet Theater in Los Angeles, for which she produced and starred in *Out of Gas on Lover's Leap* and *Vanities*. She also produced *Scooter Thomas Makes It to the Top of the World* for the theater. In 1993, Heather received an Emmy Award for Outstanding Younger Actress in a Drama Series, and has received five nominations in the same category.

Granville Van Dusen (Keith Dennison)
Birthplace: Grand Rapids, Minnesota / Birthdate: March 16

Granville joined *Y&R* in 1996. He was raised in Grand Rapids and later moved to Anoka where he was an All State basketball player. He majored in theater at St. Cloud University. He has guest starred in *Lois and Clark*; *Diagnosis Murder*; *Murder, She Wrote*; *Matlock*; *Doogie Howser*; *Hill Street Blues*; *Highway to Heaven*; *Silk Stalkings*; and *Magnum P.I.*; and also starred in the TV movies *The Memoirs of Abraham Lincoln*, *Breaking Up*, *The Jackal and the Rose*, *The War between the Tates*, and *Someone I Touched*. Granville costarred in the feature films *It Ain't Easy*; *The Statue*; and *Run, Johnny, Run*. He has appeared in Los Angeles theater productions of *Habeas Corpus* and *A Bed Facing North*, and the San Francisco production of *Interior Decoration*. Granville is an award-winning member of the Matrix Theater Company. He lives with his wife, June, and two children, Megan and Mitch, and enjoys playing golf, gardening, and fishing. He is also a registered pilot.

Jess Walton (Jill Abbott)
Birthplace: Grand Rapids, Michigan / Birthdate: February 18

Jess joined *Y&R* in 1987. She grew up in Toronto, Canada, and studied at the Toronto Workshop Productions' Repertory Theater. Jess appeared in summer stock and repertory company productions such as *Uncle Vanya* and *The Right Honorable Gentleman*. She starred in *Capitol* for three years, and guest starred in numerous TV series, including *The Rockford Files*; *Cannon*; *Marcus Welby, M.D.*; *The Six Million Dollar Man*; *The Streets of San Francisco*; *Barnaby Jones*; *Ironside*; *Starsky & Hutch*; and *Kojak*. She also starred in the TV movies *Montserrat*, *You'll Never See Me Again*, *The Storm*, *Diary of a Madman*, and *Mod Squad II*. Jess received Emmy Awards as Outstanding Lead Actress (1997), and Outstanding Supporting Actress (1991). She was also nominated as supporting actress in 1990. She earned a Soap Opera Digest Award as Outstanding Lead Actress in 1993. Jess is married to the internationally renowned grief recovery authority John W. James, founder of the Grief Recovery Institute, and volunteers for the Grief Recovery Help Line. The couple lives in Los Angeles with their son, Cole; daughter, Allison; and two dogs and a cat.

Patty Weaver (Gina Roma)
Birthplace: Clarkesburg, West Virginia / Birthdate: September 23

Patty joined the cast of *Y&R* in 1982. She was raised in Dayton, Ohio. Patty keeps busy on the nightclub circuit, and has opened for Bob Newhart, Don Rickles, Jerry Lewis, and the late George Burns in Las Vegas and Atlantic City. She appears on some of the most prominent telethons and has helped raise millions of dollars for charity. Before launching her acting career, she formed a rock 'n' roll band called The Loved Ones. She has recorded several albums and continues her singing career. Her television credits include *Days of Our Lives*, *Maude*, and *All in the Family*. Patty is married to *Y&R* writer Jerry Birn.

Tonya Lee Williams (Dr. Olivia Barber Winters)
Birthplace: London, England / Birthdate: July 12

Tonya joined *Y&R* in 1990. She was born in London and a year later, her family relocated to Kingston, Jamaica. She and her mother returned to London before moving to Oshawa, Canada. Tonya graduated from Ryerson College in Toronto, a school specializing in theater arts. As a teenager, she was the milk girl in the famous "Wear a Mustache" milk campaign. Her TV credits include *Generations*, *Falcon Crest*, *Hill Street Blues*, *Matlock*, *Gimme a Break*, *Silk Stalkings*, and *A Very Brady Christmas*. She appeared in the Canadian television programs *For the Record*, *Seeing Things*, *In Good Company*, *Street Legal*, *Time of Your Life*, *Check It Out*, and *Polka Dot Door*, the Canadian version of *Sesame Street*. Her feature film credits include *Spaced Invaders* and *Hearts of Fire*. Tonya currently lives in Los Angeles. She donates her time to the Sickle Cell Association of Toronto, and enjoys tennis, horseback riding, and hiking.

William J. Bell accepted the Governor's Lifetime Achievement Award from the National Academy of Television Arts and Sciences in 1992. Bell and his colleagues at *The Young and the Restless* have received numerous awards and honors throughout the show's 25-year history. This includes more Emmy nominations for Outstanding Daytime Drama Series than any other show—an award *Y&R* has won five times! In all, *Y&R* has earned 177 Emmy nominations and 61 Emmy awards. In addition, *Y&R* has been the recipient of countless honors and commendations for service to the community resulting from the socially relevant issue–oriented stories that have always been a mainstay of the show.

1997

24TH ANNUAL DAYTIME EMMY AWARDS
Outstanding Drama Series Writing Team
Outstanding Drama Series Directing Team
Outstanding Lead Actress in a Drama
Series—Jess Walton
Outstanding Supporting Actress in a Drama
Series—Michelle Stafford
Outstanding Art Direction / Set Decoration /
Scenic Design for a Drama Series
Outstanding Technical Direction / Electronic
Direction / Video Control for a Drama Series
Outstanding Lighting Direction for a Drama
Series

1997 DIRECTORS GUILD AWARDS
Directing for a Daytime Series—Mike Denney
and Kathryn Foster
13TH ANNUAL SOAP OPERA AWARDS
Outstanding Lead Actor—Eric Braeden
Outstanding Supporting Actor—Doug
Davidson
Outstanding Villainess—Michelle Stafford
Outstanding Younger Leading Actress—
Heather Tom
29TH ANNUAL NAACP IMAGE AWARDS
Outstanding Daytime Drama Series
Outstanding Actress in a Daytime Drama
Series—Victoria Rowell

Outstanding Actor in a Daytime Drama
Series—Kristoff St. John

1996

23RD ANNUAL DAYTIME EMMY AWARDS
Outstanding Drama Series Directing Team
STRIVING FOR EXCELLENCE AWARDS
Minorities in Broadcasting Pacesetter
Presentation—William J. Bell and Lee
Phillip Bell
SOAP OPERA UPDATE AWARDS
Best Actor in a Daytime Drama Series—
Peter Bergman
Best Actress in a Daytime Drama Series—
Melody Thomas Scott
NOSOTROS SILVER ANNIVERSARY AWARDS
Golden Eagle Award—Anthony Peña
28TH ANNUAL NAACP IMAGE AWARDS
Outstanding Daytime Drama Series
Outstanding Actor in a Daytime Drama
Series—Kristoff St. John
Outstanding Actress in a Daytime Drama
Series—Victoria Rowell
12TH ANNUAL SOAP OPERA AWARDS
Outstanding Younger Lead Actor—Joshua
Morrow
Outstanding Female Newcomer—Michelle
Stafford
THE NANCY SUSAN REYNOLDS AWARDS
Nick / Sharon / Matt storyline—The Young
and the Restless
HEROES AND LEGENDS AWARDS
Victoria Rowell
THE MICHAEL BOLTON FOUNDATION
Humanitarian Award—William J. Bell
THE VISION AWARDS
Lifetime Achievement Award—William J. Bell
EMERSON COLLEGE / THE EVVY AWARDS
Lifetime Achievement Award—William J. Bell
& Lee Phillip Bell

1995

22ND ANNUAL DAYTIME EMMY AWARDS
Outstanding Achievement in Art Direction /
Set Decoration / Scenic Design for a Drama
Series
SOAP OPERA UPDATE AWARDS
Best Actor in a Daytime Drama Series—Peter
Bergman
Best Actress in a Daytime Drama Series—
Melody Thomas Scott
16TH ANNUAL YOUTH IN FILM AWARDS
Best Performance by a Youth Actor in a Soap
Opera—Courtland Mead
11TH ANNUAL SOAP OPERA AWARDS
Outstanding Supporting Actress—Signy
Coleman

1994

21ST ANNUAL DAYTIME EMMY AWARDS
Outstanding Achievement in Lighting
Direction for a Drama Series
10TH ANNUAL SOAP OPERA AWARDS
Outstanding Younger Leading Actor—Scott
Reeves
Outstanding Lead Actress—Jess Walton
Outstanding Scene Stealer—Victoria Rowell
THE BLACK ACHIEVERS AWARD
Victoria Rowell

SOAP OPERA UPDATE AWARDS
Outstanding Actor in a Daytime Drama—Eric
Braeden
Outstanding Actress in a Daytime Drama—
Signy Coleman
27TH ANNUAL NAACP IMAGE AWARDS
Outstanding Daytime Drama
Outstanding Lead Actor—Kristoff St. John
Outstanding Lead Actress—Victoria Rowell

1993

20TH ANNUAL DAYTIME EMMY AWARDS
Outstanding Drama Series
Outstanding Younger Actress in a Drama
Series—Heather Tom
Outstanding Achievement in Technical
Direction / Electronic Camera / Video Control
for a Drama Series
Outstanding Achievement in Live and Tape
Sound Mixing and Sound Effects for a Drama
Series
Outstanding Achievement in Costume Design
for a Drama Series
26TH ANNUAL NAACP IMAGE AWARDS
Outstanding Daytime Drama
Outstanding Lead Actor—Kristoff St. John
Outstanding Lead Actress—Victoria Rowell
1993 DIRECTORS CHOICE AWARDS
The National Women's Economic Alliance
Foundation Outstanding Women Directors—
Lee Phillip Bell
THE NANCY SUSAN REYNOLDS AWARDS
Outstanding Daytime Drama—Christine
Romalotti / Michael Baldwin sexual harass-
ment storyline
AMERICAN WOMEN IN RADIO AND TELEVI-
SION AWARDS
Broadcaster of the Year—Lee Phillip Bell
19TH ANNUAL PEOPLE'S CHOICE AWARDS
Favorite Daytime Drama Series
1993 DIRECTORS GUILD AWARDS
Directing for a Daytime Serial—Frank Pacelli
9TH ANNUAL SOAP OPERA AWARDS
Outstanding Lead Actor—Peter Bergman
Outstanding Villainess—Kimberlin Brown
SOAP OPERA UPDATE AWARDS
Outstanding Lead Actor in a Daytime
Drama—Scott Reeves
Outstanding Lead Actress in a Daytime
Drama—Melody Thomas Scott
THE GOLDEN EAGLE AWARDS
Outstanding Lead Actor—Kristoff St. John
THE YOUTH IN FILM AWARDS
Outstanding Lead Actor—Paul Walker
Outstanding Lead Actress—Heather Tom

1992

19TH ANNUAL DAYTIME EMMY AWARDS
The Governor's Lifetime Achievement Award—
William J. Bell
Outstanding Drama Series Writing Team
Outstanding Lead Actor in a Drama Series—
Peter Bergman
Outstanding Younger Actress in a Drama
Series—Tricia Cast
Outstanding Younger Actor in a Drama
Series—Kristoff St. John

Outstanding Achievement in Multiple Camera
Editing for a Drama Series
Outstanding Achievement in Live and Tape
Sound Mixing and Sound Effects for a
Drama Series
25TH ANNUAL NAACP IMAGE AWARDS
Outstanding Daytime Drama Series
Outstanding Actor in a Daytime Drama
Series—Kristoff St. John
Outstanding Actress in a Daytime Drama
Series—Victoria Rowell
THE NANCY SUSAN REYNOLDS AWARDS
Outstanding Daytime Drama Series
1992 SELF-ESTEEM AWARDS
Special Award—William J. Bell
8TH ANNUAL SOAP OPERA AWARDS
Editor's Award—William J. Bell
Outstanding Younger Leading Actress—Tricia
Cast
Outstanding Supporting Actor—Doug
Davidson
18TH ANNUAL PEOPLE'S CHOICE AWARDS
Favorite Male Performer in a Daytime
Series—Eric Braeden
THE NATIONAL SOCIETY OF THE DAUGHTERS
OF THE AMERICAN REVOLUTION
Certificate of Appreciation Award for
Outstanding Achievement in Telling the
Concerns, Problems and Values of Youth

1991

18TH ANNUAL DAYTIME EMMY AWARDS
Outstanding Lead Actor in a Drama Series—
Peter Bergman
Outstanding Supporting Actress in a Drama
Series—Jess Walton
Outstanding Achievement in Technical
Direction / Electronic Camera / Video Control
for a Drama Series
Outstanding Achievement in Live and Tape
Sound Mixing for a Drama Series
Outstanding Achievement in Videotape
Editing for a Drama Series
CALIFORNIA GOVERNOR'S COMMITTEE FOR
EMPLOYMENT OF DISABLED PERSONS
Outstanding Achievement Awards—William J.
Bell and Christopher Templeton
CHICAGO MUSEUM OF BROADCAST
COMMUNICATIONS
Tribute to The Young and the Restless and
its Creators, William J. Bell and Lee Phillip
Bell

MEN'S FASHION ASSOCIATION ALDO AWARD
For Distinguished Fashion Contributions in
Daytime Television
7TH ANNUAL SOAP OPERA AWARDS
Outstanding Hero—Doug Davidson
SOAP OPERA UPDATE AWARDS
Outstanding Lead Actor in a Daytime
Drama—Peter Bergman
Outstanding Lead Actress in a Daytime
Drama—Melody Thomas Scott

1990

17TH ANNUAL DAYTIME EMMY AWARDS
Outstanding Achievement in Technical
Direction / Electronic Camera / Video Control
for a Drama Series
Outstanding Achievement in Makeup for a
Drama Series
Outstanding Achievement in Videotape
Editing for a Drama Series
Outstanding Achievement in Live and Tape
Sound Mixing and Sound Special Effects for
a Drama Series
ENTERTAINMENT INDUSTRIES COUNCIL, INC.
Certificate of Commendation—Outstanding
Efforts in the Fight Against Alcohol and Drug
Abuse
THE NANCY SUSAN REYNOLDS AWARDS
Outstanding Daytime Drama—Cricket Blair
date rape storyline
MEDIA ACCESS AWARDS
Outstanding Daytime Drama Series for the
development of the Carole Robbins Evans
storyline utilizing handicapped actress
Christopher Templeton
MUSEUM OF BROADCASTING TRIBUTE
A Salute to 17 years of Outstanding
Television Drama
6TH ANNUAL SOAP OPERA AWARDS
Outstanding Hero—Doug Davidson
SOAP OPERA UPDATE AWARDS
Outstanding Lead Actor in a Daytime
Drama—Eric Braeden
Outstanding Lead Actress in a Daytime
Drama—Jeanne Cooper

1989

16TH ANNUAL DAYTIME EMMY AWARDS
Outstanding Drama Series Directing Team
Outstanding Achievement in Live and
Tape Sound Mixing and Sound Effects
for a Drama Series

Complete